THE MODERN LIBRARY
of the World's Best Books

MEDIEVAL PHILOSOPHY

MEDIEVAL PHILOSOPHY

Selected Readings from Augustine to Buridan

EDITED AND INTRODUCED BY

HERMAN SHAPIRO,

Department of Philosophy,
San Jose State College

The Modern Library

New York

Library of Congress Catalog Card Number: 64–11996

THE MODERN LIBRARY
is published by RANDOM HOUSE, INC.
BENNETT CERF • DONALD S. KLOPFER

Manufactured in the United States of America by H. Wolff

For Charlotte and Pip

Preface

❀ ❀

At a time when medieval philosophy is receiving more serious attention than for some hundreds of years, no apologies need be offered for undertaking to present this book. Its purpose is to provide a convenient and simple introduction to the history of medieval philosophy through the presentation of selected primary source materials in English translation. It is intended for use not only by those studying this area of intellectual history as part of a formal course leading to a degree, but also for members of a wide public who may hitherto have been excluded from firsthand acquaintance with the medieval thinkers by the scarcity or inaccessibility of reliable translations of their works.

Clearly, one could hardly even begin to fairly represent the swarms of thinkers crowding the centuries between Augustine and Buridan in fifty volumes, each twice the size of the present one. The particular selections offered are the result of eliminations necessary to bring within the covers of a single, reasonably-sized volume, those readings regarded by the editor as best suited for introducing the reader to some of the immensely diverse, rich and profound currents of medieval thought. Hence the intermixture of important texts dealing with a broad variety of philosophical topics, with such standard items as the selections from St. Anselm, Roger Bacon, and St. Thomas Aquinas.

As we see it, the wide range of subject materials displayed in our selections in no way detracts from our primary purpose in presenting this book. Certainly, there is no reason *a priori* why a volume of readings in the history of medieval philosophy must be restricted to tracing out the development of but one skein of thought. Where this volume is used to supply the basic readings for a college course in the history of medieval philosophy, that history itself, as set forth by the lecturer, will provide the unifying thread binding the selections. Again, should he choose to employ them in that manner, the materials contained herein will lend themselves nicely to a "Problems," "Currents," or "Landmarks" approach. But we shall not presume further: in any case, the classroom instructor will best know how to utilize the selections.

For the general reader, we have appended to each selection a list of *Suggestions for Further Reading*. As these lists cite works available in English in which the particular author's doctrines are authoritatively interpreted and evaluated, our own introductions to each selection were restricted, for the most part, to brief biographical sketches. The *Suggestions* contain, in addition, references to three superb histories of medieval philosophy: F. C. Copleston's *A History of Philosophy* (London, 1947–60), abbreviated in our lists as *FCC;* E. Gilson's *History of Christian Philosophy in the Middle Ages* (New York, 1955), abbreviated *EG;* and A. A. Maurer's *Medieval Philosophy* (New York, 1962), abbreviated *AAM*. The reader will find his appreciation and understanding of the original texts profoundly deepened by consulting any—or, better still, all three—of these histories. Additional primary sources, too, are listed. A reference of *RMcK* is meant to direct the reader to R. McKeon's fine two-volume anthology: *Selections from Medieval Philosophers* (New York, 1929). None of Professor McKeon's selections are duplicated in this volume.

Although specialists may question our inclusion of just *this* selection rather than some other, there can be no serious doubt regarding the intrinsic merits of each of the selections offered. Three of them, however—selections VII, IX, and XVI—call for special remarks. Obviously, even a minimal handling of the medieval controversy over universals would require the presentation of three selections: one representing the realist, one the moderate realist or conceptualist, and one the so-called "nominalist" point of view. Since three such inclusions would have necessitated the exclusion of yet other significant writings, we chose to present all of these positions through the eyes of the Humanist thinker, John of Salisbury. In this way we were able to include *four* medieval approaches to the problem within the compass of but one selection. Thus selection VII. We faced a similar difficulty when it came to ensuring the Arab and Jewish thinkers adequate representation, and adopted a similar solution. Thus, in selection XVI, original and significant passages drawn from the philosophical works of Avicenna, Averroes, Maimonides, and others are presented for our understanding from the point of view of the influential Christian thinker, Giles of Rome. Selection IX consists of a number of documents relating to the great medieval University of Paris. The university, it should be noted, is a medieval creation; and it simply did not seem reasonable to us to present a sequence of writings chronicling the development of Scholastic thought without giving some indication of the educational facilities available to those who contributed to its growth. But two more general remarks: for obvious reasons there has been no attempt to make the selections represent the entire range of thought of an individual; and the amount of space allotted to the respective authors should not be construed as a measure of their relative importance.

For the purpose of this volume, entirely original translations were required for the selections from Albert the Great, Peter of Spain, Siger of Brabant, and Nicolaus of Autrecourt. The first three were rendered into English by the precise scholarship of my former colleague, Professor J. P. Mullally of Queens College in New York. The fourth was graciously offered for inclusion in this volume by my former teacher, the outstanding medieval scholar, Professor E. A. Moody of the University of California in Los Angeles. The selections from John Scotus Erigena and Giles of Rome were newly translated by the editor especially for this volume. For all other selections, the translations—chosen on the basis of textual fidelity as well as general excellence—were followed faithfully with only minor alterations in a few instances.

The present editor wishes to make grateful acknowledgment to Professor F. C. Dommeyer, Chairman of the Department of Philosophy at San Jose State College, and indeed, to all of his colleagues at San Jose State, whose genuine interest and many suggestions contributed greatly to the execution of this work.

HERMAN SHAPIRO

Contents

❁ ❁

MEDIEVAL PHILOSOPHY

St. Augustine

St. Aurelius Augustine was born in 354 at Tagaste, North Africa. His mother, Monica, was a devout Christian. His father, Patricius, remained a pagan until shortly before his death. Augustine was sent to Carthage to study, and early displayed a promising literary gift. When, in later life, he wrote his *Confessions,* Augustine portrayed his youth as wayward and misspent. Like most converts, however, he probably judged his preconversion days much too harshly.

While still in his early twenties, Augustine underwent what are referred to as his "two conversions." The first of these, primarily intellectual, arose from the reading of certain—as he called them—"Platonic" works. Actually, these consisted in such Neo-Platonic writings as Plotinus' *Enneads,* then newly rendered into Latin by Marius Victorinus. Their effect upon Augustine appears to have been immediate and profound: the call of Neo-Platonism, with its vision of a supersensible realm which is but poorly shadowed forth in the material and sensible, led Augustine to finally reject both the materialism and the skepticism to which he had earlier subscribed.

The second conversion, moral and practical in nature, was owing to an accumulation of Christian influences—chiefly that of St. Ambrose—and to a close study of the New Testament read in the light of the Neo-Platonic philosophy. As a result of these experiences, Augustine was at last won over to Christianity. In the year 387 he received baptism at the hands of St. Ambrose.

In 391 Augustine entered the priesthood, and in 395 was appointed Bishop of Hippo, a city near Carthage in North Africa. He spent the remainder of his life working zealously in the affairs of his diocese, and managed as well to pen an immense number of writings, many of which were in confutation of such heresies as Manichaeism, Donatism, and Pelagianism. Augustine died in Hippo in 430—the very year in which the Vandals laid the city siege.

Reprinted below in its entirety is Augustine's *On the Teacher:* an early work in which is set forth his unique approach to the problem of human knowledge. The work is written in the form of a dialogue between Augustine and the natural son of his preconversion days, Adeodatus.

ST. AUGUSTINE ON THE TEACHER *

i, 1. *Augustine.*—What do you suppose is our purpose when we use words? *Adeodatus.*—The answer that occurs to me at the moment is, we want to let people know something, or we want to learn something. *Augustine.*—I agree at once with the former, for it is clear that when we use words we want to let somebody know something. But in what way do we show that we wish to learn? *Adeodatus.*—When we ask questions, of course. *Aug.*—Even then, as I understand it, we want to let somebody know something. Do you ask a question for any other reason than to show the person questioned what you want to know? *Ad.*—No. *Aug.*—You see, then, that when we use words we desire nothing but to let someone know something. *Ad.*—Not quite, perhaps. If speaking means using words, I see that we do so when we sing. Now we often sing when we are alone, with no one present to hear us; and then I cannot think we want to tell anyone anything. *Aug.*—And yet I think there is a kind of teaching, and a most important kind, which consists in reminding people of something. I believe this will be made clear as our conversation proceeds. If,

* From *Augustine: Earlier Writings.* Translated by J. H. S. Burleigh. The Westminster Press, 1953. Used by permission.

however, you do not think that we learn by remembering, or that he who reminds us of something really teaches us, I do not press the point. I assert that there are two reasons for our using words, either to teach, or to remind others or, it may be, ourselves. And we do this also when we sing. Don't you agree?

Ad.—Well, hardly. For I very rarely sing to remind myself of anything, almost always simply to give myself pleasure. *Aug.*—I see what you mean. But don't you notice that what pleases you in singing is the melody? Now this can be added to the words or not added, so that singing is not the same thing as speaking. Flutes and harps make melody. Birds sing. Sometimes we hum a bit of music without words. All these things may be called singing but not speaking. Do you disagree? *Ad.*—No. Not at all.

2. *Aug.*—You agree, then, that there is no other reason for the use of words than either to teach or to call something to mind? *Ad.*—I would agree were I not impressed by the fact that we use words when we pray; and it is not proper to believe that we teach God anything or remind him of anything. *Aug.*—I dare say you do not know that we have been commanded to pray in closed chambers, by which is meant our inmost mind, for no other reason than that God does not seek to be reminded or taught by our speech in order that he may give us what we desire. He who speaks gives by articulate sounds an external sign of what he wants. But God is to be sought and prayed to in the secret place of the rational soul, which is called "the inner man." This he wants to be his temple. Have you not read in the Apostle: "Know ye not that ye are the temple of God, and the Spirit of God dwelleth in you?" (1 Cor. 3:16) and "that Christ may dwell in the inner man" (Eph. 3:17)? Have you not observed in the Prophet: "Commune with your own hearts and be stricken on your beds. Offer the sacrifice of righteousness and hope in the Lord" (Ps. 4:4-5)? Where do you think the sacrifice of righteousness is offered save in the temple of the mind and on the bed of the heart? Where sacrifice is to be offered, there is prayer to be made. Wherefore when we pray there is no need

of speech, that is of articulate words, except perhaps as priests use words to give a sign of what is in their minds, not that God may hear, but that men may hear and, being put in remembrance, may with some consent be brought into dependence on God. What do you think? *Ad.*—I entirely agree. *Aug.*—And you are not disturbed by the fact that our great Master, in teaching his disciples to pray, taught them certain words, so that it looks as if he had taught them actually what words to use in prayer? *Ad.*—No. That does not disturb me. For he did not teach them words merely, but by words, by means of which they could keep themselves in constant remembrance, he taught them realities—what they should pray for, and from whom, when they prayed in their inmost mind, as we said. *Aug.*—You have correctly understood the point. And I believe you have also noticed a further point. It might be contended that, though we utter no sound, we nevertheless use words in thinking and therefore use speech within our minds. But such speech is nothing but a calling to remembrance of the realities of which the words are but the signs, for the memory, which retains the words and turns them over and over, causes the realities to come to mind. *Ad.*—I understand and follow.

ii, 3. *Aug.*—We agree, then, that words are signs. *Ad.*—We do. *Aug.*—That alone can be a sign which signifies something? *Ad.*—Certainly. *Aug.*—How many words are there in this verse?

> *Si nihil ex tanta superis placet urbe relinqui*
> [If it pleases the gods that nothing be left of so great a city]

Ad.—Eight. *Aug.*—Then there are eight signs? *Ad.*—There are. *Aug.*—I suppose you understand the meaning of the verse. *Ad.*—Yes, I think so. *Aug.*—Tell me what each word signifies. *Ad.*—I know what *si* signifies, but I can think of no other word to explain it. *Aug.*—At least you can explain the state of mind signified by that word. *Ad.*—It seems to me to signify doubt, and doubt is found in the mind. *Aug.*—I accept that in the meantime. Go on to the next word. *Ad.*—*Nihil* signifies simply what is not. *Aug.*—Perhaps you are right. But I am prevented from giving my assent by what you admitted a moment ago. You agreed that only that can be a sign which signifies something. Now, what is not cannot be something. So the second word in the verse is not a sign, because it does not signify something. We were wrong, therefore, in laying it down that all words are signs, or that all signs must signify something. *Ad.*—You press me sore. But surely it is utterly foolish to use a word if we have no meaning to attach to it. When you are speaking with me I believe that you do not utter any merely empty sound, but that in everything that proceeds from your mouth you are giving me a sign by which I may understand something. So you ought not in speaking to pronounce these two syllables unless by them you mean something. If you see that they are necessary to set forth some idea and to teach and remind us of something when they sound in our ears, you assuredly also see what I wish to say but cannot clearly explain. *Aug.*—What then are we to do? Shall we say that the word, *nihil,* signifies a state of mind rather than a thing which is nothing; the state of a mind, I mean, which does not see an object, and discovers or thinks it has discovered nonentity? *Ad.*—Perhaps that was what I was trying to explain. *Aug.*—However it may be, let us go on to the next point lest something most absurd happen to us. *Ad.*—What do you mean? *Aug.*—If "nothing" should detain us, and yet we should suffer delay. *Ad.*—It is indeed ridiculous, and yet somehow I see it can happen and indeed has happened.

4. *Aug.*—At the proper time we shall understand more clearly this kind of difficulty, if God will. Now go back to the verse and do your best to unfold what the other words signify. *Ad.*—The third word is the preposition *ex* for which I think we can substitute *de*. *Aug.*—But I am not asking you to substitute for one well-known word another equally well-known word which you say means the same thing, if indeed it does mean the same thing. But let that pass meantime. If the poet had written not *ex tanta urbe* but *de tanta urbe,* and I asked what *de* signified, you would say *ex,* since these two words, that is, signs, signify, you think, one and the same thing. But I am looking for the one thing which is signified

by these two signs. *Ad.*—I think they mean a separation of a thing A, from a thing, B, in which it had formerly existed. A is said to be "of" or "out of" B. And this in one or other of two ways. Either B does not remain, as in this verse. For Troy has been destroyed but some Trojans could still exist. Or B remains, as when we say that businessmen of the City of Rome are in Africa. *Aug.*—I shall concede your point, and not seek to enumerate the many exceptions that can be found to your rule. But you can at least observe that you have been explaining words by means of words, that is, signs by means of signs, well-known words and signs by words and signs also well-known. But I want you to show me, if you can, what are the things of which these are the signs.

iii, 5. *Ad.*—I am surprised that you do not know, or rather that you pretend not to know, that what you ask cannot be done in conversation, where we cannot answer questions except by means of words. You ask for things which, whatever they may be, are certainly not words, and yet you too use words in asking me. First put your questions without using words, and I shall reply on the same terms. *Aug.*—I admit your challenge is just. But if I were to ask what was signified when these three syllables, *par-i-es,* are pronounced couldn't you point with your finger, so that I should immediately see the thing itself of which that trisyllabic word is the sign? You would be pointing it out without using any words. *Ad.*—I agree that is possible, but only in the case of names signifying corporeal objects, if these objects were at hand. *Aug.*—But surely we do not call a colour a corporeal object? Is it not rather a quality of a corporeal object? *Ad.*—It is so. *Aug.*—Why then can it, too, be pointed out with the finger? Do you include the qualities of corporeal objects among corporeal objects, at least so far as they can be brought to knowledge without words? *Ad.*—When I said corporeal objects I meant all corporeal things to be understood, that is, all the qualities of bodies which are susceptible to sense-perception. *Aug.*—Consider, however, whether some exceptions are to be made. *Ad.* —You do well to warn me. I should have said not all corporeal objects but all visible objects. For I admit that sound, smell, taste, weight, heat, etc., which belong to the other senses, though they cannot be perceived apart from bodies and are therefore corporeal, cannot, nevertheless, be pointed out with the finger. *Aug.*—Have you never seen how men carry on conversation, as it were, with deaf people by means of gesture, and how deaf people, similarly by gesture, ask questions and reply, teach and indicate all their wishes, or at least most of them? Thus not only visible things are pointed out without the use of words, but also sounds, tastes and other such things. Actors, too, in the theatres often unfold and set forth whole stories by dancing simply and without using a single word. *Ad.*—I have no adverse comment to make except that neither I nor your dancing actor will ever be able to point out to you what the preposition, *ex,* signifies without using words.

6. *Aug.*—Perhaps you are right. But suppose he could. You would, I imagine, have no hesitation in saying that whatever movement of his body he used in trying to show me the thing signified by that word, it would still be a sign and not the thing itself. Therefore, though he indeed would not explain a word by a word, he would, none the less, explain a sign by a sign. So that both the monosyllable, *ex,* and his gesture would signify one thing, which I was asking to have pointed out to me without a sign, directly. *Ad.*—Pray, how can that possibly be done? *Aug.*—The way a wall does it. *Ad.*—But even a wall, as our reasoning showed, cannot be shown without a pointing finger. The holding out of the finger is not the wall but the sign by means of which the wall is pointed out. So far as I can see there is nothing which can be shown without signs. *Aug.*—Suppose I were to ask you what walking is, and you were to get up and do it, wouldn't you be using the thing itself to show me, not words or any other signs? *Ad.*—Yes, of course. I am ashamed that I did not notice so obvious a fact. Now thousands of examples come to my mind of things which can be demonstrated immediately and without signs, such as eating, drinking, sitting, standing, shouting and other things innumerable. *Aug.*—Well then, tell me this. Supposing I had no idea of the meaning of the word "walking," and I were to ask you when you were walking what "walking" means, how

would you teach me? *Ad.*—I should walk a little more quickly. The change in speed would give notice that I was replying to your question, and I should still be doing what I was asked to demonstrate. *Aug.*—But you know there is a difference between walking and hastening. He who walks does not suddenly hasten, and he who hastens does not necessarily walk. We speak of hastening in writing, reading and very many other things. Consequently, if, after my query, you did what you had been doing, only a little more quickly, I should conclude that walking was the same thing as hastening, for the acceleration was the new feature of your behaviour. So I should be misled. *Ad.*—I admit that a thing cannot be demonstrated without a sign, at any rate if the thing is an action in which we are engaged when we are questioned. If we add nothing new to what we are doing, our questioner will think that we don't want to show him, but are continuing in what we were doing without paying any attention to him. But if his inquiry is about actions which we can perform, and if we are not doing them when he inquires, by doing it after he has inquired we can demonstrate what he asks by the actual thing and not merely by a sign. A special case would arise if, while I was speaking, someone asked me what "speaking" was. In order to let him know I must speak, whatever I actually may say. And I shall continue to show him until I make plain to him what he wants to know, not departing from the actual thing which he wished to have demonstrated to him, and yet not seeking signs apart from the thing itself wherewith to demonstrate it.

iv, 7. *Aug.*—Most acutely stated. Are we, now, agreed that there are two classes of things that can be demonstrated without signs; those which we are not engaged in doing when we are asked and can immediately start doing, and those in which the action consists in simply giving signs? For when we speak we make signs, whence is derived the verb, *to signify*. *Ad.*—Agreed. *Aug.*—When the question concerns signs merely, signs can be demonstrated by signs. But when the question is about things which are not signs, they can be demonstrated by carrying out the action, if possible, after the question has been asked, or by giving signs by means of which the things can be brought to mind. *Ad.*—That is so. *Aug.*—Here, then, we have a threefold classification. Let us first consider, if you please, the case of signs being demonstrated by signs. Words are not the only signs? *Ad.*—No. *Aug.*—It seems to me that in speaking we use words to signify words or other signs, as when we say "gesture" or "letter"; for these two words also signify signs. Or we may express in words something which is not a sign, as for example when we say the word "stone." The word is a sign for it signifies something, but what it signifies is not a sign. But this kind of case where words signify things that are not signs does not concern our present discussion. For we undertook to consider those cases where signs are demonstrated by signs, and we found that they fall into two classes; those in which we teach or call to remembrance by signs similar signs, and those in which we teach or call to remembrance different signs. Do you agree? *Ad.*—Clearly.

8. *Aug.*—Tell me, to what sense do verbal signs pertain? *Ad.*—To the sense of hearing. *Aug.*—And gesture? *Ad.*—To sight. *Aug.*—What about written words? Surely they are words? Or are they better understood as signs of words? A word is a meaningful articulate sound, and sound is perceived by no other sense than hearing. When a word is written, a sign is given to the eyes whereby something that properly belongs to the ears is brought to mind. *Ad.*—I agree entirely. *Aug.*—You will also agree, I imagine, that when we pronounce the word, *nomen* [name], we signify something. *Ad.*—True. *Aug.*—What, then? *Ad.*—That by which something or somebody is called; for example, Romulus, Rome, Virtue, a River, etc., etc. *Aug.*—These four names signify something. *Ad.*—Indeed they do. *Aug.*—Is there a difference between these names and the things they signify? *Ad.*—A great difference. *Aug.*—I should like you to tell me what is the difference. *Ad.*—In the first place, the names are signs; the things are not. *Aug.*—Shall we call things which can be signified by signs but are not signs "significables," as we call things that can be seen visible? It will simplify our discussion of them.

Ad.—Very well. *Aug.*—Can these four signs you have just mentioned be signified by no other sign? *Ad.*—I am surprised that you should think I have already forgotten that we found that written words are signs of spoken words, signs, therefore, of signs. *Aug.*—What is the difference? *Ad.*—Written words are visible. Spoken words are audible. Why should we not use the word, audible, if we allow "significable"? *Aug.*—I allow it at once, and am grateful for your suggestion. But I ask again whether these four signs cannot be signified by any other audible sign as well as by the visible signs you have called to mind. *Ad.*—I recall that this too was said recently in our discussion. I said that a name signified some thing and I gave these four examples. I recognize that the word "name" and these four names are all audible when spoken. *Aug.*—What, then, is the difference between an audible sign and other audible signs signified by it? *Ad.*—So far as I can see the difference between the word "name" and the four examples is this; it is the audible sign of audible signs; they are the audible signs not of signs but of things, partly visible, like Romulus, Rome, River, partly intelligible, like Virtue.

9. *Aug.*—I understand and approve. But you know that every articulate sound pronounced with some meaning is called a word. *Ad.*—I do. *Aug.*—A name, therefore, is a word when it is pronounced articulately with a meaning. When we say of a fluent man that he uses good words, we mean also that he uses names. When the slave in Terence said to his aged master, "Good words, I pray you," he used many names. *Ad.*—I agree. *Aug.*—So when we pronounce these two syllables, *ver-bum,* we also signify a name, and the one word is the sign of the other. *Ad.*—I agree. *Aug.*—Here is another question I should like you to answer. You have said that "word" is a sign pointing to "name," and "name" is a sign pointing to "river," and "river" is the sign of a thing which can be seen. Also you have explained the difference between this "thing" and "river," which is its sign, and between "river" and "name," which is the sign of a sign. What do you think is the difference between the sign of a name, that is a word, and the name itself of which it is the sign? *Ad.*—I understand the difference to be

this. What is signified by "name" is also signified by "word." A name is a word, and "river" is a word. But everything that has a verbal sign does not have a nominal sign. For *si* at the beginning of the verse you quoted, and *ex,* where this long course of reasoning started, are words but they are not names. And there are many other such words. All names are words, but all words are not names. So the difference between a word and a name is, I think, clear, that is, between the sign of a sign which signifies no other signs, and the sign of a sign that points to other signs. *Aug.*—Every horse is an animal, but every animal is not a horse? *Ad.*—Indubitably. *Aug.*—There is the same difference between "name" and "word" as between horse and animal. Unless perhaps you are prevented from assenting by the fact that we use the word "verb" in a special sense to signify those things which have tenses—I write, I wrote; I read, I have read. Clearly these are not names. *Ad.*—You have mentioned exactly what caused me to hesitate. *Aug.*—Don't let that trouble you. In all cases where words are employed and something is signified we speak of signs universally and without qualification. On the other hand, we speak of military signs which are properly called signs because words are not used. If I were to say to you that just as every horse is an animal but every animal is not a horse, so every word is a sign but every sign is not a word, you would not hesitate, I believe. *Ad.*—Now I understand and agree that there is the same difference between a word, universally, and a name as between animal and horse.

10. *Aug.*—You know that when we say "animal," that trisyllabic name pronounced by the voice is a different thing from that which it signifies? *Ad.*—We have admitted that is true for all signs and "significables." *Aug.*—Do you think that all signs signify something different from themselves, just as the three syllables of the word animal cannot signify the word itself. *Ad.*—Not altogether. For when we say the word "sign" it signifies not only all other signs but also itself. For it is a word, and all words are signs. *Aug.*—Does not the same thing happen when we say the word *verbum?* If that word signifies every meaningful articulate sound, it is itself included in that

category. *Ad.*—It is. *Aug.*—Isn't it the same with the word "name"? It signifies names of all categories, and is itself the name of no category. If I were to ask you what part of speech is a name, could you answer correctly except by saying it is a noun? *Ad.*—No, indeed. *Aug.*—There are therefore signs which signify themselves as well as other signs. *Ad.*—There are. *Aug.*—Do you think that the same is true with the quadrisyllabic sign "conjunction" when spoken? *Ad.*—By no means. It is a name, but the things it signifies are not names.

v, 11. *Aug.*—You have been most attentive. Now consider whether there are signs which signify each other mutually, the one being signified by the other. This is not the case with the word "conjunction" and the words signified by it, such as if, or, for, unless, therefore, since, and the like. All these are signified by that one word, but by none of them is that word signified. *Ad.*—I see. And I should like to learn what signs signify one another mutually. *Aug.*—When we say "name" and "word" we use two words. *Ad.*—Yes. *Aug.*—And when we use these two words we at the same time use two names. *Ad.*—Yes. *Aug.*—So that "name" signifies "word" just as "word" signifies "name." *Ad.*—I agree. *Aug.*—Can you say how they differ except that they sound differently and are spelt differently? *Ad.*—Perhaps I can, remembering what I said a little while ago. By "words" we mean everything articulately spoken and with some meaning. So every name, including the word "name," is a word; but every word is not a name, though the word "word" is itself a name.

12. *Aug.*—If someone were to affirm and prove that, just as every name is a word, so every word is a name, could you point out the difference except in sound and spelling? *Ad.*—I could not. And I do not think there is a difference. *Aug.*—If all articulate and meaningful sounds are both words and names, but for one reason they are called words and for another names, will there be no difference? *Ad.*—I don't understand how that could be. *Aug.*—You understand at any rate that every coloured thing is visible, and that every visible thing is coloured, though these two words have quite different meanings. *Ad.*—I do. *Aug.*—What if similarly every word is

a name and every name a word, though these two words, viz., "name" and "word," have different meanings? *Ad.*—I now see it might be so, but I wait for you to show me how. *Aug.*—You are aware, I suppose, that every articulate significant sound smites the ear in order that it may be perceived, remembered and known? *Ad.*—I am aware of that. *Aug.*—Therefore, whenever we speak, two things happen. *Ad.*—That is so. *Aug.*—What if words are so called from one of these two things, and names from the other? That is to say, if *verbum* derives from *verberare, nomen* from *noscere,* the former would receive its due appellation from something that happens to the ear, the latter from something that happens in the mind.

13. *Ad.*—I shall agree when you show me how we can correctly say that all words are names. *Aug.*—That is easy. I suppose you once learned and still remember that a pronoun is so called because it can stand for a noun (name), though it characterizes its object less fully than the noun it has replaced. I believe this is the definition which you used to repeat to your grammar teacher: A pronoun is a part of speech which, when put in place of a noun, designates the same object but less fully. *Ad.*—I remember and I approve. *Aug.*—You see, then, that, according to this definition, pronouns can serve only in place of nouns, and can be put only in the place of nouns. For example, we say, "this man," "the king himself," "the same woman," "this gold," "that silver." "This," "that," "himself," "the same" are pronouns. "Man," "king," "woman," "gold," "silver" are nouns, by means of which the things are more fully described than by the pronouns. *Ad.*—I see and agree. *Aug.*—Now name a few conjunctions, whichever you like. *Ad.*—"And," "but," "also." *Aug.*—Don't you think that all these you have mentioned are names [nouns]? *Ad.*—Not at all. *Aug.*—Do you think that I have used correct language in saying "all these you have mentioned"? *Ad.*—Quite correct. And now I understand that you have been showing me in a wonderful way that these were nouns which I mentioned, for otherwise it would not be correct to refer to them as "these." But I have still a suspicion that I judged your language to be correct because these conjunctions are undeniably words.

Therefore we can correctly refer to them as "all these," viz., "all these words." If you ask me what part of speech is "words" I can only answer "a noun." So that your expression was correct perhaps because the pronoun was implicitly attached to this noun.

14. *Aug.*—An acute observation. But you are wrong. To correct your error listen attentively to what I say, if I can manage to express myself as I wish. To use words to treat of words is as complicated as to rub fingers together and expect someone else to distinguish which fingers tingle with warmth and which help others to tingle. *Ad.*—I give you all my attention, for your similitude has aroused my interest. *Aug.*—Words are a compound of sound and letters. *Ad.*—That is right. *Aug.*—Let us use a citation from an authority, dearest of all to us. When the Apostle Paul says: "In Christ there was not Yea [*est*] and Nay, but in him was Yea [*est*]" we are not to think, I suppose, that these three letters, e-s-t, were in Christ, but rather that which is signified by them. *Ad.*—Quite true. *Aug.*—When he says: "In him was *Est,*" he is to be understood as meaning, "In him was what we call *Est* [being]." If he had said: "In him was virtue," he would have to be understood to mean: "In him was what we call virtue." We should not have to think that these two syllables which we use when we speak of virtue were in him, but rather that the quality denoted by the word "virtue" was in him. *Ad.*—I follow you. *Aug.*—You understand that there is no difference between "is called virtue" and "is named virtue"? *Ad.*—That is clear. *Aug.*—It is equally clear that there is no difference between, "in him was what is called *Est,*" and, "in him was what is named *Est.*" *Ad.*—I see there is no difference. *Aug.*—Do you see now what I am trying to point out to you? *Ad.*—Not quite. *Aug.*—You see that a name is that by which a thing is named. *Ad.*—Nothing is clearer. *Aug.*—Then you see that *Est* is a name [noun] if that which was in him is named *Est* [being]. *Ad.*—Undeniably. *Aug.*—But if I were to ask you what part of speech is *Est,* you would, I suppose, say it was not a noun but a verb, though our reasoning has taught us that it is also a noun. *Ad.*—It is just as you say. *Aug.*—Do you still hesi-

tate to regard as names the other parts of speech—names in the sense we have demonstrated? *Ad.*—I do not hesitate, now that I have to confess that they may be signs of something. But if you ask what the specific things signified are called or named, I cannot answer. I can refer only to those parts of speech which we do not usually call names, but which I see we are now constrained so to call.

15. *Aug.*—Are you not disturbed by the possibility that there may be someone who would weaken our argument by saying that we must attribute to the Apostle authority in the matter of realities but not in the use of words? The ground of our argument would not be so sure as we had assumed. It is possible that, though Paul lived and taught with absolute rectitude, his language was less correct when he wrote: "In him was *Est,*" especially when he himself confesses that he was unskilled in speech. How do you think we ought to refute such a man? *Ad.*—I have nothing to urge against him. I pray you, find someone among the acknowledged masters of words by whose authority you can effect what you desire. *Aug.*—You think that without authorities reason itself is hardly sufficient. But reason itself demonstrates that all the parts of speech may signify some thing, that consequently they may be names or nouns. This can be most easily seen by comparing different languages. Obviously if you ask what is the Greek name for our *quis,* the answer is *tis;* for *volo, thelo;* for *bene, kalôs;* for *scriptum, to gegrammenon;* for *et, kai;* for *ab, apo;* for *heu, oi.* The question can thus be correctly asked about all the parts of speech as I have enumerated them. This could not be done unless they were names. When we can by this process of reasoning, apart from the authority of all the eloquent men, prove that the Apostle Paul spoke correctly, what need is there to seek anyone to buttress our argument with his personal authority?

16. But possibly some man, from greater stupidity or impudence, may not agree, but on the contrary may assert that he will give way only to those authorities who with universal consent are allowed to lay down the law in regard to words. What in the Latin tongue can be found more excellent than

Cicero? And yet he, in his noblest orations, called the Verrine orations, calls *coram* a noun. Now *coram* is a preposition, or possibly an adverb in that particular passage. It may be that I do not correctly understand the passage, and others may explain it differently. But there is one point to which I think there is no possible answer. The best masters of dialectic tell us that a complete sentence, whether affirmative or negative (what Tullius somewhere also calls a pronouncement), consists of a noun and a verb; and when the verb is in the third person, the noun, they say, and rightly, must be in the nominative case. Now consider this point. When we say "the man sits" and "the horse runs" you observe there are two pronouncements. *Ad.*—I do. *Aug.*—In each of them there is one noun, in the one case, "man," in the other, "horse." There is likewise one verb, "sits" in the one case, "runs" in the other. *Ad.*—So I observe. *Aug.*—If I said simply "sits" or "runs," you would very properly ask me "who or what?" I should have to reply, "the man," "the horse," "the animal" or some other noun which, when added to the verb, completes the pronouncement or affirmative or negative sentence. *Ad.*—I understand. *Aug.*—Now listen. Suppose we see some object rather far away and are uncertain whether it is an animal or a stone or something else. Suppose I say to you: "Because it is a man it is an animal." Shouldn't I be speaking rashly? *Ad.*—You would indeed, but not if you said: "If it is a man it is an animal." *Aug.*—You are right. So in your sentence "if" satisfies us both, and in mine "because" is felt to be wrong. *Ad.*—I agree. *Aug.*—Now are these two pronouncements complete sentences: " 'if' satisfies," and, " 'because' is wrong"? *Ad.*—Yes. They are complete. *Aug.*—Now tell me which are the verbs and which the nouns. *Ad.*—The verbs are "satisfies" and "is wrong"; and the nouns must be "if" and "because." *Aug.*—It is therefore sufficiently proved that these two conjunctions can also be nouns. *Ad.*—Quite sufficiently. *Aug.*—Can you by yourself prove that the other parts of speech can be brought under the same rule? *Ad.*—I can.

vi, 17. *Aug.*—Let us, then, pass on. Tell me whether you think that, just as we have found that all words are names and all names are words, so all names are substantives and all substantives are names. *Ad.*—I see no difference between them except their sounds. *Aug.*—I make no objection provisionally. There are some who see a distinction between them in meaning too, but we need not consider their opinion just now. But at least you observe that we have reached signs which signify one another mutually, differing in nothing but sound, and which signify themselves together with all the other parts of speech. *Ad.*—I don't understand. *Aug.*—Don't you understand that "substantive" signifies "name" and "name" "substantive," and that there is no difference between them except in sound, so far as concerns the general concept, "name." For of course we use the concept, "name" (or noun), in a special sense, when we use it to denote one of the eight parts of speech over against the other seven. *Ad.*—That I understand. *Aug.*—That is what I meant when I said that substantive and name signify one another mutually.

18. *Ad.*—I understand that, but I wonder what you meant by saying they signify themselves together with the other parts of speech. *Aug.*—Didn't our previous argument teach us that all parts of speech can be used as names and substantives, that is, may be signified by the signs, "name" and "substantive"? *Ad.*—That is so. *Aug.*—If I ask you the meaning of *no-men* —I mean that disyllabic sound—wouldn't you correctly reply *nomen? Ad.*—Yes. *Aug.*—But it is not surely the same with the sign we give when we pronounce the four syllables, *con-junc-ti-o?* This name cannot be enumerated among the conjunctions which it signifies. *Ad.*—That I accept as right. *Aug.* —So you see what I meant by saying, a name which signifies itself and all the other things it signifies. You can work this out for yourself if you like in the case of the word, "substantive." *Ad.*—Easily enough. But it occurs to me that "name" is used in both a general and a special sense. "Substantive" is not accepted among the eight parts of speech. So there must be a difference in meaning besides the difference in sound. *Aug.*—What difference is there between *nomen* and *onoma* except a difference of sound, the difference between the Latin and the Greek languages? *Ad.*—In this case I see no difference

save one of sound. *Aug.*—So we have discovered signs which signify themselves, and one another mutually. Whatever is signified by the one is also signified by the other, and they differ only in sound. We have just found out this fourth characteristic. The three former ones we learned in connection with names and words. *Ad.*—Yes. That is what we have discovered.

vii, 19. *Aug.*—I should like you to recall what we have learned as a result of our conversation. *Ad.*—I shall do the best I can. To begin with I recall that we spent some time in inquiring why we use speech, and we saw that we did so in order to teach or to call to mind. Even when we ask questions our motive is simply to let the person questioned know what we want to hear. We seem to sing for the pleasure it gives us, but the pleasure derives from the melody and not properly from the words sung. In prayer, we cannot hold that God needs to be taught or reminded, so that when we use words we do so to remind ourselves or to admonish and teach others. Then we decided that words were simply signs. Things which do not signify something beyond themselves cannot be signs. Then you quoted the verse,

Si nihil ex tanta superis placet urbe relinqui

and I tried to show what each word signified. We could not discover what the second word signifies though it is a well-known obvious word. I thought it was not an empty word but did express something, perhaps the state of mind of one who discovers that the object of his search does not exist, or at least thinks he has made that discovery. You made some reply, jestingly avoiding the profundity of the question, and putting it off for another time. Don't think I have forgotten the explanation you owe me. Then I tried to explain the third word in the verse and you urged me not to explain it by means of a synonym, but to show the reality which the word signified. I said it was impossible to do this in conversation, so we came to things which can be pointed out with the finger. I thought all corporeal objects were of this kind, but we found that only visible things were. Then somehow we spoke of deaf people and actors who without words and by gestures alone signify not only visible things but much else besides, indeed nearly everything we speak about. And we decided that these gestures also were signs. Then we began again to inquire how we could without signs point out actual things, since a wall, a colour, all visible things are indicated by pointing with the finger, which is itself a sign. When I wrongly said that nothing could be found which could be shown without a sign, we agreed that it was possible in the case of actions, provided we were not performing them when we were questioned, if we could perform them when questioned. But speaking was not among such actions for even if we were asked while we were speaking what speaking is, it would clearly be easy to demonstrate the action by performing the action itself.

20. Hence we learned that signs are demonstrated by signs, also other things which are not signs. Likewise, without a sign, actions can be demonstrated which we can perform on being questioned. Of these three statements we undertook to consider diligently and to discuss the first. The discussion showed that, on the one hand, there are signs which cannot be signified by the signs they themselves signify, for example, the word "conjunction." On the other hand some can. For example, the word "sign" signifies a word, and the word "word" signifies a sign, so that "sign" and "word" are both signs and words. In the class of signs which are mutually significant it was shown that there are degrees of correspondence. The sound, *sig-num,* signifies everything by which anything is signified, but *ver-bum* is not a sign of all signs, but only of those which are articulately pronounced. Hence it is manifest that while *sig-num* signifies *ver-bum* and vice-versa, *signum* applies more widely than *verbum.* But in a general sense *verbum* and *nomen* have the same range of application. Our argument showed us that all the parts of speech can be names, because pronouns can be substituted for or added to them. Of all of them it can be said that they "name" something, and there is none of them which cannot be made the subject of a verb to form a complete sentence. But though "name" and "word" have the same range of applicability, since all words are names, yet they are

not identical in meaning. We gave a probable reason for the distinction between "word" and "name," viz., *verbum* is derived from *verberare,* to strike the ear, *nomen* from the mental process of reminding. When we want to memorize something we rightly say, "What is its name?" but we do not usually say, "What is its word?" Of absolute synonyms, differing in nothing save in sound and spelling, the only example we found was *nomen* and *onoma,* a Latin word and its Greek equivalent. In the class of mutually significant signs, it escaped me that we had found no sign which does not signify itself among the other signs it signifies. There! I have recalled as much as I am able. I am sure that in our conversation you have said nothing without conscious design, and you will know whether I have summarized our talk properly and in order.

viii, 21. *Aug.*—You have indeed repeated from memory all I wanted; and I must confess these distinctions now seem to me to be much clearer than they did when our discussion forced them out from obscurity. But it is hard to say at this point what goal we are striving to reach by all these roundabout paths. Probably you think we have just been playing a game and diverting the mind from serious things by these apparently puerile questionings, or, perhaps, that a very small gain has been made, if any. Or, if you suspect that some great advantage is to arise from our debate, you want to know it now or, at all events, to be told what it is. I want you to believe that I have not been trifling in this conversation, though perhaps we have been amusing ourselves. But the game is not to be regarded as merely puerile, nor is it to be thought that only small or moderate advantages have been gained. And yet, if I say that there is a life eternally blessed, and that my desire is that God, who is very truth, should bring us thither by steps suited to our poor abilities, I am afraid I shall appear ridiculous, because I set out on so long a journey with the consideration of signs and not of the realities they signify. You will pardon me, therefore, if I play with you to begin with, not for the sake of playing, but in order to exercise and sharpen our mental powers so that we may be able not merely to endure the heat and light of the region where lies the blessed life, but also to love them. *Ad.*—Go on as you have begun, for I shall never think unworthy of attention anything you may think it necessary to say or to do.

22. *Aug.*—Let us then consider the other side of the problem, where signs signify not other signs but what we have agreed to call "significables." And first tell me whether man is man. *Ad.*—Now I am not sure whether you are joking. *Aug.*—Why? *Ad.*—Because you think it necessary to ask me that question. *Aug.*—I dare say you would also suppose I was joking if I were to ask you whether the first syllable of that noun is *ho* and the second *mo*. *Ad.*—I certainly should. *Aug.*—But these two syllables together make *homo*. Do you agree? *Ad.*—Who could deny it? *Aug.*—Now I ask; do these two syllables together make you? *Ad.*—Of course not. But now I see your point. *Aug.*—You state it, then, so that I may not seem to be abusive. *Ad.*—You think the conclusion is that I am not a man. *Aug.*—Don't you agree, seeing you have agreed that all the premises are true from which this conclusion is reached? *Ad.*—I shall not tell you what I think until you tell me whether, in asking whether man is man, you meant these two syllables *homo,* or the thing they signify. *Aug.*—You tell me, rather, in what sense you understood my question. For if it is ambiguous you should have been careful and should not have replied until you were quite sure of the meaning of the question. *Ad.*—The ambiguity would not prevent me from answering that "*homo*" is "*homo*" in both senses. For these two syllables are nothing but these two syllables; and what they signify is exactly what is signified by them. *Aug.*—All right. But why don't you understand in two senses not only the word "*homo*" but all the other words we have used? *Ad.*—Have I not done so? *Aug.*—Take my first question. If you had understood it to be nothing but a series of syllables, you would have made no answer for I should apparently have asked no question. When I asked, *utrum homo homo sit,* I used three words, repeating one of them twice. It is clear that you took the first and last words not as mere syllables but as significant words, and so you thought you could reply with certainty and confidence. *Ad.*—That is true. *Aug.*—Why did you wish to take

the middle word only in two senses, according to its sound and according to its sense? *Ad.*—Now I take the whole sentence according to the sense of the words. I agree with you that we cannot carry on a conversation at all unless the words we hear carry the mind to the things of which they are the signs. Show me, now, the fallacy of the reasoning which proved that I am not a man. *Aug.*—I shall put the questions again so that you may yourself detect your mistake. *Ad.*—That is better.

23. *Aug.*—I shall not repeat the first question, for that has been agreed. But now think. The syllable *ho* is *ho,* and *mo* is *mo. Ad.*—Obviously. *Aug.*—Together they form *homo. Ad.*—There I went wrong. I thought, rightly, that when a sign is given one should look to what it signified, and, with that in view, should answer yes or no. But I allowed significance to separate syllables when of course they have none. *Aug.*—You are quite certain, then, that no answer should be given to questions except in terms of the things signified by the words. *Ad.*—Why not, if words are used? *Aug.*—I should like to hear how you would reply to the man in the amusing story who drew the conclusion that a lion had come out of the mouth of his fellow-disputant. He first asked whether what we say comes out of our mouth. That was, of course, undeniable. Then he had no difficulty in getting the other, in the course of the discussion, to mention a lion. Whereupon he made fun of him, and insisted that, since he had confessed that what we say comes out of our mouth, and since he could not deny that he had said "lion," therefore with the best intentions he had let out a horrid beast from his mouth. *Ad.*—It would not be difficult to answer that clever jester. I should not concede that whatever we say comes out of our mouth. For our words are signs merely of things. It is the sign and not the thing signified which comes out of the mouth of the speaker. In some cases it may be simply the sign of another sign, as we have said earlier in our discussion.

24. *Aug.*—I see you are well armed against that adversary. But if I ask whether *homo* is a noun, what answer will you give me? *Ad.*—What else could it be? *Aug.*—When I see you,

do I see a noun? *Ad.*—No. *Aug.*—Shall I point out what follows from your reply? *Ad.*—Please don't. I see for myself that it must be that I am not a man because, when you asked whether *homo* was a noun I replied that it was, though I had decided to look to the significance of words in giving an affirmative or a negative answer. *Aug.*—Still I think there was some advantage gained by your slipping into that reply. The very law of reason stamped on our minds has awakened your vigilance. If I were to ask simply what is *homo,* you would probably reply, an animal. But if I were to ask what part of speech is *homo,* the only correct answer is, a noun. So *homo* is both a noun and an animal. It is a noun when it is regarded as a sign, and an animal when regard is had to the thing signified by the sign. If anyone asks me whether *homo* is a noun I shall reply that it is, for the form of the question indicates sufficiently in what sense the word is to be taken—the sense in which it is a sign. If he asks whether *homo* is an animal I shall assent even more readily. But if he asks simply what *homo* is without mentioning either noun or animal, my mind, following the rule laid down for our discourse, would at once turn to the thing signified by these two syllables, and would give no other answer but "animal," unless it gave the whole definition, which is "a rational and mortal animal." Don't you think so? *Ad.*—I do. But if we have admitted that *homo* is a noun how shall we avoid the insulting conclusion that we are not men? *Aug.*—How else than by explaining that the conclusion is inferred by importing into the word a different sense from that which we had understood in giving our assent. And if he says that was the sense he intended, the conclusion is not to be feared in any way; for why should I fear to confess that I am not a man (*hominem*), that is, I am not these three syllables? *Ad.*—Very true. Why indeed should one be offended when one is said not to be a man in that sense? According to our argument nothing could be more true. *Aug.*—The rule, which naturally carries the greatest weight, is that as soon as signs are heard, the attention is directed to the things they signify. So, when the rule is stated, it becomes impossible not to suppose that the conclusion refers to what is signified by the two syllables, *ho-mo*. *Ad.*—I understand and agree with what you say.

ix, 25. *Aug.*—I want you now to understand that things signified are of greater importance than their signs. Whatever exists on account of something else must necessarily be of less value than that on account of which it exists. Do you agree? *Ad.*—It seems to me we must not rashly agree to that statement. The word *caenum* (filth) for example is, I think, far preferable to the thing it signifies. What offends us when it is mentioned has nothing to do with the sound of the word. Change one letter and *caenum* becomes *caelum* (heaven), but what a difference there is between the things signified by these two words! I should not, therefore, attribute to the sign the quality I loathe in the thing signified. We prefer to hear the word to being brought into contact with the thing with our other senses. Accordingly I prefer the sign to the thing signified. *Aug.*—You are most observant. It is false, therefore, that things universally are to be preferred to their signs. *Ad.*—So it seems. *Aug.*—Tell me, then, what you think people wanted to achieve when they bestowed that name on an object so nasty and revolting. Do you approve of what they did or not? *Ad.*—I do not venture to approve or to disapprove, nor do I know what they were trying to do. *Aug.*—But you can know what you intend to do when you mention the word? *Ad.*—Certainly. I want to give a sign to the man with whom I am speaking, by means of which I may let him know what I think he ought to know. *Aug.*—The knowledge, then, conveyed by this word from you to him or from him to you, is more valuable than the word itself? *Ad.*—I agree that the knowledge conveyed by the sign is more important than the sign itself. But this does not mean that the thing signified is better than its sign.

26. *Aug.*—Therefore, though it is false that things universally are to be preferred to their signs, it is nevertheless true that whatever exists on account of something else is inferior to that on account of which it exists. Knowledge of filth, for example, to convey which knowledge the name was invented, is more important than the name, while the name is also to be

preferred to the thing it designates, as we have discovered. The knowledge is superior to the sign simply because it is the end towards which the latter is the means. If some gluttonous man, a worshipper of his belly, as the Apostle says, were to say that he lived to eat, a temperate man, hearing him, and unable to bear with him, might say: "How much better it would be if you ate to live." This judgment would proceed from the same rule. What displeased him would be that the other valued his life so little that he thought less of it than of the pleasures of gluttony, saying that he lived for banqueting. The advice to eat in order to live rather than to live in order to eat, is justly praised simply because it shows understanding of what is means and what is end, that is to say, of what should be subordinate to what. Similarly you or another man of discernment, hearing some loquacious lover of verbiage say: "I teach for the sake of talking," would reply: "My man, why don't you rather talk for the sake of teaching." Now if this is right, as you know it is, you see at once how much less value we are to attribute to words than to the things on account of which we use words. The use to which words are put is superior to the words; for words exist to be used, and used to teach. Just as it is better to teach than to talk, so speech is better than words. And knowledge is much better than words. I want to hear if you have any objection to offer.

27. *Ad.*—I agree that knowledge is better than words. But I am not sure that no objection can be urged against the general rule that everything which is means to an end is inferior to the end it serves. *Aug.*—We shall have a better opportunity at another time to discuss that problem more carefully. Meantime what you have admitted is sufficient for what I am desirous of establishing now. You grant that the knowledge of things is better than the signs of things. So knowledge of the things signified by signs is preferable to knowledge of their signs. Is it not? *Ad.*—Surely I have not granted that the knowledge of things is superior to the knowledge of signs, but not superior to the signs themselves. I am afraid to give my assent to what you have said. If the word filth is better than the thing it signifies, knowledge of the word would be preferable to knowledge of

the thing. And yet the name itself is inferior to the knowledge. There are four terms here: the name, the thing, knowledge of the name, knowledge of the thing. Why is not the third better than the fourth, just as the first is better than the second? And yet surely it is not to be subordinated?

28. *Aug.*—I see you have a wonderful memory for retaining your admissions and an excellent way of expounding your views. But take the word "vice" (*vitium*). When we pronounce the word *vi-ti-um* you know that it is better than the thing it signifies. And yet mere knowledge of the word is much inferior to knowledge of the vices. Let us consider your four terms: the name, the thing, knowledge of the name, knowledge of the thing. We rightly prefer the first to the second. When Persius used the name in his poem—"This man is stupefied by vice" —he committed no fault of versification, indeed he added an ornament. And yet the thing signified by the word makes the man in whom it is found necessarily vicious. But there is not the same relation between your third and fourth terms. The fourth is obviously better than the third. Knowledge of the word vice is inferior to knowledge of the vices. *Ad.*—Do you think that knowledge is preferable even when it makes us more miserable? For above all the penalties thought of by the cruelty of tyrants or calculated by their greed, Persius sets this one penalty which tortures men who are compelled to acknowledge vices which they cannot avoid. *Aug.*—In the same way you could deny that knowledge of the virtues is preferable to knowledge of the word "virtue," for to see and not to possess virtue was the punishment which the satirist wished tryants to suffer. *Ad.* —May God avert such madness! Now I understand that the knowledge imparted to the mind by a good education is not to be blamed, but those are to be judged most miserable of all who are affected by a disease which no medicine can cure. This, I think, was Persius' view too. *Aug.*—Quite right. But it does not matter to us what Persius thought. In such matters we are not subject to the authority of such as he. It is not easy to explain how one kind of knowledge is preferable to another. It is enough for my present purpose that we agree that knowledge of things signified is better than the signs even if not better than

knowledge of the signs. Now let us discuss the greater problem. What kind of things, as we said, can be pointed out by themselves without signs such as speaking, walking, lying, and suchlike? *Ad.*—I remember the problem.

x, 29. *Aug.*—Do you think that all actions which we can perform on being interrogated can be demonstrated without a sign? Or is there any exception? *Ad.*—Considering this whole class of things I find none which can be shown without a sign, except perhaps speaking or possibly teaching. For whatever I do by way of demonstration when someone has asked a question, I see that he cannot learn immediately from the action which he wants to have demonstrated to him. Even if I am doing nothing, or am doing something else, when I am asked what walking is, and if I immediately set about walking, and try to give an answer to the question without a sign, how am I to make sure that "walking" is not taken to mean walking the exact distance that I actually walked. In that case my questioner would be deceived, and would imagine that anyone who walked further or less far than I had walked, had not in fact walked at all. And what I have said of this one action applies to all those which I thought could be demonstrated without a sign, except the two I have mentioned.

30. *Aug.*—I grant that. But now, don't you think speaking and teaching are different things? *Ad.*—Certainly. If they were the same, no one could teach without speaking. Who can doubt there is a difference, seeing that, in fact, we can teach many things with other signs besides words? *Aug.*—Is there any difference between teaching and giving signs? *Ad.*—I think they are the same thing. *Aug.*—So it is correct to say that we give signs in order to teach? *Ad.*—Quite correct. *Aug.*—If anyone says that we teach in order to give signs, he can easily be refuted by the previous sentence? *Ad.*—That is so. *Aug.*—If we give signs in order that we may teach, and do not teach in order that we may give signs, teaching and giving signs are different things. *Ad.*—You are right, and I was wrong when I said they were the same. *Aug.*—Now does he who shows us what teaching is do it by giving signs or otherwise? *Ad.*—I do not see how he can do it otherwise. *Aug.*—So you were wrong in saying a

moment ago that, when the question is what teaching is, the true answer can be given without signs. Even this, we see, cannot be done without signs, and you have agreed that giving signs is a different thing from teaching. If, as now appears, they are different, teaching cannot be demonstrated without signs and by itself alone, as you thought. So up to this point we have discovered nothing that can be demonstrated by simply performing the action except speaking, which consists in giving signs. But even speaking is itself a sign, so that it seems there is absolutely nothing which can be taught without signs. *Ad.*—I have no reason for refusing my assent.

31. *Aug.*—It is established then that: (*a*) nothing is taught without signs, (*b*) knowledge should be more precious to us than the signs by means of which we acquire it; though (*c*) possibly not all things which are signified are better than the signs which indicate them. *Ad.*—So it seems. *Aug.*—Just think what a tiny result has been reached by so long and circuitous a path. Since we began our conversation which has now continued for a long time, we have laboured to find answers to three questions: (*a*) whether anything can be taught without signs, (*b*) whether some signs are to be preferred to the things which they signify, (*c*) whether the knowledge of things is better than the knowledge of their signs. But there is a fourth question to which I should like to hear your answer. Do you think our results now stand beyond all doubt? *Ad.*—I should dearly like to think that after all these turnings and twistings we have indeed reached certainty. But your question makes me anxious, and deters me from answering in the affirmative. For it seems to me that you would not have asked the question unless you had some difficulty in mind. The complexity of our problems does not allow me to examine the whole field or to answer with complete confidence. I am afraid there is something hidden in these complexities, to penetrate to which my mind is not sharp enough. *Aug.*—I am not at all unhappy about your hesitation, for it indicates a cautious mind. And caution is the best guard of tranquillity. It is the most difficult thing in the world not to be upset when opinions which we hold, and to which we have given a too ready and too wilful approval, are shattered by

contrary arguments and are, as it were, weapons torn from our hands. It is a good thing to give in calmly to arguments that are well considered and grasped, just as it is dangerous to hold as known what in fact we do not know. We should be on our guard lest, when things are frequently undermined which we assumed would stand firm and abide, we fall into such hatred or fear of reason that we think we cannot trust even the most clearly manifest truth.

32. But come, let us consider expeditiously whether you do right to hesitate about our conclusions. Suppose someone ignorant of how birds are deceived by twigs and birdlime should meet a birdcatcher equipped with his instruments but merely travelling and not actually engaged in his work. Suppose he followed the birdcatcher step by step and wonderingly thought and inquired what could be the purpose of the man's equipment. Suppose the birdcatcher, seeing him all attention, and eager to display his skill, got ready his twigs and tubes and hawk and caught a bird, would he not teach the spectator what he wanted to know by the action itself and without any signs? *Ad.*—I suspect the same trouble would arise as I described in the case of the man who asked what "walking" was. So far as I see the whole art of birdcatching has not been demonstrated. *Aug.*—That trouble can easily be removed by adding a further supposition. Suppose the spectator were sufficiently intelligent to learn the whole art from what he saw. It is sufficient for our present purpose that some men can be taught some, not all, things without a sign. *Ad.*—I can make the same additional supposition in the other case. A man who is sufficiently intelligent will learn the exact meaning of "walking" when the action has been shown by taking a few paces. *Aug.*—I have no objection to your doing so, and indeed I approve. Both of us have now shown that some men can be taught some things without signs, and that our previous view was wrong, that nothing at all can be shown without signs. Hence not one or two things but thousands of things occur to my mind which can be shown by themselves and without any sign. Why should we doubt it? I need not mention the innumerable spectacles which men exhibit in the theatres, showing them without any

sign and just as they are. Think of the sun, the light that suffuses and clothes all things, the moon and the stars, earth and sea, and the innumerable things they bear. Does not God exhibit them in themselves to those who behold them?

33. If we consider this a little more closely, perhaps you will find that nothing is learned even by its appropriate sign. If I am given a sign and I do not know the thing of which it is the sign, it can teach me nothing. If I know the thing, what do I learn from the sign? When I read (Dan. 3:27: LXX Dan. 3:94): "Their *saraballae* were not changed," the word, *saraballae,* does not indicate what it means. If I am told that some covering of the head is so called, would I know what a head is, or a covering, unless I knew already? Knowledge of such things comes to me not when they are named by others but when I actually see them. When these two syllables first struck my ear, *ca-put,* I was as ignorant of what they meant as I was of the meaning of *saraballae* when I first heard or read it. But when the word, *caput,* was frequently repeated, observing when it was said, I discovered it was the name of a thing well known to me from my having seen it. Before I made that discovery the word was merely a sound to me. It became a sign when I had learned the thing of which it was the sign. And this I had learned not from signs but from seeing the actual object. So the sign is learned from knowing the thing, rather than vice versa.

34. To understand this better, suppose we hear the sound, *caput,* for the first time, not knowing whether it is merely a sound or whether it has some meaning. We ask what *caput* is. Remember we want to know not the thing signified but the sign, although we cannot have that knowledge so long as we do not know what it is a sign of. If, then, in answer to our question the thing is pointed out with a finger, we look at it and learn that that was a sign which we had heard but had not known before. In a sign there are two things, sound and meaning. We perceive the sound when it strikes our ear, while the meaning becomes clear when we look at the thing signified. The pointing with the finger can indicate nothing but the object pointed out, and it points not to a sign but to a part of the body which we call *caput*. In that way, accordingly, I cannot learn the thing,

because I knew it already, nor can I learn the sign because it is not pointed to. I am not greatly interested in the act of pointing. As a gesture it is a sign of something being pointed out rather than of the object pointed out. It is as when we say, "Lo"; for we are accustomed to use that adverb when we point with the finger in case one sign is not sufficient. What I am really trying to convince you of, if I can, is this. We learn nothing by means of these signs we call words. On the contrary, as I said, we learn the force of the word, that is the meaning which lies in the sound of the word, when we come to know the object signified by the word. Then only do we perceive that the word was a sign conveying that meaning.

35. The same is true of the word "coverings," and all the rest. But even when I have come to know them all, I still do not know what *saraballae* are. If someone points them out, or makes a drawing of them, or shows me something like them, I shall not say that he did not teach me what they were, though I could easily prove that that is true with a little more argument. I content myself with saying what is obvious; he did not teach me by words. If he saw them when I was present and called my attention to them by saying: "Lo, there are *saraballae,*" I should learn something I did not know, not from any words spoken but by looking at the object pointed out to me. In this way I should learn and remember the thing that gives meaning to the word. In learning the thing I did not trust the words of another but my own eyes. I trusted the words simply so far as to direct my attention to what was pointed out, that is, to find my answer by looking at a visible object.

xi, 36. The utmost value I can attribute to words is this. They bid us look for things, but they do not show them to us so that we may know them. He alone teaches me anything who sets before my eyes, or one of my other bodily senses, or my mind, the things which I desire to know. From words we can learn only words. Indeed we can learn only their sound and noise. Even if words, in order to be words really, must also be signs, I do not know that any sound I may hear is a word until I know what it means. Knowledge of words is completed by knowledge of things, and by the hearing of words not even words are learned. We learn nothing new when we know the words already, and when we don't know them we cannot say we have learned anything unless we also learn their meaning. And their meaning we learn not from hearing their sound when they are uttered, but from getting to know the things they signify. It is sound reasoning and truly said that when words are spoken we either know or do not know what they mean. If we know, we do not learn, but are rather reminded of what we know. If we do not know, we are not even reminded, but are perhaps urged to inquire.

37. But you may say: granted we cannot know those head-coverings, the sound of whose name we remember, unless we see them, and that we cannot fully know the name until we know the thing. But what about those young men of whom we have heard (Dan. 3) how they vanquished King Nebuchadnezzar and his fiery furnace by their faithfulness and religion, how they sang praises to God, and won honours from their enemy? Have we learned about them otherwise than by means of words? I reply, Yes. But we already knew the meaning of all these words. I already knew the meaning of "three youths," "furnace," "fire," "king," "unhurt by fire" and so on. But the names, Ananias, Azarias and Misael, are as unknown to me as *saraballae,* and the names did not help me to know them and could not help me. All that we read of in that story happened at that time and was written down, so that I have to confess I must believe rather than know. And the writers whom we believe were not ignorant of the difference. For the prophet says: "Unless ye believe ye shall not know" (Isa. 7:9:LXX). This he would not have said if he had thought there was no difference. What I know I also believe, but I do not know everything that I believe. All that I understand I know, but I do not know all that I believe. And I know how useful it is to believe many things which I do not know, among them this story about the three youths. I know how useful it is to believe many things of which knowledge is not possible.

38. Concerning universals of which we can have knowledge, we do not listen to anyone speaking and making sounds outside ourselves. We listen to Truth which presides over our minds

within us, though of course we may be bidden to listen by someone using words. Our real Teacher is he who is so listened to, who is said to dwell in the inner man, namely Christ, that is, the unchangeable power and eternal wisdom of God. To this wisdom every rational soul gives heed, but to each is given only so much as he is able to receive, according to his own good or evil will. If anyone is ever deceived it is not the fault of Truth, any more than it is the fault of the common light of day that the bodily eyes are often deceived. Confessedly we must pay heed to the light that it may let us discern visible things so far as we are able.

xii, 39. On the one hand we need light that we may see colours, and the elements of this world and sentient bodies that we may perceive things of sense, and the senses themselves which the mind uses as interpreters in its search for sense knowledge. On the other hand, to know intelligible things with our reason we pay attention to the interior truth. How, then can it be shown that words teach us anything besides the sound that strikes the ear? Everything we perceive we perceive either by bodily sense or by the mind. The former we call "sensible things," the latter "intelligible things"; or, to use the terminology of our Christian authors, the former we call "carnal things," the latter "spiritual things." When we are asked about the former we reply if they are present to our senses, for example if we are looking at the new moon and someone asks what it is or where. If our questioner does not see it he believes our words or perhaps often does not believe them, but he learns nothing unless he himself sees what he is asking about. When he sees he learns not from words uttered but from the objects seen and his sense of sight. Words would have the same sound whether he saw or not. When the question concerns not things which are present to our senses but which once were, we do not speak of the things themselves, but of images derived from them and imprinted on the memory. I do not know how we can call these things true, since what we have in view are only false images, unless it is because we speak of them not as things we see and feel but as things we have seen and felt. So in the halls of memory we bear the images of things once perceived as memorials which we can contemplate mentally and can speak of with a good conscience and without lying. But these memorials belong to us privately. If anyone hears me speak of them, provided he has seen them himself, he does not learn from my words, but recognizes the truth of what I say by the images which he has in his own memory. But if he has not had these sensations, obviously he believes my words rather than learns from them.

40. But when we have to do with things which we behold with the mind, that is, with the intelligence and with reason, we speak of things which we look upon directly in the inner light of truth which illumines the inner man and is inwardly enjoyed. There again if my hearer sees these things himself with his inward eye, he comes to know what I say, not as a result of my words but as a result of his own contemplation. Even when I speak what is true and he sees what is true, it is not I who teach him. He is taught not by my words but by the things themselves which inwardly God has made manifest to him. Accordingly, if asked he can make answer regarding these things. What could be more absurd than that he should suppose that by my speaking I have taught him, when, if asked, he could himself have explained these things before I spoke? It often happens that a man, when asked a question, gives a negative answer, but by further questioning can be brought to answer in the affirmative. The reason lies in his own weakness. He is unable to let the light illumine the whole problem. Though he cannot behold the whole all at once, yet when he is questioned about the parts which compose the whole, he is induced to bring them one by one into the light. He is so induced by the words of his questioner, words, mark you, which do not make statements, but merely ask such questions as put him who is questioned in a position to learn inwardly. For example, if I were to ask you the question I am at present discussing: "Can nothing be taught by means of words?" it might at first seem to you to be absurd because you cannot visualize the whole problem. So I must put my question in a way suited to your ability to hear the inward Teacher. Then, when you have admitted that what I said was true, that you are certain of it,

and assuredly know it, I should say: "Where did you learn that?" You might reply that I had taught you. Then I should say: "If I were to tell you that I had seen a man flying, would my words render you as certain of their truth as if I had said, 'Wise men are better than fools'?" You would certainly say: "No, I don't believe your first statement, or, if I believe it, I certainly do not *know* that it is true; but your second statement I know most certainly to be true." In this way you would realize that neither in the case of your not knowing what I affirmed, nor in the case of your knowing quite well, had you learned anything from my words, because in answer to each question you were able to answer confidently that you did not know this and that you did know that. When you realize that all the parts which constitute the whole are clear and certain, you will then admit what you had denied. You will agree that a man who has heard what we have said must either not know whether it is true, or know that it is false, or know that it is true. In the first case he must either believe it, or suppose it, or doubt it. In the second case he must oppose it and deny it. In the third case he must testify to its truth. In no case, therefore, will he learn. When my words have been spoken both he who does not know whether my words are true, and he who knows they are false, and he who could have given the same answers when asked are proved to have learned nothing from my words.

xiii, 41. Wherefore in matters which are discerned by the mind, whoever cannot discern them for himself listens vainly to the words of him who can, except that it is useful to believe such things so long as ignorance lasts. Whoever can discern them for himself is inwardly a disciple of the truth, and outwardly a judge of the speaker, or rather of what he says. For often enough the hearer knows what is said even when the speaker does not. For example, suppose some believer in the Epicureans, who held that the soul is mortal, should expound the arguments used by wiser men in favour of the soul's immortality in the hearing of one who can behold spiritual things. The latter judges that the former has spoken the truth, though the speaker does not know whether his words are true, and indeed believes them to be utterly false. Are we to think that he can teach what he does not know? Yet he uses the same words as he might use who does know.

42. Hence words do not even have the function of indicating the mind of the speaker, if it is uncertain whether he knows what he is saying. There are liars too and deceivers, so that you can easily understand that words not only do not reveal the mind, but even serve to conceal it. I do not of course in any way doubt that the words of truthful people are endeavouring to reveal the mind of the speaker and make some claim to do so, and would do so, all would agree, if only liars were not allowed to speak. And yet we have often experienced in ourselves and others that words do not correctly convey thoughts. This can happen in one or other of two ways. A speech committed to memory and frequently conned may be spoken when we are thinking of something else entirely. This often happens when we are singing a hymn. Or by a slip of the tongue some words will get substituted for others against our will, so that those which are heard are not signs of what is in our minds. Liars, too, think of the things they speak about, so that even if we do not know whether they speak the truth, at least we know that they intend what they say, unless either of the two accidents occur which I have mentioned. If anyone contends that this sometimes occurs and can be noticed when it occurs, I make no objection, though it often is hidden and has often escaped my notice when I have been listening.

43. There is the other kind of accident, very widespread and the seed of innumerable dissensions and strifes. The speaker indeed expresses his thoughts but is understood only by himself and by some others. What he says does not convey the same meaning to those who hear him. For example, someone might say in our hearing that some wild beasts surpass man in virtue. Our impulse would be not to endure it, but to use every effort to refute such a false and pestilential opinion. But possibly he is giving the name of virtue to bodily strength, and has correctly expressed his mind. He is not lying. He is not substantially wrong. He is not uttering words committed to memory while he has something else in mind. He has not spoken the wrong word by a slip of the tongue. He has simply called the thing he

has in mind by a different name from the one we are accustomed to use. We should at once agree with him if we could see into his thought, which he had not made clear by the words he used in expressing his opinion. It is said that definition is the remedy for this mistake. If in this question he would define virtue, it would be apparent, they say, that the controversy was not about the substance of his statement but about a word. I should agree that that is so, but how often is a man to be found who is good at definition? Many things, too, are urged against the discipline of definition, but this is not the opportune place to deal with them, and I do not approve of them.

44. I need not mention the fact that often we do not rightly hear what is said, and enter into lengthy arguments over things we wrongly thought we heard. For example, recently, when I said that a certain Punic word meant mercy, you said that you had heard from those who knew the language better that it meant piety. I objected, insisting that you had quite misunderstood what you had been told, for I thought you said not piety but faith. Now you were sitting quite close to me, and these two words are not so alike in sound as to deceive the ear. For a long time I thought you did not know what had been told you, while all the time I did not know what you had said. If I had heard you aright I should not have thought it absurd that piety and mercy should be expressed by one word in Punic. Such misunderstandings often occur, but, as I said, let us omit them lest it should put upon words the blame that is due to the negligence of listeners, or seem to be troubled by human deafness. My chief troubles are those I have mentioned, where by means of words clearly heard, Latin words when Latin is our mother-tongue, we are yet unable to learn the thoughts of those who speak to us.

xiv, 45. Putting aside all these exceptions, I agree that when words are heard by one who knows them, he can also know that the speaker has thought the things which the words signify. Now the question is, does he also learn that the words spoken are true? Do teachers profess that it is their thoughts that are learned and retained, and not the disciplines which they imagine they transmit by their speaking? Who is so foolishly curious as to send his son to school to learn what the teacher thinks? When the teachers have expounded by means of words all the disciplines which they profess to teach, the disciplines also of virtue and wisdom, then their pupils take thought within themselves whether what they have been told is true, looking to the inward truth, that is to say, so far as they are able. In this way they learn. And when they find inwardly that what they have been told is true they praise their teachers, not knowing that they really praise not teachers but learned men, if the teachers really know what they express in words. Men are wrong when they call those teachers who are not. But because very often there is no interval between the moment of speaking and the moment of knowing, and because they inwardly learn immediately after the speaker has given his admonition, they suppose that they have been taught in an external fashion by him who gave the admonition.

46. At another time, if God permit, we shall inquire into the whole problem of the usefulness of words, for their usefulness properly considered is not slight. Now I have warned you that we must not attribute to them a greater importance than they ought to have, so that now we should not only believe but also begin to understand how truly it is written by divine authority that we are to call no one on earth our teacher, for One is our teacher who is in heaven (cf. Matt. 23:10). What is meant by "in heaven" he will teach us, by whom we are admonished through human agency and by external signs to be inwardly converted to him and so to be instructed. To know and to love him is the blessed life, which all proclaim that they are seeking but few have the joy of really finding. But I should like you to tell me what you think of my whole discourse. If you know that what I have said is true, and if you had been interrogated at every point, you would have answered that you knew it to be true. You see, then, who taught you; certainly not I, for you would of your own accord have given the right answer each time I asked. If, on the other hand, you do not know that what I have said is true, neither I nor the inward teacher has taught you. Not I, because I have never the power to teach anyone; and not he, because you have not yet the power to learn. *Ad.*—

I have learned by your warning words, that by means of words a man is simply put on the alert in order that he may learn; also that very little of the thought of a speaker is made evident by his speaking. I have also learned that in order to know the truth of what is spoken, I must be taught by him who dwells within and gives me counsel about words spoken externally in the ear. By his favour I shall love him the more ardently the more I advance in learning. And I am specially grateful that latterly you have spoken without the interruption of questions and answers, because you have taken up and resolved all the difficulties I was prepared to urge against you. You omitted nothing at all that caused me to doubt; and in every case the Secret Oracle of which you have spoken has answered me exactly according to your words.

SUM.

Suggestions for Further Reading

Basic Writings of St. Augustine. W. J. Oates (ed.). 2 vols. New York, 1948; Gilson, E. *The Christian Philosophy of St. Augustine.* New York, 1960; Bourke, V. J. *Augustine's Quest of Wisdom.* Milwaukee, 1949; *FCC* vol. II, pp. 40-91; *EG* 70-81; *AAM* 3-21; *RMcK* vol. 1, pp. 3-64.

The Pseudo-Dionysius

Toward the close of the fifth century there appeared four remarkable treatises destined to have a profound and lasting effect upon subsequent Christian thought: *The Divine Names; The Mystical Theology; The Heavenly Hierarchy;* and *The Earthly Hierarchy.* The author of these writings is entirely unknown; but the reverence and authority accorded his works undoubtedly stemmed from the fact that the medieval world generally believed him to have been that Dionysius whom St. Paul converted to Christianity in Athens (Acts 13:34). Indeed, it was not until the sixteenth century that this belief was discovered to be false. Since then, although there has been lively controversy over the question of actual authorship, there is general agreement that the true author—whoever he was—flourished some four hundred years after the genuine disciple of St. Paul.

As we have already noted, it was Neo-Platonism which proved instrumental in opening the road for St. Augustine's conversion. With the Pseudo-Dionysius—"Pseudo" for obvious reasons—the Middle Ages had yet another source from which Neo-Platonism was to become channeled into Christianity. Actually, it is not at all strange that Christianity should have thus found its earliest expressions in terms drawn originally from the philosophy of Plotinus. The rapport between Neo-Platonism and Christianity had long been recognized by the early Church Fathers, and Marius Victorinus, the translator who first rendered Plotinus' *Enneads* into Latin, had himself died a Christian. Both Neo-Platonism and

Christianity laid emphasis on the contrast between the visible and the invisible worlds; both interpreted man and the universe in similar ways; both recognized a Divine Logos; and both held a doctrine of the Trinity. In the selection given below—an excerpt from *The Divine Names*—we see the Pseudo-Dionysius offering the Neo-Platonic solution to the problem of evil: a solution, it should be noted, which was, in its main features, woven into some of the most impressive Christian philosophical systems of the Middle Ages.

PSEUDO-DIONYSIUS ON THE PROBLEM OF EVIL *

Concerning "Good," "Light," "Beautiful," "Desire," "Ecstasy," "Jealousy." Also that Evil is neither existent nor sprung from anything existent nor inherent in existent things.

1. Now let us consider the name of "Good" which the Sacred Writers apply to the Supra-Divine Godhead in a transcendent manner, calling the Supreme Divine Existence Itself "Goodness" (as it seems to me) in a sense that separates It from the whole creation, and meaning, by this term, to indicate that the Good, under the form of Good-Being, extends Its goodness by the very fact of Its existence unto all things. For as our sun, through no choice or deliberation, but by the very fact of its existence, gives light to all those things which have any inherent power of sharing its illumination, even so the Good (which is above the sun, as the transcendent archetype by the very mode of its existence is above its faded image) sends forth upon all things according to their receptive powers, the rays of Its undivided Goodness. Through these all Spiritual Beings and faculties and activities (whether perceived or

---

* Reprinted by permission of the Society for Promoting Christian Knowledge, from *Dionysius the Areopagite on the Divine Names and the Mystical Theology*. Translated by C. E. Rolt. London, 1920.

percipient) began; through these they exist and possess a life incapable of failure or diminution, and are untainted by any corruption or death or materiality or birth, being separate above all instability and flux and restlessness of change. And whereas they are bodiless and immaterial they are perceived by our minds, and whereas they are minds themselves, they possess a supernatural perception and receive an illumination (after their own manner) concerning the hidden nature of things, from whence they pass on their own knowledge to other kindred spirits. Their rest is in the Divine Goodness, wherein they are grounded, and This Goodness maintains them and protects them and feasts them with Its good things. Through desiring this they possess their being and their blessedness, and, being conformed thereto (according to their powers), they are goodly, and, as the Divine Law commands, pass on to those that are below them, of the gifts which have come unto them from the Good.

2. Hence have they their celestial orders, their self-unities, their mutual indwellings, their distinct Differences, the faculties which raise the lower unto the higher ranks, the providences of the higher for those beneath them; their preservation of the properties belonging to each faculty, their unchanging introversions, their constancy and elevation in their search for the Good, and all the other qualities which we have described in our book concerning the Properties and Orders of the Angels. Moreover all things appertaining to the Celestial Hierarchy, the angelic Purifications, the Illuminations and the attainments which perfect them in all angelic perfection and come from the all-creative and originating Goodness, from whence it was given to them to possess their created goodness, and to manifest the Secret Goodness in themselves, and so to be (as it were) the angelic Evangelists of the Divine Silence and to stand forth as shining lights revealing Him that is within the shrine. And next those sacred and holy Minds, men's souls and all the excellences that belong to souls derive their being from the Super-Excellent Goodness. So do they possess intelligence; so do they preserve their living being immortal; so is it they exist at all, and can, by straining to-

wards the living angelic powers, through their good guidance mount towards the Bounteous Origin of all things; so can they (according to their measure) participate in the illuminations which stream from above and share the bounteous gift (as far as their power extends) and attain all the other privileges which we have recounted in our book, *Concerning the Soul.* Yea, and the same is true, if it must needs be said, concerning even the irrational souls, or living creatures, which cleave the air, or tread the earth, or crawl upon the ground, and those which live among the waters or possess an amphibious life, and all that live buried and covered in the earth—in a word all that possess a sensitive soul or life. All these are endowed with soul and life because the Good exists. And all plants derive from the Good that life which gives them nourishment and motion, and even whatsoever has no life or soul exists through the Good, and thus came into the estate of being.

3. Now if the Good is above all things (as indeed It is) Its Formless Nature produces all-form; and in It alone Not-Being is an excess of Being, and Lifelessness an excess of Life and Its Mindless state is an excess of Wisdom, and all the Attributes of the Good we express in a transcendent manner by negative images. And if it is reverent so to say, even that which *is not* desires the all-transcendent Good and struggles itself, by its denial of all things, to find its rest in the Good which verily transcends all being.

4. Nay, even the foundation and the boundaries of the heavens (as we forgot to say while thinking of other matters) owe their origin to the Good. Such is this universe, which lessens not nor grows, and such the noiseless movements (if noiseless they be) of the vast heavenly revolution, and such the starry orders whose light is fixed as an ornament of heaven, and such the various wanderings of certain stars—especially the repeated and returning orbits of those two luminaries to which the Scripture giveth the name of "Great," whereby we reckon our days and nights and months and years; which define the round of time and temporal events and give them measurement, sequence, and cohesion. And what shall I say concerning the sun's rays considered in themselves? From the

Good comes the light which is an image of Goodness; wherefore the Good is described by the name of "Light," being the archetype thereof which is revealed in that image. For as the Goodness of the all-transcendent Godhead reaches from the highest and most perfect forms of being unto the lowest, and still is beyond them all, remaining superior to those above and retaining those below in its embrace, and so gives light to all things that can receive It, and creates and vitalizes and maintains and perfects them, and is the Measure of the Universe and its Eternity, its Numerical Principle, its Order, its Embracing Power, its Cause and its End: even so this great, all-bright and ever-shining sun, which is the visible image of the Divine Goodness, faintly re-echoing the activity of the Good, illumines all things that can receive its light while retaining the utter simplicity of light, and expands above and below throughout the visible world the beams of its own radiance. And if there is aught that does not share them, this is not due to any weakness or deficiency in its distribution of the light, but is due to the unreceptiveness of those creatures which do not attain sufficient singleness to participate therein. For verily the light passeth over many such substances and enlightens those which are beyond them, and there is no visible thing unto which the light reacheth not in the exceeding greatness of its proper radiance. Yea, and it contributes to the birth of material bodies and brings them unto life, and nourishes them that they may grow, and perfects and purifies and renews them. And the light is the measure and the numerical principle of seasons and of days and of all our earthly Time; for 'tis the selfsame light (though then without a form) which, Moses the Divine declares, marked even that first period of three days which was at the beginning of time. And like as Goodness draweth all things to Itself, and is the great Attractive Power which unites things that are sundered (being as It is: the Godhead and the Supreme Fount and Producer of Unity); and like as all things desire It as their beginning, their cohesive power and end; and like as 'tis the Good (as saith the Scripture) from which all things were made and are (having been brought into existence thence as from a Perfect

Cause); and like as in the Good all things subsist, being kept and controlled in an almighty Receptacle; and like as unto the Good all things are turned (as unto the proper End of each); and like as after the Good all things do yearn—those that have mind and reason seeking It by knowledge, those that have perception seeking It by perception, those that have no perception seeking It by the natural movement of their vital instinct, and those that are without life and have mere existence seeking It by their aptitude for that bare participation whence this mere existence is theirs—even so doth the light (being as it were Its visible image) draw together all things and attract them unto Itself those that can see, those that have motion, those that receive Its light and warmth, those that are merely held in being by Its rays; whence the sun is so called because it summeth all things and uniteth the scattered elements of the world. All material things desire the sun, for they desire either to see or to move and to receive light and warmth and to be maintained in existence by the light. I say not (as was feigned by the ancient myth) that the sun is the God and Creator of this Universe, and therefore takes the visible world under his special care; but I say that the "invisible things of God from the creation of the world are clearly seen, being understood by the things that are made, even His eternal power and Godhead."

5. But these things are dealt with in the "Symbolic Divinity." Here I desire to declare what is the spiritual meaning of the name "Light" as belonging to the Good. The Good God is called Spiritual Light because He fills every heavenly mind with spiritual light, and drives all ignorance and error from all souls where they have gained a lodgment, and giveth them all a share of holy light and purges their spiritual eyes from the mist of ignorance that surrounds them, and stirs and opens the eyes which are fast shut and weighed down with darkness, and gives them first a moderate illumination, then (when they taste the Light and desire It more) He giveth Himself in greater measure and shineth in more abundance on them "because they have loved much," and ever He constraineth them according to their powers of looking upwards.

6. And so that Good which is above all light is called a Spiritual Light because It is an Originating Beam and an Overflowing Radiance, illuminating with its fullness every Mind above the world, around it, or within it, and renewing all their spiritual powers, embracing them all by Its transcendent compass and exceeding them all by Its transcendent elevation. And It contains within Itself, in a simple form, the entire ultimate principle of light; and is the Transcendent Archetype of Light; and, while bearing the light in its womb, It exceeds it in quality and precedes it in time; and so conjoineth together all spiritual and rational beings, uniting them in one. For as ignorance leadeth wanderers astray from one another, so doth the presence of Spiritual Light join and unite together those that are being illuminated, and perfects them and converts them toward that which truly Is—yea, converts them from their manifold false opinions and unites their different perceptions, or rather fancies, into one true, pure and coherent knowledge, and filleth them with one unifying light.

7. This Good is described by the Sacred Writers as Beautiful and as Beauty, as Love or Beloved, and by all other Divine titles which befit Its beautifying and gracious fairness. Now there is a distinction between the titles "Beautiful" and "Beauty" applied to the all-embracing Cause. For we universally distinguish these two titles as meaning respectively the qualities shared and the objects which share therein. We give the name of "Beautiful" to that which shares in the quality of beauty, and we give the name of "Beauty" to that common quality by which all beautiful things are beautiful. But the Super-Essential Beautiful is called "Beauty" because of that quality which It imparts to all things severally according to their nature, and because It is the Cause of the harmony and splendour in all things, flashing forth upon them all, like light, the beautifying communications of Its originating ray; and because It summons all things to *fare* unto Itself (from whence It hath the name of "Fairness"), and because It draws all things together in a state of mutual interpenetration. And it is called "Beautiful" because It is All-Beautiful and more than Beautiful, and is eternally, unvaryingly, unchangeably Beauti-

ful; incapable of birth or death or growth or decay; and not beautiful in one part and foul in another; nor yet at one time and not at another; nor yet beautiful in relation to one thing but not to another; nor yet beautiful in one place and not in another (as if It were beautiful for some but were not beautiful for others); nay, on the contrary, It is, in Itself and by Itself, uniquely and eternally beautiful, and from beforehand It contains in a transcendent manner the originating beauty of everything that is beautiful. For in the simple and supernatural nature belonging to the world of beautiful things, all beauty and all that is beautiful hath its unique and pre-existent Cause. From this Beautiful all things possess their existence, each kind being beautiful in its own manner, and the Beautiful causes the harmonies and sympathies and communities of all things. And by the Beautiful all things are united together and the Beautiful is the beginning of all things, as being the Creative Cause which moves the world and holds all things in existence by their yearning for their own Beauty. And It is the Goal of all things, and their Beloved, as being their Final Cause (for 'tis the desire of the Beautiful that brings them all into existence), and It is their Exemplar from which they derive their definite limits; and hence the Beautiful is the same as the Good, inasmuch as all things, in all causation, desire the Beautiful and Good; nor is there anything in the world but hath a share in the Beautiful and Good. Moreover our Discourse will dare to aver that even the Non-Existent shares in the Beautiful and Good, for Non-Existence is itself beautiful and good when, by the Negation of all Attributes, it is ascribed Super-Essentially to God. This One Good and Beautiful is in Its oneness the Cause of all the many beautiful and good things. Hence comes the bare existence of all things, and hence their unions, their differentiations, their identities, their differences, their similarities, their dissimilarities, their communions of opposite things, the unconfused distinctions of their interpenetrating elements; the providences of the Superiors, the interdependence of the Co-ordinates, the responses of the Inferiors, the states of permanence wherein all keep their own identity. And hence again the intercommunion of all things according to the power of each; their harmonies and sympathies (which do not merge them) and the co-ordinations of the whole universe; the mixture of elements therein and the indestructible ligaments of things; the ceaseless succession of the recreative process in Minds and Souls and in Bodies; for all have rest and movement in That Which, above all rest and all movement, grounds each one in its own natural laws and moves each one to its own proper movement.

8. And the Heavenly Minds are spoken of as moving (1) in a circular manner, when they are united to the beginningless and endless illuminations of the Beautiful and Good; (2) straight forward, when they advance to the providential guidance of those beneath them and unerringly accomplish their designs; and (3) with spiral motion, because, even while providentially guiding their inferiors, they remain immutably in their self-identity, turning unceasingly around the Beautiful and Good whence all identity is sprung.

9. And the soul hath (1) a circular movement—viz. an introversion from things without and the unified concentration of its spiritual powers—which gives it a kind of fixed revolution, and, turning it from the multiplicity without, draws it together first into itself, and then (after it has reached this unified condition) unites it to those powers which are a perfect Unity, and thus leads it on unto the Beautiful and Good Which is beyond all things, and is One and is the Same, without beginning or end. (2) And the soul moves with a spiral motion whensoever (according to its capacity) it is enlightened with truths of Divine Knowledge, not in the special unity of its being but by the process of its discursive reason and by mingled and alternative activities. (3) And it moves straight forward when it does not enter into itself to feel the stirrings of its spiritual unity (for this, as I said, is the circular motion), but goes forth unto the things around it and feels an influence coming even from the outward world, as from a rich abundance of cunning tokens, drawing it unto the simple unity of contemplative acts.

10. These three motions, and also the similar motions we perceive in this material world and (far anterior to these) the

individual permanence, rest and grounding of each Kind have their Efficient, Formal, and Final Cause in the Beautiful and Good; Which is above all rest and motion; through Which all rest and motion come; and from Which, and in Which, and unto Which, and for the sake of Which they are. For from It and through It are all Being and life of spirit and of soul; and hence in the realm of nature magnitudes both small, co-equal and great; hence all the measured order and the proportions of things, which, by their different harmonies, commingle into wholes made up of co-existent parts; hence this universe, which is both One and Many; the conjunctions of parts together; the unities underlying all multiplicity, and the perfections of the individual wholes; hence Quality, Quantity, Magnitude and Infinitude; hence fusions and differentiations, hence all infinity and all limitation; all boundaries, ranks, transcendences, elements and forms, hence all Being, all Power, all Activity, all Condition, all Perception, all Reason, all Intuition, all Apprehension, all Understanding, all Communion—in a word, all that *is* comes from the Beautiful and Good, hath its very existence in the Beautiful and Good, and turns towards the Beautiful and Good. Yea, all that exists and that comes into being, exists and comes into being because of the Beautiful and Good; and unto this Object all things gaze and by It are moved and are conserved, and for the sake of It, because of It and in It, existeth every originating Principle—be this Exemplar, or be it Final or Efficient or Formal or Material Cause—in a word, all Beginning, all Conservation, and all Ending, or (to sum it up) all things that have being are derived from the Beautiful and Good. Yea, and all things that have no substantial being super-essentially exist in the Beautiful and Good: this is the transcendent Beginning and the transcendent Goal of the universe. For, as Holy Scripture saith: "Of Him, and through Him, and to Him, are all things: to whom be glory for ever. Amen." And hence all things must desire and yearn for and must love the Beautiful and the Good. Yea, and because of It and for Its sake the inferior things yearn for the superior under the mode of attraction, and those of the same rank have a yearning towards their peers under the mode of mutual communion; and the superior have a yearning towards their inferiors under the mode of providential kindness; and each hath a yearning towards itself under the mode of cohesion, and all things are moved by a longing for the Beautiful and Good, to accomplish every outward work and form every act of will. And true reasoning will also dare to affirm that even the Creator of all things Himself yearneth after all things, createth all things, perfecteth all things, conserveth all things, attracteth all things, through nothing but excess of Goodness. Yea, and the Divine Yearning is naught else than a Good Yearning towards the Good for the mere sake of the Good. For the Yearning which createth all the goodness of the world, being pre-existent abundantly in the Good Creator, allowed Him not to remain unfruitful in Himself, but moved Him to exert the abundance of His powers in the production of the universe.

11. And let no man think we are contradicting the Scripture when we solemnly proclaim the title of "Yearning." For 'tis, methinks, unreasonable and foolish to consider the phrases rather than the meaning; and such is not the way of them that wish for insight into things Divine, but rather of them that receive the empty sounds without letting them pass beyond their ears, and shut them out, not wishing to know what such and such a phrase intends, nor how they ought to explain it in other terms expressing the same sense more clearly. Such men are under the dominion of senseless elements and lines, and of uncomprehended syllables and phrases which penetrate not into the perception of their souls, but make a dumb noise outside about their lips and hearing: holding it unlawful to explain the number "four" by calling it "twice two," or a straight line by calling it a "direct line" or the "Motherland" by calling it the "Fatherland," or so to interchange any other of those terms which under varieties of language possess all the same signification. Need is there to understand that in proper truth we do but use the elements and syllables and phrases and written terms and words as an aid to our senses; inasmuch as when our soul is moved by spiritual energies unto spiritual things, our senses, together with the

thing which they perceive, are all superfluous; even as the spiritual faculties are also such when the soul, becoming God-like, meets in the blind embraces of an incomprehensible union the Rays of the unapproachable Light. Now when the mind, through the things of sense, feels an eager stirring to mount towards spiritual contemplations, it values most of all those aids from its perceptions which have the plainest form, the clearest words, the things most distinctly seen, because, when the objects of sense are in confusion, then the senses themselves cannot present their message truly to the mind. But that we may not seem, in saying this, to be setting aside Holy Scripture, let those who blame the title of "Yearning" hear what the Scripture saith: "Yearn for her and she shall keep thee; exalt her and she shall promote thee; she shall bring thee to honour when thou dost embrace her." And there are many other such Scriptural passages which speak of this yearning.

12. Nay, some of our writers about holy things have thought the title of "Yearning" diviner than that of "Love." Ignatius the Divine writes: "He whom I yearn for is crucified." And in the "Introductions" of Scripture thou wilt find some one saying concerning the Divine Wisdom: "I yearned for her beauty." Let us not, therefore, shrink from this title of "Yearning," nor be perturbed and affrighted by aught that any man may say about it. For methinks the Sacred Writers regard the titles "Love" and "Yearning" as of one meaning; but preferred, when speaking of Yearning in a heavenly sense, to qualify it with the word "real" because of the inconvenient pre-notion of such men. For whereas the title of "Real Yearning" is employed not merely by ourselves but even by the Scriptures, mankind (not grasping the unity intended when Yearning is ascribed to God) fell by their own propensity into the notion of a partial, physical and divided quality, which is not true Yearning but a vain image of Real Yearning, or rather a lapse therefrom. For mankind at large cannot grasp the simplicity of the one Divine Yearning, and hence, because of the offence it gives to most men, it is used concerning the Divine Wisdom to lead and raise them up to the knowledge of the Real Yearning until they are set free from all offence

thereat; and often on the other hand when it was possible that base minds should suppose that which is not convenient, the word that is held in greater reverence is used concerning ourselves. "Thy love," says some one, "came upon me like as the love of women." To those who listen aright to Holy Scripture, the word "Love" is used by the Sacred Writers in Divine Revelation with the same meaning as the word "Yearning." It means a faculty of unifying and conjoining and of producing a special commingling together in the Beautiful and Good: a faculty which pre-exists for the sake of the Beautiful and Good, and is diffused from this Origin and to this End, and holds together things of the same order by a mutual connection, and moves the highest to take thought for those below and fixes the inferior in a state which seeks the higher.

13. And the Divine Yearning brings ecstasy, not allowing them that are touched thereby to belong unto themselves but only to the objects of their affection. This principle is shown by superior things through their providential care for their inferiors, and by those which are co-ordinate through the mutual bond uniting them, and by the inferior through their diviner tendency towards the highest. And hence the great Paul, constrained by the Divine Yearning, and having received a share in its ecstatic power, says, with inspired utterance, "I live, and yet not I but Christ liveth in me": true Sweetheart that he was and (as he says himself) being beside himself unto God, and not possessing his own life but possessing and loving the life of Him for Whom he yearned. And we must dare to affirm (for 'tis the truth) that the Creator of the Universe Himself, in His Beautiful and Good Yearning towards the Universe, is through the excessive yearning of His Goodness, transported outside of Himself in His providential activities towards all things that have being, and is touched by the sweet spell of Goodness, Love and Yearning, and so is drawn from His transcendent throne above all things, to dwell within the heart of all things, through a super-essential and ecstatic power whereby He yet stays within Himself. Hence Doctors call Him "jealous," because He is vehement

in His Good Yearning towards the world, and because He stirs men up to a zealous search of yearning desire for Him, and thus shows Himself zealous inasmuch as zeal is always felt concerning things which are desired, and inasmuch as He hath a zeal concerning the creatures for which He careth. In short, both the Yearning and its Object belong to the Beautiful and the Good, and have therein their pre-existent roots and because of it exist and come into being.

14. But why speak the Sacred Writers of God sometimes as Yearning and Love, sometimes as the Object of these emotions? In the one case He is the Cause and Producer and Begetter of the thing signified, in the other He is the Thing signified Itself. Now the reason why He is Himself on the one hand moved by the quality signified, and on the other causes motion by it, is that He moves and leads onward Himself unto Himself. Therefore on the one hand they call Him the Object of Love and Yearning as being Beautiful and Good, and on the other they call Him Yearning and Love as being a Motive-Power leading all things to Himself, Who is the only ultimate Beautiful and Good—yea, as being His own Self-Revelation and the Bounteous Emanation of His own Transcendent Unity, a Motion of Yearning simple, self-moved, self-acting, pre-existent in the Good, and overflowing from the Good into creation, and once again returning to the Good. And herein the Divine Yearning showeth especially its beginningless and endless nature, revolving in a perpetual circle for the Good, from the Good, in the Good, and to the Good, with unerring revolution, never varying its centre or direction, perpetually advancing and remaining and returning to Itself. This by Divine inspiration our renowned Initiator hath declared in his *Hymns of Yearning,* which it will not be amiss to quote and thus to bring unto a holy consummation our Discourse concerning this matter.

15. Words of the most holy Hierotheus from the *Hymns of Yearning.* "Yearning (be it in God or Angel, or Spirit, or Animal Life, or Nature) must be conceived of as an uniting and commingling power which moveth the higher things to a

care for those below them, moveth co-equals to a mutual communion, and finally moveth the inferiors to turn towards their superiors in virtue and position."

16. Words of the same, from the same *Hymns of Yearning*. "Forasmuch as we have set down in order the manifold yearnings springing from the One, and have duly explained what are the powers of knowledge and of action belonging to the yearnings springing from the One, and have duly explained what are the powers of knowledge and of action proper to the Yearnings within the world and above it (wherein, as hath been already explained, the higher place belongeth unto those ranks and orders of Yearning which are spiritually felt and perceived, and highest amongst these are the Divine Yearnings in the very core of the Spirit towards those Beauties which have their veritable Being Yonder), let us now yet further resume and compact them all together into the one and concentrated Yearning which is the Father of them all, and let us collect together into two kinds their general desiderative powers, over which the entire mastery and primacy is in that Incomprehensible Causation of all yearning which cometh from Beyond them all, and whereunto the universal yearning of all creatures presseth upwards according to the nature of each."

17. Words of the same, from the same *Hymns of Yearning*. "Let us once more collect these powers into one and declare that there is but One Simple Power Which of Itself moveth all things to be mingled in an unity, starting from the Good and going unto the lowest of the creatures and thence again returning through all stages in due order unto the Good, and thus revolving from Itself, and through Itself and upon Itself and towards Itself, in an unceasing orbit."

18. Now some one, perhaps, will say: "If the Beautiful and Good is an Object of Yearning and desire and love to all (for even that which *is not* longs for It, as was said, and strives to find its rest therein, and thus It creates a form even in formless things and thus is said super-essentially to *contain*, and does so *contain*, the non-existent)—if this is so, how is it that the company of the devils desires not the Beautiful and Good,

but, being inclined towards matter and fallen far from the fixed angelic state of desire for the Good, becomes a cause of all evils to itself and to all other beings which we describe as becoming evil? How is it that the devils, having been produced wholly out of the Good, are not good in disposition? Or how is it that, if produced good from out of the Good, they became changed? What made them evil, and indeed what is the nature of evil? From what origin did it arise and in what thing doth it lie? Why did He that is Good will to produce it? And how, having so willed, was He able so to do? And if evil comes from some other cause, what other cause can anything have excepting the Good? How, if there is a Providence, doth evil exist, or arise at all, or escape destruction? And why doth anything in the world desire it instead of Good?"

19. Thus perhaps will such bewildered discourse speak. Now we will bid the questioner look towards the truth of things, and in the first place we will venture thus to answer: "Evil cometh not of the Good; and if it cometh therefrom it is not evil. For even as fire cannot cool us, so Good cannot produce the things which are not good. And if all things that have being come from the Good (for it is natural to the Good to produce and preserve the creatures, and natural to evil to corrupt and to destroy them) then nothing in the world cometh of evil. Then evil cannot even in any wise exist, if it act as evil upon itself. And unless it do so act, evil is not wholly evil, but hath some portion of the Good whereby it can exist at all. And if the things that have being desire the Beautiful and Good and accomplish all their acts for the sake of that which seemeth good, and if all that they intend hath the Good as its Motive and its Aim (for nothing looks unto the nature of evil to guide it in its actions), what place is left for evil among things that have being, or how can it have any being at all bereft of such good purpose? And if all things that have being come of the Good and the Good is Beyond things that have being, then, whereas that which exists not yet hath being in the Good; evil contrariwise hath none (otherwise it were not wholly evil or *Non-Ens;* for that which is wholly *Non-Ens* can be but naught except this be spoken Super-Essentially of the

Good). So the Good must have Its seat far above and before that which hath mere being and that which hath not; but evil hath no place either amongst things that have being or things that have not, yea it is farther removed than the Non-Existent from the Good and hath less being than it. 'Then' (saith one perchance) 'whence cometh evil? For if' (saith he) 'evil is not, virtue and vice must needs be the same both in their whole entirety and in their corresponding particulars,'—*i.e.* even that which fighteth against virtue cannot be evil. And yet temperance is the opposite of debauchery, and righteousness of wickedness. And I mean not only the righteous and the unrighteous man, or the temperate and intemperate man; I mean that, even before the external distinction appeared between the virtuous man and his opposite, the ultimate distinction between the virtues and the vices hath existed long beforehand in the soul itself, and the passions war against the reason, and hence we must assume something evil which is contrary to goodness. For goodness is not contrary to itself, but, being come from One Beginning and being the offspring of One Cause, it rejoices in fellowship, unity, and concord. Even the lesser Good is not contrary to the greater, for that which is less hot or cold is not contrary to that which is more so. Wherefore evil lieth in the things that have being and possesseth being and is opposed and contrary to goodness. And if evil is the destruction of things which have being, that depriveth it not of its own being. It itself still hath being and giveth being to its offspring. Yea, is not the destruction of one thing often the birth of another? And thus it will be found that evil maketh contribution unto the fullness of the world, and through its presence, saveth the universe from imperfection."

20. The true answer whereunto will be that evil (*qua* evil) causes no existence or birth, but only debases and corrupts, so far as its power extends, the substance of things that have being. And if any one says that it is productive, and that by the destruction of one thing it giveth birth to somewhat else, the true answer is that it doth not so *qua* destructive. *Qua* destructive and evil it only destroys and debases; but it taketh upon it the form of birth and essence through the action of

the Good. Thus evil will be found to be a destructive force in itself, but a productive force through the action of the Good. *Qua* evil it neither hath being nor confers it; through the action of the Good, it hath being (yea, a good being) and confers being on good things. Or rather (since we cannot call the same thing both good and bad in the same relations, nor are the destruction and birth of the same thing the same function or faculty, whether productive or destructive, working in the same relations), Evil in itself hath neither being, goodness, productiveness, nor power of creating things which have being and goodness; the Good, on the other hand, wherever It becomes perfectly present, creates perfect, universal and untainted manifestations of goodness; while the things which have a lesser share therein are imperfect manifestations of goodness and mixed with other elements through lack of the Good. In fine, evil is not in any wise good, nor the maker of good; but every thing must be good only in proportion as it approacheth more or less unto the Good, since the perfect Goodness penetrating all things reacheth not only to the wholly good beings around It, but extendeth even unto the lowest things, being entirely present unto some, and in a lower measure to others, and unto others in lowest measure, according as each one is capable of participating therein. Some creatures participate wholly in the Good, others are lacking in It less or more, and others possess a still fainter participation therein, while to others the Good is present as but the faintest echo. For if the Good were not present only in a manner proportioned unto each, then the divinest and most honourable things would be no higher than the lowest! And how, pray, could all things have a uniform share in the Good, since not all are equally fit to share entirely therein? But in truth the exceeding greatness of the power of the Good is shown by this—that It giveth power even to the things which lack It, yea even unto that very lack itself, inasmuch as even here is to be found some kind of participation in It. And, if we must needs boldly speak the truth, even the things that fight against It possess through Its power their being and their capability to fight. Or rather, to speak shortly, all creatures in so far as they have being are good and come from the Good, and in so far as they are deprived of the Good, neither are good nor have they being. For in the case of other qualities, such as heat or cold, the things which have been warmed have their being even when they lose their warmth, and many of the creatures there are which have no life or mind; and in like manner God transcendeth all being and so is Super-Essential; and generally, in all other cases, though the quality be gone or hath never been present, the creatures yet have being and can subsist; but that which is utterly bereft of the Good never had, nor hath, nor ever shall have, no nor can have any sort of being whatever. For instance, the depraved sinner, though bereft of the Good by his brutish desire, is in this respect unreal and desires unrealities; but still he hath a share in the Good in so far as there is in him a distorted reflection of true Love and Communion. And anger hath a share in the Good, in so far as it is a movement which seeks to remedy apparent evils, converting them to that which appears to be fair. And even he that desires the basest life, yet in so far as he feels desire at all and feels desire for life, and intends what he thinks the best kind of life, so far participates in the Good. And if you wholly destroy the Good, there will be neither being, life, desire, nor motion, or any other thing. Hence the birth of fresh life out of destruction is not the function of evil but is the presence of Good in a lesser form, even as disease is a disorder, yet not the destruction of all order, for if this happen the disease itself will not exist. But the disease remains and exists. Its essence is order reduced to a *minimum;* and in this it consists. For that which is utterly without the Good hath neither being nor place amongst the things that are in being; but that which is of mixed nature owes to the Good its place among things in being, and hath this place amongst them and hath being just so far as it participates in the Good. Or rather all things in being will have their being more or less in proportion as they participate in the Good. For so far as mere Being is concerned, that which hath not being in any respect will not exist at all; that which hath being in one respect but not in another doth not exist in so far as it hath fallen away from the everlasting Being; while in so far as it hath a share of being, to that extent it exists; and thus both an element of existence and an element of non-existence in it are kept and preserved. So too with evil. That which is utterly fallen from Good can have no place either in the things which are more good or in the things which are less so. That which is good in one respect but not in another is at war with some particular good but not with the whole of the Good. It also is preserved by the admixture of the Good, and thus the Good giveth existence to the lack of Itself through some element of Itself being present there. For if the Good be entirely removed, there will not remain aught at all, either good or mixed or absolutely bad. For if evil is imperfect Goodness, the perfect absence of the Good will remove both the perfect and the imperfect Good, and evil will only exist and appear because, while it is evil in relation to one kind of good (being the contrary thereof), yet it depends for its existence on another kind of good and, to that extent, is good itself. For things of the same kind cannot be wholly contradictory to one another in the same respects. Hence evil is Non-Existent.

21. Neither inhereth evil in existent creatures. For if all creatures are from the Good, and the Good is in them all and embraces them all, either evil can have no place amongst the creatures, or else it must have a place in the Good. Now it cannot inhere in the Good, any more than cold can inhere in fire; just so the quality of becoming evil cannot inhere in that which turns even evil into good. And if evil doth inhere in the Good, what will the mode of its inherence be? If you say: It cometh of the Good, I answer: That is absurd and impossible. For (as the infallible Scriptures say), a good tree cannot bring forth evil fruit, nor yet is the converse possible. But if it cometh not of the Good, it is plainly from another origin and cause. Either evil must come from the Good, or the Good from evil, or else (if this is impossible) both the Good and evil must be from another origin or cause. For no duality can be an origin: some unity must be the origin of all duality. And yet it is absurd to suppose that two entirely opposite things can owe their birth and their being to the same thing. This

would make the origin itself not a simple unity but divided, double, self-contradictory and discordant. Nor again is it possible that the world should have two contradictory origins, existing in each other and in the whole and mutually at strife. For, were this assumed, God cannot be free from pain, nor without a feeling of ill, since there would be something causing Him trouble, yea, all things must in that case be in a state of disorder and perpetual strife; whereas the Good imparts a principle of harmony to all things and is called by the Sacred Writers Peace and the Bestower of Peace. And hence it is that all good things display a mutual attraction and harmony, and are the offspring of one Life and are disposed in fellowship towards one Good, and are kindly, of like nature, and benignant to one another. And so evil is not in God, and is not divine. Nor cometh it of God. For either He is not good, or else He worketh goodness and bringeth good things unto existence. Nor acts He thus only at some times and not at others, or only in the case of some things but not of all. For were He to act thus, He must suffer a change and alteration, and that in respect of the divinest quality of all—causality. And if the Good is in God as His very substance, God must, in changing from the Good, sometimes exist and sometimes not exist. Doubtless if you feign that He hath the Good by mere participation therein, and derives It from another, in that case He will, forsooth, sometimes possess It and sometimes not possess It. Evil, therefore, doth not come from God, nor is it in God either absolutely or temporally.

22. Neither inhereth evil in the angels. For if the good angel declares the Divine Goodness, he is in a secondary manner and by participation that which the Subject of his message is in a primary and causal manner. And thus the angel is an image of God, a manifestation of the invisible light, a burnished mirror, bright, untarnished, without spot or blemish, receiving (if it is reverent to say so) all the beauty of the Absolute Divine Goodness, and (so far as may be) kindling in itself, with unallowed radiance, the Goodness of the Secret Silence. Hence evil inhereth not in the angels; they are evil only in so far as they must punish sinners. But in this respect even

those who chastise wrong-doers are evil, and so are the priests who exclude the profane man from the Divine Mysteries. But, indeed, 'tis not the suffering of the punishment that is evil but the being worthy thereof; nor yet is a just exclusion from the sacrifices evil, but to be guilty and unholy and unfit for those pure mysteries is evil.

23. Nor are the devils naturally evil. For, were they such, they would not have sprung from the Good, nor have a place amongst existent creatures, nor have fallen from Goodness (being by their very nature always evil). Moreover, are they evil with respect to themselves or to others? If the former they must also be self-destructive; if the latter, how do they destroy, and what do they destroy? Do they destroy Essence, or Faculty, or Activity? If Essence, then, first, they cannot destroy it contrary to its own nature; for they cannot destroy things which by their nature are indestructible, but only the things which are capable of destruction. And, secondly, destruction itself is not evil in every case and under all circumstances. Nor can any existent thing be destroyed so far as its being and nature act; for its destruction is due to a failure of its natural order, whereby the principle of harmony and symmetry grows weak and so cannot remain unchanged. But the weakness is not complete; for, were it complete, it would have annihilated both the process of destruction and the object which suffers it and such a destruction as this must be self-destructive. Hence such a quality is not evil but imperfect good; for that which is wholly destitute of the Good can have no place among things that have being. And the same is true of destruction when it works upon a faculty or activity. Moreover, how can the devils be evil since they are sprung from God? For the Good produceth and createth good things. But it may be said that they are called evil not in so far as they exist (for they are from the Good and had a good existence given them), but in so far as they do not exist, having been unable (as the Scripture saith) to keep their original state. For in what, pray, do we consider the wickedness of the devils to consist except their ceasing from the quality and activity of divine virtues? Otherwise, if the devils are naturally evil, they must be always evil.

But evil is unstable. Hence if they are always in the same condition, they are not evil; for to remain always the same is a property of the Good. But if they are not always evil, then they are not evil by their natural constitution, but only through a lack of angelic virtues. Hence they are not utterly without the Good, seeing that they exist and live and form intuitions and have within them any movement of desire at all; but they are called evil because they fail in the exercise of their natural activity. The evil in them is therefore a warping, a declension from their right condition; a failure, an imperfection, an impotence, and a weakness, loss and lapse of that power which would preserve their perfection in them. Moreover what is the evil in the devils? Brutish wrath, bland desire, headstrong fancy. But these qualities, even though they exist in the devils, are not wholly, invariably, and essentially evil. For in other living creatures, not the possession of these qualities but their loss is destructive of the creature and hence is evil; while their possession preserves the creature and enables the creature possessing them to exist. Hence the devils are not evil in so far as they fulfil their nature, but in so far as they do not. Nor hath the Good bestowed complete upon them been changed; rather have they fallen from the completeness of that gift. And we maintain that the angelic gifts bestowed upon them have never themselves suffered change, but are unblemished in their perfect brightness, even if the devils themselves do not perceive it through blinding their faculties of spiritual perception. Thus, so far as their existence is concerned, they possess it from the Good, and are naturally good, and desire the Beautiful and Good in desiring existence, life, and intuition, which are existent things. And they are called evil through the deprivation and the loss whereby they have lapsed from their proper virtues. And hence they are evil in so far as they do not exist; and in desiring evil they desire that which is nonexistent.

24. But perhaps someone will say that human souls are the seat of evil. Now if the reason alleged is that they have contact with evil temptations when they take forethought to preserve themselves therefrom, this is not evil but good and

cometh from the Good that turns even evil into good. But if we mean the depravation which souls undergo, in what do they undergo depravation except in the deficiency of good qualities and activities and in the failure and fall therefrom due to their own weakness? Even so we say that the air is darkened around us by a deficiency and absence of the light; while yet the light itself is always light and illuminates the darkness. Hence the evil inhereth not in the devils or in us, *as* evil, but only as a deficiency and lack of the perfection of our proper virtues.

25. Neither inhereth evil in the brute beasts. For if you take away the passions of anger, desire, etc. (which are not in their essential nature evil, although alleged to be so), the lion, having lost its savage wildness, will be a lion no longer; and the dog, if it become gentle to all, will cease to be a dog, since the virtue of a dog is to watch and to allow its own masters to approach while driving strangers away. Wherefore 'tis not evil for a creature so to act as preserveth its nature undestroyed; evil is the destruction of its nature, the weakness and deficiency of its natural qualities, activities, and powers. And if all things which the process of generation produces have their goal of perfection in time, then even that which seemeth to be their imperfection is not wholly and entirely contrary to nature.

26. Neither inhereth evil in nature as a whole. For if all natural laws together come from the universal system of Nature, there is nothing contrary to Nature. 'Tis but when we consider the nature of particular things, that we find one part of Nature to be natural and another part to be unnatural. For one thing may be unnatural in one case, and another thing in another case; and that which is natural in one is unnatural in another. Now the evil taint of a natural force is something unnatural. It is a lack of the thing's natural virtues. Hence, no natural force is evil: the evil of nature lies in a thing's inability to fulfil its natural functions.

27. Neither inhereth evil in our bodies. For ugliness and disease are a deficiency in form and a want of order. But this is not wholly evil, being rather a lesser good. For were there

a complete destruction of beauty, form, and order, the very body must disappear. And that the body is not the cause of evil in the soul is plain in that evil can be nigh at hand even without a body, as it is in the devils. Evil in spirits' souls and bodies is a weakness and lapse in the condition of their natural virtues.

28. Nor is the familiar notion true that "Evil inheres in matter *qua* matter." For matter, too, hath a share in order, beauty, and form. And if matter is without these things, and in itself hath no quality or form, how can it produce anything, since in that case it hath not of itself even the power of suffering any affection? Nay, how can matter be evil? For it hath no being whatever, it is neither good nor evil; but it hath a kind of being, then (since all things that have being come from the Good) matter must come from the Good. And thus either the Good produces evil (*i.e.* evil, since it comes from the Good, is good), or else the Good Itself is produced by evil (*i.e.* the Good, as coming thus from evil, is evil). Or else we are driven back again to two principles. But if so, these must be derived from some further single source beyond them. And if they say that matter is necessary for the whole world to fulfil its development, how can that be evil which depends for its existence upon the Good? For evil abhors the very nature of the Good. And how can matter, if it is evil, produce and nourish Nature? For evil, *qua* evil, cannot produce or nourish anything, nor create or preserve it at all. And if they reply that matter causes not the evil in our souls, but that it yet draws them down towards evil, can that be true? For many of them have their gaze turned towards the Good. And how can that be, if matter doth nothing except drag them down towards evil? Hence evil in our souls is not derived from matter but from a disordered and discordant motion. And if they say that this motion is always the consequence of matter; and if the unstable medium of matter is necessary for things that are incapable of firm self-subsistence, then *why* is it that evil is thus necessary or that this necessary thing is evil?

29. Nor is the common saying true that Deprivation or Lack fights by its natural power against the Good. For a com-

plete lack is utterly impotent; and that which is partial hath its power, not in so far as it is a lack, but in so far as it is not a perfect lack. For when the lack of the Good is partial, evil is not as yet; and when it becomes perfect, evil itself utterly vanishes.

30. In fine, Good cometh from the One universal Cause; and evil from many partial deficiencies. God knows evil under the form of good, and with Him the causes of evil things are faculties productive of good. And if evil is eternal, creative, and powerful, and if it hath being and activity, whence hath it these attributes? Come they from the Good? Or from the evil by the action of the Good? Or from some other cause by the action of them both? All natural results arise from a definite cause; and if evil hath no cause or definite being, it is unnatural. For that which is contrary to Nature hath no place in Nature, even as unskilfulness hath no place in skilfulness. Is the soul, then, the cause of evils, even as fire is the cause of warmth? And doth the soul, then, fill with evil whatsoever things are near it? Or is the nature of the soul in itself good, while yet in its activities the soul is sometimes in one state, and sometimes in another? Now, if the very existence of the soul is naturally evil, whence is that existence derived? From the Good Creative Cause of the whole world? If from this Origin, how can it be, in its essential nature, evil? For all things sprung from out this Origin are good. But if it is evil merely in its activities, even so this condition is not fixed. Otherwise (*i.e.* if it doth not itself also assume a good quality) what is the origin of the virtues? There remains but one alternative: Evil is a weakness and deficiency of Good.

31. Good things have all one cause. If evil is opposed to the Good, then hath evil many causes. The efficient causes of evil results, however, are not any laws and faculties, but an impotence and weakness and an inharmonious mingling of discordant elements. Evil things are not immutable and unchanging but indeterminate and indefinite: the sport of alien influences which have no definite aim. The Good must be the beginning and the end even of all evil things. For the Good is the final Purpose of all things, good and bad alike. For even

when we act amiss we do so from a longing for the Good; for no one makes evil his definite object when performing any action. Hence evil hath no substantial being, but only a shadow thereof; since the Good, and not itself, is the ultimate object for which it comes into existence.

32. Unto evil we can attribute but an accidental kind of existence. It exists for the sake of something else, and is not self-originating. And hence our action appears to be right (for it hath Good as its object) while yet it is not really right (because we mistake for good that which is not good). 'Tis proven, then, that our purpose is different from our action. Thus evil is contrary to progress, purpose, nature, cause, principle, end, law, will, and being. Evil is, then, a lack, a deficiency, a weakness, a disproportion, an error, purposeless, unlovely, lifeless, unwise, unreasonable, imperfect, unreal, causeless, indeterminate, sterile, inert, powerless, disordered, incongruous, indefinite, dark, unsubstantial, and never in itself possessed of any existence whatever. How, then, is it that an admixture of the Good bestows any power upon evil? For that which is altogether destitute of Good is nothing and hath no power. And if the Good is Existent and is the Source of will, power, and action, how can Its opposite (being destitute of existence, will, power, and activity) have any power against It? Only because evil things are not all entirely the same in all cases and in all relations. In the case of a devil evil lieth in the being contrary to spiritual goodness; in the soul it lieth in the being contrary to reason; in the body it lieth in the being contrary to nature.

33. How can evil things have any existence at all if there is a Providence? Only because evil (as such) hath no being, neither inhereth it in things that have being. And naught that hath being is independent of Providence; for evil hath no being at all, except when mingled with the Good. And if no thing in the world is without a share in the Good, and evil is the deficiency of Good and no thing in the world is utterly destitute of Good, then the Divine Providence is in all things, and nothing that exists can be without It. Yea, even the evil effects that arise are turned by Providence to a kindly purpose, for

the succour of themselves or others (either individually or in common), and thus it is that Providence cares individually for each particular thing in all the world. Therefore we shall pay no heed to the fond argument so often heard that "Providence shall lead us unto virtue even against our will." 'Tis not worthy of Providence to violate nature. Wherefore Its Providential character is shown herein: that It preserves the nature of each individual, and, in making provision for the free and independent, it hath respect unto their state, providing, both in general and in particular, according as the nature of those It cares for can receive Its providential benefactions, which are bestowed suitably on each by Its multiform and universal activity.

34. Thus evil hath no being, nor any inherence in things that have being. Evil is nowhere *qua* evil; and it arises not through any power but through weakness. Even the devils derive their existence from the Good, and their mere existence is good. Their evil is the result of a fall from their proper virtues, and is a change with regard to their individual state, a weakness of their true angelical perfections. And they desire the Good in so far as they desire existence, life, and understanding; and in so far as they do not desire the Good, they desire that which hath no being. And this is not desire, but an error of real desire.

35. By "men who sin knowingly" Scripture means them that are weak in the *exercised* knowledge and performance of Good; and by "them that know the Divine Will and do it not," it means them that have heard the truth and yet are weak in faith to trust the Good or in action to fulfil it. And some desire not to have understanding in order that they may do good, so great is the warping or the weakness of their will. And, in a word, evil (as we have often said) is weakness, impotence, and deficiency of knowledge (or, at least, of exercised knowledge), or of faith, desire, or activity as touching the Good. Now, it may be urged that weakness should not be punished, but on the contrary should be pardoned. This would be just were the power not within man's grasp; but if the power is offered by the Good that giveth without stint (as saith the Scripture) that which is needful to each, we must

not condone the wandering or defection, desertion, and fall from the proper virtues offered by the Good. But hereon let that suffice which we have already spoken (to the best of our abilities) in the treatise *Concerning Justice and Divine Judgment:* a sacred exercise wherein the Truth of Scripture disallowed as lunatic babbling such nice arguments as despitefully and slanderously blaspheme God. In this present treatise we have, to the best of our abilities, celebrated the Good as truly Admirable, as the Beginning and the End of all things, as the Power that embraces them, as That which gives form to non-existent things, as That which causes all good things and yet causes no evil things, as perfect Providence and Goodness surpassing all things that are, and all that are not, and turning base things and the lack of Itself unto good, as That Which all must desire, yearn for, and love; and as possessed of many other qualities the which a true argument hath, methinks, in this chapter expounded.

Suggestions for Further Reading

FCC vol. II, ch. IX; *EG* part III, ch.2.

Boethius

Anicius Manlius Severinus Boethius was born into a distinguished Roman family about A.D. 480. His father had been a consul; he was himself consul under Theodoric the Ostrogoth in 510; his two sons served as joint consuls in 522. Boethius' public career was brilliant and honorable up until the time when he incurred the displeasure of Theodoric. He was then charged with treasonable activities, thrown into prison, and brutally executed in 524.

Boethius' brief life was marked not only by eminence in affairs of state, but as well by great literary productivity. He was a scholar of wide learning, and early conceived the idea of translating into Latin the complete works of Plato and Aristotle in order to make them available to his countrymen. To have conceived such a plan constitutes a judgment upon the learning of the day; to have executed it, however, was next to impossible. How far Boethius actually succeeded in this ambitious enterprise is still a matter of dispute. He did, however, certainly translate the *Isagoge* of Porphyry, and Aristotle's *Organon.* He composed two commentaries on the *Isagoge,* and commentaries on the *Categories,* and the *On Interpretation* of Aristotle. He wrote also original treatises on the categorical and hypothetical syllogism, on division, topics, music, rhetoric, arithmetic, and theology, as well as the famous *Consolation of Philosophy,* composed while he was in prison.

Had Boethius managed to accomplish either more or less of the gigantic task that he had undertaken, it is most probable that subsequent intellectual history would have been profoundly altered. As it was, he transmitted to the early Middle Ages the greatest part of the knowledge of Aristotle then available. In addition, as is well known, it was Boethius who, in his commentary on the *Isagoge,* brought the problem of universals into focus for the Schoolmen. Further, his application of the Aristotelian philosophical categories to theology instituted scholastic theological science; while his use and definition of philosophical terms was to serve centuries of philosophers and theologians. Finally, we may note that it was Boethius who bequeathed to the medievals what was to become their most characteristic form of philosophical composition: the commentary.

In the selection which follows—the whole of Boethius' little tract *On The Trinity*—we see Boethius employing the Aristotelian categories as an instrument for resolving a most profound theological question.

BOETHIUS ON THE TRINITY *

I have long pondered this problem with such mind as I have and all the light that God has lent me. Now, having set it forth in logical order and cast it into literary form, I venture to submit it to your judgment, for which I care as much as for the results of my own research. You will readily understand what I feel whenever I try to write down what I think if you consider the difficulty of the topic and the fact that I discuss it only with the few—I may say with no one but yourself. It is indeed no desire for fame or empty popular applause that prompts my pen; if there be any external reward, we may not look for more warmth in the verdict than the subject itself arouses. For, apart from yourself, wherever I turn my eyes, they fall on either the apathy of the dullard or the jealousy of the shrewd, and a man who casts his thoughts before the common herd—I will not say to consider but to trample under

---

* Reprinted by permission of Harvard University Press, Cambridge, Mass., from the Loeb Classical Library. Boethius. *The Theological Tracts.* Translated by H. F. Stewart and E. K. Rand. 1926.

foot, would seem to bring discredit on the study of divinity. So I purposely use brevity and wrap up the ideas I draw from the deep questionings of philosophy in new and unaccustomed words which speak only to you and to myself, that is, if you deign to look at them. The rest of the world I simply disregard: they cannot understand, and therefore do not deserve to read. We should not of course press our inquiry further than man's wit and reason are allowed to climb the height of heavenly knowledge. In all the liberal arts we see the same limit set beyond which reason may not reach. Medicine, for instance, does not always bring health to the sick, though the doctor will not be to blame if he has left nothing undone which he ought to do. So with the other arts. In the present case the very difficulty of the quest claims a lenient judgment. You must however examine whether the seeds sown in my mind by St. Augustine's writings have borne fruit. And now let us begin our inquiry.

I

There are many who claim as theirs the dignity of the Christian religion; but that form of faith is valid and only valid which, both on account of the universal character of the rules and doctrines affirming its authority, and because the worship in which they are expressed has spread throughout the world, is called catholic or universal. The belief of this religion concerning the Unity of the Trinity is as follows: the Father is God, the Son is God, the Holy Spirit is God. Therefore Father, Son, and Holy Spirit are one God, not three Gods. The principle of this union is absence of difference: difference cannot be avoided by those who add to or take from the Unity, as for instance the Arians, who, by graduating the Trinity according to merit, break it up and convert it to Plurality. For the essence of plurality is otherness; apart from otherness plurality is unintelligible. In fact, the difference between three or more things lies in genus or species or number. Difference is the necessary correlative of sameness. Sameness is predicated in three ways: By genus; *e.g.* a man and a horse, because of their common genus, animal. By species; *e.g.* Cato and Cicero, because of their common species, man. By number; *e.g.* Tully and Cicero, because they are numerically one. Similarly difference is expressed by genus, species, and number. Now numerical difference is caused by variety of accidents; three men differ neither by genus nor species but by their accidents, for if we mentally remove from them all other accidents, still each one occupies a different place which cannot possibly be regarded as the same for each, since two bodies cannot occupy the same place, and place is an accident. Wherefore it is because men are plural by their accidents that they are plural in number.

II

We will now begin a careful consideration of each several point, as far as they can be grasped and understood; for it has been wisely said, in my opinion, that it is a scholar's duty to formulate his belief about anything according to its real nature.

Speculative Science may be divided into three kinds: Physics, Mathematics, and Theology. Physics deals with motion and is not abstract or separable (*i.e.* ἀνυπεξαίρετος); for it is concerned with the forms of bodies together with their constituent matter, which forms cannot be separated in reality from their bodies. As the bodies are in motion—the earth, for instance, tending downwards, and fire tending upwards, form takes on the movement of the particular thing to which it is annexed.

Mathematics does not deal with motion and is not abstract, for it investigates forms of bodies apart from matter, and therefore apart from movement, which forms, however, being connected with matter cannot be really separated from bodies.

Theology does not deal with motion and is abstract and separable, for the Divine Substance is without either matter or motion. In Physics, then, we are bound to use scientific, in Mathematics, systematical, in Theology, intellectual concepts;

and in Theology we will not let ourselves be diverted to play with imaginations, but will simply apprehend that Form which is pure form and no image, which is very Being and the source of Being. For everything owes its being to Form. Thus a statue is not a statue on account of the brass which is its matter, but on account of the form whereby the likeness of a living thing is impressed upon it: the brass itself is not brass because of the earth which is its matter, but because of its form. Likewise earth is not earth by reason of unqualified matter, but by reason of dryness and weight, which are forms. So nothing is said to be because it has matter, but because it has a distinctive form. But the Divine Substance is Form without matter, and is therefore One, and is its own essence. But other things are not simply their own essences, for each thing has its being from the things of which it is composed, that is, from its parts. It is This *and* That, *i.e.* it is the totality of its parts in conjunction; it is not This *or* That taken apart. Earthly man, for instance, since he consists of soul and body, is soul *and* body, not soul *or* body, separately; therefore he is not his own essence. That on the other hand which does not consist of This and That, but is only This, is really its own essence, and is altogether beautiful and stable because it is not grounded in anything. Wherefore that is truly One in which is no number, in which nothing is present except its own essence. Nor can it become the substrate of anything, for it is pure Form, and pure Forms cannot be substrates. For if humanity, like other forms, is a substrate for accidents, it does not receive accidents through the fact that it exists, but through the fact that matter is subjected to it. Humanity appears indeed to appropriate the accident which in reality belongs to the matter underlying the conception Humanity. But Form which is without matter cannot be a substrate, and cannot have its essence in matter, else it would not be form but a reflexion. For from those forms which are outside matter come the forms which are in matter and produce bodies. We misname the entities that reside in bodies when we call them forms; they are mere images; they only resemble those forms which are not incorporate in matter. In Him, then, is no difference, no plurality arising out of difference, no multiplicity arising out of accidents, and accordingly no number.

III

Now God differs from God in no respect, for there cannot be divine essences distinguished either by accidents or by substantial differences belonging to a substrate. But where there is no difference, there is no sort of plurality and accordingly no number; here, therefore, is unity alone. For whereas we say God thrice when we name the Father, Son, and Holy Spirit, these three unities do not produce a plurality of number in their own essences, if we think of what we count instead of what we count with. For in the case of abstract number a repetition of single items does produce plurality; but in the case of concrete number the repetition and plural use of single items does not by any means produce numerical difference in the objects counted. There are as a fact two kinds of number. There is the number with which we count (abstract) and the number inherent in the things counted (concrete). "One" is a thing—the thing counted. Unity is that by which oneness is denoted. Again "two" belongs to the class of things as men or stones; but not so duality; duality is merely that whereby two men or two stones are denoted; and so on. Therefore a repetition of unities produces plurality when it is a question of abstract, but not when it is a question of concrete things, as, for example, if I say of one and the same thing, "one sword, one brand, one blade." It is easy to see that each of these names denotes a sword; I am not numbering unities but simply repeating one thing, and in saying "sword, brand, blade," I reiterate the one thing and do not enumerate several different things any more than I produce three suns instead of merely mentioning one thing thrice when I say "Sun, Sun, Sun."

So then if God be predicated thrice of Father, Son, and Holy Spirit, the threefold predication does not result in plural number. The risk of that, as has been said, attends only on those who distinguish Them according to merit. But Catholic

Christians, allowing no difference of merit in God, assuming Him to be Pure Form and believing Him to be nothing else than His own essence, rightly regard the statement "the Father is God, the Son is God, the Holy Spirit is God, and this Trinity is one God," not as an enumeration of different things but as a reiteration of one and the same thing, like the statement, "blade and brand are one sword" or "sun, sun, and sun are one sun."

Let this be enough for the present to establish my meaning and to show that not every repetition of units produces number and plurality. Still in saying "Father, Son, and Holy Spirit," we are not using synonymous terms. "Brand and blade" are the same and identical, but "Father, Son, and Holy Spirit," though the same, are not identical. This point deserves a moment's consideration. When they ask, "Is the Father the same as the Son?" Catholics answer "No." "Is the One the same as the Other?" The answer is in the negative. There is not, therefore, complete indifference between Them; and so number does come in—number which we explained was the result of diversity of substrates. We will briefly debate this point when we have done examining how particular predicates can be applied to God.

IV

There are in all ten categories which can be universally predicated of things, namely, Substance, Quality, Quantity, Relation, Place, Time, Condition, Situation, Activity, Passivity. Their meaning is determined by the contingent subject; for some of them denote substance in making predication of other things, others belong to the class of accidents. But when these categories are applied to God they change their meaning entirely. Relation, for instance, cannot be predicated at all of God; for substance in Him is not really substantial but supersubstantial. So with quality and the other possible attributes, of which we must add examples for the sake of clearness.

When we say God, we seem to denote a substance; but it is a substance that is supersubstantial. When we say of Him,

"He is just," we mention a quality, not an accidental quality—rather a substantial and, in fact, a supersubstantial quality. For God is not one thing because He is, and another thing because He is just; with Him to be just and to be God are one and the same. So when we say, "He is great or the greatest," we seem to predicate quantity, but it is a quantity similar to this substance which we have declared to be supersubstantial; for with Him to be great and to be God are all one. Again, concerning His Form, we have already shown that He is Form, and truly One without Plurality. The categories we have mentioned are such that they give to the thing to which they are applied the character which they express; in created things they express divided being, in God, conjoined and united being—in the following manner. When we name a substance, as man or God, it seems as though that of which the predication is made were substance itself, as man or God is substance. But there is a difference: since a man is not simply and entirely man, and in virtue of this he is not substance. For what man is he owes to other things which are not man. But God is simply and entirely God, for He is nothing else than what He is, and therefore is, through simple existence, God. Again we apply just, a quality, as though it were that of which it is predicated; that is, if we say "a just man or just God," we assert that man or God is just. But there is a difference, for man is one thing, and a just man is another thing. But God is justice itself. So a man or God is said to be great, and it would appear that man is substantially great or that God is substantially great. But man is merely great; God is greatness.

The remaining categories are not predicable of God nor yet of created things. For place is predicated of man or of God—a man is in the market-place; God is everywhere—but in neither case is the predicate identical with the object of predication. To say "A man is in the market" is quite a different thing from saying "he is white or long," or, so to speak, encompassed and determined by some property which enables him to be described in terms of his substance; this predicate of place simply declares how far his substance is given a particular setting amid other things.

It is otherwise, of course, with God. "He is everywhere" does not mean that He is in every place, for He cannot be in any place at all—but that every place is present to Him for Him to occupy, although He Himself can be received by no place, and therefore He cannot anywhere be in a place, since He is everywhere but in no place. It is the same with the category of time, as, "A man came yesterday; God is ever." Here again the predicate of "coming yesterday" denotes not something substantial, but something happening in terms of time. But the expression "God is ever" denotes a single Present, summing up His continual presence in all the past, in all the present—however that term be used—and in all the future. Philosophers say that "ever" may be applied to the life of the heavens and other immortal bodies. But as applied to God it has a different meaning. He is ever, because "ever" is with Him a term of present time, and there is this great difference between "now," which is our present, and the divine present. Our present connotes changing time and sempiternity; God's present, abiding, unmoved, and immovable, connotes eternity. Add *semper* to *eternity* and you get the constant, incessant and thereby perpetual course of our present time, that is to say, sempiternity.

It is just the same with the categories of condition and activity. For example, we say, "A man runs, clothed," "God rules, possessing all things." Here again nothing substantial is asserted of either subject; in fact all the categories we have hitherto named arise from what lies outside substance, and all of them, so to speak, refer to something other than substance. The difference between the categories is easily seen by an example. Thus, the terms "man" and "God" refer to the substance in virtue of which the subject is—man or God. The term "just" refers to the quality in virtue of which the subject is something, viz. just; the term "great" to the quantity in virtue of which He is something, viz. great. No other category save substance, quality, and quantity refer to the substance of the subject. If I say of one "he is in the market" or "everywhere," I am applying the category of place, which is not a category of the substance, like "just" in virtue of justice. So if I say, "he runs, He rules, he is now, He is ever," I make reference to activity or time—if indeed God's "ever" can be described as time—but not to a category of substance, like "great" in virtue of greatness.

Finally, we must not look for the categories of situation and passivity in God, for they simply are not to be found in Him.

Have I now made clear the difference between the categories? Some denote the reality of a thing; others its accidental circumstances; the former declare that a thing is something; the latter say nothing about its being anything, but simply attach to it, so to speak, something external. Those categories which describe a thing in terms of its substance may be called substantial categories; when they apply to things as subjects they are called accidents. In reference to God, who is not a subject at all, it is only possible to employ the category of substance.

V

Let us now consider the category of relation, to which all the foregoing remarks have been preliminary; for qualities which obviously arise from the association of another term do not appear to predicate anything concerning the substance of a subject. For instance, master and slave are relative terms; let us see whether either of them are predicates of substance. If you suppress the term slave, you simultaneously suppress the term master. On the other hand, though you suppress the term whiteness, you do not suppress some white thing, though, of course, if the particular whiteness inhere as an accident in the thing, the thing disappears as soon as you suppress the accidental quality whiteness. But in the case of master, if you suppress the term slave, the term master disappears. But slave is not an accidental quality of master, as whiteness is of a white thing; it denotes the power which the master has over the slave. Now since the power goes when the slave is removed, it is plain that power is no accident to the substance of master, but is an adventitious augmentation arising from the possession of slaves.

It cannot therefore be affirmed that a category of relation increases, decreases, or alters in any way the substance of the thing to which it is applied. The category of relation, then, has nothing to do with the essence of the subject; it simply denotes a condition of relativity, and that not necessarily to something else, but sometimes to the subject itself. For suppose a man standing. If I go up to him on my right and stand beside him, he will be left, in relation to me, not because he is left in himself, but because I have come up to him on my right. Again, if I come up to him on my left, he becomes right in relation to me, not because he is right in himself, as he may be white or long, but because he is right in virtue of my approach. What he is depends entirely on me, and not in the least on the essence of his being.

Accordingly those predicates which do not denote the essential nature of a thing cannot alter, change, or disturb its nature in any way. Wherefore if Father and Son are predicates of relation, and, as we have said, have no other difference but that of relation, and if relation is not asserted of its subject as though it were the subject itself and its substantial quality, it will effect no real difference in its subject, but, in a phrase which aims at interpreting what we can hardly understand, a difference of persons. For it is a canon of absolute truth that distinctions in incorporeal things are established by differences and not by spatial separation. It cannot be said that God became Father by the addition to His substance of some accident; for he never began to be Father, since the begetting of the Son belongs to His very substance; however, the predicate father, as such, is relative. And if we bear in mind all the propositions made concerning God in the previous discussion, we shall admit that God the Son proceeded from God the Father, and the Holy Ghost from both, and that They cannot possibly be spatially different, since They are incorporeal. But since the Father is God, the Son is God, and the Holy Spirit is God, and since there are in God no points of difference distinguishing Him from God, He differs from none of the Others. But where there are no differences there is no plurality; where there is no plurality there is Unity. Again, nothing but God can be begotten of God, and lastly, in concrete enumerations the repetition of units does not produce plurality. Thus the Unity of the Three is suitably established.

VI

But since no relation can be affirmed of one subject alone, since a predication referring to one substance is a predication without relation, the manifoldness of the Trinity is secured through the category of relation, and the Unity is maintained through the fact that there is no difference of substance, or operation, or generally of any substantial predicate. So then, the category of substance preserves the Unity, that of relation brings about the Trinity. Hence only terms belonging to relation may be applied singly to Each. For the Father is not the same as the Son, nor is either of Them the same as the Holy Spirit, Yet Father, Son, and Holy Spirit are each the same God, the same in justice, in goodness, in greatness, and in everything that can be predicated of substance. One must not forget that predicates of relativity do not always involve relation to something other than the subject, as slave involves master, where the two terms are different. For equals are equal, like are like, identicals are identical, each with other, and the relation of Father to Son, and of both to Holy Spirit is a relation of identicals. A relation of this kind is not to be found in created things, but that is because of the difference which we know attaches to transient objects. We must not in speaking of God let imagination lead us astray; we must let the Faculty of pure Knowledge lift us up and teach us to know all things as far as they may be known.

I have now finished the investigation which I proposed. The exactness of my reasoning awaits the standard of your judgment; your authority will pronounce whether I have seen a straight path to the goal. If, God helping me, I have furnished some support in argument to an article which stands by itself on the firm foundation of Faith, I shall render joyous praise for the finished work to Him from whom the invitation comes. But if human nature has failed to reach beyond its limits, whatever is lost through my infirmity must be made good by my intention.

Suggestions for Further Reading

Boethius. *The Consolation of Philosophy.* I. Edman (ed.). New York, 1943; Barrett, H. M. *Boethius—Some Aspects of his Times and Work.* Cambridge, 1940; Patch, H. R. *The Tradition of Boethius.* New York, 1935; *FCC* vol. II, 101-104; *EG* 97-106; *AAM* 22-34; *RMcK* vol. 1, 65-105.

John Scotus Erigena

After Boethius, no really significant philosophical figure appeared in the west for some three hundred years. The thinkers of this interval seem to have been almost exclusively engaged in appropriating the heritage of the past and adapting it to the needs of the new age. It appears, therefore, all the more startling when, in the midst of this prolonged period of intellectual conservation and assimilation, there suddenly springs upon the philosophical scene a speculative thinker of the very highest order: John Scotus Erigena.

Very little is known of Erigena's life. He was born in Ireland around 810, and appears to have studied in the land of his birth, where he received an education far superior to that which was available to students on the continent. It was doubtless in an Irish monastery that he acquired his mastery of Greek; for by the ninth century, knowledge of the Greek tongue was almost exclusively limited to the Irish monks.

Around 840, Erigena went to France. We know that he was at the court of Charles the Bald sometime before 850, where it is assumed that he headed the Palace school. Although probably not himself a member of the clergy, Erigena took an active role in the theological controversies of his day. Unfortunately, many of the arguments by means of which he sought to defend Catholic views were considered to be just as dangerous to orthodoxy as those of his adversaries; and in 855 the Synod of Valence condemned some nineteen theses drawn from his works.

It is doubtful that Erigena outlived Charles the Bald, who died in 877. Various chroniclers have given differing versions of his death. One tradition has it that Erigena became Abbot of Athelney, and was murdered by the monks; still another holds that Erigena, having been called to England by Alfred the Great to teach, ran afoul of a particularly critical body of students who responded to his lectures by stabbing him to death with their pens.

Aside from his theological tracts and commentaries, Erigena left a rich heritage of translations from the Greek, the most important of these being a rendering into Latin of the four books of the Pseudo-Dionysius. His masterpiece, however, was an original work on metaphysics written in dialogue form—*The Division of Nature*—from which we present an excerpt.

JOHN SCOTUS ERIGENA ON THE DIVISION OF NATURE *

Master: While thinking about and inquiring as diligently as my faculties permit into the first and highest division of all things capable of being perceived by the soul, or into those which transcend its reach—into those things which are, and those which are not—a general term embracing all of these occurred to me: in Greek the term is *phusis,* in Latin, *natura.* Does the case seem otherwise to you?

Disciple: No; I quite agree. Indeed, even I, although just a novice when it comes to reasoning, can see this is the case.

Master: Consequently, *nature* is the general name for all things which are and which are not?

Disciple: Yes. For nothing that can be thought of as obtaining in the universe would remain outside this designation.

Master: As we are thus agreed with respect to the utter generality of this designation, I should enjoy hearing you discourse on the principle of its division, through *differentiae,* into spe-

* Translated by H. Shapiro especially for this volume from J. S. Erigena's *De Divisione Naturae*, Book I, as found in J. P. Migne, *Patrologia Latina*, vol. CXXII.

cies. Or would you prefer that I attempt this dividing while you evaluate my divisions?

Disciple: You go ahead, please. I am quite anxious to learn the true principle of these things from you.

Master: Now as I see it the division of nature consists in four species derived by means of four *differentia.* The first of these divisions being *that which creates and is not created;* the second, *that which is created and creates;* the third, *that which is created and does not create;* and the fourth, *that which neither creates nor is created.* In these four there are two pairs of opposites: the third division, that is, is opposed to the first, while the fourth is opposed to the second. Note, however, that the fourth is classed with the impossibles—*i.e.,* those things whose *differentia* is not-being-able-to-be. Does it seem to you that such a division obtains?

Disciple: Yes it does. But will you expand a bit, so that I may more clearly grasp the oppositions of which you spoke?

Master: Now, unless I'm mistaken, you do see the opposition between the first and third species. The first, that is, creates and is not created so that, *ex contrario,* that which is created and does not create is in opposition to it. Again, the second is opposed to the fourth inasmuch as the second—which is both created and creates—is universally contradicted by the fourth—which neither creates nor is created.

Disciple: I see. Yet the fourth species puzzles me. I feel no hesitation with respect to the other three, since the first is understood (if I see it correctly) in the cause of all that which is and which is not; while the second is understood in the primordial causes; and the third is understood in that of which we become aware in temporally and spatially located generations. Still, as I see it, it would help if we discuss each of these a bit more in detail.

Master: You are quite right. But which species of nature should be discussed first?

Disciple: It seems proper to me to speak of the first before discussing the others.

Master: So be it. But first of all I think that we should speak briefly of the highest and principal division of all things—that is, the division into those things which are and those which are not.

Disciple: All right. As a matter of fact, I can see that reasoning should proceed from this starting point; not only because this is the first *differentia* of all things, but because it appears that this is more obscure than the others.

Master: All right. Now, this basic class-producing *differentia* of all things is to be approached in various ways. The first of these ways leads us to observe that all things capable of being perceived by the senses or grasped by the intellect can reasonably be said to-be; while it seems just as reasonable that those things—owing to the excellence of their natures—which elude both the sensitive faculties and the intellect, be said not-to-be. This last group of things is not correctly understood save in God alone, and in matter, and in the principles and essences of all things constituted by Him. There is a good reason for this: only He who alone truly is, is the essence of all things. To quote Dionysius the Areopagite, "the being of all things is superbeing Divinity." Gregory the Theologian, too, adduces many reasons to prove that no intellect can grasp the *what* of any substance or essence, whether of a visible or invisible creature. For just as God Himself, in Himself, and beyond every creature can be understood by no intellect, just so the essence obtaining in the most secret recesses of his creations remains incomprehensible. For whatever is perceived by the corporeal senses, or grasped by the intellect, as being in any creature, is but a certain accident of each essence which remains, in itself, incomprehensible. The essence, that is, approached through the quality, quantity, form, matter, *differentia*, place or time, is not the *what* but the *that*.

Hence, this is the first and highest mode of the division of things which are said to-be and not-to-be. As I see it, that mode which appears to be reasonable—*i.e.*, the mode which consists in privations of relations with respect to substances (such as sight and blindness with respect to the eyes)—should not be admitted at all. For it seems to me to be wholly inadmissible to hold that that which entirely is-not, or is not-able-to-be, or which transcends the intellect owing to the excellence of its nature, can ever be received into the divisions of things unless one were to hold that the absences and privations of things which are, are not entirely nothing, but are rather supported in some unbelievable manner by the natural power of the things of which they are the privations, absences or oppositions, so that in this sense, they could be held to-be.

Now let the second way of approaching being and not-being be that which is accomplished by considering the orders and *differentiae* of the natures of creatures. This, which begins with the most pre-eminent intellectual power obtaining closest to God, descends to the lowest point of the rational and irrational creature—*i.e.*, from the most elevated angel to the lowest portion of the rational and irrational soul. Now in this way each order, including the very lowest one—the order of bodies in which the entire division is terminated—can in a certain extraordinary sense be said to-be and not-to-be. Affirmation, that is, of the inferior is a negation of the superior; while negation of the inferior is an affirmation of the superior. Similarly, affirmation of the superior is a negation of the inferior; while negation of the superior is an affirmation of the inferior. Clearly, the affirmation of man, insofar as he is mortal, is the negation of the angel. Again, negation of man is an affirmation of the angel, and so on. For if it is the case that man is a rational animal, mortal and visible, then clearly an angel is neither a rational animal, nor mortal, nor visible. Again, if an angel is an essential intellectual motion contemplating God and the causes of things, then man is not an essential intellectual motion contemplating God and the causes of things. And this same law obtains with respect to all celestial essences until the highest order of all things is attained. But this highest order terminates in a supreme upward negation. For its negation affirms no creature superior to itself.

Now upwards, there obtains three orders, the first of which are Cherubim, Seraphim and Thrones; the second, Virtues, Powers and Dominations; the third, Principles, Archangels and Angels. Downward, however, the lowest order of bodies only negates or affirms that which is superior to itself. Nothing, that is, obtains below this order to either affirm or negate, since it is preceded by all superiors but itself precedes no inferior. For this reason, every order of the rational and intellectual creature is said to-be and not-to-be. *It is,* that is to say, to the degree that it is known by superiors or by itself; while *it is not,* to the degree that it is incapable of comprehension by an inferior.

The third way is fittingly approached by observing those things by which the plenitude of this visible world is perfected, and by their prior causes obtaining in the most hidden of nature's recesses. Now, whichever of these causes obtain, formed-matter—that which is known through generation in space and time—is said by a peculiar human speech-pattern, to-be. Nevertheless, whatever does obtain within the recesses of nature and does not appear as formed-matter either in place, time or other accidents, is said by the same curious speech-pattern, not-to-be.

There are numerous examples of this approach, especially when it comes to regarding human nature. For as God made all men simultaneously in that first, single man created in His image; and as He did not constitute all of them at once, but rather in particular times and places; and that He thus brought the singly created nature of man into visible being in accordance with a certain order known to Himself; so it is the case that those who have already appeared and do now appear in the visible world are said to-be; while those who are yet latent, but nonetheless going-to-be, are said not-to-be.

Thus, this difference obtains between the first and third modes: the first appears generally in all things which have been made simultaneously and singly in causes and effects. The third obtains particularly with respect to those things which are as yet partly latent in respect of their causes, and partly apparent in their effects. To this mode belongs that principle which refers to seeds—be they of animal, tree or herb. For the power of seed—at the time when it is quietly in repose within the recesses of nature—is said not-to-be, because it is not yet become manifest; but directly it has manifested itself by the generation of animals, or flowers or fruit, it is said to-be.

Now the fourth approach is that adopted by the philosophers who hold—not without reason—that only those things truly are, which are grasped by the intellect; while those things subject to generation and which are varied, united and separated by the additions and subtractions of matter, or intervals, or motions of time and place as are all bodies subject to generation and corruption, are held truly not-to-be.

A fifth approach derives from that which obtains in human nature alone. For when the human nature, through sin, has violated the dignity of the Divine image in which it subsists, and has thus deservedly lost its being, it is said, as a consequence, not-to-be. When human nature, however, restored by the grace of God's only-begotten Son, is led back to the original condition of its substance, in which it has been made according to the image of God, it then begins to-be, and begins to live in him who was made in God's image. The Apostle seems to be speaking in this mode when he says: "and He calls those things that are not, as those that are"—*i.e.*, God the Father calls through faith in his Son those who have been lost in the first man, so that they may be just as those who have been reborn in Christ. Again, this could also be understood as referring to those whom God calls daily out of the secret recesses of nature (where they are held not-to-be) into visible form and matter, and in all other ways in which hidden things can appear. But as I see it, enough has been said of these things for now. Does it seem so to you?

Disciple: Enough, indeed . . .

Master: Then let us return to those things which we have already mentioned; that is, to the division of nature. . . . Now of these, the first *differentia,* as we saw, was into that which creates and is not created. Such a species of nature is correctly predicated of God alone: for He alone is understood as without beginning and creator of all things. And in virtue of the fact that He is thus principal cause of all things which have been made from Him and through Him, He is also the end of all that which is from Him. All things desire Him. He is, consequently, beginning, middle and end. Beginning, because all things participating in essence are from Him;

middle, because they subsist and are moved in and through Him; and end, because they are moved to Him seeking the termination of their motion and the permanence of their perfection.

Disciple: This I do believe most devoutly; and to the degree that it is capable of being understood, I understand that this is predicated correctly only of the Divine cause of all things, since this cause alone causes all things which are from it, while it is itself created by nothing superior or precedent. For it is itself the highest and only cause of all things which subsist from it and in it.

Yet, I am puzzled, and should like to hear your opinion on this. Quite often—and it is this which puzzles me—I find that in the books of the holy fathers, when they are attempting to argue about the Divine Nature, they maintain that it not only creates all things which are, but is itself, as well, created. Hence, if this is the case, I don't see how our view can obtain: for we say that the Divine Nature alone creates, but is created by nothing.

Master: You have good reason to be disturbed. I, too, wonder about this, and I should have wished to know from you how these views, which appear to be contrary, could fail to be opposed to each other and what true reason could say about it.

Disciple: Please begin. I am anxious to hear what your opinion is on this, not mine.

Master: I suggest that we first consider the name itself—God—which is employed in sacred scripture. For although Divine Nature is called by many names, as Goodness, Being, Truth, and others of a like kind, nonetheless scripture most frequently employs this Divine name.

Disciple: That is clearly the case.

Master: Now, the etymology of this name is Greek. It derives either from the verb *theoreo* [I see], or from the verb *theo* [I run]. Or, as is more probable, it can be said to derive from both, because one and the same meaning is present. For when *theos* [God], is deduced from the verb *theoreo* [I see], He is interpreted as seeing. For He Himself sees in Himself all things which are, while He looks upon nothing outside Himself because there is nothing outside Himself. But when *theos* [God], is deduced from the verb *theo* [I run], *theos* [God], is correctly understood as running. For He Himself runs in all things, and is in no way quiescent, but fills all things by running. As the saying is: "His speech runs swiftly." Despite this, He is in no way moved; as restful-motion, and mobile-rest, are most truly predicated of God. God, that is, rests absolutely within Himself, never relapsing from His natural immobility. Still, He moves Himself through all things which subsist essentially from Him, so that they may *be* those things; for all things are made by His motion. Consequently, one and the same meaning obtains in the two interpretations of His name—God. To run through all things, that is, is nothing other to God than to see all things; and just as by seeing, so also by running are all things made.

Disciple: So much for the name. Still, I do not fully see how He moves Himself. For He who is everywhere; He without which nothing else can be; He, outside of whom nothing is extended; He is the place and limit of all things.

Master: Now, I have not said that God is moved outside Himself; but by Himself, in Himself, and to Himself. For no motion aside from the appetite of His will should be believed to be in Him; and it is by this appetite that He wills that all things be made. Similarly, His rest is not to be understood as following on motion; but rather as the incommutably commanded object of this same will by means of which He defines the permanence of all things in the incommutable stability of their principles. Neither rest nor motion are properly said to be in Him. These two, indeed, appear to be opposed to one another, and true reason forbids the attribution of opposites to Him. Rest is properly the end of motion, but God does not begin to be moved in order that He attain a certain state. Consequently, these names—as many such similar ones—are predicated by the creature to the creator as a kind of Divine metaphor. Now this is not unreasonable, since He is the cause of all things which are at rest and in motion. It is, indeed, by Him that they begin to run so that they may be, as He is the principle of all things; further, it is through Him that they are brought to Him by natural motion, so that they may rest in Him eternally and incommutably. For He is the end and the rest of all things, and they desire nothing beyond Him. It is in Him that they find the beginning and the end of their motion. Hence, God is said to be running; not because He, who stands immutably in Himself and fills all things, runs outside Himself, but because He makes everything run from non-existence to existence.

Disciple: This seems reasonable; let us now return to what was proposed.

Master: What proposal are you referring to? Often when we digress we forget the principal question.

Disciple: Haven't we proposed that we inquire—so far as we are able—into the reason that those who discuss the Divine Nature say that it both creates and is created? That it does create all things, surely no intelligent being can doubt; but in what manner it is said to be created has, so it seemed to us, not been sufficiently clarified.

Master: You are right. But as I see it, from what has been said before, a key to the solution of this problem has been provided. For we have deduced that by the motion of the Divine Nature we are to understand a proposal of the Divine Will as to the establishment of those things which are to be made. Divine Nature, which *is* Divine Will, is therefore said to be made in all things. For being and willing obtain in respect of the establishment of all things which are made. That is, for example, that one can hold that the motion of the Divine Will occurs so that those things which are, might be; and that therefore it creates all things out of nothing so that they may be in being from non-being; but that it is nonetheless created, since besides itself nothing else essentially is, for it is the essence of all things. Just, that is, as there is no natural good beside itself, but all which is said to be good is good by participation in the one highest good, so everything which is said to exist, does not exist in itself, but exists by participating in the Divine Nature. Thus, not only, as we have seen, is the Divine Nature said to be made in existing things, but as well in those who are reformed by faith, hope, charity and the other virtues. The word of God is thus born in a marvelous and ineffable way, as the Apostle says when saying of Christ: "Who has been made in wisdom from God, and justification and redemption." Again, it is not improper to say that it has been made, because it—which is invisible *per se*—appears in all things which are. Our intellect, too, in this way, is not improperly said to-be, even before it arrived at thought and memory; for it, too, is invisible *per se* and unknowable to all save God and ourselves. However, as soon as it has arrived at thought, and takes a form from certain phantasms, it is said, not without reason, to be made. For the intellect which was unformed prior to its attainment of memory, is made in memory by receiving certain forms of things, or words, or colors, or other sensibles. Then it receives, so to speak, a second formation: when by certain signs of forms, or of words—*i.e.*, letters, which are signs of words; and figures, which are signs of forms—it is formed by the mathematical or other sensible signs by which means it is suggested to the sense of those who experience these signs. This similarity, then (although far removed from the Divine Nature), I judge nonetheless as significant in showing how the Divine Nature—while it creates everything and cannot be created by anything—is yet created in a marvelous way in all the things that are from it. Hence, just as the mind's intelligence, or plan, or advice—or whatever manner this our innermost motion can be spoken of when it has arrived at thought and has received certain forms of phantasms, and has then proceeded by the sign of words, or the signs of sensible motions—is said, not without rectitude, to be made, just so the Divine Essence—which subsisting *per se* transcends every intellect—is correctly said to be created in those things which have been made from it, and through it, and in it, and for it, so that it can be known in them whether by the intellect (if they are intellectual), or by sense (if they are sensible), by those who investigate the Divine Essence by correct study.

Disciple: As I see it, enough has now been said of this. . . . Still, I find that I cannot grant motion to God who alone is immutable. There is nothing in respect of which He could move Himself, inasmuch as all things are in Him: or, and this is even stronger, since He himself *is* all things. Nonetheless, I cannot deny Him making, since He is the maker of all things.

Master: Therefore you see motion as separate from making?

Disciple: No; not that; for I see that they are inseparable from each other.

Master: Well then, what are you going to do?

Disciple: I don't know. I therefore fervently request that you clear some path for me and rid me of this difficulty.

Master: Very well. Now does it seem to you that God was before He made all things?

Disciple: Yes; it seems to me that He was.

Master: Consequently, making was an accident in respect of Him. For what is not co-eternal and co-essential with Him is either something outside of Him or something befalling Him.

Disciple: I find it hard to believe that there is something outside Him; for all things are in Him and there is nothing outside Him. Indeed, I should rather have said that He is not subject to accident; for if He were, He would not be simple but rather a certain composite of essence and accidents. Clearly, if something other than He is understood together with Him, or if in any manner something befalls Him, then He is neither infinite nor simple. This, however, is repugnant to the Catholic faith and true reason. For these hold God to be infinite: more than infinite, as He is the infinity of infinities; and simple: more than simple, as He is the simplicity of simples. Further, it believes or understands that there is nothing with Him, since He is Himself the limit of all things which are and are not, and which can and cannot be, and which appear to be either contrary and opposed, or similar and dissimilar, to Him. For He is the similitude of similars; the dissimilitude of dissimilars; the opposition of opposites and the contrariety of contraries. Indeed, He gathers and compounds all these things into one concord by means of a beautiful and ineffable harmony. For everything in the parts of the universe that appear to be opposed, contrary and dissonant with respect to one another, are harmonious and in consonance when considered in the most general harmony of the universe itself.

Master: You are correct in your understanding. But take care or you may leave yourself open to the charge of having granted to other things what you have just granted of these.

Disciple: What I have conceded, I shall not retract. Proceed now in any order that you wish and I shall follow.

Master: God, then, as you say, was not before He made all things?

Disciple: True. For if He was, He would have been subject to the accident of making all things; and were He thus subject, motion and time could be predicated of Him. For He would then have moved Himself in order to make those things which He had not yet made; and He would have thus preceded His action in time which was then neither co-essential nor co-eternal with Him.

Master: Therefore His making is co-eternal and co-essential with Him.

Disciple: I believe and understand this to be the case.

Master: Is it the case that God and His making—*i.e.,* his action—are two distinct things? Or are they one thing, simple and individual?

Disciple: They are one, as I see it. For God is innumerable and does not receive number in Himself. He is number without number, beyond all numbers, and the cause of all numbers.

Master: Hence, in God there is not one thing which is being and another which is making, but for Him being is also making?

Disciple: I cannot deny this conclusion.

Master: Therefore, when we are told that God made anything, what we should take this to mean is that God is in all things—*i.e.,* subsists as the essence of all things. For He alone truly is *per se;* and only He is that which is said to be in those things which are. For none of the things which are, truly are *per se,* except insofar as they receive their true being by a participation in Him—the one who alone truly is *per se.*

Disciple: I do not deny this.

Master: Do you not, therefore, see how it is that true reason completely separates the category of making from the Divine Nature, and from changes and places, and assigns the category of making to those mutable, temporal things which cannot lack a beginning and end?

Disciple: I now see this clearly; and I quite understand that no category is attributable to God.

Master: And now what? Shall we go on, for the same reason, to examine the force of all the verbs which the sacred scripture predicates of Divine Nature so that we may assure ourselves that nothing other is meant beyond the simple, incommutable, Divine Essence—nay, *more* than essence—which is incomprehensible to every intellect and sign? For example: when we hear it said that God wishes, loves, chooses, sees, hears and other such verbs which can be predicated of Him, we are to think nothing more than that His ineffable essence and power are being suggested by these significations which come natural to us. Still, we must employ such verbs or else the true, pious Christian religion will be silenced with respect to the creator of all, so that it dare say nothing of Him for the instruction of simple souls, or [to combat] the heretics always plotting against the truth, or [to accomplish] the purpose of refuting the subtleties of those who seek to defeat the wise in these matters. Hence, it is not one thing for God to be, and another for Him to wish, make, love, esteem, see, and other activities of this kind which are predicated of Him; but rather all of these should be taken as one and the same in Him, and as suggesting His ineffable essence in that mode in which he allows Himself to be signified.

Disciple: It is as you say. For where simplicity *per se,* true, eternal and incorruptible obtains, there a variegated multitude cannot be. But will you enlighten me further so that I may the more clearly see how, when I hear it said that God loves or is loved, I am to understand this only as a reference to His nature without involving any motion of loving or being loved? For when I have been shown this, I shall in no way be puzzled when I read or hear that He wishes, or desires and is desired, values and is valued, sees and is seen, searches and is sought, or moves and is moved. Indeed, these are all to be understood as one and the same thing. For just as will, love, delight, sight, desire and motion are, when predicated of Him, to be taken as suggesting one and the same thing to us; so, as I see it, the verbs—be they active, passive or neutral, or whatever mode they signify—are to be understood as differing not at all as respects their meaning.

Master: In this, you are correct. It is just as you say. Now listen to this definition of love: love is the link and the chain by means of which the totality of all things is bound in ineffable friendship and indissoluble unity. It may also be defined in this way: love is the natural motion of all things which are in motion, and a restful abode at the terminus beyond which no motion of the creature can go. Clearly, Holy Dionysius holds to these definitions in his *Hymns of Love,* where he says:

> We understand by love—whether divine, angelic, intellectual, or animal or natural—a certain unitive and continuative virtue, moving higher things into the providence of lower things, and equiformed things into sociable interchange, and the least subjects to the place of the better and superior.

Again, in the same *Hymns,* he says:

> Since we have described many loves arising out of one, let us now once again roll together and garner all of them into one all-embracing love: the father of them all. First, into two amatory virtues embracing the father of them all; that by which every love receives its power and principle; the very peak of all things to which is extended the love co-naturally existing in each thing, and universal in all existing things.

Or again:

> Come now and once again let us speak the virtues of love gathered together into one; that it is one simple virtue moving itself to a certain unitive state from the best to the least of existences; and from it again consequently through all, as far as the best; limiting itself from itself and through itself and to itself, and always revolved in itself in the same manner.

Hence, God—because He is the cause of every love; and because He is diffused through all existents; and because He collects all things into one, and returns to Himself in an ineffable regression while terminating in Himself the amatory motions of the whole creature—is correctly called love. This love of the Divine Nature in all the things which are in it, and from it, is also called a loving diffusion in all things; not because that which lacks all motion is diffused in any manner and fills all things at once, but rather because it diffuses and moves the vision of the rational mind through all things, insofar as it is the cause of the diffusion and the motion of the soul—causing it to seek, and find, and (so far as this is possible) to understand, that love fills all things in order that they may be; and by a blissful union, so to say, of universal love in an inseparable unity—which is that which He is Himself—gathers all things and comprehends them as one. Similarly, He is said to be loved by all the things which are from Him, not because He is patient to their activity, but rather because all things seek Him, and His beauty draws all things to Him. He alone is truly lovable. He alone is the highest goodness, the true goodness, and beauty. For He is everything which is understood to be truly good and truly lovable, and truly beautiful, in creatures. Just as there is no essential good other than He, so no beautiful or lovable thing is essentially so apart from Him. Consequently, just as that stone which is called a magnet causes iron to be drawn to it by means of a natural power, while it itself does not move in any way in order to bring this motion about; nor is it patient to the iron which it draws to itself; so also the cause of all things draws back to itself all things which are from it without any motion on its part, but only by the power of its beauty. Hence, the Holy Dionysius, among others, says:

> But why do theologians call God at one time love, but at another time delight, and at another time lovable and delectable?

And this he concludes in this way:

> Because He is moved by the former, but He moves by the latter.

Speaking still more clearly on this same topic, the venerable Maximus says:

> As subsisting love and delight God is moved; but as lovable and delectable, He moves all things receptive of love and delight to Himself.

Or again, even more plainly:

> He is moved indeed, as it were, pouring forth the inseparable conjunction of love and delight on those receptive of them; but He moves as if attracting an ardent desire through the nature of those things which are moved in Himself; and again He moves and is moved as if thirsting to be thirsted for, and loving to be loved, and delighting to be delighted in.

For even this visible light which fills the entire visible world is immobile; although its vehicle—the sun—revolves in an eternal motion through the middle spaces of the ether surrounding the earth. Still, the light which proceeds from this vehicle, pouring forth, as it were, from a certain inexhaustible fount, floods the entire world by a limitless diffusion of its rays in such manner that there is no place left untouched to which it might move itself: and it remains, thus, immobile forever. It is, indeed, always abundant and complete in all places in the world. It neither deserts nor seeks a place, saving only a certain little part of that lower air girding the earth which it leaves in order to receive earth's shadow, called night. Again, it is light which moves the vision of all animals capable of seeing; and it draws to itself so that through its light they may see, to the degree that they are capable of seeing; as a consequence of which it is thought to be moved: *i.e.,* it moves the rays of the eyes so that they may be moved to it. It is the cause, put in another way, of the motion of the eyes for seeing. Do not then be puzzled when you hear that the nature of light—which is fire—fills the entire sensible world and is immutably everywhere. Even Holy Dionysius teaches this in the *Celestial Hierarchy*. So does the Holy Basil affirm the same in his *Hexaemeron:*

> Indeed the substance of light is everywhere, bursting forth by a natural operation in the luminous things of the world, whether they be great or small, not only to illuminate, but to distinguish the various times by the motions of the celestial bodies.

Now what shall we say of the arts—sometimes called the disciplines—which, although complete, integral and immutable in themselves and through themselves, are nonetheless said to be moved when they excite a vision of the rational soul which causes it to seek and find them? The arts draw men, that is, to consider them so that even these arts, which are *per se* immutable, are nonetheless seen to be moved in the minds of wise men, since they move their minds. Besides this, there are many other things in which there obtains a hidden similarity to Divine Virtue. Still, Divine Virtue itself is beyond all similitude and transcends all instances in excellence. Further, the Divine Virtue, while itself remaining immutably and eternally at rest in itself, is nonetheless said to move all things, as all things subsist in and through it and have been brought thus from non-being into being. For it is by being; while all other things proceed from nothing into being. Again, it draws all things to itself, but is also itself said to be moved, since it moves itself to itself and in this way it moves itself and, as it were, is moved by itself. In this way, God is love *per se,* sight *per se,* and motion *per se*. Still, He is neither love, nor sight, nor motion—but more than love, more than sight, more than motion. Again, He is *per se* loving, seeing and moving. Still, He is *per se* neither loving, seeing nor moving, since He is more than loving, seeing and moving. Similarly, He is *per se* being-loved, being-seen, and being-moved. Yet He is not *per se* being-loved, being-seen, nor being-moved, since He is more than able-to-be-loved, able-to-be-seen, and able-to-be-moved. Consequently, He loves Himself, and is loved by Himself, in us and in Himself. Still, neither does He love Himself nor is He loved by Himself, in us and in Himself. He sees Himself, and is seen by Himself, in Himself and in us. Yet, he neither sees Himself nor is He seen by Himself, in Himself or in us; for He more than sees and is seen in Himself and in us. He moves

Himself and is moved by Himself, in Himself and in us. Still, He does not move Himself, nor is He moved by Himself, in Himself and in us.

And here is the careful, efficacious and catholic profession to be predicated of God. First: that according to *catafatica*—affirmation—we should predicate all things, whether nouns or verbs, translatively and not properly of Him. Then we may through *apofatica*—negation—deny all that which we have predicated of Him by *catafatica;* and this negation not translatively, but properly. Indeed, it is more true to deny than affirm God to be any of the things which are predicated of Him. Hence, that super-essential nature which creates all but is not itself created is to be super-essentially, super-praised above all which is predicated of Him. Consequently, that which God, the Word made flesh, said to His disciples:

> you are not you who speak, but the spirit of your Father, who speaks in you

true reason compels us to believe, to speak, and to understand in a like vein all other similar [spoken] things. You are not you who loves, who sees, who moves—but the spirit of your Father who speaks the truth in you concerning me and my Father and itself. The truth loves and sees me and my Father and itself in you; and moves itself in you that you may love me and my Father. Consequently, if the holy Trinity loves itself in us and in itself, and sees and moves itself, then it is surely loved, seen and moved by itself in the highest mode. Since it [the Trinity] is beyond all that which is said of it, it is known to none of the creatures by which it loves, sees and moves itself, both in itself and in us. Who, indeed, can say—and what can be said—concerning the ineffable of which neither a proper noun or verb or indeed any word is found, or can be formed? Who alone has immortality and dwells in inaccessible light? Who, indeed, has known the Lord's intellect? . . .

Disciple: As I see it, it is a requisite of good order that you now put together a summary statement of that which no one is able to predicate properly of God—doing and suffering, or making and being made—and in this way bring this little book to a close.

Master: Unless I am in error, you granted a little while ago that God's being is not different from His acting and making: that to Him being and acting and making are one and the same. A simple nature, that is, does not allow for the concept of substance and accident?

Disciple: Yes, I have firmly granted this.

Master: Consequently, although being is predicated of Him, while He is properly being—aye, more than being, and the cause of all being and essence and substance—so also doing and making are predicated of Him—although He is more than doing and making, and the cause of all making and doing without any accidental motion, since He is beyond all motion. He is the cause and the beginning of all motions, all accidents and even of all essences.

Disciple: I have no doubt whatsoever of this.

Master: What else, therefore, remains except that you understand that it is entirely necessary that since being and doing and making are properly denied of Him, so suffering and being-made are to be denied of Him. For I fail to see how suffering and being-made could obtain in respect of that which does not submit to doing and making.

Disciple: Let this then be the end of the book. Quite enough has been encompassed within it.

Suggestions for Further Reading

Bett, H. *Johannes Scotus Erigena: A Study in Medieval Philosophy.* Cambridge, 1925; *FCC* vol. II, ch. XII-XIII; *EG* Part IV, ch. 1; *RMcK* vol. 1, 100-141; *AAM* Part I, ch. III.

St. Anselm and Gaunilon

St. Anselm was born in 1033 at Aosta, Italy. After completing his preliminary studies in France, at Avranches and Bec, Anselm entered the Benedictine Order. In 1068 he was made Prior of Bec; and, in 1078, Abbot. He was appointed Archbishop of Canterbury in 1093 and remained at that important post until his death in 1109.

Anselm's philosophical affiliations are clearly Augustinian. Like the great African saint, Anselm practiced philosophy as a kind of prayer: as a means of devoting his talents to the praise and glory of God. Whereas the bulk of men praise God in rather different ways, Anselm sought to praise Him with logic and dialectic. Indeed, the title of the work from which we shall below present an excerpt —*Proslogium*—is usually translated as *Discourse;* but the work is a very special kind of discourse, and the title might better be rendered *Prayer*.

The main argument from Anselm's *Proslogium*—long famous as "the ontological argument" for the existence of God—is one of the most influential and baffling philosophical arguments ever presented. In one guise or another it appears time after time in the history of philosophy in spite of the fact that it has been repeatedly "refuted." In Anselm's own day the argument was subjected to attack by Gaunilon, a monk of Marmoutier, whose arguments against it are below appended to Anselm's own. Anselm, however, replied to Gaunilon, claiming that Gaunilon had misunderstood his position. Anselm's entire reply to Gaunilon is also reprinted below.

ST. ANSELM

ON THE EXISTENCE OF GOD *

PREFACE

In this brief work the author aims at proving in a single argument the existence of God, and whatsoever we believe of God.—The difficulty of the task.—The author writes in the person of one who contemplates God, and seeks to understand what he believes. To this work he had given this title: Faith Seeking Understanding. He finally named it Proslogium—that is, A Discourse.

After I had published, at the solicitous entreaties of certain brethren, a brief work (the *Monologium*) as an example of meditation on the grounds of faith, in the person of one who investigates, in a course of silent reasoning with himself, matters of which he is ignorant; considering that this book was knit together by the linking of many arguments, I began to ask myself whether there might be found a single argument which would require no other for its proof than itself alone; and alone would suffice to demonstrate that God truly exists, and that there is a supreme good requiring nothing else, which all other things require for their existence and well-being; and whatever we believe regarding the divine Being.

Although I often and earnestly directed my thought to this end, and at some times that which I sought seemed to be just within my reach, while again it wholly evaded my mental vision, at last in despair I was about to cease, as if from the search for a thing which could not be found. But when I wished to exclude this thought altogether, lest, by busying my mind to no purpose, it should keep me from other thoughts,

* Reprinted by permission of the Open Court Publishing Company, La Salle, Illinois, from *St. Anselm: Proslogium, Monologium, an Appendix in Behalf of the Fool by Gaunilon; and Cur Deus Homo.* Translated by S. N. Deane. 1951.

in which I might be successful; then more and more, though I was unwilling and shunned it, it began to force itself upon me, with a kind of importunity. So, one day, when I was exceedingly wearied with resisting its importunity, in the very conflict of my thoughts, the proof of which I had despaired offered itself, so that I eagerly embraced the thoughts which I was strenuously repelling.

Thinking, therefore, that what I rejoiced to have found, would, if put in writing, be welcome to some readers, of this very matter, and of some others, I have written the following treatise, in the person of one who strives to lift his mind to the contemplation of God, and seeks to understand what he believes. In my judgment, neither this work nor the other, which I mentioned above, deserved to be called a book, or to bear the name of an author; and yet I thought they ought not to be sent forth without some title by which they might, in some sort, invite one into whose hands they fell to their perusal. I accordingly gave each a title, that the first might be known as, An Example of Meditation on the Grounds of Faith, and its sequel as, Faith Seeking Understanding. But, after both had been copied by many under these titles, many urged me, and especially Hugo, the reverend Archbishop of Lyons, who discharges the apostolic office in Gaul, who instructed me to this effect on his apostolic authority—to prefix my name to these writings. And that this might be done more fitly, I named the first, *Monologium,* that is, A Soliloquy; but the second, *Proslogium,* that is, A Discourse.

CHAPTER I

Exhortation of the mind to the contemplation of God.—It casts aside cares, and excludes all thoughts save that of God, that it may seek Him. Man was created to see God. Man by sin lost the blessedness for which he was made, and found the misery for which he was not made. He did not keep this good when he could keep it easily. Without God it is ill with us. Our labors and attempts are in vain without God. Man cannot seek God, unless God himself teaches him; nor find him, unless he reveals himself. God created man in his image, that he might be mindful of him, think of him, and love him. The believer does not seek to understand, that he may believe, but he believes that he may understand: for unless he believed he would not understand.

Up now, slight man! flee, for a little while, thy occupations; hide thyself, for a time, from thy disturbing thoughts. Cast aside, now, thy burdensome cares, and put away thy toilsome business. Yield room for some little time to God; and rest for a little time in him. Enter the inner chamber of thy mind; shut out all thoughts save that of God, and such as can aid thee in seeking him; close thy door and seek him. Speak now, my whole heart! speak now to God, saying, I seek thy face; thy face, Lord, will I seek (Psalms xxvii. 8). And come thou now, O Lord my God, teach my heart where and how it may seek thee, where and how it may find thee.

Lord, if thou art not here, where shall I seek thee, being absent? But if thou art everywhere, why do I not see thee present? Truly thou dwellest in unapproachable light. But where is unapproachable light, or how shall I come to it? Or who shall lead me to that light and into it, that I may see thee in it? Again, by what marks, under what form, shall I seek thee? I have never seen thee, O Lord, my God; I do not know thy form. What, O most high Lord, shall this man do, an exile far from thee? What shall thy servant do, anxious in his love of thee, and cast out afar from thy face? He pants to see thee, and thy face is too far from him. He longs to come to thee, and thy dwelling-place is inaccessible. He is eager to find thee, and knows not thy place. He desires to seek thee, and does not know thy face. Lord, thou art my God, and thou art my Lord, and never have I seen thee. It is thou that hast made me, and hast made me anew, and hast bestowed upon me all the blessings I enjoy; and not yet do I know thee. Finally, I was created to see thee, and not yet have I done that for which I was made.

O wretched lot of man, when he hath lost that for which he was made! O hard and terrible fate! Alas, what has he lost, and what has he found? What has departed, and what remains? He has lost the blessedness for which he was made, and has found the misery for which he was not made. That has departed without which nothing is happy, and that remains which, in itself, is only miserable. Man once did eat the bread of angels, for which he hungers now; he eateth now the bread of sorrows, of which he knew not then. Alas! for the mourning of all mankind, for the universal lamentation of the sons of Hades! He choked with satiety, we sigh with hunger. He abounded, we beg. He possessed in happiness, and miserably forsook his possession; we suffer want in unhappiness, and feel a miserable longing, and alas! we remain empty.

Why did he not keep for us, when he could so easily, that whose lack we should feel so heavily? Why did he shut us away from the light, and cover us over with darkness? With what purpose did he rob us of life, and inflict death upon us? Wretches that we are, whence have we been driven out; whither are we driven on? Whence hurled? Whither consigned to ruin? From a native country into exile, from the vision of God into our present blindness, from the joy of immortality into the bitterness and horror of death. Miserable exchange of how great a good, for how great an evil! Heavy loss, heavy grief, heavy all our fate!

But alas! wretched that I am, one of the sons of Eve, far removed from God! What have I undertaken? What have I accomplished? Whither was I striving? How far have I come? To what did I aspire? Amid what thoughts am I sighing? I sought blessings, and lo! confusion. I strove toward God, and I stumbled on myself. I sought calm in privacy, and I found tribulation and grief, in my inmost thoughts. I wished to smile in the joy of my mind, and I am compelled to frown by the sorrow of my heart. Gladness was hoped for, and lo! a source of frequent sighs!

And thou too, O Lord, how long? How long, O Lord, dost thou forget us; how long dost thou turn thy face from us? When wilt thou look upon us, and hear us? When wilt thou enlighten our eyes, and show us thy face? When wilt thou restore thyself to us? Look upon us, Lord; hear us, enlighten us, reveal thyself to us. Restore thyself to us, that it may be well with us—thyself, without whom it is so ill with us.

Pity our toilings and strivings toward thee, since we can do nothing without thee. Thou dost invite us; do thou help us. I beseech thee, O Lord, that I may not lose hope in sighs, but may breathe anew in hope. Lord, my heart is made bitter by its desolation; sweeten thou it, I beseech thee, with thy consolation. Lord, in hunger I began to seek thee; I beseech thee that I may not cease to hunger for thee. In hunger I have come to thee; let me not go unfed. I have come in poverty to the Rich, in misery to the Compassionate; let me not return empty and despised. And if, before I eat, I sigh, grant, even after sighs, that which I may eat. Lord, I am bowed down and can only look downward; raise me up that I may look upward. My iniquities have gone over my head; they overwhelm me; and, like a heavy load, they weigh me down. Free me from them; unburden me, that the pit of iniquities may not close over me.

Be it mine to look up to thy light, even from afar, even from the depths. Teach me to seek thee, and reveal thyself to me, when I seek thee, for I cannot seek thee, except thou teach me, nor find thee, except thou reveal thyself. Let me seek thee in longing, let me long for thee in seeking; let me find thee in love, and love thee in finding. Lord, I acknowledge and I thank thee that thou hast created me in this thine image, in order that I may be mindful of thee, may conceive of thee, and love thee; but that image has been so consumed and wasted away by vices, and obscured by the smoke of wrong-doing, that it cannot achieve that for which it was made, except thou renew it, and create it anew. I do not endeavor, O Lord, to penetrate thy sublimity, for in no wise do I compare my understanding with that; but I long to understand in some degree thy truth, which my heart believes and loves. For I do not seek to understand that I may believe, but I believe in order to understand. For this also I believe —that unless I believed, I should not understand.

CHAPTER II

Truly there is a God, although the fool hath said in his heart, There is no God.

And so, Lord, do thou, who dost give understanding to faith, give me, so far as thou knowest it to be profitable, to understand that thou art as we believe; and that thou art that which we believe. And, indeed, we believe that thou art a being than which nothing greater can be conceived. Or is there no such nature, since the fool hath said in his heart, there is no God? (Psalms xiv. 1). But, at any rate, this very fool, when he hears of this being of which I speak—a being than which nothing greater can be conceived—understands what he hears, and what he understands is in his understanding; although he does not understand it to exist.

For, it is one thing for an object to be in the understanding, and another to understand that the object exists. When a painter first conceives of what he will afterwards perform, he has it in his understanding, but he does not yet understand it to be, because he has not yet performed it. But after he has made the painting, he both has it in his understanding, and he understands that it exists, because he has made it.

Hence, even the fool is convinced that something exists in the understanding, at least, than which nothing greater can be conceived. For, when he hears of this, he understands it. And whatever is understood, exists in the understanding. And assuredly that, than which nothing greater can be conceived, cannot exist in the understanding alone. For, suppose it exists in the understanding alone: then it can be conceived to exist in reality; which is greater.

Therefore, if that, than which nothing greater can be conceived, exists in the understanding alone, the very being, than which nothing greater can be conceived, is one, than which a greater can be conceived. But obviously this is impossible. Hence, there is no doubt that there exists a being, than which nothing greater can be conceived, and it exists both in the understanding and in reality.

CHAPTER III

God cannot be conceived not to exist.—God is that, than which nothing greater can be conceived.—That which can be conceived not to exist is not God.

And it assuredly exists so truly, that it cannot be conceived not to exist. For, it is possible to conceive of a being which cannot be conceived not to exist; and this is greater than one which can be conceived not to exist. Hence, if that, than which nothing greater can be conceived, can be conceived not to exist, it is not that, than which nothing greater can be conceived. But this is an irreconcilable contradiction. There is, then, so truly a being than which nothing greater can be conceived to exist, that it cannot even be conceived not to exist; and this being thou art, O Lord, our God.

So truly, therefore, dost thou exist, O Lord, my God, that thou canst not be conceived not to exist; and rightly. For, if a mind could conceive of a being better than thee, the creature would rise above the Creator; and this is most absurd. And, indeed, whatever else there is, except thee alone, can be conceived not to exist. To thee alone, therefore, it belongs to exist more truly than all other beings, and hence in a higher degree than all others. For, whatever else exists does not exist so truly, and hence in a less degree it belongs to it to exist. Why, then, has the fool said in his heart, there is no God (Psalms xiv. 1), since it is so evident, to a rational mind, that thou dost exist in the highest degree of all? Why, except that he is dull and a fool?

CHAPTER IV

How the fool has said in his heart what cannot be conceived.—A thing may be conceived in two ways: (1) when the word signifying it is conceived; (2) when the thing itself is understood. As far as the word goes, God can be conceived not to exist; in reality he cannot.

But how has the fool said in his heart what he could not conceive; or how is it that he could not conceive what he said in his heart? since it is the same to say in the heart, and to conceive.

But, if really, nay, since really, he both conceived, because he said in his heart; and did not say in his heart, because he could not conceive; there is more than one way in which a thing is said in the heart or conceived. For, in one sense, an object is conceived, when the word signifying it is conceived; and in another, when the very entity, which the object is, is understood.

In the former sense, then, God can be conceived not to exist; but in the latter, not at all. For no one who understands what fire and water are can conceive fire to be water, in accordance with the nature of the facts themselves, although this is possible according to the words. So, then, no one who understands what God is can conceive that God does not exist; although he says these words in his heart, either without any, or with some foreign, signification. For, God is that than which a greater cannot be conceived. And he who thoroughly understands this, assuredly understands that this being so truly exists, that not even in concept can it be non-existent. Therefore, he who understands that God so exists, cannot conceive that he does not exist.

I thank thee, gracious Lord, I thank thee; because what I formerly believed by thy bounty, I now so understand by thine illumination, that if I were unwilling to believe that thou dost exist, I should not be able not to understand this to be true. . . .

❁

GAUNILON IN BEHALF OF THE FOOL

An answer to the argument of Anselm in the Proslogium. *By Gaunilon, a monk of Marmoutier.*

1. If one doubts or denies the existence of a being of such a nature that nothing greater than it can be conceived, he receives this answer:

The existence of this being is proved, in the first place, by the fact that he himself, in his doubt or denial regarding this being, already has it in his understanding; for in hearing it spoken of he understands what is spoken of. It is proved, therefore, by the fact that what he understands must exist not only in his understanding, but in reality also.

And the proof of this is as follows.—It is a greater thing to exist both in the understanding and in reality than to be in the understanding alone. And if this being is in the understanding alone, whatever has even in the past existed in reality will be greater than this being. And so that which was greater than all beings will be less than some being, and will not be greater than all: which is a manifest contradiction.

And hence, that which is greater than all, already proved to be in the understanding, must exist not only in the understanding, but also in reality: for otherwise it will not be greater than all other beings.

2. The fool might make this reply:

This being is said to be in my understanding already, only because I understand what is said. Now could it not with equal justice be said that I have in my understanding all manner of unreal objects, having absolutely no existence in themselves, because I understand these things if one speaks of them, whatever they may be?

Unless indeed it is shown that this being is of such a character that it cannot be held in concept like all unreal objects, or objects whose existence is uncertain: and hence I am not able to conceive of it when I hear of it, or to hold it in concept; but I must understand it and have it in my understanding; because, it seems, I cannot conceive of it in any other way than by understanding it, that is, by comprehending in my knowledge its existence in reality.

But if this is the case, in the first place there will be no distinction between what has precedence in time—namely, the having of an object in the understanding—and what is subsequent in time—namely, the understanding that an object exists; as in the example of the picture, which exists first in the mind of the painter, and afterwards in his work.

Moreover, the following assertion can hardly be accepted: that this being, when it is spoken of and heard of, cannot be conceived not to exist in the way in which even God can be conceived not to exist. For if this is impossible, what was the object of this argument against one who doubts or denies the existence of such a being?

Finally, that this being so exists that it cannot be perceived by an understanding convinced of its own indubitable existence, unless this being is afterwards conceived of—this should be proved to me by an indisputable argument, but not by that which you have advanced: namely, that what I understand, when I hear it, already is in my understanding. For thus in my understanding, as I still think, could be all sorts of things whose existence is uncertain, or which do not exist at all, if some one whose words I should understand mentioned them. And so much the more if I should be deceived, as often happens, and believe in them: though I do not yet believe in the being whose existence you would prove.

3. Hence, your example of the painter who already has in his understanding what he is to paint cannot agree with this argument. For the picture, before it is made, is contained in the artificer's art itself; and any such thing, existing in the art of an artificer, is nothing but a part of his understanding itself. A joiner, St. Augustine says, when he is about to make a box in fact, first has it in his art. The box which is made in fact is not life; but the box which exists in his art is life. For the

artificer's soul lives, in which all these things are, before they are produced. Why, then, are these things life in the living soul of the artificer, unless because they are nothing else than the knowledge or understanding of the soul itself?

With the exception, however, of those facts which are known to pertain to the mental nature, whatever, on being heard and thought out by the understanding, is perceived to be real, undoubtedly that real object is one thing, and the understanding itself, by which the object is grasped, is another. Hence, even if it were true that there is a being than which a greater is inconceivable: yet to this being, when heard of and understood, the not yet created picture in the mind of the painter is not analogous.

4. Let us notice also the point touched on above, with regard to this being which is greater than all which can be conceived, and which, it is said, can be none other than God himself. I, so far as actual knowledge of the object, either from its specific or general character, is concerned, am as little able to conceive of this being when I hear of it, or to have it in my understanding, as I am to conceive of or understand God himself: whom, indeed, for this very reason I can conceive not to exist. For I do not know that reality itself which God is, nor can I form a conjecture of that reality from some other like reality. For you yourself assert that that reality is such that there can be nothing else like it.

For, suppose that I should hear something said of a man absolutely unknown to me, of whose very existence I was unaware. Through that special or general knowledge by which I know what man is, or what men are, I could conceive of him also, according to the reality itself, which man is. And yet it would be possible, if the person who told me of him deceived me, that the man himself, of whom I conceived, did not exist; since that reality according to which I conceived of him, though a no less indisputable fact, was not that man, but any man.

Hence, I am not able, in the way in which I should have this unreal being in concept or in understanding, to have that being of which you speak in concept or in understanding, when I hear the word *God* or the words, *a being greater than all other beings*. For I can conceive of the man according to a fact that is real and familiar to me: but of God, or a being greater than all others, I could not conceive at all, except merely according to the word. And an object can hardly or never be conceived according to the word alone.

For when it is so conceived, it is not so much the word itself (which is, indeed, a real thing—that is, the sound of the letters and syllables) as the signification of the word, when heard, that is conceived. But it is not conceived as by one who knows what is generally signified by the word; by whom, that is, it is conceived according to a reality and in true conception alone. It is conceived as by a man who does not know the object, and conceives of it only in accordance with the movement of his mind produced by hearing the word, the mind attempting to image for itself the signification of the word that is heard. And it would be surprising if in the reality of fact it could ever attain to this.

Thus, it appears, and in no other way, this being is also in my understanding, when I hear and understand a person who says that there is a being greater than all conceivable beings. So much for the assertion that this supreme nature already is in my understanding.

5. But that this being must exist, not only in the understanding but also in reality, is thus proved to me:

If it did not so exist, whatever exists in reality would be greater than it. And so the being which has been already proved to exist in my understanding, will not be greater than all other beings.

I still answer: if it should be said that a being which cannot be even conceived in terms of any fact, is in the understanding, I do not deny that this being is, accordingly, in my understanding. But since through this fact it can in no wise attain to real existence also, I do not yet concede to it that existence at all, until some certain proof of it shall be given.

For he who says that this being exists, because otherwise the being which is greater than all will not be greater than all, does not attend strictly enough to what he is saying. For

I do not yet say, no, I even deny or doubt that this being is greater than any real object. Nor do I concede to it any other existence than this (if it should be called existence) which it has when the mind, according to a word merely heard, tries to form the image of an object absolutely unknown to it.

How, then, is the veritable existence of that being proved to me from the assumption, by hypothesis, that it is greater than all other beings? For I should still deny this, or doubt your demonstration of it, to this extent, that I should not admit that this being is in my understanding and concept even in the way in which many objects whose real existence is uncertain and doubtful, are in my understanding and concept. For it should be proved first that this being itself really exists somewhere; and then, from the fact that it is greater than all, we shall not hesitate to infer that it also subsists in itself.

6. For example: it is said that somewhere in the ocean is an island, which, because of the difficulty, or rather the impossibility, of discovering what does not exist, is called the lost island. And they say that this island has an inestimable wealth of all manner of riches and delicacies in greater abundance than is told of the Islands of the Blest; and that having no owner or inhabitant, it is more excellent than all other countries, which are inhabited by mankind, in the abundance with which it is stored.

Now if some one should tell me that there is such an island, I should easily understand his words, in which there is no difficulty. But suppose that he went on to say, as if by a logical inference: "You can no longer doubt that this island which is more excellent than all lands exists somewhere, since you have no doubt that it is in your understanding. And since it is more excellent not to be in the understanding alone, but to exist both in the understanding and in reality, for this reason it must exist. For if it does not exist, any land which really exists will be more excellent than it; and so the island already understood by you to be more excellent will not be more excellent."

If a man should try to prove to me by such reasoning that

this island truly exists, and that its existence should no longer be doubted, either I should believe that he was jesting, or I know not which I ought to regard as the greater fool: myself, supposing that I should allow this proof; or him, if he should suppose that he had established with any certainty the existence of this island. For he ought to show first that the hypothetical excellence of this island exists as a real and indubitable fact, and in no wise as any unreal object, or one whose existence is uncertain, in my understanding.

7. This, in the meantime, is the answer the fool could make to the arguments urged against him. When he is assured in the first place that this being is so great that its non-existence is not even conceivable, and that this in turn is proved on no other ground than the fact that otherwise it will not be greater than all things, the fool may make the same answer, and say:

When did I say that any such being exists in reality, that is, a being greater than all others?—that on this ground it should be proved to me that it also exists in reality to such a degree that it cannot even be conceived not to exist? Whereas in the first place it should be in some way proved that a nature which is higher, that is, greater and better, than all other natures, exists; in order that from this we may then be able to prove all attributes which necessarily the being that is greater and better than all possesses.

Moreover, it is said that the non-existence of this being is inconceivable. It might better be said, perhaps, that its non-existence, or the possibility of its non-existence, is unintelligible. For according to the true meaning of the word, unreal objects are unintelligible. Yet their existence is conceivable in the way in which the fool conceived of the non-existence of God. I am most certainly aware of my own existence; but I know, nevertheless, that my non-existence is possible. As to that supreme being, moreover, which God is, I understand without any doubt both his existence, and the impossibility of his non-existence. Whether, however, so long as I am most positively aware of my existence, I can conceive of my non-existence, I am not sure. But if I can, why can I not conceive of the non-existence of whatever else I know with the same certainty? If, however, I cannot, God will not be the only being of which it can be said, it is impossible to conceive of his non-existence.

8. The other parts of this book are argued with such truth, such brilliancy, such grandeur; and are so replete with usefulness, so fragrant with a certain perfume of devout and holy feeling, that though there are matters in the beginning which, however rightly sensed, are weakly presented, the rest of the work should not be rejected on this account. The rather ought these earlier matters to be reasoned more cogently, and the whole to be received with great respect and honor.

ANSELM'S REPLY TO GAUNILON

It was a fool against whom the argument of my *Proslogium* was directed. Seeing, however, that the author of these objections is by no means a fool, and is a Catholic, speaking in behalf of the fool, I think it sufficient that I answer the Catholic.

CHAPTER I

A general refutation of Gaunilon's argument. It is shown that a being than which a greater cannot be conceived exists in reality.

You say—whosoever you may be, who say that a fool is capable of making these statements—that a being than which a greater cannot be conceived is not in the understanding in any other sense than that in which a being that is altogether inconceivable in terms of reality, is in the understanding. You say that the inference that this being exists in reality, from the fact that it is in the understanding, is no more just than the inference that a lost island most certainly exists, from the fact that when it is described the hearer does not doubt that it is in his understanding.

But I say: if a being than which a greater is inconceivable is not understood or conceived, and is not in the understanding or in concept, certainly either God is not a being than which a greater is inconceivable, or else he is not understood or conceived, and is not in the understanding or in concept. But I call on your faith and conscience to attest that this is most false. Hence, that than which a greater cannot be conceived is truly understood and conceived, and is in the understanding and in concept. Therefore either the grounds on which you try to controvert me are not true, or else the inference which you think to base logically on those grounds is not justified.

But you hold, moreover, that supposing that a being than which a greater cannot be conceived is understood, it does not follow that this being is in the understanding; nor, if it is in the understanding, does it therefore exist in reality.

In answer to this, I maintain positively: if that being can be even conceived to be, it must exist in reality. For that than which a greater is inconceivable cannot be conceived except as without beginning. But whatever can be conceived to exist, and does not exist, can be conceived to exist through a beginning. Hence what can be conceived to exist, but does not exist, is not the being than which a greater cannot be conceived. Therefore, if such a being can be conceived to exist, necessarily it does exist.

Furthermore: if it can be conceived at all, it must exist. For no one who denies or doubts the existence of a being than which a greater is inconceivable, denies or doubts that if it did exist, its non-existence, either in reality or in the understanding, would be impossible. For otherwise it would not be a being than which a greater cannot be conceived. But as to whatever can be conceived, but does not exist—if there were such a being, its non-existence, either in reality or in the understanding, would be possible. Therefore if a being than which a greater is inconceivable can be even conceived, it cannot be non-existent.

But let us suppose that it does not exist, even if it can be conceived. Whatever can be conceived, but does not exist, if it existed, would not be a being than which a greater is inconceivable. If, then, there were a being a greater than which is inconceivable, it would not be a being than which a greater is inconceivable: which is most absurd. Hence, it is false to deny that a being than which a greater cannot be conceived exists, if it can be even conceived; much the more, therefore, if it can be understood or can be in the understanding.

Moreover, I will venture to make this assertion: without doubt, whatever at any place or at any time does not exist—even if it does exist at some place or at some time—can be conceived to exist nowhere and never, as at some place and at some time it does not exist. For what did not exist yesterday, and exists to-day, as it is understood not to have existed yesterday, so it can be apprehended by the intelligence that it never exists. And what is not here, and is elsewhere, can be conceived to be nowhere, just as it is not here. So with regard to an object of which the individual parts do not exist at the same places or times: all its parts and therefore its very whole can be conceived to exist nowhere or never.

For, although time is said to exist always, and the world everywhere, yet time does not as a whole exist always, nor the world as a whole everywhere. And as individual parts of time do not exist when others exist, so they can be conceived never to exist. And so it can be apprehended by the intelligence that individual parts of the world exist nowhere, as they do not exist where other parts exist. Moreover, what is composed of parts can be dissolved in concept, and be non-existent. Therefore, whatever at any place or at any time does not exist as a whole, even if it is existent, can be conceived not to exist.

But that than which a greater cannot be conceived, if it exists, cannot be conceived not to exist. Otherwise, it is not a being than which a greater cannot be conceived: which is inconsistent. By no means, then, does it at any place or at any time fail to exist as a whole: but it exists as a whole everywhere and always.

Do you believe that this being can in some way be conceived or understood, or that the being with regard to which these things are understood can be in concept or in the understanding? For if it cannot, these things cannot be understood with reference to it. But if you say that it is not understood and that it is not in the understanding, because it is not thoroughly understood; you should say that a man who cannot face the direct rays of the sun does not see the light of day, which is none other than the sunlight. Assuredly a being than which a greater cannot be conceived exists, and is in the understanding, at least to this extent—that these statements regarding it are understood.

CHAPTER II

The argument is continued. It is shown that a being than which a greater is inconceivable can be conceived, and also, in so far, exists.

I have said, then, in the argument which you dispute, that when the fool hears mentioned a being than which a greater is inconceivable, he understands what he hears. Certainly a man who does not understand when a familiar language is spoken, has no understanding at all, or a very dull one. Moreover, I have said that if this being is understood, it is in the understanding. Is that in no understanding which has been proved necessarily to exist in the reality of fact?

But you will say that although it is in the understanding, it does not follow that it is understood. But observe that the fact of its being understood does necessitate its being in the understanding. For as what is conceived, is conceived by conception, and what is conceived by conception, as it is conceived, so is in conception; so what is understood, is understood by understanding, and what is understood by understanding, as it is understood, so is in the understanding. What can be more clear than this?

After this, I have said that if it is even in the understanding alone, it can be conceived also to exist in reality, which is greater. If, then, it is in the understanding alone, obviously the very being than which a greater cannot be conceived is one than which a greater can be conceived. What is more logical? For if it exists even in the understanding alone, can it not be conceived also to exist in reality? And if it can be so conceived, does not he who conceives of this conceive of a thing greater than that being, if it exists in the understanding alone? What more consistent inference, then, can be made than this: that if a being than which a greater cannot be conceived is in the understanding alone, it is not that than which a greater cannot be conceived?

But, assuredly, in no understanding is a being than which a greater is conceivable a being than which a greater is inconceivable. Does it not follow, then, that if a being than which a greater cannot be conceived is in any understanding, it does not exist in the understanding alone? For if it is in the understanding alone, it is a being than which a greater can be conceived, which is inconsistent with the hypothesis.

CHAPTER III

A criticism of Gaunilon's example, in which he tries to show that in this way the real existence of a lost island might be inferred from the fact of its being conceived.

But you say, it is as if one should suppose an island in the ocean, which surpasses all lands in its fertility, and which, because of the difficulty, or rather the impossibility, of discovering what does not exist, is called a lost island; and should say that there can be no doubt that this island truly exists in reality, for this reason, that one who hears it described easily understands what he hears.

Now I promise confidently that if any man shall devise anything existing either in reality or in concept alone (except that than which a greater cannot be conceived) to which he can adapt the sequence of my reasoning, I will discover that thing, and will give him his lost island, not to be lost again.

But it now appears that this being than which a greater is inconceivable cannot be conceived not to be, because it exists on so assured a ground of truth; for otherwise it would not exist at all.

Hence, if any one says that he conceives this being not to exist, I say that at the time when he conceives of this either he conceives of a being than which a greater is inconceivable, or he does not conceive at all. If he does not conceive, he does not conceive of the non-existence of that of which he does not conceive. But if he does conceive, he certainly conceives of a being which cannot be even conceived not to exist. For if it could be conceived not to exist, it could be conceived to have a beginning and an end. But this is impossible.

He, then, who conceives of this being conceives of a being which cannot be even conceived not to exist; but he who conceives of this being does not conceive that it does not exist; else he conceives what is inconceivable. The non-existence, then, of that than which a greater cannot be conceived is inconceivable.

CHAPTER IV

The difference between the possibility of conceiving of non-existence, and understanding non-existence.

You say, moreover, that where as I assert that this supreme being cannot be *conceived* not to exist, it might better be said that its non-existence, or even the possibility of its non-existence, cannot be *understood*.

But it was more proper to say, it cannot be conceived. For if I had said that the object itself cannot be understood not to exist, possibly you yourself, who say that in accordance with the true meaning of the term what is unreal cannot be understood, would offer the objection that nothing which is can be understood not to be, for the non-existence of what exists is unreal: hence God would not be the only being of which it could be said, it is impossible to understand its non-existence. For thus one of those beings which most certainly exist can be understood not to exist in the same way in which certain other real objects can be understood not to exist.

But this objection, assuredly, cannot be urged against the term *conception,* if one considers the matter well. For although no objects which exist can be understood not to exist, yet all objects, except that which exists in the highest degree, can be conceived not to exist. For all those objects, and those alone, can be conceived not to exist, which have a beginning or end or composition of parts: also, as I have already said, whatever at any place or at any time does not exist as a whole.

That being alone, on the other hand, cannot be conceived not to exist, in which any conception discovers neither beginning nor end nor composition of parts, and which any conception finds always and everywhere as a whole.

Be assured, then, that you can conceive of your own non-existence, although you are most certain that you exist. I am surprised that you should have admitted that you are ignorant of this. For we conceive of the non-existence of many objects which we know to exist, and of the existence of many which we know not to exist; not by forming the opinion that they so exist, but by imagining that they exist as we conceive of them.

And indeed, we can conceive of the non-existence of an object, although we know it to exist, because at the same time we can conceive of the former and know the latter. And we cannot conceive of the non-existence of an object, so long as we know it to exist, because we cannot conceive at the same time of existence and non-existence.

If, then, one will thus distinguish these two senses of this statement, he will understand that nothing, so long as it is known to exist, can be conceived not to exist; and that whatever exists, except that being than which a greater cannot be conceived, can be conceived not to exist, even when it is known to exist.

So, then, of God alone it can be said that it is impossible to conceive of his non-existence; and yet many objects, so long as they exist, in one sense cannot be conceived not to exist. But in what sense God is to be conceived not to exist, I think has been shown clearly enough in my book.

CHAPTER V

A particular discussion of certain statements of Gaunilon's. In the first place, he misquoted the argument which he undertook to refute.

The nature of the other objections which you, in behalf of the fool, urge against me it is easy, even for a man of small wisdom, to detect; and I had therefore thought it unnecessary to show this. But since I hear that some readers of these objections think they have some weight against me, I will discuss them briefly.

In the first place, you often repeat that I assert that what is greater than all other beings is in the understanding; and if it is in the understanding, it exists also in reality, for otherwise the being which is greater than all would not be greater than all.

Nowhere in all my writings is such a demonstration found. For the real existence of a being which is said to be *greater than all other beings* cannot be demonstrated in the same way with the real existence of one that is said to be *a being than which a greater cannot be conceived.*

If it should be said that a being than which a greater cannot be conceived has no real existence, or that it is possible that it does not exist, or even that it can be conceived not to exist, such an assertion can be easily refuted. For the non-existence of what does not exist is possible, and that whose non-existence is possible can be conceived not to exist. But whatever can be conceived not to exist, if it exists, is not a being than which a greater cannot be conceived; but if it does not exist, it would not, even if it existed, be a being than which a greater cannot be conceived. But it cannot be said that a being than which a greater is inconceivable, if it exists, is not a being than which a greater is inconceivable; or that if it existed, it would not be a being than which a greater is inconceivable.

It is evident, then, that neither is it non-existent, nor is it possible that it does not exist, nor can it be conceived not to exist. For otherwise, if it exists, it is not that which it is said to be in the hypothesis; and if it existed, it would not be what it is said to be in the hypothesis.

But this, it appears, cannot be so easily proved of a being which is said to be *greater than all other beings*. For it is not so evident that what can be conceived not to exist is not greater than all existing beings, as it is evident that it is not a being than which a greater cannot be conceived. Nor is it so indubitable that if a being greater than all other things exists, it is no other than the being than which a greater cannot be conceived; or that if it were such a being, some other might not be this being in like manner; as it is certain with regard to a being which is hypothetically posited as one than which a greater cannot be conceived.

For consider: if one should say that there is a being greater than all other beings, and that this being can nevertheless be conceived not to exist; and that a being greater than this, although it does not exist, can be conceived to exist: can it be so clearly inferred in this case that this being is therefore not a being greater than all other existing beings, as it would be most positively affirmed in the other case, that the being under discussion is not, therefore, a being than which a greater cannot be conceived?

For the former conclusion requires another premise than the predication, *greater than all other beings*. In my argument, on the other hand, there is no need of any other than this very predication, *a being than which a greater cannot be conceived*.

If the same proof cannot be applied when the being in question is predicated to be greater than all others, which can be applied when it is predicated to be a being than which a greater cannot be conceived, you have unjustly censured me for saying what I did not say; since such a predication differs so greatly from that which I actually made. If, on the other hand, the other argument is valid, you ought not to blame me so for having said what can be proved.

Whether this can be proved, however, he will easily decide who recognizes that this being than which a greater cannot be conceived is demonstrable. For by no means can this being than which a greater cannot be conceived be understood as any other than that which alone is greater than all. Hence, just as that than which a greater cannot be conceived is understood, and is in the understanding, and for that reason is asserted to exist in the reality of fact: so what is said to be greater than all other beings is understood and is in the understanding, and therefore it is necessarily inferred that it exists in reality.

You see, then, with how much justice you have compared me with your fool, who, on the sole ground that he understands what is described to him, would affirm that a lost island exists.

CHAPTER VI

A discussion of Gaunilon's argument in his second chapter: that any unreal beings can be understood in the same way, and would, to that extent, exist.

Another of your objections is that any unreal beings, or beings whose existence is uncertain, can be understood and be in the understanding in the same way with that being which I discussed. I am surprised that you should have conceived this objection, for I was attempting to prove what was still uncertain, and contented myself at first with showing that this being is understood in any way, and is in the understanding. It was my intention to consider, on these grounds, whether this being is in the understanding alone, like an unreal object, or whether it also exists in fact, as a real being. For if unreal objects, or objects whose existence is uncertain, in this way are understood and are in the understanding, because, when they are spoken of, the hearer understands what the speaker means, there is no reason why that being of which I spoke should not be understood and be in the understanding.

How, moreover, can these two statements of yours be reconciled: (1) the assertion that if a man should speak of any unreal objects, whatever they might be, you would understand, and (2) the assertion that on hearing of that being which does exist, and not in that way in which even unreal objects are held in concept, you would not say that you conceive of it or have it in concept; since, as you say, you cannot conceive of it in any other way than by understanding it, that is, by comprehending in your knowledge its real existence?

How, I ask, can these two things be reconciled: that unreal objects are understood, and that understanding an object is comprehending in knowledge its real existence? The contradiction does not concern me: do you see to it. But if unreal objects are also in some sort understood, and your definition is applicable, not to every understanding, but to a certain sort of understanding, I ought not to be blamed for saying that a being than which a greater cannot be conceived is understood and is in the understanding, even before I reached the certain conclusion that this being exists in reality.

CHAPTER VII

In answer to another objection: that the supremely great being may be conceived not to exist, just as by the fool God is conceived not to exist.

Again, you say that it can probably never be believed that this being, when it is spoken of and heard of, cannot be conceived not to exist in the same way in which even God may be conceived not to exist.

Such an objection could be answered by those who have attained but little skill in disputation and argument. For is it compatible with reason for a man to deny the existence of what he understands, because it is said to be that being whose existence he denies because he does not understand it? Or, if at some times its existence is denied, because only to a certain extent is it understood, and that which is not at all understood is the same to him: is not what is still undetermined more easily proved of a being which exists in some understanding than of one which exists is no understanding?

Hence it cannot be credible that any man denies the existence of a being than which a greater cannot be conceived, which, when he hears of it, he understands in a certain degree:

it is incredible, I say, that any man denies the existence of this being because he denies the existence of God, the sensory perception of whom he in no wise conceives of.

Or if the existence of another object, because it is not at all understood, is denied, yet is not the existence of what is understood in some degree more easily proved than the existence of an object which is in no wise understood?

Not irrationally, then, has the hypothesis of a being a greater than which cannot be conceived been employed in controverting the fool, for the proof of the existence of God: since in some degree he would understand such a being, but in no wise could he understand God.

CHAPTER VIII

The example of the picture, treated in Gaunilon's third chapter, is examined.—From what source a notion may be formed of the supremely great being, of which Gaunilon inquired in his fourth chapter.

Moreover, your so careful demonstration that the being than which a greater cannot be conceived is not analogous to the not yet executed picture in the understanding of the painter, is quite unnecessary. It was not for this purpose that I suggested the preconceived picture. I had no thought of asserting that the being which I was discussing is of such a nature; but I wished to show that what is not understood to exist can be in the understanding.

Again, you say that when you hear of a being than which a greater is inconceivable, you cannot conceive of it in terms of any real object known to you either specifically or generally, nor have it in your understanding. For, you say, you neither know such a being in itself, nor can you form an idea of it from anything like it.

But obviously this is not true. For everything that is less good, in so far as it is good, is like the greater good. It is therefore evident to any rational mind, that by ascending from the lesser good to the greater, we can form a considerable notion of a being than which a greater is inconceivable.

For instance, who (even if he does not believe that what he conceives of exists in reality) supposing that there is some good which has a beginning and an end, does not conceive that a good is much better, which, if it begins, does not cease to be? And that as the second good is better than the first, so that good which has neither beginning nor end, though it is ever passing from the past through the present to the future, is better than the second? And that far better than this is a being —whether any being of such a nature exists or not—which in no wise requires change or motion, nor is compelled to undergo change or motion?

Is this inconceivable, or is some being greater than this conceivable? Or is not this to form a notion from objects than which a greater is conceivable, of the being than which a greater cannot be conceived? There is, then, a means of forming a notion of a being than which a greater is inconceivable.

So easily, then, can the fool who does not accept sacred authority be refuted, if he denies that a notion may be formed from other objects of a being than which a greater is inconceivable. But if any Catholic would deny this, let him remember that the invisible things of God, from the creation of the world, are clearly seen, being understood by the things that are made, even his eternal power and Godhead. (Romans i. 20.)

CHAPTER IX

The possibility of understanding and conceiving of the supremely great being. The argument advanced against the fool is confirmed.

But even if it were true that a being than which a greater is inconceivable cannot be conceived or understood; yet it would not be untrue that a being than which a greater cannot be conceived is conceivable and intelligible. There is nothing to prevent one's saying *ineffable,* although what is said to be ineffable cannot be spoken of. *Inconceivable* is conceivable, although that to which the word *inconceivable* can be applied is not conceivable. So, when one says, *that than which nothing greater is conceivable,* undoubtedly what is heard is conceivable and intelligible, although that being itself, than which a greater is inconceivable, cannot be conceived or understood.

Or, though there is a man so foolish as to say that there is no being than which a greater is inconceivable, he will not be so shameless as to say that he cannot understand or conceive of what he says. Or, if such a man is found, not only ought his words to be rejected, but he himself should be contemned.

Whoever, then, denies the existence of a being than which a greater cannot be conceived, at least understands and conceives of the denial which he makes. But this denial he cannot understand or conceive of without its component terms; and a term of this statement is *a being than which a greater cannot be conceived*. Whoever, then, makes this denial, understands and conceives of that than which a greater is inconceivable.

Moreover, it is evident that in the same way it is possible to conceive of and understand a being whose non-existence is impossible; but he who conceives of this conceives of a greater being than one whose non-existence is possible. Hence, when a being than which a greater is inconceivable is conceived, if it is a being whose non-existence is possible that is conceived, it is not a being than which a greater cannot be conceived. But an object cannot be at once conceived and not conceived. Hence he who conceives of a being than which a greater is inconceivable, does not conceive of that whose non-existence is possible, but of that whose non-existence is impossible. Therefore, what he conceives of must exist; for anything whose non-existence is possible, is not that of which he conceives.

CHAPTER X

The certainty of the foregoing argument.—The conclusion of the book.

I believe that I have shown by an argument which is not weak, but sufficiently cogent, that in my former book I proved the real existence of a being than which a greater cannot be conceived; and I believe that this argument cannot be invalidated by the validity of any objection. For so great force does the signification of this reasoning contain in itself, that this being which is the subject of discussion, is of necessity, from the very fact that it is understood or conceived, proved also to exist in reality, and to be whatever we should believe of the divine substance.

For we attribute to the divine substance anything of which it can be conceived that it is better to be than not to be that thing. For example: it is better to be eternal than not eternal; good, than not good; nay, goodness itself, than not goodness itself. But it cannot be that anything of this nature is not a property of the being than which a greater is inconceivable. Hence, the being than which a greater is inconceivable must be whatever should be attributed to the divine essence.

I thank you for your kindness both in your blame and in your praise for my book. For since you have commended so generously those parts of it which seem to you worthy of acceptance, it is quite evident that you have criticized in no unkind spirit those parts of it which seemed to you weak.

Suggestions for Further Reading

Rule, M. *The Life and Times of St. Anselm.* 2 vols. London, 1883; Church, A. W. *St. Anselm.* London, 1873; Rigg, J. M. *St. Anselm of Canterbury.* London, 1896; *FCC* vol. II, ch. XV; *EG* 128-139; *AAM* 47-58; *RMcK* vol. 1, 142-184.

Peter Abelard

Peter Abelard, one of the most impressive and energetic personalities among the twelfth-century thinkers, was born in the year 1079 at Pallet, in the county of Nantes, France. We learn from his autobiographical sketch, *The History of My Calamities,* that he was destined by his father to pursue a military career. Abelard, however, early decided for himself to "desert the court of Mars for the bosom of Minerva"; accordingly, he turned to the study of dialectics, receiving his education from some of the most famous men of the day. Eventually, Abelard opened a school of his own, first at Melun, then at Corbeil, and finally at Paris, where he entered into a bitter philosophical dispute with one of his former masters. Abelard's brilliance and skill easily won the day, and his reputation as a philosopher, which had been growing all the while, was firmly established.

Apparently not satisfied with recognition in but one field of intellectual endeavor, Abelard next directed his energies to the study of theology; and he started teaching theology himself, with similar success, at Paris, in 1113. After his famous and tragic love affair with Héloïse, Abelard retired from Paris to the Abbey of St. Denis. In 1121, the same year in which he ably defended himself against a charge of heresy before the Council of Soissons, Abelard founded yet another school—the famous Paraclete—and taught there until 1125, when he resigned to become Abbot of St. Gildas. He remained at St. Gildas until 1129, at which time he returned to Paris to teach. Abelard taught at Paris for the next twelve years until accused of heresy by St. Bernard. As a consequence of this accusation, Abelard, in 1141, was condemned by the Council of Sens. His appeal to Pope Innocent II led not only to a further condemnation, but as well to an injunction against any further teaching. At this point Abelard, broken and dejected, retired to Cluny and remained there until his death, in 1142.

Abelard is best known to the historians of philosophy for his dialectical skill and for his handling of the problem of universals. (His position in this important problem will be sketched in the excerpt from John of Salisbury's works.) Abelard's original and brilliant contribution to ethics, however, has never really received the attention which it merits, nor the acclaim which is its due. Presented below are the first sixteen chapters of his unfinished tract, *The Ethics* or *Know Thyself.*

ABELARD ON ETHICS*

PROLOGUE

In the study of morals we deal with the defects or qualities of the mind which dispose us to bad or good actions. Defects and qualities are not only mental, but also physical. There is bodily weakness; there is also the endurance which we call strength. There is sluggishness or speed; blindness or sight. When we now speak of defects, therefore, we pre-suppose defects of the mind, so as to distinguish them from the physical ones. The defects of the mind are opposed to the qualities; injustice to justice; cowardice to constancy; intemperance to temperance.

* Printed by permission of B. H. Blackwell, London, from *Abailard's Ethics*, translated by J. R. McCallum, 1935.

CHAPTER I

THE DEFECT OF MIND BEARING UPON CONDUCT

Certain defects or merits of mind have no connection with morals. They do not make human life a matter of praise or blame. Such are dull wits or quick insight; a good or a bad memory; ignorance or knowledge. Each of these features is found in good and bad alike. They have nothing to do with the system of morals, nor with making life base or honourable. To exclude these we safeguarded above the phrase "defects of mind" by adding "which dispose to bad actions," that is, those defects which incline the will to what least of all either should be done or should be left undone.

CHAPTER II

HOW DOES SIN DIFFER FROM A DISPOSITION TO EVIL?

Defect of this mental kind is not the same thing as sin. Sin, too, is not the same as a bad action. For example, to be irascible, that is, prone or easily roused to the agitation of anger is a defect and moves the mind to unpleasantly impetuous and irrational action. This defect, however, is in the mind so that the mind is liable to wrath, even when it is not actually roused to it. Similarly, lameness, by reason of which a man is said to be lame, is in the man himself even when he does not walk and reveal his lameness. For the defect is there though action be lacking. So, also, nature or constitution renders many liable to luxury. Yet they do not sin because they are like this, but from this very fact they have the material of a struggle whereby they may, in the virtue of temperance, triumph over themselves and win the crown. As Solomon says: "Better a patient than a strong man; and the Lord of his soul than he that taketh a city." (Prov. xvi, 32.) For religion does not think it degrading to be beaten by man; but it is degrading to be beaten by one's lower self. The former defeat has been the fate of good men. But, in the latter, we fall below ourselves. The Apostle commends victory of this sort; "No one shall be crowned who has not truly striven." (2 Tim. ii, 5.) This striving, I repeat, means standing less against men than against myself, so that defects may not lure me into base consent. Though men cease to oppose us, our defects do not cease. The fight with them is the more dangerous because of its repetition. And as it is the more difficult, so victory is the more glorious. Men, however much they prevail over us, do not force baseness upon us, unless by their practice of vice they turn us also to it and overcome us through our own wretched consent. They may dominate our body; but while our mind is free, there is no danger to true freedom. We run no risk of base servitude. Subservience to vice, not to man, is degradation. It is the overlordship of defects and not physical serfdom which debases the soul.

CHAPTER III

DEFINITION OF "DEFECT" AND OF SIN

Defect, then, is that whereby we are disposed to sin. We are, that is, inclined to consent to what we ought not to do, or to leave undone what we ought to do. Consent of this kind we rightly call sin. Here is the reproach of the soul meriting damnation or being declared guilty by God. What is that consent but to despise God and to violate his laws? God cannot be set at enmity by injury, but by contempt. He is the highest power, and is not diminished by any injury, but He avenges contempt of Himself. Our sin, therefore, is contempt of the Creator. To sin is to despise the Creator; that is, not to do for Him what we believe we should do for Him, or, not to renounce what we think should be renounced on His behalf. We have defined sin negatively by saying that it means not doing or not renouncing what we ought to do or renounce. Clearly, then, we have shown that sin has no reality. It exists rather in *not being* than in *being*. Similarly we could define shadows by saying: The absence of light where light usually is.

Perhaps you object that sin is the desire or will to do an evil deed, and that this will or desire condemns us before God in the same way as the will to do a good deed justifies us. There is as much quality, you suggest, in the good will as there is sin in the evil will; and it is no less "in being" in the latter than in the former. By willing to do what we believe to be pleasing to God we please Him. Equally, by willing to do what we believe to be displeasing to God, we displease Him and seem either to violate or despise His nature.

But diligent attention will show that we must think far otherwise of this point. We frequently err; and from no evil will at all. Indeed, the evil will itself, when restrained, though it may not be quenched, procures the palm-wreath for those who resist it. It provides, not merely the materials for combat, but also the crown of glory. It should be spoken of rather as a certain inevitable weakness than as sin. Take, for example, the case of an innocent servant whose harsh master is moved with fury against him. He pursues the servant, drawing his sword with intent to kill him. For a while the servant flies and avoids death as best he can. At last, forced all unwillingly to it, he kills his master so as not to be killed by him. Let anyone say what sort of evil will there was in this deed. His will was only to flee from death and preserve his own life. Was this an evil will? You reply: "I do not think this was an evil will. But the will that he had to kill the master who was pursuing him was evil." Your answer would be admirable and acute if you could show that the servant really willed what you say that he did. But, as I insisted, he was unwillingly forced to his deed. He protracted his master's life as long as he could, knowing that danger also threatened his own life from such a crime. How, then, was a deed done voluntarily by which he incurred danger to his own life?

Your reply may be that the action was voluntary because the man's will was to escape death even though it may not have been to kill his master. This charge might easily be preferred against him. I do not rebut it. Nevertheless, as has been said, that will by which he sought to evade death, as you urge, and not to kill his master, cannot at all be condemned as bad. He did, however, fail by consenting, though driven to it through fear of death, to an unjust murder which he ought rather to have endured than committed. Of his own will, I mean, he took the sword. It was not handed to him by authority. The Truth saith: "Everyone that taketh the sword shall perish by the sword." (Matt. xxvi, 52.) By his rashness he risked the death and damnation of his soul. The servant's wish then, was not to kill his master, but to avoid death. Because he *consented,* however, as he should not have done, to murder, this wrongful consent preceding the crime was sin.

Someone may interpose: "But you cannot conclude that he wished to kill his master because, in order to escape death, he was willing to kill his master. I might say to a man; I am willing for you to have my cape so that you may give me five shillings. Or, I am glad for you to have it at this price. But I do not hand it over because I desire you to have possession of it." No, and if a man in prison desired under duress, to put his son there in his place that he might secure his own ransom, should we therefore admit that he wished to send his son to prison?

It was only with many a tear and groan that he consented to such a course.

The fact is that this kind of will, existing with much internal regret, is not, if I may say so, *will,* but a passive submission of mind. It is so because the man wills one thing on account of another. He puts up with *this* because he really desires *that.* A patient is said to submit to cautery or lancet that he may obtain health. Martyrs endured that they might come to Christ; and Christ, too, that we may be saved by his passion.

Yet we are not bound to admit simply that these people therefore wish for this mental unease. Such unease can only be where something occurs contrary to wish. No man suffers so long as he fulfils his wish and does what he likes to experience. The Apostle says: "I desire to depart and to be with Christ" (Phil. i, 23), that is, to die so that I may attain to him.

Elsewhere this apostle says: "We desire not to be despoiled of our garments, but to be clothed from above, that our mortal part may be swallowed up in life." This notion, Blessed Augustine reminds us, was contained in the Lord's address to Peter: "Thou shalt extend thy hands and another shall gird thee, and lead thee whither thou willest not." (John xxi, 18.) The Lord also spoke to the Father out of the weakness of the human nature which he had taken upon himself: "If it be possible, let this cup pass from me; nevertheless not as I will, but as thou willest." (Matt. xxvi, 39.) His spirit naturally trembled before the great terror of death: and he could not speak of what he knew to be punishment as a matter of his own will. When elsewhere it is written of Him: "He was offered because He himself willed it" (Isaiah liii, 7), it must be understood either of His divine nature, in whose will it was that He should suffer as a man, or "He himself willed it" must be taken according to the Psalmist's phrase: "Whatsoever he willed, that he did." (Ps. cxiii, 3.)

Sin, therefore, is sometimes committed without an evil will. Thus sin cannot be defined as "will." True, you will say, when we sin under constraint, but not when we sin willingly, for instance, when we will to do something which we know ought not to be done by us. There the evil will and sin seem to be the same thing. For example a man sees a woman; his concupiscence is aroused; his mind is enticed by fleshly lust and stirred to base desire. This wish, this lascivious longing, what else can it be, you say, than sin?

I reply: What if that wish may be bridled by the power of temperance? What if its nature is never to be entirely extinguished but to persist in struggle and not fully fail even in defeat? For where is the battle if the antagonist is away? Whence the great reward without grave endurance? When the fight is over nothing remains but to reap the reward. Here we strive in contest in order elsewhere to obtain as victors a crown. Now, for a contest, an opponent is needed who will resist, not one who simply submits. This opponent is our evil will over which we triumph when we subjugate it to the divine will. But we do not entirely destroy it. For we needs must ever expect to encounter our enemy. What achievement before God is it if we undergo nothing contrary to our own will, but merely practice what we please? Who will be grateful to us if in what we say we do for him we merely satisfy our own fancy?

You will say, what merit have we with God in acting willingly or unwillingly? Certainly none: I reply. He weighs the intention rather than the deed in his recompense. Nor does the deed, whether it proceed from a good or an evil will, add anything to the merit, as we shall show shortly. But when we set His will before our own so as to follow His and not ours, our merit with God is magnified, in accordance with that perfect word of Truth: "I came not to do mine own will, but the will of Him that sent me." (John vi, 38.) To this end He exhorts us: "If anyone comes to me, and does not hate father, and mother . . . yea his own soul also, he is not worthy of me." (Luke xiv, 26.) That is to say, "unless a man renounces his parents' influence and his own will and submits himself to my teaching, he is not worthy of me." Thus we are bidden to hate our father, not to destroy him. Similarly with our own will. We must not be led by it; at the same time, we are not asked to root it out altogether.

When the Scripture says: "Go not after your own desires" (Eccles. xviii, 30), and: "Turn from your own will" (ibid.), it instructs us not to fulfil our desires. Yet it does not say that we are to be wholly without them. It is vicious to give in to our desires; but not to have any desires at all is impossible for our weak nature.

The sin, then, consists not in desiring a woman, but in consent to the desire, and not the wish for whoredom, but the consent to the wish is damnation.

Let us see how our conclusions about sexual intemperance apply to theft. A man crosses another's garden. At the sight of the delectable fruit his desire is aroused. He does not, however, give way to desire so as to take anything by theft or rapine, although his mind was moved to strong inclination by the thought of the delight of eating. Where there is desire, there, without doubt, will exists. The man desires the eating of that fruit wherein he doubts not that there will be delight. The weakness of nature in this man is compelled to desire the fruit which, without the master's permission, he has no right to take. He conquers the desire, but does not extinguish it. Since, however, he is not enticed into consent, he does not descend to sin.

What, then, of your objection? It should be clear from such instances, that the wish or desire itself of doing what is not seemly is never to be called sin, but rather, as we said, the consent is sin. We consent to what is not seemly when we do not draw ourselves back from such a deed, and are prepared, should opportunity offer, to perform it completely. Whoever is discovered in this intention, though his guilt has yet to be completed in deed, is already guilty before God in so far as he strives with all his might to sin, and accomplishes within himself, as the blessed Augustine reminds us, as much as if he were actually taken in the act.

But while wish is not sin, and, as we have said, we sometimes commit sin unwillingly, there are nevertheless those who assert that every sin is voluntary. In this respect they discover a certain difference between sin and will. Will is one thing, they say, but a voluntary act is another. They mean that there is a distinction between will and what is done willingly. If, however, we call sin what we have already decided that it essentially is, namely, contempt of God or consent to that which we believe should not, for God's sake, be done how can we say that sin is voluntary? I mean, how can we say that we wish to despise God? What is sin but sinking below a standard, or becoming liable to damnation? For although we desire to do what we know deserves punishment, yet we do not desire to be punished. Thus plainly we are reprobate. We are willing to do wrong; but we are unwilling to bear the just punishment of wrong-doing. The punishment which is just displeases: the deed which is unjust pleases. Often we woo a married woman because of her charm. Our wish is not so much to commit adultery as a longing that she were unmarried. On the other hand, many covet the wives of influential men for the sake of their own fame, and not for the natural attractiveness of these ladies. Their wish is for adultery rather than sexual relationship, the major in preference to the minor excess. Some, too, are ashamed altogether of being betrayed into any consent to concupiscence or evil will; and thus from the weakness of the flesh are compelled to wish what they least of all wish to wish.

How, then, a wish which we do not wish to have can be called voluntary, as it is according to those thinkers I have mentioned, so that all sin becomes a matter of voluntary action, I assuredly do not understand, unless by voluntary is meant that no action is determined, since a sin is never a predestined event. Or perhaps we are to take "voluntary" to be that which proceeds from some kind of will. For although the man who slew his master had no will to perform the actual murder, nevertheless he did it from some sort of will, because he certainly wished to escape or defer death.

Some are intensely indignant when they hear us assert that the act of sinning adds nothing to guilt or damnation before God. Their contention is that in this act of sinning a certain delight supervenes, which increases the sin, as in sexual intercourse or indulgence in food which we referred to above. Their statement is absurd unless they can prove that physical delight of this kind is itself sin, and that such pleasure cannot be taken without a sin being thereby committed. If it be as they suppose, then no one is permitted to enjoy physical pleasure. The married do not escape sin when they employ their physical privilege; nor yet the man who eats with relish his own fruits.

Invalids, too, who are treated to more delicate dishes to aid their recovery of strength would likewise be guilty, since they are not able to eat without a sense of delight and should this be lacking, the food does them no good. Finally, God, the Creator of nourishment and of the bodies which receive it, would not be without guilt for having instilled savours which necessarily involve in sin those who ignorantly use them. Yet how should He supply such things for our consumption, or permit them to be consumed, if it were impossible for us to eat them without sin? How, again, can it be said that there is sin in doing what is allowed? In regard to those matters which once were unlawful and forbidden, if they are later allowed and made lawful, they can be done entirely without sin. For instance, the eating of pork and many other things once out of bounds to the Jews are now free to us Christians. When, therefore, we see Jews turned Christian gladly eating food of this sort which the law had probihited, how can we defend their rectitude except by affirming that this latitude has now been conceded to them by God?

Well, in what was formerly a food restriction and is now food freedom, the concession of freedom excludes sin and eliminates contempt of God. Who then shall say that a man sins in respect of a matter which the divine permission has made lawful for him? If the marriage-bed or the eating of even delicate food was permitted from the first day of our creation, when we lived in Paradise without sin, who can prove that we transgress in these enjoyments, so long as we do not pass the limits of the permission? Another objection is that matrimonial intercourse and the eating of tasty food are only allowed on condition of being taken without pleasure. But, if this is so, then they are allowed to be done in a way in which they never can be done. That concession is not reasonable which concedes that a thing shall be so done as it is certain that it cannot be done. By what reasoning did the law aforetime enforce matrimony so that each might leave his seed to Israel? Or, how did the Apostle oblige wives to fulfil the mutual debt if these acts could not be done without sinning? How can he refer to this debt when already it is of necessity sin? Or how should a man be compelled to do what he will grieve God by doing? Hence, I think that it is plain that no natural physical delight can be set down as sin, nor can it be called guilt for men to delight in what, when it is done, must involve the feeling of delight.

For example, if anyone obliged a monk, bound in chains, to lie among women, and the monk by the softness of the couch and by contact with his fair flatterers is allured into delight, though not into consent, who shall presume to designate guilt the delight which is naturally awakened?

You may urge, with some thinkers, that the carnal pleasure, even in lawful intercourse, involves sin. Thus David says: "Behold in sin was I conceived." (Ps. I, 7.) And the Apostle, when he had said: "Ye return to it again" (1 Cor. vii, 5), adds, nevertheless, "This I say by way of concession, not of command." (ibid., v, 6.) Yet authority rather than reason, seems to dictate the view that we should allow simple physical delight to be sin. For, assuredly, David was conceived not in fornication, but in matrimony: and concession, that is forgiveness, does not, as this standpoint avers, condone when there is no guilt to forgive. As for what David meant when he says that he had been conceived "in iniquity" or "in sin" and does not say "whose" sin, he referred to the general curse of original sin, wherein from the guilt of our first parents each is subject to damnation, as it is elsewhere stated: "None are pure of stain, not the infant a day old, if he has life on this earth." As the blessed Jerome reminds us and as manifest reason teaches, the soul of a young child is without sin. If, then, it is pure of sin, how is it also impure by sinful corruption? We must understand the infant's purity from sin in reference to its personal guilt. But its contact with sinful corruption, its "stain," is in reference to penalty owed by mankind because of Adam's sin. He who has not yet perceived by reason what he ought to do cannot be guilty of contempt of God. Yet he is not free from the contamination of the sin of his first parents, from which he contracts the penalty, though not the guilt, and bears in penalty what they committed in guilt. When, therefore, David says that he was conceived in iniquity or sin, he sees himself subject to the general sentence of damnation from the guilt of his racial parents, and he assigns these sins, not to his father and mother but to his first parents.

When the Apostle speaks of indulgence, he must not be understood as some would wish to understand him, to mean permission to be equivalent to pardon for sin. His statement is: "By way of indulgence not of command." He might equally have said: "By permission, not by force." If husband and wife wish and decide upon mutual agreement they can abstain altogether from intercourse, and may not be compelled to it by command. But should they not so decide they have indulgence, that is, permission to substitute a less perfect for a more perfect rule of life. The Apostle, in this passage, did not therefore refer to pardon for sin, but to the permission of a less strict life for the avoidance of fornication. He meant that this lower level might elude the peaks of sin, and by its inferior standing escape the greater guilt.

We come, then, to this conclusion, that no one who sets out to assert that all fleshly desire is sin may say that the sin itself is increased by the doing of it. For this would mean extending the consent of the soul into the exercise of the action. In short, one would be stained not only by consent to baseness, but also by the mire of the deed, as if what happens externally in the body could possibly soil the soul. Sin is not, therefore, increased by the doing of an action: and nothing mars the soul except what is of its own nature, namely consent. This we affirmed was alone sin, preceding action in will, or subsequent to the performance of action. Although we wish for, or do, what is unseemly, we do not therefore sin. For such deeds not uncommonly occur without there being any sin. On the other hand, there may be consent without the external effects, as we have indicated. There was wish without consent in the case of the man who was attracted by a woman whom he caught sight of, or who was tempted by his neighbour's fruit, but who was not enticed into consent. There was evil consent without evil desire in the servant who unwillingly killed his master.

Certain acts which ought not to be done often are done, and without any sin, when, for instance, they are committed under force or ignorance. No one, I think, ignores this fact. A woman under constraint of violence, lies with another's husband. A man, taken by some trick, sleeps with one whom he supposed to be his wife, or kills a man, in the belief that he himself has the right to be both judge and executioner. Thus to desire the wife of another or actually to lie with her is not sin. But to consent to that desire or to that action is sin. This consent to covetousness the law calls covetousness in saying: "Thou shalt not covet." (Deut. v, 21.) Yet that which we cannot avoid ought not to be forbidden, nor that wherein, as we said, we do not sin. But we should be cautioned about the consent to covetousness. So, too, the saying of the Lord must be understood: "Whosoever shall look upon a woman to desire her." (Matt. v, 28.) That is, whosoever shall so look upon her as to slip into consent to covetousness, "has already committed adultery with her in his heart" (Matt. v, 28), even though he may not have committed adultery in deed. He is guilty of sin, though there be no sequel to his intention.

Careful account will reveal that wherever actions are restricted by some precept or prohibition, these refer rather to will and consent than to the deeds themselves. Otherwise nothing relative to a person's moral merit could be included under a precept. Indeed, actions are so much the less worth prescribing as they are less in our power to do. At the same time, many things we are forbidden to do for which there exists in our will both the inclination and the consent.

The Lord God says: "Thou shalt not kill. Thou shalt not bear false witness." (Deut. v, 17, 20.) If we accept these cautions as being only about actions, as the words suggest, then guilt is not forbidden, but simply the activity of guilt. For we have seen that actions may be carried out without sin, as that it is not sin to kill a man or to lie with another's wife. And even the man who desires to bear false testimony, and is willing to utter it, so long as he is silent for some reason and does not speak, is innocent before the law, that is, if the probibition in this matter be accepted literally of the action. It is not said that we should not *wish* to give false witness, or that we should not *consent* in bearing it, but simply that we should not bear false witness.

Similarly, when the law forbids us to marry or have intercourse with our sisters, if this prohibition relates to deed rather than to intention, no one can keep the commandment, for a sister unless we recognize her, is just a woman. If a man, then, marries his sister in error, is he a transgressor for doing what the law forbade? He is not, you will reply, because, in acting ignorantly in what he did, he did not consent to a transgression. Thus a transgressor is not one who *does* what is prohibited. He is one who *consents* to what is prohibited. The prohibition is, therefore, not about action, but about consent.

It is as though in saying: "Do not do this or that," we meant: "Do not consent to do this or that," or "Do not wittingly do this."

Blessed Augustine,[1] in his careful view of this question, reduces every sin or command to terms of charity and covetousness, and not to works. "The law," he says, "inculcates nothing but charity, and forbids nothing but covetousness." The Apostle, also, asserts: "All the law is contained in one word: thou shalt love thy neighbour as thyself," (Rom. xiii, 8, 10), and again, "Love is the fulfilling of the law." (ibid.)

Whether you actually give alms to a needy person, or charity makes you ready to give, makes no difference to the merit of the deed. The will may be there when the opportunity is not. Nor does it rest entirely with you to deal with every case of need which you encounter. Actions which are right and actions which are far from right are done by good and bad men alike. The intention alone separates the two classes of men.

Augustine reminds us that in the self-same action we find God the Father, the Lord Jesus Christ, and also Judas the betrayer. The betrayal of the Son was accomplished by God the Father, and by the Son, and by the betrayer. For "the Father delivered up the Son, and the Son Himself" (Rom. viii, 32; Gal. ii, 22), as the Apostle says, and Judas delivered up his Master. The traitor, therefore, did the same thing as God Himself. But did Judas do anything well? No. Good certainly came of his act; but his act was not well done, nor was it destined to benefit him.

God considers not the action, but the spirit of the action. It is the intention, not the deed wherein the merit or praise of the doer consists. Often, indeed, the same action is done from different motives: for justice' sake by one man, for an evil reason by another. Two men, for instance, hang a guilty person. The one does it out of zeal for justice; the other in resentment for an earlier enmity. The action of hanging is the same. Both men do what is good and what justice demands. Yet the diversity

[1] Abailard cites the Fathers to buttress particular points without implying their full agreement with his main argument. In the *Sic et Non* he showed that the Fathers frequently contradicted themselves!

of their intentions causes the same deed to be done from different motives, in the one case good, in the other bad.

Everyone knows that the devil himself does nothing without God's permission, when he either punishes a wicked man according to his deserts, or is allowed to afflict a just man for moral cleansing or for an example of endurance. Since, however, in doing what God permits the devil moves at the spur of his own malice, the power which he has may be called good, or even just, while his will is for ever unjust. He receives, that is, the power from God, but his will is of himself.

Who, among the elect, can ever emulate the deeds of hypocrites? Who, for the love of God, ever endures or undertakes so much as they do from thirst for human praise? Who does not agree that sometimes what God forbids may rightly be done, while, contrarily, He may counsel certain things which of all things are least convenient? We note how He forbade certain miracles, whereby He had healed infirmities, to be made public. He set an example of humility lest any man should claim glory for the grace bestowed on him. Nevertheless, the recipients of those benefits did not cease to broadcast them, to the praise of Him who had done such things, and yet, had forbidden them to be revealed. Thus we read: "As much as He bade them not to speak, so much the more did they publish abroad, etc." Will you judge these men guilty of a fault who acted contrary to the command which they had received, and did so wittingly? Who can acquit them of wrong-doing, unless by finding that they did not act out of contempt for the One who commanded, but decided to do what was to His honour? How, then, did the matter stand? Did Christ command what ought not to have been commanded? Or, did the newly-healed men disobey when they should have obeyed? The command was a good thing; yet it was not good for it to be obeyed.

In the case of Abraham, also, you will accuse God for first enjoining the sacrifice of Abraham's son, and then revoking the command. Has, then, God never *wisely commanded* anything which, if *it had come about,* would not have been good? If good, you will object, why was it afterwards forbidden? But conceive that it was good for the same thing to be prescribed and also to be prohibited. God, we know, permits nothing, and does not himself consent to achieve anything apart from rational cause. Thus it is the pure intention of the command, not the execution of the action which justifies God in wisely commanding what would not in actual fact be good. God did not intend Abraham to sacrifice his son, or command this sacrifice to be put into effect. His aim was to test Abraham's obedience, constancy of faith, and love towards Him, so that these qualities should be left to us as an example. This intention the Lord God plainly asserts afterwards in saying: "Now know I that thou fearest the Lord." (Gen. xxii, 12.) It is as if he frankly said: "I commanded you: you showed yourself ready to obey Me. Both these things were done so that others might know what I had Myself known of you from the beginning." There was a right intention on God's part; but it was not right for it to be put in practice. The prohibition, too, in the case of the miracles of healing was right. The object of this prohibition was not for it to be obeyed, but for an example to be given to our weak spirit in avoiding empty applause. God, in the one case enjoined an action which, if obeyed, would not have been good. In the other case, He forbade what was worth putting into fact, namely, a knowledge of Christ's miracles. The intention excuses Him in the first matter, just as the intention excuses the men who, in the second instance, were healed and did not carry out His injunction. They knew that the precept was not given to be practised, but in order that the aforenamed example of moderation in a successful miracle might be set. In keeping, then, the spirit of the command they showed, by actually disobeying no contempt for Him with whose intention they knew that they were acting.

A scrutiny of the deed rather than of the intention will reveal, then, cases where men frequently not only wish to go against God's bidding, but carry their wish knowingly into effect, and do so without any guilt of sin. An action or a wish must not be called bad because it does not in actual fact fall in with God's command. It may well be that the doer's intention does not at all differ from the will of his divine superior. The intention exonerates Him who gave a practically unseemly command: the intention excuses the man who, out of kindness, disobeyed the command to conceal the miracle.

Briefly to summarize the above argument: Four things were postulated which must be carefully distinguished from one another.

1. Imperfection of soul, making us liable to sin.
2. Sin itself, which we decided is consent to evil or contempt of God.
3. The will or desire of evil.
4. The evil deed.

To wish is not the same thing as to fulfil a wish. Equally, to sin is not the same as to carry out a sin. In the first case, we sin by consent of the soul: the second is a matter of the external effect of an action, namely, when we fulfil in deed that whereunto we have previously consented. When, therefore, temptation is said to proceed through three stages, suggestion, delight, consent, it must be understood that, like our first parents, we are frequently led along these three paths to the commission of sin. The devil's persuasion comes *first* promising from the taste of the forbidden fruit immortality. Delight follows. When the woman sees the beautiful tree, and perceives that the fruit is good, her appetite is whetted by the anticipated pleasure of tasting. This desire she ought to have repressed, so as to obey God's command. But in consenting to it, she was drawn *secondly* into sin. By penitence she should have put right this fault, and obtained pardon. Instead, she *thirdly* consummated the sin by the deed. Eve thus passed through the three stages to the commission of sin.

By the same avenues we also arrive not at sin, but at the action of sin, namely, the doing of an unseemly deed through the suggestion or prompting of something within us. If we already know that such a deed will be pleasant, our imagination is held by anticipatory delight and we are tempted thereby in thought. So long as we give consent to such delight, we sin. Lastly, we pass to the third stage, and actually commit the sin.

It is agreed by some thinkers that carnal suggestion, even

though the person causing the suggestion be not present, should be included under sinful suggestion. For example, a man having seen a woman falls into a sensual desire of her. But it seems that this kind of suggestion should simply be called delight. This delight, and other delights of the like kind, arise naturally and, as we said above, they are not sinful. The Apostle calls them "human temptations." "No temptation has taken you yet which was not common to men. God is faithful, and will not suffer you to be tempted above what you are able; but will, with the temptation make a way of escape, that you may be able to bear it." By temptation is meant, in general, any movement of the soul to do something unseemly, whether in wish or consent. We speak of human temptation without which it is hardly or never possible for human weakness to exist. Such are sexual desire, or the pleasures of the table. From these the Psalmist asks to be delivered when he says: "Deliver me from my wants, O Lord" (Ps. xxiv, 17); that is, from the temptations of natural and necessary appetites that they may not influence him into sinful consent. Or, he may mean: "When this life is over, grant me to be without those temptations of which life has been full."

When the Apostle says: "No temptation has taken you but what is human," his statement amounts to this: Even if the soul be stirred by that delight which is, as we said, human temptation, yet God would not lead the soul into that consent wherein sin consists. Someone may object: But by what power of our own are we able to resist those desires? We may reply: "God is faithful, who will not allow you to be tempted," as the Scripture says. In other words: We should rather trust him than rely upon ourselves. He promises help, and is true to his promises. He is faithful, so that we should have complete faith in him. Out of pity God diminishes the degree of human temptation, "does not suffer us to be tempted above what we are able," in order that it may not drive us to sin at a pace we cannot endure, when, that is, we strive to resist it. Then, too, God turns the temptation to our advantage: for He trains us thereby so that the recurrence of temptation causes us less care, and we fear less the onset of a foe over whom we have already triumphed, and whom we know how to meet.

Every encounter, not as yet undertaken, is for that reason, to us, a matter of more anxiety and dismay. But when such an encounter comes to those accustomed to victory, its force and terror alike vanish.

CHAPTER IV

DIABOLICAL SUGGESTION

There are suggestions of demons, as well as of men. Demons stimulate to sin not so much by words as by opportunities. Skilled in natural matters, both by subtlety of spirit and long experience, whence they are called "daemones," i.e., *skilful,*[1] they know the inherent nature of force of things whereby human frailty can easily be led into lust and other impulses.

With God's permission they also often send men into a stupor and provide remedies for it when men ask their aid. When they cease to injure 'tis said, they begin to cure. In Egypt they were allowed, through magicians, to work wonderfully against Moses. Indeed, by their insight into the nature of things they must be named "promoters" rather than creators of what they accomplish; just as the man who, in Virgil (*Georg.,* Bk. IV, v, 310), made bees come out of the tanned hide of a bull, would be called not a creator of bees, so much as a fitter of nature's parts.

Demons, by this skill in the nature of things, bewitch us into lust or other passions, arousing them by some art we wot not of, bestirring them as we eat or lie a-bed; or somehow insinuating them from within or without. In herbs or seeds, or in the nature of trees and stones, are many powers apt to stimulate or mollify the mind. Diligent study of them brings facility in their use.

---

[1] Cf. The Greek legendary figure, Daedalus, whose name with the same root, signifies "cunning workman." Abailard is mediaeval rather than modern in this chapter; but there is a scientific view in his notion of incitement through material objects.

CHAPTER V

CRIME AND INWARD GUILT: THEIR RESPECTIVE PUNISHMENTS

"The sinful action is not strictly sin; it adds nothing to the sum of sin." Our axiom, so enunciated, falls on dissentient ears. "Why, then," it is asked, "give a more severe penance for sins of commission than for guilty thoughts?" But let them reflect whether sometimes a grave penance be not imposed where no guilt called for pardon. Are there not times when we must punish those whom we know to be innocent?

A poor woman has a child at the breast. She lacks the clothing needful for herself and for the babe in the cradle. Prompted by pity, she lays the infant in her own bed so as to cherish him with her clothes. Nature, however, overcomes her, and, in sleep, she stifles the child whom she yet embraces with the greatest love. "Have love," says Augustine, "and do as thou wilt." Yet when she goes to the bishop for penance, a heavy penalty is pronounced upon her, not for the fault, but that she herself a second time, and other women, may be more careful in such a situation.

Again, a man may be accused by his enemies before the judge, and a charge made against him whereof the judge knows that the man is innocent. His enemies, however, persist and are importunate for a hearing. On the appointed day they begin the case and adduce false witnesses to get their man convicted. By no clear reasons can the judge take exception to these witnesses; and he is compelled by law to admit them. Their proof prevails. The judge has to punish an innocent man who ought not to be punished. The accused merited no penalty; but the judge, justly in the legal aspect, had to impose one. Plainly, therefore, a man may frequently be the subject of a justifiable sentence without the anterior fault. Is it any wonder, then, if there be preceding guilt, that the subsequent act of crime should increase the penalty required by men in this life, although the guilt and not the act of crime is what begets the penalty required by God in a future life? Men judge of visible, and not of invisible fact. They do not estimate the error, so much as the effect of an action. God alone considers the spirit in which a thing is done, rather than merely what is done. He weighs accurately the guilt in our intention, and assesses our fault by a true test. Hence he "proves the heart and reins" (Jer. xx, 12), and "sees in secret." (Matt. vi, 4.) Where no man sees, there God sees. In punishing sin he regards not the work, but the will. We, contrarily, regard not the will, which we do not see, but the work which we do see. Frequently, therefore, by mistake, or, as we have said, under stress of law, we punish the innocent or acquit the guilty. "He tries the heart and reins." God discerns, that is to say, the *intentions,* of whatever sort, which spring from the disposition or weakness of the soul, or from physical delight.

CHAPTER VI

SPIRITUAL AND CARNAL SINS

All sins are of the mind only, for there alone can be the crime and the contempt of God, where is the seat of the knowledge of Him, and where reason resides. Certain sins, nevertheless, are called spiritual, others carnal. The spiritual sins proceed from the imperfection of the mind, the carnal from the weakness of the flesh. Now it is impossible to lust after or desire anything except by an act of will. Although, therefore, desire belongs to the mind alone, will concerns both the flesh and also the spirit. "The flesh," says the Apostle, "lusteth against the spirit, and the spirit against the flesh." (Gal. v, 7.) Out of fleshly delight the soul desires certain things which, on the verdict of reason, it either recoils from or rebukes.

CHAPTER VII

WHY IS GOD CALLED "INSPECTOR CORDIS ET RENUM," I.E., SAID TO TRY THE HEART AND REINS?

These two desires of the flesh, and of the spirit are, then, distinguished. Now God has been called the "one who tries the heart and reins." He scrutinizes, that is to say, intentions and the consents which proceed from them. We on our part cannot discuss and decide these issues of intention, but address our censure to deeds. We punish facts rather than faults. Injury to the soul we do not regard as so much a matter for punishment as injury to others. Our object is to avoid public mischief, rather than to correct personal mistakes. The Lord said to Peter: "If thy brother sin against thee, correct him between thyself and him." (Matt. xviii, 15.) "Sin against thee." Is the meaning here that we ought to correct and punish injuries done to us and not those done to others, as though "against thee" meant "not against another"? By no means. The phrase "if he sin against thee" means that he acts publicly so as to corrupt you by his example. For if he sins against himself only, his sin, being hidden, involves in guilt merely the man himself. The sin does not, by the sinner's bad example, induce others to indiscretion. Although the evil action has no imitators, or even none who recognize it as wrong, nevertheless, in so far as it is a public act it must, in human society, be chastised more than private guilt, because it can occasion greater mischief, and can be more destructive, by the example it sets, than the hidden failing. Everything which is likely to lead to common loss or to public harm must be punished by a greater requital. Where a sin involves more serious injury the penalty must therefore be heavier. The greater the social stumbling-block, the more stringent must be the social correction, even though the original guilt be relatively light.

Suppose, for example, that someone has, by evil intercourse, corrupted a woman in a church. The people hear of the incident. But they are not roused so much by the violation of a woman, the true temple of God, as by the desecration of the material temple, the church. This is the case even though, admittedly, a wall is of less consequence than a woman, and it is more grievous to harm a human being than a place. Again, the setting fire to houses we punish more severely than fornication. But with God the latter incurs a far greater sentence.

The punishment of public guilt is not so much a debt paid to justice as the exercise of economy. We consult the common interest, as has been said by checking social mischief. Frequently we punish minor misdeeds with major penalties. In doing so, we do not, in a spirit of pure justice ponder what guilt preceded; but, by shrewd foresight, we estimate the damage which may ensue if the deed be lightly dealt with. We reserve, therefore, sins of the soul for the divine judgment. But the effect of these sins, about which we have to determine, we follow up, by our own judgment, employing a certain economy, that is, the rule of prudence referred to above, rather than the precept of equity.

God assigns the penalty of each crime according to the measure of guilt. The degree of contempt displayed by men to God is afterwards proportionately punished, whatever be their condition or calling. Suppose that a monk and a lay-brother both fall into consent to an act of fornication. If the mind of the lay-brother be so inflamed that he would not abstain from shame out of reverence for God, even if he had been a monk, then the lay-brother deserves the same penalty as the monk.

The same notion applies where one man, sinning openly, offends many, and corrupts them by his example; while another man sins in secret, and injures only himself. For the secret sinner, if his intention and his contempt of God are identical with those of the open sinner, rather by accident does not corrupt others. The man who does not restrain himself out of respect for God would hardly refrain, for the same reason, from public crime. In God's sight, assuredly, he is committed on a similar charge to that of the open sinner. For, in the recompense of good or evil, God notes the soul alone, not its external effects, and counts what comes from our guilt or good will. It is the soul in its scheme of intention, not in the outward result of its action, that God assesses. There are actions, as we said, common to sinners and saints, all of them in themselves indifferent and only to be called bad or good according to the intention of the agent. Such actions are so described not because it is good or bad for them to be done, but because they are done *well,* or *ill;* that is, they are performed with a seemly, or unseemly intention.

For, as Blessed Augustine reminds us, it is good for a man to be bad since God may use him for a good end, and may not allow him to be otherwise even though his condition be altogether evil.

When, therefore, we call the intention of a man good, and his deed good also, we distinguish two things, intention and deed. Nevertheless, there is only one goodness of intention. It is like speaking of a good man, and the son of a good man. We imagine two men, but not two goodnesses. A man is called good because of his own goodness. But when the son of a good man is spoken of, it is clear that he cannot have good in him just because he is a good man's son. Similarly, everyone's intention is called good in itself. But the deed is not called good in itself, for it only proceeds from a good intention. Thus, there is one goodness, whence both intention and deed are designated good, just as there is one goodness from which a good man and the son of a good man are named; or one goodness by which a good man, and the will of a good man can each be explained.

The objection of some who say that the deed merits equal recompense with the intention, or even an additional recompense, may be proved nonsensical. "There are two goods," they exclaim, "the good intention, and the carrying out of the good intention. Good added to good ought to be worth more than a single good."

Our reply is: "Granted that the whole is worth more than the separate parts, must we admit that it merits greater reward?" Not at all. There are many animate and inanimate things which, in large numbers, are useful for more purposes than any one of the number would be alone. Nevertheless, no additional reward is thought to be due to them on that account. For instance, an ox joined to another ox or a horse to a horse; or, again, wood added to wood or iron to iron; these things are good, and a number of them is worth more than each singly. Yet they are not more highly praised when it is seen that two of them put together can do more than one by itself.

True, you say, it is so; but only because these things could never deserve anything, being without reason. Well; but has our deed any reason, so as to be able to deserve praise or blame? None, you say; but our action is said to have merit because it imparts merit to us, making us worthy of reward, or, at any rate, of greater reward. Now it is this very statement which we have denied above. Consider why it is false, apart from what we have already said. Two men set about the same scheme of building poor-houses. One man completes the object to which he devotes himself. The other has the money which he put by stolen forcibly from him, and through no fault of his own—prevented simply by burglary—is not able to conclude what he intended to do. Can the external fact, that the almshouses are unbuilt, lessen his merit with God, or shall the malice of another make the man who did what he could for God less acceptable to God?

Otherwise, the size of his purse could make a man better and worthier, if property had any bearing upon moral merit or the increase of merit. The richer men were, the better they could be, since from their stock of wealth they would be able to augment their piety by their philanthropy.[1] But it is the height of insanity to assume that wealth can confer true bliss or dignity of the soul, or detract from the merit of poor men. If property cannot make a soul better, then it cannot make the soul dearer to God, nor get any bliss of moral merit.

---

1 Two almshouses built by a very rich man would be of greater merit to him than one built by a well-off man, even though the piety of both, in their motive of serving God and man, was the same.

CHAPTER VIII

RECOMPENSE OF ACTIONS

We do not, however, deny that in this life some recompense should be made for good and bad deeds, so that by means of reward and punishment in the present we may be stirred to good actions or restrained from bad ones. People may also profit by the examples of others in this way. They can copy what is fit and agreeable, and avoid what is not.

CHAPTER IX

GOD AND MAN UNITED IN CHRIST IS NOT SOMETHING BETTER THAN GOD ALONE

Let us resume the argument (Ch. VII). When it is asserted that good added to good achieves something better than one of these goods by itself, beware of being led to say that Christ, that is, God and man united mutually in a person, is something better than the divinity of Christ or than the humanity of Christ, that is to say that this union is more than God united with man, or man's nature taken by God. It is agreed that, in Christ, man's nature was assumed, and that God, who assumed it, was good. Both substances, human and divine, can only be understood as good. Similarly in individual men, the body and the soul, the corporeal and the incorporeal, are alike good. The goodness of the body does not effect the honour or merit of the soul. But who will dare to prefer the whole which is called Christ, namely, God and man, or any group of things to God Himself, as though there could be anything better than Him, Who is the highest good, and from Whom all things receive whatever good they possess? For although some things seem to be so necessary to achieving action that God cannot, as it were, do without them, as being auxiliary or originative causes, yet let there be the largest assembly of things imaginable, nothing can possibly surpass

God. Suppose that the number of good things be known, so that we have goodness in many particular cases, still it does not come about, for that reason, that the goodness itself is greater. The same is true of knowledge, which may exist in many minds; or the number of known things may increase, but on that account, knowledge itself does not necessarily grow and become greater than it was before. So, since God is good in Himself, and creates innumerable things, which would neither exist nor be good apart from Him, goodness exists in many things through Him, and the number of good things may get greater, yet no goodness can be preferred to or equal His goodness. Goodness exists in man, and goodness exists in God. The substances or natures wherein goodness exists are different: and the goodness of a thing can never be preferred to or equal the divine goodness. For this reason, we cannot speak of anything as better, that is to say, a greater good than God, or of anything equally good.

CHAPTER X

A NUMBER OF GOOD THINGS IS NOT BETTER THAN ONE OF THESE GOOD THINGS

The number of actions is of no importance for their intention. For to speak of good intention and good action, that is action proceeding from good intention, is to refer merely to the goodness of the intention. We cannot retain the term good in this same sense and talk of many "goods."

When we say that a man is simple, and speech simple, we do not therefore allow that there exist many "simples" just because this word "simple" is employed in the first instance of a man, and in the second instance of speech. No one can then compel us to concede that when the good act is added to the good intention, good is added to good, as though there could be many goods in proportion to whose number recompense ought to be increased. As we have said, we cannot call those actions "additional goods," for the word "good" does not properly apply to them.

CHAPTER XI

THE GOOD ACTION SPRINGS FROM THE GOOD INTENTION

We call the intention good which is right in itself, but the action is good, not because it contains within it some good, but because it issues from a good intention. The same act may be done by the same man at different times. According to the diversity of his intention, however, this act may be at one time good, at another bad. So goodness and badness vary. Compare the proposition: "Socrates sits." One conceives this statement either truly or falsely according as Socrates actually does sit, or stands. This alternation in truth and falsity, Aristotle affirms, comes about not from any change in the circumstances which compose the true or false situation, but because the subject-matter of the statement (that is, Socrates) moves in itself, I mean changes from sitting to standing or vice versa.[1]

CHAPTER XII

WHAT ARE THE GROUNDS OF GOOD INTENTION?

Good or right intention is held by some to be when anyone believes that he acts well, and that what he does pleases God. An example is supplied by those who persecuted the martyrs. About them the Gospel Truth says: "The hour comes when everyone who kills you will think that he is obedient to God." (John xvi, 2.) In sympathy with the ignorance of such the Apostle exclaims: "I bear this testimony on their behalf, that they are zealous for God but not according to knowledge." That is to say, they are fervently eager to do what they believe

---

[1] We may do the same action twice, just as we may say "Socrates sits" twice. But just as the same statement will be true when Socrates sits and false when he stands, so the same action will be good when the intention is good, and bad when the intention is bad.

pleases God. Since, however, in this desire or keenness of mind they are deceived, their intention is a mistake. The eye of the heart is not so simple as to be capable of seeing clearly and to guard itself from error. For this reason the Lord, when he distinguished works according to right and wrong intention, spoke of the eye of the mind, that is the intention, as either *single,* pure, as it were, from spot, so that it could see clearly, or, on the contrary, as *clouded*. "If thine eye be single, thy whole body shall be full of light." This means that, provided the intention was right, all the acts proceeding from the intention which can possibly be foreseen in the manner of mortal affairs, will be worthy of the light; that is to say, good. And, contrarily, from wrong intention arise dark deeds.

The intention, therefore, must not be called good, merely because it seems good, but over and above this, because it is such as it is estimated to be. I mean that, if it thinks to please God in what it aims as its aim therein should not be mistaken. Otherwise the heathen, just like us, could count their good works, since they no less than we believe themselves either to be saved or to please God by their deeds.

CHAPTER XIII

NO SIN SAVE THAT AGAINST CONSCIENCE

The question may be asked whether the persecutors of the martyrs or of Christ erred because they believed that they were pleasing God, or whether they could do without sin what they at heart thought should never be done, especially in view of the above analysis of sin as "contempt of God," or "consent to that whereto consent ought not to be given." We cannot say that they did sin in this respect: nor can we call anyone's ignorance or even the infidelity (having which no man may be saved) a sin. They who know not Christ, and reject the Christian faith because they believe that it is contrary to God, what contempt of God do they show in this act which is really done on behalf of God? On this latter account, indeed, they think to do well, particularly when the

Apostle says: "If our heart does not condemn us, we have confidence with God." (1 John iii, 2), as though he said: "when we do not violate our conscience, we have little fear of God holding us guilty of a fault." If ignorance must least of all be reckoned as sin, how, it may be urged, does the Lord Himself pray for those who crucify Him saying: "Father, forgive them: for they know not what they do."—(Luke xxiii, 34) or, taught by this example, how can Stephen supplicate for the men who stone him: "Father, lay not this sin to their charge." (Acts vii, 59)? We must proceed to deal with this question. For, it will be insisted, where guilt does not go first there is no need, later, of pardon. And to be pardoned is simply to have the penalty remitted which the crime warranted. Moreover, Stephen clearly calls sin that which came about from ignorance.

CHAPTER XIV

VARIOUS USES OF THE WORD "SIN"

To reply more fully to these objections it must be understood that the term "sin" can be taken in different ways, although, properly speaking, sin is the actual *contempt of God,* or *consent to evil* as we recalled just now. The young are immune from sin; so, too, are idiots. These two classes, lacking reason, cannot claim merit and nothing can be imputed to them for sin. They are saved only by the sacraments. Sin is spoken of with the meaning "a sacrifice for sin." The Apostle, for instance, says that our Lord Jesus Christ was made "sin." [1] The "penalty of sin" is called simply sin or "curse" when we say sin is destroyed, that is the penalty remitted; and, again, when it is said that Jesus Christ bore our sins, that is, He endured the punishment of our sins or their possible punishment.

The statement that infants have original sin or that all, as the Apostle says, have sinned in Adam is the same as saying that from Adam's sin arose the sense of our punishment or

[1] i.e., "a sacrifice for sin."

damnation for sin. Sinful deeds, provided we either do not rightly know them as such, or do not really wish to do them, are not at all to be termed sins. For what is sinning against anyone but the putting into effect of the evil intention? It is not unusual when, contrariwise, we refer, with Athanasius, to sins as if they were deeds. "And they shall give an account," he says, "of their own deeds. They who have done good deeds shall go into eternal life; they who have done evil, into everlasting fire." What, then, is "their own deeds"? Is judgment merely to be about what has been fulfilled in action, that a man may receive more in recompense in proportion as he offers more in effects? Is he who came short in effecting what he intended immune from damnation, like the devil who designed cunningly, but failed in fact? Certainly not. In speaking of "their own deeds" the scripture means what they consented to, what they determined to carry out, that is, about sins of intention, the things which, in God's sight, they are considered to have actually done, since He punishes intentions as we punish deeds.

Stephen, however, speaks of the sin which the Jews, out of ignorance, committed against him. By this he means the punishment itself which he was enduring and which resulted from the sin of our first parent, just like other punishment issuing from the same source, or, in a word, the injustice of their action in stoning him. And when Stephen prayed that it might not be laid to their charge, he meant that they should not be physically punished for it. For not seldom God punishes some people physically when no fault of theirs warrants it. God does so not without a reason, as when He sends affliction upon the just to purge or prove them; or again, when he permits some to be in distress that they may afterwards be freed and glorify God for the benefit obtained. We have, for instance, the case of the blind man about whom the Saviour says: "Neither did this man sin, nor his parents that he was born blind, but that the works of God might become manifest in him." (John ix, 2.)

You may notice, too, that innocent sons may be endangered or afflicted along with their evil parents and because of their parents' guilt, as was the case at Sodom, and as often occurs. The object is to inspire the wicked to greater terror as they see the punishment more widely extended. It was therefore this kind of sin, namely the punishment which he endured from the Jews and which they unjustly put into effect, which Blessed Stephen contemplated with patience. He prayed that it might not be laid to their charge. That is, that they should not suffer the physical punishment which God gives for peoples' well-being even though they have not sinned in intention.

Our Master also was of this mind in saying: "Father, forgive them." (Luke xxiii, 34.) He meant: "Do not avenge their action against Me with a physical penalty." This could reasonably have come about even had no guilt of theirs gone before. By such punishment other people, and those Jews themselves, would have realized that in their deed they had not done rightly. Well did the Lord by this example of His prayer exhort us to the power of patience and to an expression of the highest love. Thereby through His own example He showed to us in deed what He had taught in word, that we also should pray for our enemies. The saying, "forgive," did not refer to preceding guilt or contempt of God, but to God's reasonable right of inflicting punishment. A divine penalty might, as we said, ensue for which there could be good reason even though actual guilt had not preceded it. An instance occurs in the case of the prophet sent to speak against Samaria, who passed the time in eating, God having forbidden him to do this. He was tricked by another prophet, and could not be charged with contempt of God. He incurred death innocently, and more because he had done a deed than from real guilt. For Blessed Gregory reminds us: "God sometimes alters his sentence, but never His plan." God often withdraws from effect a lesson or threat which He had been disposed to employ. His plan, however, remains firm. What He wills, in prescience, to accomplish never comes short of attainment. He did not abide, for instance, by His injunction to Abraham to immolate his son, nor by His threat against the Ninevites. He changed, as we said, His sentence. Similarly the afore-mentioned prophet, whom God had forbidden to eat on his journey, believed that God had altered his resolution. The prophet thought that he would be in the wrong if he gave no heed to the other prophet, who asserted that he had been sent by God for the very purpose of refreshing that prophet's faintness with food. He acted without fault, therefore, in as much as he determined to avoid a fault. The sudden death did not harm him. It set him free from the cares of this life and was a salutary caution to many. For they might behold the punishment of a man, just and faultless, and the fulfillment of the saying: "Thou, O God, art just and disposest all things justly: him also who deserves no penalty thou dost condemn." "Thou condemest," the scripture implies, "not to eternal, but to physical death." We may compare the fact that some are saved without merit of their own, as for instance, infants, and attain eternal life by grace alone. Equally, it is not fantastic that some should endure physical penalties which they have not merited. This is the case with infants deceased without the grace of baptism. They are damned, physically and eternally. Many innocent people are also afflicted. What wonder, therefore, if those who crucified the Lord should reasonably incur punishment, though not eternal, albeit their ignorance excuses them from real guilt! Thus was said: "forgive them," or "do not put into effect the punishment which they may, with good reason, incur from this insult."

The actions which those men committed out of ignorance, or, if you will, ignorance itself is not properly called sin, that is contempt of God. Nor, also, is infidelity, under these circumstances, to be called sin, although of necessity it involves exclusion from eternal life for those who are rationally full-grown. Disbelief in the Gospel, not to recognize Christ, refusal of the Church sacraments, each of these, though they come less from malice than as a result of ignorance are reasons for damnation. The Truth speaks of such: "He who believes not is already judged." (John iii, 18.) The Apostle also: "He who does not know shall not be known." (I Cor. xiv, 38.) But when we say that we sin ignorantly, that is, do what is not seemly, we take sin of this sort to be not in real contempt, but in action only. Philosophers call it a fault to express an idea in unfitting fashion, even though this mistake may not seem to do offence to God. Aristotle, for instance, speaks somewhere about the wrong description of relations. Unless the terms of a statement are properly placed a wrong notion will be the result. Thus a wing may be predicated as "of a bird," but it would be a fault to make a phrase "the bird of a wing."

Now, if in this sort of fashion we can speak of sin, then everything which we do unsuitably or which we cling to contrary to our well-being—infidelity and ignorance of beliefs which are necessary to salvation—all this we can speak of as "sins," although no contempt of God appears in them. But I feel that, properly speaking, sin is that which can never come about without personal guilt. Not to know God, to have no belief in Him, to do wrongly under a misapprehension—such things can be found in many a life without there being real fault. A man, for example, may not believe in the Gospel or in Christ because he has heard no preacher. "How shall they believe who have not heard? How shall they hear without a preacher?" (Romans x, 14.) What blame is to be attributed to such a man for not believing? Cornelius did not believe in Christ until Peter came and gave him instruction. He had known and loved God before by natural law, and, by reason of this, deserved to be heard in his prayer and to find favour in his almsgiving. But if, prior to faith in Christ, he had perchance been untrue to the light of conscience, we should not dare to promise him life, however good his deeds, and we should have to count him not among the faithful, but rather, despite his zeal of salvation, among the unfaithful. Many of God's decisions are a mystery. He draws to Himself those who hold back or are least concerned with their own salvation, but, in the profound wisdom of his plan he rejects the forward convert and the overwilling believer. Thus the zealous volunteer—"Master, I will follow thee whithersoever thou goest"—met with reproof. When another excused himself on the ground of solicitude for his father, the Saviour did not even for a moment admit this plea of filial regard. Again, in his onslaught on the obstinacy of certain cities the Lord says: "Woe to thee, Chorazin! Woe to thee, Bethsaida! For if the mighty works had been done in Tyre and Sidon which have been done among you, they would have repented long ago in sackcloth and ashes." (Matt. xi, 21.) He confronted these cities, Bethsaida and Chorazin, not only with his preaching, but also with his miracles, though he had anticipated that they would not receive them with respect. The other Gentile cities, Tyre and Sidon, as he knew, would easily have received the evangel. While he thought that a visit to them was unwarranted, he knew that certain people in these cities had been ready to accept the word of preaching. And yet these people perished with their cities. Who, then, can impute to their guilt the destruction which undoubtedly came about through no disregard of theirs? [2] Nevertheless, we affirm that their infidelity, wherein they died, suffices for damnation, although the reason for this blindness in which the Lord left them remains less clear. One may, perhaps, set it down to their sin, which was a mistake but not a guilty mistake. For, is it not absurd for such persons to be damned if they have not done some kind of sinful deed?

The contention, however, which for some time we have kept in mind is that sin is simply guilty neglect. It cannot exist in anyone, young or old, without their deserving damnation thereby. I do not see how it can be ascribed to guilt if infants or those to whom the Gospel has not been announced do not believe in Christ. It is infidelity; but not guilt, any more than anything which occurs through invincible ignorance, and which we cannot foresee is guilt, e.g., when a man accidentally kills another in a forest with an arrow, not seeing the man and thinking to slay only birds or wild beasts. In such a case we say that he "sins" from ignorance just as we may say that we "sin" not only in consent, but in imagination. But we do not here mean sin to be the same as guilt. We use the term

---

[2] The people of Tyre and Sidon sinned in not knowing Christ, but they did so in ignorance, and their sin has, therefore, not the guilt of the cities of Bethsaida and Chorazin, who sinned knowingly, since Christ had preached to them.

"sin" widely for what little beseems us to do, whether it come about from a mistake, from neglect, or from some other remissness. This, then, is our definition of the sin of ignorance: to do without guilt what we should not do: to do or, if you like, sin in imagination, i.e., to wish for what is not fitting for us; or in speech, or in act, speaking or doing what we ought not; and to do such things out of ignorance and unwittingly. The persecutors of Christ and of their own kinsfolk whom they thought ought to be persecuted, may be said to have sinned in action only (*per operationem*). But they would have sinned really and more grievously, had they contrary to their conscience, permitted their victims to go free.

CHAPTER XV

IS EVERY SIN PROHIBITED?

It may be asked whether God forbids us altogether to sin. If so, then He appears to act unreasonably. This life of ours cannot be lived without at least venial sins. If God meant us to avoid all sins, which is impossible, He would then have promised us no easy yoke and placed on us no light burden, but one which exceeds our strength and which we should support feebly like that yoke of the law of which the apostle Peter spoke. For who can provide against the idle word so as ever without contumely to preserve that perfection whereof James says: "If any stumbleth not in word, the same is a perfect man." (James iii, 2.) The same writer, however, observes: "In many things we have all offended." And another apostle of great excellence says: "If we say that we have no sin we deceive ourselves and the truth is not in us." (1 John i, 18.) All, I think, are aware how difficult and, indeed, impossible, it seems to our weak nature for us to remain entirely immune from sin. Thus, if we take the term "sin" generally we shall affirm sin to be everything which we do unfittingly. On the other hand, if strictly speaking we understand by sin simply contempt of God, then it is truly possible for our life to be passed without sin, though this will involve the greatest difficulty. Sin, as we said, is not prohibited by God, but only consent to evil whereby we despise God: and this is forbidden even though it seems, in the practice of it, to give moral instruction. This has been explained above, where we have also shown that in no other way can we keep God's commandments.

Some sins are spoken of as venial or light, and others are called damnable or grave. Again of damnable sins some are called criminous, which can make a person infamous or criminous if they become known; while others are hardly of this sort at all. Venial sins are such as we consent to, knowing that we should not give consent. But the memory of what we know does not at the moment recur to our mind. For we can know many things even when asleep or when we are unconscious of knowing them. We do not lose our knowledge in sleep. If we did, we should become fools, or else develop wisdom by keeping awake. When, therefore, we give way to flippancy or excessive eating or drinking, we know that this ought not to be done. But at the time we are least aware of the restriction. Such consent, arising from absent-mindedness, is called venial or slight; and not needing correction by a grave penalty. For such sin we are not excluded from the Church, or put under the strain of severe self-denial. These peccadillos are remitted for the penitent by the words of daily confession wherein is no mention of the more grievous but only of small faults; and in daily prayer we are not to avow: "I have sinned by perjury, homicide, adultery, and the like," which are mortal and more serious sins. These latter, unlike the former, are not entered upon from shortsightedness. We commit that kind of crime with close attention and set purpose: and become anathema to God, as the Psalmist says: "They have become abominable in their ways." (Ps. xiii, 2.) He refers to men who were unholy and hateful inasmuch as they offended wittingly. Of this sort of sin some is called criminous which, being of known effect, demoralizes a man by the stain of great guilt. Such are conscious perjury, homicide or adultery, which chief of all are a scandal to the Church. If, however, we exceed sufficiency by over-eating at table, or adorn our person, out of vain glory, in extravagant attire, and are conscious of going to an excess in this way, our fault is not commonly reckoned criminous. Many, indeed, give these foibles more praise than blame.

CHAPTER XVI

SLIGHT AND SERIOUS SINS, OF WHICH IS IT BEST TO BEWARE

The avoidance of venial in contrast to criminal sins is by some thinkers insisted on, because, as they hold, such is the more complete and the better method of conduct, and in its greater difficulty calls for a stricter effort. Our immediate reply to this argument is in a line of Cicero. *The laborious is not therefore the glorious.* But if they are right, then those who bore the heavy weight of the law had more worth before God than those who serve Him with the Gospel freedom. Fear has punishment which perfect love casteth out, and to be driven by fear makes men drudge more than they would if they acted spontaneously out of love. For this reason the heavy-laden are urged by the Lord to His easy yoke, and to take up a light burden. They are to leave the slavery of the law whereby they are weighed down, for the liberty of the Gospel: so that though beginning in fear they may end in love which, without difficulty, "beareth all things, endureth all things." Nothing is hard to one who loves. The love of God is spiritual, not carnal, and all the stronger because it is truer.

Who doubts that it is harder for us to guard against a flea than an enemy, or the injury of a little flint than of a large stone?

But as to that which gives us greater difficulty in guarding against it, do we consider it to be therefore the better and more sound achievement? We do not. And why not? Because what is more difficult to beware of is less likely to injure.

Although, then, our view is that it is harder to be rid of venial than of criminal faults, yet it is the latter that should be avoided as compared with the former. We ought to steer clear of those sins by which we believe that God is most likely to be offended. These merit the greater condemnation and displease Him the more. As love brings us nearer to God we should be more carefully averse from giving Him an affront and from doing what He more plainly disapproves. The lover is anxious less on account of his own loss than for any injury or contempt of his friend. Thus the Apostle: "Love seeketh not her own." (1 Cor. xiii, 5); and again: "Let no one look to the things of himself, but to those of others." If it is our duty, then, to avoid faults not so much in view of our own loss, but of their offence to God, it is evident that those sins should be guarded aganst whereby God will be the more grieved. We may listen to the line of the poet on moral honour:

From love of virtue good men hate to sin.

It is evident that certain things must give rise to particular disgust as being objectionable in themselves and causing hurt to other people.

Finally, in order to distinguish faults by a closer inspection, let us compare the venial and the criminous. Take, for instance, over-indulgence at the table and compare it with perjury and adultery. Let us ask, by which of these trespasses is the greater sin committed, or by which of them is God the more despised and affronted. "I know not," you may perhaps reply, "for some philosophers have thought all faults to be equal." But if you desire to follow this philosophy or rather avowed foolishness, then it is equally good to abstain either from criminious or venial faults, for to commit either the one or the other is alike bad. Why, too, should anyone aver that it is preferable to abstain from venial rather than from criminal faults? Should any one ask how we can tell that the transgression of adultery displeases God more than excess of eating, it is, as I think, the divine law which instructs us. For the punishment of over-eating there has been laid down no penalty, whereas adultery is to be avenged not by this or that punishment but by death. In proportion as love—which the Apostle calls "fulfilling of the law"—is injured, by so much is the action contrary to love, and therefore the sin is the more grievous.

Even when we set particular sins of a venial and criminous kind side by side and compare them so as to satisfy every possibility I still hold to my point. Assume that a man uses every care to abstain from the venial and yet makes no attempt to avoid criminal faults. Now because he keeps clear of all light contamination there arises this question: who shall decide that he sins more lightly or is better for avoiding venial sin, but being liable to criminal? There is no "worse" or "better" in his case because he has left the light sins and given an opening for the grave ones. In fact, should we compare sins singly, as I said, or in general, the conclusion is that to avoid the venial rather than the criminal is not a superior way or the sign of greater perfection. Anyone, however, who by avoiding first the venial fault is strengthened to combat later the criminal has, in this respect, come towards perfection. But we must beware of regarding these later victories, which elicit the height of courage, as overtopping the earlier points of valour or meriting a great recompense. Often in the building of an edifice those do less who bring the job to a finish than the men who have toiled from the first. For they lay the coping and carry the work to its conclusion, so that the house is builded. But while the house was in building there was no need of their finishing touches.

To endeavour to know our faults so far as memory directs us is enough. Where we recognize a thing more closely we can be the more cautious over it. Knowledge of evil cannot be lacking to a just man: and there is no sense in avoiding sins which are not known.

Suggestions for Further Reading

Abelard, P. *The Story of My Misfortunes.* Translated by H. A. Bellows. St. Paul, 1922; *The Letters of Abelard and Heloïse.* Translated by C. K. S. Moncrieff. New York, 1926; Sikes, J. G. *Peter Abelard.* Cambridge, 1932; Gilson, E. *Heloise and Abelard.* Chicago, 1951; *FCC* vol. II, 148-151; *EG* 153-164; *AAM* 59-70; *RMcK* vol. 1, 202-262.

John of Salisbury

Nothing is better designed to give a vivid impression of the diversity of intellectual currents in the Middle Ages than a perusal of the writings of John of Salisbury. John was born in Salisbury, England, sometime between 1115 and 1120. In 1136 he went to France in order to further his education, and was fortunate enough to study under some of the most able teachers of his day—among them, the brilliant Peter Abelard. He entered the priesthood around 1148. After some six to ten years more of training and service with the papal court, John—possibly through the good offices of St. Bernard—was recalled to England to become Secretary to the Archbishop of Canterbury. He served in this capacity on many important diplomatic missions. In 1176, having consistently conducted the affairs of the church with delicacy and distinction, he was appointed Bishop of Chartres. Four short years after his appointment, John died. His body was interred in the monastery of Josaphat, just outside his cathedral city.

Although quite influential in the affairs of his day, John is especially admired by posterity for his writings. Of these, the *Metalogicon,* a treatise on education, and the *Policraticus,* a political treatise, are the most important. In these works we meet with the type of cultured mind and interest which was to become general only in the Renaissance. John, who had the typically Humanist horror of mere verbalism and "logic-chopping," persistently denounced the Scholastics for what he considered to be the sterility of their dialectical disputes: a particular instance of which was manifested, according to John, in the hotly contested controversy over universals.

The problem of universals was transmitted to the early Middle Ages through Boethius' commentary on Porphyry's *Isagoge*. In the selection that follows—an excerpt from John of Salisbury's *Metalogicon*—we see the controversy through the eyes of our author. We have chosen to present it from John's point of view not only for the reason cited in our Preface, but as well because he catalogues clearly and succinctly the kinds of solutions that were current in his day. John himself, as we shall see, proposes a kind of "common sense" solution designed to dissolve what he referred to as "a problem over which more time has been lost than the Caesars ever spent in conquering the world, and more money than ever filled the coffers of Croesus."

JOHN OF SALISBURY AND THE CONTROVERSY OVER UNIVERSALS *

In what a pernicious manner logic is sometimes taught; and the ideas of moderns about [*the nature of*] *genera and species.*

To show off their knowledge, our contemporaries dispense their instruction in such a way that their listeners are at a loss to understand them. They seem to have the impression that every letter of the alphabet is pregnant with the secrets of Minerva. They analyze and press upon tender ears everything that anyone has ever said or done. Falling into the error condemned by Cicero, they frequently come to be unintelligible to their hearers more because of the multiplicity than the profundity of their statements. "It is indeed useful and advantageous for disputants," as Aristotle observes, "to take cognizance of several opinions on a topic." From the mutual

---

* Reprinted by permission of the University of California Press, Berkeley, California, from *The Metalogicon of John of Salisbury*, translated by D. D. McGarry, 1955.

disagreement thus brought into relief, what is seen to be poorly stated may be disproved or modified. Instruction in elementary logic does not, however, constitute the proper occasion for such procedure. Simplicity, brevity, and easy subject matter are, so far as is possible, appropriate in introductory studies. This is so true that it is permissible to expound many difficult points in a simpler way than their nature strictly requires. Thus, much that we have learned in our youth must later be amended in more advanced philosophical studies. Nevertheless, at present, all are here [in introductory logical studies] declaiming on the nature of universals, and attempting to explain, contrary to the intention of the author, what is really a most profound question, and a matter [that should be reserved] for more advanced studies. One holds that universals are merely word sounds, although this opinion, along with its author Roscelin, has already almost completely passed into oblivion. Another maintains that universals are word concepts, and twists to support his thesis everything that he can remember to have ever been written on the subject. Our Peripatetic of Pallet, Abelard, was ensnared in this opinion. He left many, and still has, to this day, some followers and proponents of his doctrine. They are friends of mine, although they often so torture the helpless letter that even the hardest heart is filled with compassion for the latter. They hold that it is preposterous to predicate a thing concerning a thing, although Aristotle is author of this monstrosity. For Aristotle frequently asserts that a thing is predicated concerning a thing, as is evident to anyone who is really familiar with his teaching. Another is wrapped up in a consideration of acts of the [intuitive] understanding, and says that genera and species are nothing more than the latter. Proponents of this view take their cue from Cicero and Boethius, who cite Aristotle as saying that universals should be regarded as and called "notions." "A notion," they tell us, "is the cognition of something, derived from its previously perceived form, and in need of unravelment." Or again [they say]: "A notion is an act of the [intuitive] understanding, a simple mental comprehension." They accordingly distort everything written, with an eye to making acts of [intuitive] understanding or "notions" include the universality of universals. Those who adhere to the view that universals are things, have various and sundry opinions. One, reasoning from the fact that everything which exists is singular in number, concludes that either the universal is numerically one, or it is non-existent. But since it is impossible for things that are substantial to be non-existent, if those things for which they are substantial exist, they further conclude that universals must be essentially one with particular things. Accordingly, following Walter of Mortagne, they distinguish [various] states [of existence], and say that Plato is an individual in so far as he is Plato; a species in so far as he is a man; a genus of a subaltern [subordinate] kind in so far as he is an animal; and a most general genus in so far as he is a substance. Although this opinion formerly had some proponents, it has been a long time since anyone has asserted it. Walter now upholds [the doctrine of] ideas, emulating Plato and imitating Bernard of Chartres, and maintains that genus and species are nothing more nor less than these, namely, ideas. "An idea," according to Seneca's definition, "is an eternal exemplar of those things which come to be as a result of nature." And since universals are not subject to corruption, and are not altered by the changes that transform particular things and cause them to come and go, succeeding one another almost momentarily, ideas are properly and correctly called "universals." Indeed, particular things are deemed incapable of supporting the substantive verb, [i.e., of being said "to be"], since they are not at all stable, and disappear without even waiting to receive names. For they vary so much in their qualities, time, location, and numerous different properties, that their whole existence seems to be more a mutable transition than a stable status. In contrast, Boethius declares: "We say that things 'are' when they may neither be increased nor diminished, but always continue as they are, firmly sustained by the foundations of their own nature." These [foundations] include their quantities, qualities, relations, places, times, conditions, and whatever is found in a way united with bodies. Although these adjuncts of bodies may seem to be changed, they remain immutable in their own nature. In like manner, although individuals [of species] may change, species remain the same. The waves of a stream wash on, yet the same flow of water continues, and we refer to the stream as the same river. Whence the statement of Seneca, which, in fact, he has borrowed from another: "In one sense it is true that we may descend twice into the same river, although in another sense this is not so." These "ideas," or "exemplary forms," are the original plans of all things. They may neither be decreased nor augmented: and they are so permanent and perpetual, that even if the whole world were to come to an end, they could not perish. They include all things, and, as Augustine seems to maintain in his book *On Free Will,* their number neither increases nor diminishes, because the ideas always continue on, even when it happens that [particular] temporal things cease to exist. What these men promise is wonderful, and familiar to philosophers who rise to the contemplation of higher things. But, as Boethius and numerous other authors testify, it is utterly foreign to the mind of Aristotle. For Aristotle very frequently opposes this view, as is clear from his books. Bernard of Chartres and his followers labored strenuously to compose the differences between Aristotle and Plato. But I opine that they arrived on the scene too late, so that their efforts to reconcile two dead men, who disagreed as long as they were alive and could do so, were in vain. Still another, in his endeavor to explain Aristotle, places universality in "native forms," as does Gilbert, Bishop of Poitiers, who labors to prove that "native forms" and universals are identical. A "native form" is an example of an original [exemplar]. It [the native form, unlike the original] inheres in created things, instead of subsisting in the divine mind. In Greek it is called the *idos,* since it stands in relation to the idea as the example does to its exemplar. The native form is sensible in things that are perceptible by the senses; but insensible as conceived in the mind. It is singular in individuals, but universal in all [of a kind]. Another, with Joscelin, Bishop of Soissons, attributes universality to collections of things, while denying it to things as individuals. When Joscelin tries to explain the authorities, he has his troubles and is hard put, for in many places he cannot bear the gaping astonishment of the indignant letter. Still another takes refuge in a new tongue, since he does not have sufficient command of Latin. When he hears the words "genus" and "species," at one time he says they should be understood as universals, and at another that they refer to the *maneries* of things. I know not in which of the authors he has found this term or this distinction, unless perhaps he has dug it out of lists of abstruse and obsolete words, or it is an item of jargon [in the baggage] of present-day doctors. I am further at a loss to see what it can mean here, unless it refers to collections of things, which would be the same as Joscelin's view, or to a universal thing, which, however, could hardly be called a *maneries*. For a *maneries* may be interpreted as referring to both [collections and universals], since a number of things, or the status in which a thing of such and such a type continues to exist may be called a *maneries*. Finally, there are some who fix their attention on the status of things, and say that genera and species consist in the latter.

That men always alter the opinions of their predecessors.

It would take too long, and [also] be entirely foreign to my purpose, to propound the opinions and errors of everyone. The saying of the comic poet that "There are as many opinions as heads," has almost come to hold true. Rarely, if ever, do we find a teacher who is content to follow in the footsteps of his master. Each, to make a name for himself, coins his own special error. Wherewith, while promising to correct his master, he sets himself up as a target for correction and condemnation by his own disciples as well as by posterity. I recognize that the same rule threatens to apply in my own case. By disagreeing with others and committing my dissent to writing, I am, in fact, laying myself open to be criticized by many. He who speaks is judged merely by one or a few persons; whereas he who writes thereby exposes himself to criticism by all, and appears before the tribunal of the whole world and every age. However, not to be overly harsh with the doctors, I must observe that, very often, many of them seem to be wrangling over words, rather than disputing about facts. Nonetheless there is nothing that is less appropriate for a professor of this art [of logic], since such procedure ill befits a serious man. As Aristotle declares, "To dispute in this wise over a word is utterly abhorrent in dialectic, unless it be the sole possible way in which a proposition may be discussed." Of a truth, on points where they seem to be in profound disagreement, such [professors of logic] admit one another's interpretations, even though they may maintain that the latter are inadequate. They are mutually condemning, not the meaning, but the words of one another's statements.

Wherein teachers of this kind are not to be forgiven.

I do not criticize their opinions, which [probably] do not actually disagree, as would be shown if it were possible to compare their meanings. Still, they are guilty of certain offenses which, in my opinion, should not be overlooked. In the first place, they load "insupportable burdens" on the frail shoulders of their students. Second, they pay no attention to proper order in teaching, and diligently take care lest "All things be suitably arranged, each in its own place." Thus they, so to speak, read the whole art into its title. With them, Porphyry practically teaches beforehand the contents of the *Topics*, the *Analytics*, and the *Elenchi*. Finally, they go against the mind of the author, and comb, as it were, in the wrong direction. For the [supposed] purpose of simplifying Aristotle, they teach the doctrine of Plato, or [perhaps even] some false opinion, which differs with equal error from the views of both Aristotle and Plato. At the same time, they all profess to be followers of Aristotle.

Aristotle's opinion concerning genera and species, supported by numerous confirmatory reasons and references to written works.

Aristotle stated that genera and species do not exist [as such], but are only understood. What is the point, then, in inquiring as to what genus is, when Aristotle has definitely asserted that it does not exist? Is it not inane to try to determine the nature, quantity, and quality of something that has no existence? If substance be lacking, then none of these other attributes can be present. If Aristotle, who says that genera and species do not exist [as such], is right, then the labors of the foregoing inquiry as to their substance, quantity, quality, or origin, are futile. We cannot describe the quality or quantity of something that lacks substance. Neither can we give the reason why something that does not exist is one thing or another, and of this or that size or kind. Wherefore, unless one wants to break with Aristotle, by granting that universals exist, he must reject opinions which would identify universals with word sounds, word concepts, sensible things, ideas, native forms, or collections. For all of the latter doubtless exist. In short, one who maintains that universals exist, contradicts Aristotle. We should not, however, fear that our understanding is empty when it perceives universals as abstracted from particular things, although the former have no [actual] existence apart from the latter. Our understanding [has two different modes of operation:] at times [it] looks directly at the simple essence of things, apart from composition, as when it conceives of "man" *per se,* or "stone" *per se,* in which operation it is simple. But at times it proceeds gradually, step by step, as when it considers a man as white, or a horse as running, in which case its operation is composite. A simple act of the understanding at times considers a thing as it is, as when it considers Plato; but at other times it conceives of a thing as otherwise. Sometimes it combines things that are [in actual life] uncombined, at other times it separates things that cannot [in reality] be dissociated. One who imagines a goat-stag or a centaur, conceives of a combination of man and beast that is alien to nature, or a combination of two species of animals. On the other hand, one who considers line or surface apart from a given mass, dissociates form from matter by the keen blade of his contemplative insight, although, actually, it is impossible for them to exist apart from each other. However, the abstracting intellect does not in this case conceive of form as existing apart from matter. If it did, its operation would be composite. Rather, it simply contemplates the form, without considering the matter, even though in fact the former cannot exist apart from the latter. Such an operation agrees with the intellect's simplicity, which comes into sharper relief in proportion as it considers simpler things in themselves, namely, apart from composition with other things. Nor is this procedure contrary to the order of nature, which has bestowed on the [human] intellect this faculty of distinguishing things that are combined, and putting together things that exist separately, in order to facilitate its investigation of nature itself. The combining process of the intellect, whereby things that are not united are copulated, lacks objectivity; but its abstracting process is both accurate and true to reality. The latter constitutes, as it were, the common factory of all the arts. While things possess but one manner of existence which they have received from nature, they may nevertheless be understood or signified in more than one way. Although a man who is not a specific man cannot exist, "man" may still be conceived mentally and represented in such a way that no given individual man is thought of or denoted. Therefore genera and species may be conceived by the abstracting intellect in order to signify things [as considered] apart from composition. But if one were, ever so diligently, to search for the latter in nature, dissociated from sensible things, he would be wasting his time, and laboring in vain, as nature does not count anything of the sort among her brood. Reason, on considering the substantial mutual resemblances of certain individual things, has discerned genera and species. Thus it has, as Boethius tells us, defined the general concept: "Rational mortal animal," which it has, on reflection, concluded from the mutual conformity existing among men, even though such a "rational mortal animal" [actually] exists only in individual cases. Consequently, genera and species are not things that are really and by their nature unrelated to individual things. Rather, they are mental representations of actual, natural things, intellectual images of the mutual likenesses of real things, reflected, as it were, in the mirror of the soul's native purity. These concepts the Greek call *ennoyas* or *yconoyfanas,* that is to say images of things clearly discernible by the mind. For the soul, as it were by the reflected ray of its own contemplation, finds in itself what it defines. The exemplar of what is defined exists in the mind, while the example exists among actual things. A similar condition maintains when we say in grammar: "Names which have such and such an ending are feminine or neuter." A general rule is laid down, which provides, so to speak, an exemplar for many declinable words. The examples, in turn, are to be found in all the words with a given termination. In like manner, certain exemplars are mentally conceived after their examples have been formed and presented to the senses by nature. According to Aristotle, these exemplars are conceptual, and are, as it were, images and shadows of things that really exist. But if one attempts to lay hold of them, supposing them to have an existence of their own, apart from particular things, they vanish [into thin air] as do dreams. "For they are representations," apparent only to the intellect. When universals are said to be substantial for individual things, reference is made to causality in the cognitive order, and to the nature of individual things. It is clear in particular cases that subordinate things cannot exist or be understood without superior ones. Thus the non-existence of animals would preclude the existence of man [a particular kind of animal]. And we must understand what an "animal" is, in order to understand what "man" is. For man is a certain kind of animal. In the same way "man" is in Plato, as Plato both exists and is understood, though Plato actually is a particular given man. While the idea and existence of animal are postulated by the idea and existence of man, this proposition is not convertible, as the concept and existence of man are not postulated by those of animal. For although the concept of man includes that of animal, the concept of animal does not include that of man. Since, therefore, both essentially and in the order of cognition, a species requires its genus, but is not itself required by its genus, the latter [genus] is said to be substantial for the former [species]. The same [general principle] holds true for individual things, which require [their] species and genus, but are not themselves necessitated by their species and genus. A particular thing cannot possess substance or be known by us, unless it is a [certain] species or genus, that is unless it is some [sort of] thing, or is known as this or that. Despite the fact that universals are called things, and are frequently spoken of as existing, without [any] qualification, neither the physical mass of bodies, nor the tenuity of spirits, nor the distinct essence of particular things is for this reason to be found in them. In a similar way, although matters that are the subject of affirmation or negation are called "things," and we very often say that what is true "is," still we do not classify such as substances or accidents. Neither do we refer to them as "Creator" or "creature." In the mart of the various branches of knowledge, free mutual exchange of words between one discipline and another ought to prevail, as observes Ulger, venerable Bishop of Angers. Liberality reigns in the market place of philosophers, where words may be borrowed without restriction or charge. Accordingly, even if it were granted that universals "exist" and are "things," to please the obstinate, still it would not, on this account, follow that the [total] number of things would be increased or diminished by adding or subtracting universals. If one examines universals, he will find that, while they can be numbered, this number cannot be added to the number of individual things. As with corporate colleges or other bodies, the number of heads cannot be added to that of the bodies, or vice versa, so with universals and particular things, the number of universals cannot be added to that of particular things, or vice versa. Only things of the same sort, which are by nature distinct in each given kind of things, can be numbered together with one another. Nothing can be universal unless it is found in particular things. Despite this, many have sought to find the universal, in itself, apart from individual things. But at the end of their search, they have all come out empty-handed. For the universal, apart from particular things, is not an entity, unless perhaps in the sense that truths and like meanings of combined words are entities. It does not make any difference that particular material things are examples of universal immaterial things, as every mode of activity (according to Augustine) is immaterial and insensible, although what is done, together with the act whereby it is done, is generally perceptible by the senses. That which is understood in a general way by the mind, as pertaining equally to many particular things, and that which is signified in a general way by a word, as referring equally to several beings, is beyond doubt universal. But even the terms "that which is understood," and "that which is signified," must be accepted in a broad manner, and cannot be subjected either to the narrow straits of disputation or to the subtle analysis of the grammatical art. The latter, of its nature, does not allow demonstrative expressions to be unlimited in application, except after one has sought and obtained such permission. Neither does it tolerate relative expressions that are vague. It requires, rather, that the meaning of such expressions be fixed by determining the person, or [his] act, or the action of another. A relative expression is, in fact, one which designates something as the subject of foregoing speech or thought. In the saying: "Wise and happy is the man who has recognized goodness, and has faithfully conformed his actions to this," the relative words "who" and "this," even though they do not designate the specific person [and act], are nevertheless in a way limited, and freed of their indefiniteness, by specification as to how they are to be recognized. There must be someone who corresponds to the statement, someone who, recognizing what is right, has acted accordingly, and is consequently happy. Only in cases where there is a mistake or a figure does it happen that there is nothing sure and definite to which a relative expression refers. Whence if a horse in general [in a generic manner] is promised, and the one to whom the promise was made says: "The horse which is promised to me is either healthy or sickly, since every horse is either healthy or sickly," he is clearly quibbling. For there is no horse that was promised to him. I do not say "There is no horse" because the horse does not or will not exist. Even that which does not exist, such as Arethusa's giving birth to child, may be the subject of a very definite promissory obligation. Rather, I say, "There is no horse," because the promise of a general kind of thing [a generic promise] does not involve the promise of the specific, that is a distinct thing. For when I say, "That which is promised," "That which is signified," "That which is understood," and the like, some definite thing is promised or meant if the relation is proper. However, there are also relations that are general [generic], which, if they are to remain true and are to be properly understood, cannot be tied down to some particular subject [the specific]. Examples of such are provided by the sayings: "A woman, both saved [us], and damned [us]"; "A tree both bore the cause of our death, and that of our life"; "The green leaves, which the freezing north wind bears off, the mild west wind restores." In the instances which I have just mentioned, I believe that these relative expressions should not be conceived as descending to the specific, and pointing out some particular person or thing, but rather that they should be understood as remaining general [generic]. In brief, what is signified by the noun "man" is a species, because man is signified, and man is a special kind of animal. What is signified by the word "animal" is a genus, as an animal is signified, and an animal is a general [generic] kind of thing. For what is signified by a word is that to which it directly refers, or that which the mind reasonably conceives on hearing the word. When one hears the word "man," one does not mentally run through all men, for this would be a task both endless and impossible. Neither does he restrict his concept to one particular man, for this would be inadequate, and would not really correspond to the meaning of the term. Likewise, when one defines an animal as a substance possessing life and the power of sensation, one is not simply describing a single particular animal, lest his definition be incomplete. Neither is he trying to give a description of every animal, lest his labor be endless. Each of these universals signifies or defines, not merely "what," but rather "what kind of what," not merely a given [particular] thing, but rather a certain kind of thing. Thus Galen, in his *Techne,* defines medicine as "the science of healthful, unhealthful, and intermediate things." He does not say, "the science of everything," since this would be infinite.

Neither does he say, "the science of certain [particular] things," since this would be inadequate for the definition of an art. Rather, he defines medicine as the science of a given kind of things. Aristotle tells us: "Genera and species determine the kind of a substance. They do not merely designate 'what,' but, in a way, 'what kind of a thing.' " In like vein, Aristotle declares in his *Elenchi:* "General terms, such as 'man,' do not denote some particular thing, but rather a certain kind of thing, or [a thing in] some sort of relation to something, or something like this." A little further on he says: "It is evident that a general, universal predication [concerning things of a class] is not to be understood as referring to some particular thing, but rather as signifying quality, relation, quantity, or something of the sort." In fact, what is not a particular thing cannot be described in detail. Real things have from nature certain limitations, and are distinguished from one another by their properties, even though frequently our knowledge of them is not very definite, and our concept of them rather vague. The well-known principle that what common names mean and what they name are not identical, does not militate against what has just been said. For their meaning is universal, even though they name particular things. Evidently, if one looks only for a simple general relationship, he will have no trouble understanding the foregoing, but if he insists on trying to find the precise determination of some individual thing, he may well be at a loss to put his finger on anything of the sort. There is a rule that "Demonstrative expressions provide primary cognition, relative expressions knowledge of a secondary kind." In fact [our] cognition, in apprehending something, circumscribes and defines the latter for itself by a certain [comprehensive] capacity of the mind, so that if a thing presents itself to the mind as absolutely unlimited in every respect, neither primary nor secondary cognition can proceed. All knowledge or cognition possessed by creatures is limited. Infinite knowledge belongs solely to God, because of His infinite nature. However limitless things may be, they are at the same time most certainly circumscribed by His infinite immensity, and defined by His boundless knowledge and wisdom, which cannot be counted and have no limit. But we are imprisoned within the petty dimensions of our human capacity, wherefore we attain neither primary, nor secondary, nor tertiary, nor any distinction of knowledge of what is infinite, save the realization that it is unknown because it is infinite. Accordingly, all demonstrative and relative expressions must refer to a specific, definite subject if they are correctly posited. Otherwise they will miss their mark. For cognition naturally seeks or possesses certitude as its object. However, language is often conscripted to serve in extraordinary senses, and frequently incorrect expressions are used as a matter of convenience. Thus the axiom that "All men love themselves," is generally accepted, not merely to provide material for the pedantic bickering of those who are content to chatter on any sort of topic that permits disputation, but also to convey knowledge of a truth to hearers who are in good faith. However, if one analyzes this principle according to the strict and proper meaning of a relative expression, one will perhaps charge that it is improperly stated and false. For it is evident that all men do not love all men. Neither do all men love any given man. So whether the expression: "all men," be understood collectively or distributively, the relative pronoun "themselves," which follows, cannot correctly be understood as referring either to every man or to any one man. The relation [here] is accordingly not a strict one. Begging, as it were, indulgent forgiveness from its own rule, it refutes the reliability of the universal with reference to the truth of particular things. While it is true in individual cases that everyone loves himself, and this is affirmed of all men in general in a distributive sense by the saying that "all men love themselves," the relation is to be understood in a broad and free way. It should not be taken in a narrow, grammatical sense, whereby it would either compass all men, or single out some particular individual from this universality. Hence, according to those who always seize upon difficulties and subtleties, and decline to use good faith as their principle in [interpreting] conversation or reading, this is "a form of statement" rather than "a statement of regular form." They also assert the same whenever a pronoun refers to a common noun, since a pronoun, which is always demonstrative or relative, stands in the place of a proper noun, at least when it correctly fulfills the purpose for which it was originally invented. For occasionally, by indulgence, pronouns have a wider meaning. Thus, when it is said that "If a being is a man, it is also an animal," we have not so much a consequence in a hypothetical statement, as a form of a consequence when something is expressed in a hypothetical manner. For the word "it," according to the strict laws of disputation, does not refer to a man. Nor can we see any definite thing to which it may be referred. Whence come many meaningless and vexatious objections, raised by such as delight in harassing the ignorant and those of a more liberal and less petty disposition. Such tireless wranglers, who refuse to desist from their stubborn objections [must] do so out of either ignorance, or perversity, or greed. Just as cognition seeks certitude, so demonstrative and relative expressions, which convey either primary or other cognition, depend on certain and definite subjects, which such expressions, when they are properly employed, present to our mind as particular things. Let us suppose that common names signify some general status (for I have already declared that I side with the Academicians in regard to things that are doubtful to a wise man, and that I do not care for contentious argumentation). Although I can somehow dream of a status wherein particular things are united, yet [wherein] no particular thing exists, I am still at a loss to see how this can be reconciled with the opinion of Aristotle, who contends that universals do not exist. Even the designations "incorporeal" and "insensible," which, as I have previously mentioned, are appropriate for universals, are only privative with reference to them. They do not attribute to universals any properties whereby the nature of the latter may be ascertained. For a universal is not an incorporeal or insensible thing. Something that is incorporeal is either a spirit or the property of a body or spirit. As universals are neither of these, they cannot strictly be called incorporeal. What incorporeal thing is not a substance created by God, or something united with a substance created by God? If universals were incorporeal [things], they would either be substances, that is, bodies or spirits, or things in composition with the same. They would depend on the Creator as the cause of their existence and the originator and support of their substance. For they would bid farewell and vanish, were they not subject to Him. "By Him, all things were made" to be what they are called from their qualities or effects, whether they are the subjects of forms or the forms of subjects. If a substance is a substance made by the Creator, it must have a certain size, kind, and existence relative to something else, in a given place at a specific time. It must also possess, do, or undergo something, with Him as author through Whom exists every substance and property of a substance, every part or combination of parts. Substantial and accidental forms alike receive from Him their existence and power to produce certain effects in their subjects. If anything exists, it is [necessarily] dependent on Him. The Stoics suppose that matter is coeternal with God, and maintain that form had no beginning. They posit three principles: matter, form, and God, saying that the latter is not indeed the Creator, but only the conciliator of the aforesaid. Others, who, although they profess and affect to be philosophers, by no means attain full cognition of the truth, falsely maintain that there are even more principles. Notwithstanding, there is but one principle of all things, from Whom has proceeded everything that is correctly considered and called something. As Augustine says, "God has created matter possessing [given] form." Although matter is sometimes spoken of as "formless," it has never existed utterly destitute of form. Reason is subservient to inquiry rather than to actuality. *Ylen,* which neither exists, nor can exist, nor can be fully understood without form, is, by our intellect, relentlessly divested, so to speak, of the forms wherewith it is attired, and stripped down to its own particular nudity and deficiency. But the strength of reason seemingly melts when confronted by the [first] principles of things. Hence it is that Boethius, defining "nature" in his book *Against Nestorius and Eutyches,* says that it "pertains to things, which, since they exist, may, at least in some way, be understood by the intellect." Explaining the force of the expression "at least in some way," used in his definition, Boethius states that this qualification is included because of God and matter, since in the investigation of the latter the human intellect is deficient. Indeed, God made matter from nothing, while form, likewise simultaneously created from nothing, is united with this matter, in such a way that, just as the privilege of determination is granted to the form, so that of existence is accorded to the matter. Thus, in a way, the form exists through the matter, while conversely the matter is determined by the form. Neither does the form exist of itself, nor would the matter be determinate without the form. Chaos would reign, or rather the sensible world would come to an end, if nature did not compose the figures of things by means of forms. To the point here is what Boethius says in the first part of his work *On the Trinity:* "Every existence is the result of a form." This proposition he clarifies by examples. "A statue," he points out, "is so called, not because of the bronze, the matter whereof it is made, but because of the form of Hector or Achilles, into which the bronze has been molded. The bronze itself is called bronze, not from the earth, which is its matter, but from the forms allotted it by nature. Even earth itself obtains its name, not from *poutou yle,* its matter, but from dryness and weight, its forms." To its form everything, accordingly, owes the fact that it is what it is, possesses such and such qualities, and has this or that quantity. Just as matter has the potentiality of becoming something of a certain size and kind, so forms have from their Creator the power of making this or that, for example, an animal or a tree, or something of a given size and kind. It is true that mathematics, which deals theoretically with abstractions, and in its subtle analysis separates things that are united in nature, treats matter and form apart from one another, so that the nature of what is composite may be more accurately and definitely understood. Still, the one cannot exist apart from the other, as [in this case] either matter would be without form, or form would lack a subject and hence be ineffective. "Even so the one requires the assistance of the other, and they work together in friendly fashion." It is recorded that in the beginning, heaven and earth were created, and then their various embellishments were created and interposed between the fire and water, which God had, so to speak, established as the first foundations of the world's body. In this account, reference is made to species. I do not refer here to the sort of "species" which logicians have dreamt of as being independent of the Creator. I speak rather of the forms in which things have been born, first in their own essence, and subsequently in our human understanding. The very fact that we call something "heaven" or "earth" is due to its form. It is likewise said that "The earth brought forth the green grass and the various kinds of trees." This shows that forms are united to matter, and also teaches that God is the author, not only of the grass, but also of its greenness. "Without Him, nothing was made." And verily whatever comes from the one principle, not only is one in number, but also is itself good, yea, "exceedingly good." For it proceeds from the supreme good. God willed to make all things similar to Himself, so far as the nature of each was, by His divinely established order, receptive of goodness. And so, in the approving judgment of the Divine Artisan, all the things which He had made were "exceedingly good." If genera and species do not proceed from God, they are nothing. But if each of them does proceed from Him, it is certainly one, and likewise good. And if a thing is numerically one, it is forthwith singular. The fact that some people call a thing "one" simply because it unites several things by expressing their conformity, although it is not one in itself, does not contradict our point. In the latter case, what is called "one" is neither immediately nor adequately one. If it were, it would be singular. However similar God's works may be, they are singular and distinct, one from another. Such is the arrangement decreed by Him, Who has created all things in number for their differentiation, in "weight" for their generic value, and in measure for their quantitative determination, all the while reserving to Himself universal authority. All things other than God are finite. Every substance is subject to number because it has just so many, and no more accidents. Every accident and every form is likewise subject to number, although in this case because of the singular nature of its subject, rather than a participation of accidents or forms. Everything also has its own "weight," either according to the respect due its form, if it is a substance, or according to the worth of its effects, if it is a form. Hence it is that, in comparing substances, we place man above the brute animals, out of esteem for his form, which is rational, as we deem external appearance less important than rationality, which provides the ability to reason. Measure, for its part, consists in the fact that everything has no more than a certain quantity. An accident or form cannot exceed the limits of its subject, and the subject itself cannot be greater than its accidents or form allow. The "color" of a body is both diffused throughout the whole body, and bounded by the external surfaces of the latter. On the other hand, the body itself extends only as far as its "color," neither going beyond, nor stopping short of the latter. In like manner, every subject is considered to extend as far as its accidents, while every accident which pertains to an entire subject exists complete throughout its whole subject, or if it pertains only to a part of the subject, it exists solely in that part. I do not hesitate to affirm that either genera and species are from God, or they are nothing at all; and I would do so even if the whole world were to hold the opposite. Dionysius the Areopagite makes clear that he holds the same view, and says that the number whereby all things are distinguished, the "weight" wherein they are established, and the measure wherewith they are limited, image God. For, of a truth, God is number innumerable, weight incalculable, and measure inestimable. And in Him alone all things that have been made in number, in "weight," and in measure, have been created. Whence Augustine says: "The invisible differences of invisible things are determinable only by Him, Who has ordained all things in [their] number, weight, and measure, and in Him, Who is measure, fixing the extent of all things; number, giving everything its specific existence; and "weight," drawing each entity to a stable existence, or, in other words, delimiting, forming, and ordering all things. In the account of the works of the six days [of creation], although we read that all good things were created, each according to its own kind, we find no allusion whatsoever to universals. Nor could there properly be such, if universals are essentially united with particular things, or [even] if the Platonic doctrine is correct. Furthermore, I cannot remember ever having read anywhere whence universals have derived existence, or when they have originated. According to Aristotle, universals are only understood, and there is no actual thing that is universal. These representations have licitly, and for instructional purposes, been given names that denote the way in which they are understood. It is true that every man is this or that [particular] man, that is to say, an individual. But "man" can be understood in such a way that neither this nor that [given] man, nor any being that is one in the singularity of its essence, is understood. And by means of this concept we can reason about man in general, that is man in general can be actually represented because of the general nature of the intellect. Accordingly, something that can be so understood, even though it may not be [at a given time actually] understood by anyone, is said to be general. For [certain] things resemble one another, and our intellect, abstracting from consideration of the [particular] things themselves, considers this conformity. One man has the same form as another, inasmuch as they are both men, even though they [assuredly] differ in their personal qualities. Man also has in common with the horse (from which he differs completely in species, that is, in the whole form of his nature, and so to speak, in his entire appearance) that they both live and have sensation, or, in other words, that they are both animals. That in which men, who are alike in the form of their nature, and distinct only in number (whereby so and so is one, and so and so another man), correspond, is called their "species." And that which is, so to speak, a general image of various forms, is known as "genus." Therefore, in Aristotle's judgment, genera and species are not merely "what" [things are], but also are, in a way, conceptions of "what kind of what" [they are]. They are, as it were, fictions, employed by [human] reason as it delves deeper in its investigation and explanation of things. Reason does this validly, for, whenever there is need, it can point to a manifest example in the world of reality to substantiate its concepts. Civil law does likewise, and has its own fictions. So, in fact, do all branches of learning, which unhesitatingly devise fictions to expedite their investigations. Each of them even, in a way, prides itself on its own special figments. "We may dispense with forms," says Aristotle, "for they are representations (or, according to a new translation: chatter) and even if they did exist, they would have no bearing on our discussion." Although Aristotle may be understood as referring here to Platonic ideas, genera and species may still both, not without reason, be said to "exist," if one bears in mind the diverse meanings of which "being" and "existence" are susceptible when applied to various subjects. For our reason prompts us to say that things exist, when we can see that they are exemplified by particular instances, of whose existence no one can doubt. It is not because genera and species are exemplary forms in the Platonic sense, "and existed as concepts in the Divine mind before they emanated into entities of the external physical world," that they are said to be exemplars of particular things. It is rather because, when one looks for an example of what is represented in a general way by [e.g.] the word "man," and what is defined when we say [e.g.] that "man is a mortal rational animal," forthwith Plato or some other particular man can be pointed out, in order firmly to establish the general meaning or definition. Genera and species may be called "representations," because on the one hand they represent particular things, and, on the other, they are represented by the latter. Things are made manifest sometimes by what is prior, sometimes by what is posterior. More general things are, in themselves, prior, for they are also understood in other things; while particular things are posterior. Frequently, however, things which are naturally prior, and of themselves more properly objects of knowledge, are actually less known by us. The more solidly substantial things are, the more readily we can recognize them with our senses; the more subtile they become, the more difficult it is to perceive them. As Aristotle observes, "The point is prior to, and in itself more evident than the line. The same may be said of the line relative to the plane surface, and of the plane surface with reference to the solid. It is likewise true of unity in relation to plurality, for which unity is the principle. This also holds in regard to the letter relative to the syllable." The foregoing list could be extended. [Aristotle continues:] "The reverse, however, sometimes occurs in the case of our knowledge. Generally the average mind more readily perceives what is posterior, whereas the comprehension of what is prior is reserved to the more profound and learned intellect." Whence, even though it is true that what is posterior is best defined by what is prior, and this is always more scientific, still, frequently, of necessity, and to provide subject matter within the ken of our senses, what is prior is actually explained by what is posterior. A point is thus said to be the end of a line; a line, the edge of a surface; a surface, the side of a solid. In like manner, unity is said to be the elementary principle of number, the moment that of time, the letter that of speech. Genera and species are accordingly exemplars of particular things, but rather as instruments of learning than as essential causes of particular things. And this representative (to use the term with considerable license) contemplation of fictions even goes to the extent of completely dispensing with the consideration of individual things. Since every substance is comprised of its own properties, the same collection of which is not found in any other substance, the abstracting intellect proceeds to consider each thing as it is in itself. Although Plato could not exist without form, and divorced from place or time, reason regards him as, so to speak, "nude," stripped of his quantity, quality, and other accidents. It thus gives the individual a [common] name. This, it must be admitted, is a fiction, designed to expedite learning and deeper inquiry. No such thing [as "man" in general] can actually be found. Still, the concept of "man" in general is a valid act of understanding. This is perhaps why, in the *Analytics,* we find the statement: "Aristomenes is always intelligible, even though Aristomenes does not always exist, as he must one day disintegrate." What is uniquely individual can only, according to some, be predicated of a certain subject. Plato, [as] the son of Aristides, is individual neither in quantity, as an atom, nor by solidity, as a diamond, nor even, so they say, by predication. I, personally, neither strongly oppose nor sponsor this opinion. Nor do I think that it is a matter of moment, since I advocate recognition of the fact that words may be used in various senses. This is, I believe, an indispensable condition, if one is accurately to understand what authors mean. What is there to forbid lest, just as a genus may, with truth, be predicated of its species, so this particular Plato, perceptible by the senses, may, with truth, be predicated of the son of Aristides, if he is Aristides' only son. Then, just as man is an animal, so the son of Aristides is Plato. Some believe that this was what Aristotle meant when he said in his *Analytics:* "Of all the things that exist, some are such that they cannot be predicated of anything else with true universality. Such is the case, for example, with Cleon and Callias, as well as with whatever is singular and perceptible by the senses. However, other things may be predicated of them, as each [Cleon, Callias] is both a man and an animal. Some things are themselves predicated of other things, but other things that are prior are not predicated of them. With certain things, however, it is true that both they themselves are predicated of other things, and other things are predicated of them. Thus, for example, man is predicated of Callias, while, in turn, animal is predicated of man. Certain things which exist are clearly fated by their nature not to be predicated of anything. Almost all sensible things fall in this category, and cannot be predicated of anything save as accidents, as when we say, 'That white figure is Socrates'; and 'That object approaching [in the distance] is Callias.' " This distribution would seem entirely out of place if a sensible thing could not be predicated. But while the latter is predicated of something else, it is predicated only as an accident. If it could not be predicated as an accident concerning itself or something else, what Aristotle says would be false, and his example would be pointless. And if a sensible thing could not be made the subject of a predication, then, doubtless, Aristotle would be either lying or talking nonsense. Here, as elsewhere, Aristotle has proceeded in the manner which one should use in teaching the liberal arts, and has discussed his subject in a greatly simplified fashion, so that he may [more easily] be understood. Accordingly, he has not introduced into genera and species a difficulty which the doctors themselves are unable to understand, much less to explain to others. The statement found in the *Topics* that "In the case of animals, all differences must be either species or individuals, since every animal is either a species or an individual," exemplifies the sovereignty of this principle of simplicity. Similar simplification is found in the statement of Boethius that "Every species is its own genus." For every man is an animal, and all whiteness is color. By the same token, what prevents sensible things being predicated, or made the subject of predications, in like extended sense? I do not believe that the authors have so done violence to words as to tie them down to a single meaning in all contexts. Rather, I am confident that they express their teachings so as always to serve understanding, which is highly adaptable [to varying meanings], and which reason requires should be here the first and foremost consideration. Predication has several different meanings, which vary according to the context. Still it probably everywhere denotes some sort of conformity or intrinsic connection. For when a word shows an aptness to be joined with another word in the terms of a true affirmation, and when a word is said to be predicated of a thing, it is evident that such an appellation must suit it. At times, to predicate something about a thing denotes that the latter is such and such, as when we say that Plato is a man. At other times, such predication denotes that the subject partakes of something, as for instance that a subject has a certain accident. I do not have any misgivings about declaring that a thing may be predicated of a thing in a proposition, even though the thing is not [explicitly stated] in the proposition. For a thing may be signified by the predicate term of a true affirmation, in whose subject some [given] thing is involved or signified. In fine, instead of fighting against what is written, I believe that we should accept [and try to understand] it in a friendly manner. Our policy should be to admit the liberal interpretation of words that are susceptible of more than one meaning. It is unbefitting a reader or listener to snap like a dog at every figure of speech, or employment of what is deemed poor diction. "Become used to what is hard to bear, and you will bear it." Certainly one is rash, ungrateful, and imprudent if he contradicts his teacher at every turn, and refuses to agree with him on any point. Let us fall [gracefully] into step, therefore, with the figurative speech used by the authors, and let us weigh whatever they say in the light of the causes behind their saying it. In this way we will arrive at an accurate understanding of what they have written. Thus the word "thing" may admit of a wider extension, whereby it may apply to universals, even though Aristotle says that the latter are to be understood as abstracted from particular things in such a way that they would have no existence in the absence of the aforesaid. But those who maintain that genus is numerically one assert the independent existence of universals, according to Aristotle. This they do who suppose the [separate] existence of forms, that is to say "ideas." Aristotle vigorously opposed this doctrine, together with its author, Plato, whenever he had the opportunity. It is true that a great host of philosophers, including not only Augustine, but also several of our contemporaries, have [adopted and] championed Plato's doctrine of ideas. Still we by no means follow Plato in his analysis of the nature of universals. On this question we acknowledge Aristotle, the prince of the Peripatetics, as the master. To judge between the opinions of such great men is a tremendous matter, a task which Boethius in his second commentary on Porphyry, declares to be beyond his abilities. But one embarking upon a study of the works of the Peripatetics, should accept the judgment of Aristotle, if not because it is truer, then certainly because it will serve him better in his studies. Those who declare that genera and species are merely word sounds or word concepts, as well as those who are led astray by other of the aforesaid opinions in their investigations, have all alike obviously strayed far afield from Aristotle's teaching. Indeed, they diverge from his views even more childishly and stupidly than do the followers of Plato, whose opinion they will not even deign to recognize. I believe that what we have said should suffice to show that those who review every opinion that has ever been advanced concerning genera and species, in order to disagree with all of them, and at length establish some plausibility for their own [pet] notion, are neither [really] trying to explain Porphyry with accuracy, nor treating what is introductory in a suitable manner. Such a procedure, entirely foreign to the mind of the author, dulls the mental faculties of students, and usurps time that ought to be given to the study of other points whose knowledge is equally necessary.

Suggestions for Further Reading

On the problem of universals: Carré, M. H. *Realists and Nominalists.* Oxford, 1956. On John of Salisbury: Webb, C. C. J. *John of Salisbury.* London, 1932; *FCC* vol. II, ch. XIV; *EG* 150-153; *AAM* 79-81.

Hugh of St. Victor

Hugh was born of noble parentage in Saxony, around 1096. His early studies were pursued in the monastery of Hamersleben near Halberstadt. After taking the habit, Hugh, in 1115, journeyed to Paris in order to further his education at the famous school in the Abbey of St. Victor. His own teaching career commenced in 1125; and in 1131 he became head of the school of St. Victor. He remained as head until his death in 1141.

Hugh was one of the foremost theologians and educators of the day. He was also a devoted friend of the arts, regarding such studies not only as conducive to progress in theology, but also of great utility in all other pursuits. Although Hugh wrote profusely both mystical and exegetical works, we have chosen to present below an excerpt from his *Didascalicon*, a work which typifies the twelfth-century tendency to classify and systematize the learning of the day.

HUGH OF ST. VICTOR ON THE ORIGIN OF THE ARTS*

PREFACE

There are many persons whose nature has left them so poor in ability that they can hardly grasp with their intellect even easy things, and of these persons I believe there are two kinds. There are those who, while they are not unaware of their own dullness, nonetheless struggle after knowledge with all the effort they can put forth and who, by tirelessly keeping up their pursuit, deserve to obtain as a result of their will power what they by no means possess as a result of their work. Others, however, because they know that they are in no way able to compass the highest things, neglect even the least, and, as it were, carelessly at rest in their own sluggishness, they all the more lose the light of truth in the greatest matters for their refusal to learn those smallest of which they are capable. It is of such that the Psalmist declares, "They were unwilling to understand how they might do well." Not knowing and not wishing to know are far different things. Not knowing, to be sure, springs from weakness; but contempt of knowledge springs from a wicked will.

There is another sort of man whom nature has enriched with the full measure of ability and to whom she shows an easy way to come at truth. Among these, even granting inequality in the strength of their ability, there is nevertheless not the same virtue or will in all for the cultivation of their natural sense through practice and learning. Many of this sort, caught up in the affairs and cares of this world beyond what is needful or given over to the vices and sensual indulgences of

---

* From *The Didascalicon of Hugh of St. Victor*, translated by J. Taylor. Published 1961, Columbia University Press. Used by permission.

the body, bury the talent of God in earth, seeking from it neither the fruit of wisdom nor the profit of good work. These, assuredly, are completely detestable. Again, for others of them, lack of family wealth and a slender income decrease the opportunity of learning. Yet, we decidedly do not believe that these can be altogether excused by this circumstance, since we see many laboring in hunger, thirst, and nakedness attain to the fruit of knowledge. And still it is one thing when one is not able, or to speak more truly, when one is not easily able to learn, and another when one is able but unwilling to learn. Just as it is more glorious to lay hold upon wisdom by sheer exertion, even though no resources support one, so, to be sure, it is more loathsome to enjoy natural ability and to have plenty of wealth, yet to grow dull in idleness.

The things by which every man advances in knowledge are principally two—namely, reading and meditation. Of these, reading holds first place in instruction, and it is of reading that this book treats, setting forth rules for it. For there are three things particularly necessary to learn for reading: first, each man should know what he ought to read; second, in what order he ought to read, that is, what first and what afterwards; and third, in what manner he ought to read. These three points are handled one by one in this book. The book, moreover, instructs the reader as well of secular writings as of the Divine Writings. Therefore, it is divided into two parts, each of which contains three subdivisions. In the first part, it instructs the reader of the arts, in the second, the reader of the Sacred Scripture. It instructs, moreover, in this way: it shows first what ought to be read, and next in what order and in what manner it ought to be read. But in order to make known what ought to be read, or what ought especially to be read, in the first part it first of all enumerates the origin of all the arts, and then their description and division, that is, how each art either contains some other or is contained by some other, thus dividing up philosophy from the peak down to the lowest members. Then it enumerates the authors of the arts and afterwards makes clear which of these arts ought principally to be read; then, likewise, it reveals in what order and in what manner. Finally, it lays down for students their discipline of life, and thus the first part concludes.

In the second part it determines what writings ought to be called divine, and next, the number and order of the Divine Books, and their authors, and the interpretations of the names of these Books. It then treats certain characteristics of Divine Scripture which are very important. Then it shows how Sacred Scripture ought to be read by the man who seeks in it the correction of his morals and a form of living. Finally, it instructs the man who reads in it for love of knowledge, and thus the second part too comes to a close.

BOOK ONE

Chapter 1. Concerning the origin of the arts.

Of all things to be sought, the first is that Wisdom in which the Form of the Perfect Good stands fixed. Wisdom illuminates man so that he may recognize himself; for man was like all the other animals when he did not understand that he had been created of a higher order than they. But his immortal mind, illuminated by Wisdom, beholds its own principle and recognizes how unfitting it is for it to seek anything outside itself when what it is in itself can be enough for it. It is written on the tripod of Apollo: *γνῶθι οεαυτον*, that is "Know thyself," for surely, if man had not forgotten his origin, he would recognize that everything subject to change is nothing.

An opinion approved among philosophers maintains that the soul is put together out of all the parts of nature. And Plato's *Timaeus* formed the entelechy out of substance which is "dividual" and "individual" and mixed of these two; and likewise out of nature which is "same" and "diverse" and a mixture of this pair, by which the universe is defined. For the entelechy grasps "not only the elements but all things that are made from them," since, through its understanding, it comprehends the invisible causes of things and, through sense impressions, picks up the visible forms of actual objects. "Divided, it gathers movement into twin spheres" because, whether it goes out to sensible things through its senses or ascends to invisible things through its understanding, it circles about, drawing to itself the likenesses of things; and thus it is that one and the same mind, having the capacity for all things, is fitted together out of every substance and nature by the fact that it represents within itself their imaged likeness.

Now, it was a Pythagorean teaching that similars are comprehended by similars: so that, in a word, the rational soul could by no means comprehend all things unless it were also composed of all of them; or, as a certain writer puts it:

> Earth we grasp with the earthly, fire with flame,
> Liquid with moisture, air with our breath.

But we ought not to suppose that men most familiar with all the natures of things thought that simple essence was in any way distended in quantitative parts. Rather, in order to demonstrate the soul's marvelous power more clearly did they declare that it consists of all natures, "not as being physically composed of them, but as having an analogous type of composition." For it is not to be thought that this similitude to all things comes into the soul from elsewhere, or from without; on the contrary, the soul grasps the similitude in and of itself, out of a certain native capacity and proper power of its own. As Varro says in the *Periphysion:* Not all change comes upon things from without and in such a way that whatever changes necessarily either loses something it had or gains from the outside some other and different thing which it did not have before. We see how a wall receives a likeness when the form of some image or other is put upon it from the outside. But when a coiner imprints a figure upon metal, the metal, which itself is one thing, begins to represent a different thing, not just on the outside, but from its own power and its natural aptitude to do so. It is in this way that the mind, imprinted with the likenesses of all things, is said to *be* all things and to receive its composition from all things and to contain them not as actual components, or formally, but virtually and potentially.

This, then, is that dignity of our nature which all naturally possess in equal measure, but which all do not equally understand. For the mind, stupefied by bodily sensations and enticed out of itself by sensuous forms, has forgotten what it was, and, because it does not remember that it was anything different, believes that it is nothing except what is seen. But we are restored through instruction, so that we may recognize our nature and learn not to seek outside ourselves what we can find within. "The highest curative in life," therefore, is the pursuit of Wisdom: he who finds it is happy, and he who possesses it, blessed.

Chapter 2. That philosophy is the pursuit of wisdom.

"Pythagoras was the first to call the pursuit of Wisdom philosophy" and to prefer to be called *philosophos:* for previously philosophers had been called *sophoi,* that is, wise men. Fitly indeed did he call the seekers of truth not wise men but lovers of Wisdom, for certainly the whole truth lies so deeply hidden that the mind, however much it may ardently yearn toward it or however much it may struggle to acquire it, can nonetheless comprehend only with difficulty the truth as it is. Pythagoras, however, established philosophy as the discipline "of those things which truly exist and are of themselves endowed with unchangeable substance."

"Philosophy, then, is the love and pursuit of Wisdom, and, in a certain way, a friendship with it: not, however, of that 'wisdom' which is concerned with certain tools and with knowledge and skill in some craft, but of that Wisdom which, wanting in nothing, is a living Mind and the sole primordial Idea or Pattern of things. This love of Wisdom, moreover, is an illumination of the apprehending mind by that pure Wisdom and, in a certain way, a drawing and a calling back to Itself of man's mind, so that the pursuit of Wisdom appears like friendship with that Divinity and pure Mind. This Wisdom bestows upon every manner of souls the benefit of its own divinity, and brings them back to the proper force and purity of their nature. From it are born truth of speculation and of thought and holy and pure chastity of action."

"But since this most excellent good of philosophy has been prepared for human souls, we must begin with those very powers of the soul, so that our exposition may follow an orderly line of progression."

Chapter 3. Concerning the threefold power of the soul, and the fact that man alone is endowed with reason.

"Altogether, the power of the soul in vivifying bodies is discovered to be of three kinds: one kind supplies life to the body alone in order that, on being born, the body may grow and, by being nourished, may remain in existence; another provides the judgment of sense perception; a third rests upon the power of mind and reason.

"Of the first, the function is to attend to the forming, nourishing, and sustaining of bodies; its function is not, however, to bestow upon them the judgment either of sense perception or of reason. It is the vivifying force seen at work in grasses and trees and whatever is rooted firmly in the earth.

"The second is a composite and conjoint power which subsumes the first and makes it part of itself, and which exercises judgment of several different kinds upon such objects as it can compass; for every animal endowed with sense perception is likewise born, nourished, and sustained; but the senses it possesses are diverse and are found up to five in number. Thus, whatever receives nutriment only, does not also have sense perception; but whatever has sense perception does also receive nutriment, and this fact proves that to such a being the first vivifying power of the soul, that of conferring birth and nourishment, also belongs. Moreover, such beings as possess sense perception not only apprehend the forms of things that affect them while the sensible body is present, but even after the sense perception has ceased and the sensible objects are removed, they retain images of the sense-perceived forms and build up memory of them. Each animal retains these images more or less enduringly, according to its ability. However, they possess them in a confused and unclear manner, so that they can achieve nothing from joining or combining them, and, while they are therefore able to remember them all, they cannot do so with equal distinctness; and, having once forgotten them, they are unable to recollect or re-evoke them. As to the future, they have no knowledge of it.

"But the third power of the soul appropriates the prior nutritional and sense-perceiving powers, using them, so to speak, as its domestics and servants. It is rooted entirely in the reason, and it exercises itself either in the most unfaltering grasp of things present, or in the understanding of things absent, or in the investigation of things unknown. This power belongs to humankind alone. It not only takes in sense impressions and images which are perfect and well founded, but, by a complete act of the understanding, it explains and confirms what imagination has only suggested. And, as has been said, this divine nature is not content with the knowledge of those things alone which it perceives spread before its senses, but, in addition, it is able to provide even for things removed from it names which imagination has conceived from the sensible world, and it makes known, by arrangements of words, what it has grasped by reason of its understanding. For it belongs to this nature, too, that by things already known to it, it should seek after things not known, and it requires to know of each thing not only whether it exists, but of what nature it is, and of what properties, and even for what purpose.

"To repeat, this threefold power of soul is the exclusive endowment of human nature, whose power of soul is not lacking in the movements of understanding. By this power it exercises its faculty of reason properly upon the following four heads: either it inquires whether a thing exists, or, if it has established that it does, it searches out the thing's nature; but if it possesses reasoned knowledge of both these things, it investigates the properties of each object, and sifts the total import of all other accidents; and knowing all these things, it nevertheless further inquires and searches rationally why the object exists as it does.

"While the mind of man, then, so acts that it is always concerned with the apprehension of things before it or the understanding of things not present to it or the investigation and discovery of things unknown, there are two matters upon which the power of the reasoning soul spends every effort: one is that it may know the natures of things by the method of inquiry; but the other is that there may first come to its knowledge those things which moral earnestness will thereafter transform into action."

Chapter 4. What matters pertain to philosophy.

But, as I perceive, the very course of our discussion has already led us into "a trap from which there is no escape." However, it is not involved words but an obscure subject matter that gives rise to our difficulty. Because we have undertaken to speak of the pursuit of Wisdom, and have affirmed that this pursuit belongs to men alone by a distinct prerogative of their nature, we must consequently seem committed now to the position that Wisdom is a kind of moderator over *all* human actions. For while the nature of brute animals, governed by no rational judgment, produces movements guided only by sense impressions and in pursuing or fleeing anything uses no discretion born of understanding but is driven by a certain blind inclination of the flesh: it remains true that the actions of the rational soul are not swept away by blind impulse but are always preceded by Wisdom as their guide. If this is settled as true, then we shall say that not only such studies as are concerned with the nature of things or the regulation of morals but also those concerned with the theoretical consideration of *all* human acts and pursuits belong with equal fitness to philosophy. Following this view, we can define philosophy thus: Philosophy is the discipline which investigates comprehensively the ideas of all things, human and divine.

And yet we ought not to retract what we said at the outset, namely, that philosophy is the love and the pursuit of Wisdom, not, however, of that "wisdom" which is deployed with tools, like building and farming and other activities of this kind, but of that Wisdom which is the sole primordial Idea or Pattern of things. For the same action is able to belong to philosophy as concerns its ideas and to be excluded from it as concerns its actual performance. For example, to speak in terms of instances already before us, the theory of agriculture belongs to the philosopher, but the execution of it to the farmer. Moreover, the products of artificers, while not nature, imitate nature, and, in the design by which they imitate, they express the form of their exemplar, which is nature.

You see, then, for what reason we are compelled to extend philosophy to all the actions of men, so that necessarily the parts of philosophy are equal in number to the different types of those things over which its extension has now been established.

Chapter 5. Concerning the rise of the theoretical, the practical, and the mechanical.

Of all human acts or pursuits, then, governed as these are by Wisdom, the end and the intention ought to regard either the restoring of our nature's integrity, or the relieving of those weaknesses to which our present life lies subject. What I have just said, let me more fully explain.

In man are two things—the good and the evil, his nature and the defective state of his nature. The good, because it is his nature, because it has suffered corruption, because it has been lessened, requires to be restored by active effort. The evil, because it constitutes a deficiency, because it constitutes a corruption, because it is not our nature, requires to be removed, or, if not able to be removed completely, then at least to be alleviated through the application of a remedy. This is our entire task—the restoration of our nature and the removal of our deficiency.

The integrity of human nature, however, is attained in two things—in knowledge and in virtue, and in these lies our sole likeness to the supernal and divine substances. For man, since he is not simple in nature but is composed of a twofold substance, is immortal in that part of himself which is the more important part—that part which, to state the case more clearly, he in fact *is*. In his other part, however—that part which is transitory and which is all that has been recognized by those too ignorant to give credit to anything but their senses—he is subject to death and to change. In this part man must die as often as he loses concrete substantiality. This part is of that lowest category of things, things having both beginning and end.

Chapter 6. Concerning the three "manners" of things.

Among things there are some which have neither beginning nor end, and these are named eternal; there are others which have a beginning but are terminated by no end, and these are called perpetual; and there are yet others which have both beginning and end, and these are temporal.

In the first category we place that in which the very being (*esse*) and "that which is" (*id quod est*) are not separate, that is, in which cause and effect are not different from one another, and which draws its subsistence not from a principle distinct from it but from its very self. Such alone is the Begetter and Artificer of nature.

But that type of thing in which the very being (*esse*) and "that which is" (*id quod est*) are separate, that is, which has come into being from a principle distinct from it, and which, in order that it might begin to be, flowed into actuality out of a preceding cause—this type of being, I say, is nature, which includes the whole world, and it is divided into two parts: it is that certain being which, in acquiring existence from its primordial causes, came forth into actuality not as moved thereto by anything itself in motion, but solely by the decision of the divine will, and, once in existence, stood immutable, free from all destruction or change (of this type are the substances of things, called by the Greeks *ousiai*) and it is all the bodies of the superlunary world, which, from their knowing no change, have also been called divine.

The third type of things consists of those which have both beginning and end and which come into being not of their own power but as works of nature. These come to be upon the earth, in the sublunary world, by the movement of an artifacting fire which descends with a certain power to beget all sensible objects.

Now, of the second sort it is said, "Nothing in the world

perishes," for no essence suffers destruction. Not the essences but the forms of things pass away. When the form is said to pass away, this is to be understood as meaning not that some existing thing is believed to have perished altogether and lost its being, but rather that it has undergone change, perhaps in one of the following ways: that things once joined are now apart, or once apart are now joined; or that things once standing here now move there; or that things which now are only "have-beens" once subsisted; in all these instances the being of the things suffers no loss. Of the third sort it is said, "All things which have arisen fall, and all which have grown decline": for all the works of nature, as they have a beginning, so have they an end. Of the second sort, again, it is said, "Nothing comes from nothing, and into nothingness can nothing revert," from the fact that all of nature has both a primordial cause and a perpetual subsistence. And of the third sort, once more, "That which before was nothing returns again thereto": for just as every work of nature flows temporarily into actuality out of its hidden cause, so when its actuality has temporarily been destroyed, that work will return again to the place from which it came.

Chapter 7. Concerning the superlunary and sublunary world.

Because of these facts, astronomers (*mathematici*) have divided the world into two parts: into that, namely, which stretches above the sphere of the moon and that which lies below it. The superlunary world, because in it all things stand fixed by primordial law, they called "nature," while the sublunary world they called "the work of nature," that is, the work of the superior world, because the varieties of all animate beings which live below by the infusion of life-giving spirit, take their infused nutriment through invisible emanations from above, not only that by being born they may grow but also that by being nourished they may continue in existence. Likewise they called that superior world "time" because of the course and movement of the heavenly bodies in it, and the inferior world they called "temporal" because it is moved in accordance with the movements of the superior. Again, the superlunary, from the perpetual tranquillity of its light and stillness, they called *elysium,* while the sublunary, from the instability and confusion of things in flux, they called the underworld or *infernum.*

Into these things we have digressed somewhat more broadly in order to explain how man, in that part in which he partakes of change, is likewise subject to necessity, whereas in that in which he is immortal, he is related to divinity. From this it can be inferred, as said above, that the intention of all human actions is resolved in a common objective: either to restore in us the likeness of the divine image or to take thought for the necessity of this life, which, the more easily it can suffer harm from those things which work to its disadvantage, the more does it require to be cherished and conserved.

Chapter 8. In what man is like unto God.

Now there are two things which restore the divine likeness in man, namely the contemplation of truth and the practice of virtue. For man resembles God in being wise and just—though, to be sure, man is but changeably so while God stands changelessly both wise and just. Of those actions which minister to the necessity of this life, there are three types: first, those which take care of the feeding of nature; second, those which fortify against harms which might possibly come from without; and third, those which provide remedy for harms already besieging us. When, moreover, we strive after the restoration of our nature, we perform a divine action, but when we provide the necessaries required by our infirm part, a human action. Every action, thus, is either divine or human. The former type, since it derives from above, we may not unfittingly call "understanding" (*intelligentia*); the latter, since it derives from below and requires, as it were, a certain practical counsel, "knowledge" (*scientia*).

If, therefore, Wisdom, as declared above, is moderator over all that we do deliberately, we must consequently admit that it contains two parts, understanding and knowledge. Understanding, again, inasmuch as it works both for the investigation of truth and the delineation of morals, we divide into two kinds—into theoretical, that is to say speculative, and practical, that is to say active. The latter is also called ethical, or moral. Knowledge, however, since it pursues merely human works, is fitly called "mechanical," that is to say adulterate.

Chapter 9. Concerning the three works.

"Now there are three works—the work of God, the work of nature, and the work of the artificer, who imitates nature." The work of God is to create that which was not, whence we read, "In the beginning God created heaven and earth"; the work of nature is to bring forth into actuality that which lay hidden, whence we read, "Let the earth bring forth the green herb," etc.; the work of the artificer is to put together things disjoined or to disjoin those put together, whence we read, "They sewed themselves aprons." For the earth cannot create the heaven, nor can man, who is powerless to add a mere span to his stature, bring forth the green herb.

Among these works, the human work, because it is not nature but only imitative of nature, is fitly called mechanical, that is adulterate, just as a skeleton key is called a "mechanical" key. How the work of the artificer in each case imitates nature is a long and difficult matter to pursue in detail. For illustration, however, we can show the matter briefly as follows: The founder who casts a statue has gazed upon man as his model. The builder who has constructed a house has taken into consideration a mountain, for, as the Prophet declares, "Thou sendest forth springs in the vales; between the midst of the hills the waters shall pass"; as the ridges of mountains retain no water, even so does a house require to be framed into a high peak that it may safely discharge the weight of pouring rains. He who first invented the use of clothes had considered how each of the growing things one by one has its proper covering by which to protect its nature from offense. Bark encircles the tree, feathers cover the bird, scales encase the fish, fleece clothes the sheep, hair garbs cattle and wild beasts, a shell protects the tortoise, and ivory makes the elephant unafraid of spears. But it is not without reason that while each living thing is born equipped with its own natural armor, man alone is brought forth naked and unarmed. For it is fitting that nature should provide a plan for those beings which do not know how to care for themselves, but that from nature's example, a better chance for trying things should be provided to man when he comes to devise for himself by his own reasoning those things naturally given to all other animals. Indeed, man's reason shines forth much more brilliantly in inventing these very things than ever it would have had man naturally possessed them. Nor is it without cause that the proverb says: "Ingenious want hath mothered all the arts." Want it is which has devised all that you see most excellent in the occupations of men. From this the infinite varieties of painting, weaving, carving, and founding have arisen, so that we look with wonder not at nature alone but at the artificer as well.

Chapter 10. What "nature" is.

But since we have already spoken so many times of "nature," it seems that the meaning of this word ought not to be passed over in complete silence, even though as Tully says, " 'Nature' is difficult to define." Nor, because we are unable to say of it all we might wish, ought we to maintain silence about what we can say.

Men of former times, we find, have said a great deal concerning "nature," but nothing so complete that no more should seem to remain to be said. So far as I am able to conclude from their remarks, they were accustomed to use this word in three special senses, giving each its own definition.

In the first place, they wished by this word to signify that archetypal Exemplar of all things which exists in the divine Mind, according to the idea of which all things have been formed; and they said that nature was the primordial cause of each thing, whence each takes not only its being (*esse*) but its "being such or such a thing" (*talis esse*) as well. To the word in this sense they assigned the following definition: "Nature is that which gives to each thing its being."

In the second place they said that "nature" meant each thing's peculiar being (*proprium esse*), and to "nature" in this sense they assigned this next definition: "The peculiar difference giving form to each thing is called its nature." It is with this meaning in mind that we are accustomed to say, "It is the nature of all heavy objects to tend toward the earth, of light ones to rise, of fire to burn, and of water to wet."

The third definition is this: "Nature is an artificer fire coming forth from a certain power to beget sensible objects." For physicists tell us that all things are procreated from heat and moisture. Therefore Vergil calls Oceanus "father," and Valerius Soranus, in a certain verse which treats Jove as a symbol of aethereal fire, says:

> Jupiter omnipotent, author of things as of kings,
> Of all true gods the father and womb in one!

Chapter 11. Concerning the origin of logic.

Having demonstrated the origin of the theoretical, the practical, and the mechanical arts, we must now therefore investigate as well the derivation of the logical; and these I have left to the end because they were the last to be discovered. All the other arts were invented first; but that logic too should be invented was essential, for no man can fitly discuss things unless he first has learned the nature of correct and true discourse. For, as Boethius declares, when the ancients first applied themselves to searching out the natures of things and the essentials of morality, they of necessity erred frequently, for they lacked discrimination in the use of words and concepts: "This is frequently the case with Epicurus, who thinks that the universe consists of atoms, and who falsely maintains that pleasure is virtue. Clearly, such errors befell Epicurus and others because, being unskilled in argument, they transferred to the real world whatever conclusion they had reached by reasoning. This is a great error indeed, for real things do not precisely conform to the conclusions of our reasoning as they do to a mathematical count. In counting, whatever result obtains in the figures of one who computes correctly is sure to obtain in reality as well, so that if a count of one hundred is registered, one hundred objects will also necessarily be found as the basis for that count. In argument, however, such a relationship does not obtain with equal force, and whatever emerges in the course of a discussion does not find a fixed counterpart in nature, either. Thus it is that the man who brushes aside knowledge of argumentation falls of necessity into error when he searches out the nature of things. For unless he has first come to know for certain what form of reasoning keeps to the true course of argument, and what form keeps only to a seemingly true course, and unless he has learned what form of reasoning can be depended upon and what form must be held suspect, he cannot attain, by reasoning, the imperishable truth of things.

"Since, therefore, the ancients, having fallen often into many errors, came to certain conclusions and arguments which were false and contrary to each other; and since it seemed impossible, when contrary conclusions had been constructed concerning the same matter, either that both the conclusions which mutually inconsistent trains of reasoning had established should be true, or that there should be ambiguity concerning which train of reasoning should be credited, it was apparent that the true and whole nature of argument itself should be considered first. Once this was known, then they could also know whether the results discovered by argument were truly held. Hence, skill in the discipline of logic began—that discipline which provides ways of distinguishing between modes of argument and the trains of reasoning themselves, so that it can be known which trains of reasoning are sometimes true, sometimes false, which moreover are always false, and which never false." And so logic came last in time, but is first in order. It is logic which ought to be read first by those beginning the study of philosophy, for it teaches the nature of words and concepts, without both of which no treatise of philosophy can be explained rationally.

Logic is so called from the Greek word *logos*, which has a double sense. For *logos* means either word (*sermo*) or reason, and hence logic can be called either a linguistic (*sermocinalis*) or a rational science. Rational logic, which is called argumentative, contains dialectic and rhetoric. Linguistic logic stands as genus to grammar, dialectic, and rhetoric, thus containing argumentative logic as a subdivision. It is linguistic logic that we put forth after the theoretical, practical, and mechanical. It must not be supposed, however, that this science is called logical, that is, linguistic, because before its discovery there were no words, or as if men before its time did not have conversations with one another. For both spoken and written words existed previously, but the theory of spoken and written language was not yet reduced to an art; no rules for speaking or arguing correctly had yet been given. All sciences, indeed, were matters of use before they became matters of art. But when men subsequently considered that use can be transformed into art, and what was previously vague and subject to caprice can be brought into order by definite rules and precepts, they began, we are told, to reduce to art the habits which had arisen partly by chance, partly by nature—correcting what was bad in use, supplying what was missing, eliminating what was superfluous, and furthermore prescribing definite rules and precepts for each usage.

Such was the origin of all the arts; scanning them all, we find this true. Before there was grammar, men both wrote and spoke; before there was dialectic, they distinguished the true from the false by reasoning; before there was rhetoric, they discoursed upon civil laws; before there was arithmetic, there was knowledge of counting; before there was an art of music, they sang; before there was geometry, they measured fields; before there was astronomy, they marked off periods of time from the courses of the stars. But then came the arts, which, though they took their rise in usage, nonetheless excel it.

This would be the place to set forth who were the inventors

of the separate arts, when these persons flourished and where, and how the various disciplines made a start in their hands: first, however, I wish to distinguish the individual arts from one another by dividing philosophy into its parts, so to say. I should therefore briefly recapitulate the things I have said thus far, so that the transition to what follows may more easily be made.

We have said that there are four branches of knowledge only, and that they contain all the rest: they are the theoretical, which strives for the contemplation of truth; the practical, which considers the regulation of morals; the mechanical, which supervises the occupations of this life; and the logical, which provides the knowledge necessary for correct speaking and clear argumentation. And so, here, we may not incongruously understand that number "four" belonging to the soul—that "four" which, for reverence of it, the ancients called to witness in their oaths, whence we read:

> "By him who gave the quaternary number to our soul!"

How these sciences are comprised under philosophy, and again what they themselves comprise we shall now show, briefly repeating first the definition of philosophy.

Suggestions for Further Reading

Taylor, J. *The Didascalicon of Hugh of St. Victor*. New York, 1961; *FCC* vol. II, 175-178; *EG* 169-171.

The Universities

Universities are a creation of the Middle Ages. It is difficult to assign any specific date for their foundation. In fact, like Topsy, they seem to have "just growed"; and when eventually they were issued formal charters, these merely recognized what was an already existing state of affairs. In the year 1200, for example, the great University of Paris received a charter from Philip Augustus; in 1215, its statutes were approved by the papal legate, Robert de Courçon; but for all practical purposes the schools of Paris had for some time previously existed as a "university," in the sense of an institution dedicated to higher learning, possessed of a teaching faculty, and open to all qualified scholars and students. Oxford was founded a little later than Paris; but again, there were certainly schools at Oxford in the early part of the twelfth century, although the university did not become a legal entity until later. The term "university" in the Middle Ages denoted not a handsome campus and venerable old buildings, but rather the body of professors and students studying together at a certain city; while the charter—normally granted by papal or imperial authority—formally constituted them as a corporation with specified rights, privileges, and immunities. Reprinted below are a number of documents in which are spelled out some of the "rights, privileges, and immunities" attaching to the great medieval University of Paris. Included also are some other documents touching on university life at Paris.

❁

RULES OF THE UNIVERSITY OF PARIS, 1215 *

Chartularium universitatis Parisiensis, I, 78-79.

Robert, cardinal legate, prescribes the mode of lecturing in arts and in theology, indicates what books the masters of arts should not read, formulates the discipline of the scholars and the state of the university generally.

Robert, servant of the cross of Christ by divine pity cardinal priest of the title, St. Stephen in Mons Caelius, legate of the apostolic see, to all the masters and scholars of Paris eternal greeting in the Lord. Let all know that, since we had a special mandate from the pope to take effective measures to reform the state of the Parisian scholars for the better, wishing with the counsel of good men to provide for the tranquillity of the scholars in the future, we have decreed and ordained in this wise:

No one shall lecture in the arts at Paris before he is twenty-one years of age, and he shall have heard lectures for at least six years before he begins to lecture, and he shall promise to lecture for at least two years, unless a reasonable cause prevents; which he ought to prove publicly or before examiners. He shall not be stained by any infamy, and when he is ready to lecture, he shall be examined according to the form which is contained in the writing of the lord bishop of Paris, where is contained the peace confirmed between the chancellor and scholars by judges delegated by the pope, namely, by the bishop and dean of Troyes and by P. the bishop and J. the chancellor of Paris approved and confirmed. And they shall lecture on the books of Aristotle on dialectic old and new in the schools ordinarily and not *ad cursum*. They shall also lec-

* Reprinted by permission of Columbia University Press, New York, from L. Thorndike, *University Records and Life in the Middle Ages*, 1944.

ture on both Priscians ordinarily, or at least on one. They shall not lecture on feast days except on philosophers and rhetoric and the quadrivium and *Barbarismus* and ethics, if it please them, and the fourth book of the *Topics*. They shall not lecture on the books of Aristotle on metaphysics and natural philosophy or on summaries of them or concerning the doctrine of master David of Dinant or the heretic Amaury or Mauritius of Spain.

In the *principia* and meetings of the masters and in the responsions or oppositions of the boys and youths there shall be no drinking. They may summon some friends or associates, but only a few. Donations of clothing or other things as has been customary, or more, we urge should be made, especially to the poor. None of the masters lecturing in arts shall have a cope except one round, black and reaching to the ankles, at least while it is new. Use of the pallium is permitted. No one shall wear with the round cope shoes that are oramented or with elongated pointed toes. If any scholar in arts or theology dies, half of the masters of arts shall attend the funeral at one time, the other half the next time, and no one shall leave until the sepulture is finished, unless he has reasonable cause. If any master in arts of theology dies, all the masters shall keep vigils, each shall read or cause to be read the Psalter, each shall attend the church where is celebrated the watch until midnight or the greater part of the night, unless reasonable cause prevent. On the day when the master is buried, no one shall lecture or dispute.

We fully confirm to them the meadow of St. Germain in that condition in which it was adjudicated to them.

Each master shall have jurisdiction over his scholar. No one shall occupy a classroom or house without asking the consent of the tenant, provided one has a chance to ask it. No one shall receive the licentiate from the chancellor or another for money given or promised made or other condition agreed upon. Also, the masters and scholars can make both between themselves and with other persons obligations and constitutions supported by faith or penalty or oath in these cases: namely, the murder or mutilation of a scholar or atrocious injury done a scholar, if justice should not be forthcoming, arranging the prices of lodgings, costume, burial, lectures and disputations, so, however, that the university be not thereby dissolved or destroyed.

As to the status of the theologians, we decree that no one shall lecture at Paris before his thirty-fifth year and unless he has studied for eight years at least, and has heard the books faithfully and in classrooms, and has attended lectures in theology for five years before he gives lectures himself publicly. And none of these shall lecture before the third hour on days when masters lecture. No one shall be admitted at Paris to formal lectures or to preachings unless he shall be of approved life and science. No one shall be a scholar at Paris who has no definite master.

Moreover, that these decrees may be observed inviolate, we by virtue of our legatine authority have bound by the knot of excommunication all who shall contumaciously presume to go against these our statutes, unless within fifteen days after the offense they have taken care to emend their presumption before the university of masters and scholars or other persons constituted by the university. Done in the year of Grace 1215, the month of August.

RULES FOR DETERMINATIONS IN ARTS, 1252

STATUTES OF THE ARTISTS OF THE ENGLISH NATION CONCERNING BACHELORS OF ARTS WHO ARE TO DETERMINE DURING LENT

Chartularium universitatis Parisiensis, I, 227-30.

This selection depicts in detail the exercise of determining or Determinations, prolonged public disputations during Lent by which the candidates for the licentiate, each in his own classroom, gave proof of their ability. For further discussion of this institution as it developed subsequently the reader may consult Rashdall, I (1936),

450-56. Incidentally the required texts in logic are listed, and explicit mention is made of the "university of artists" with its rector and common chest, and of the four Nations into which the university was divided with their proctors and statutes such as the present selection.

In the year since the Incarnation, 1251, the masters of the English nation, teaching in arts at Paris and for the good of the university and of learning taking multifold measures, and by God's grace continuing in the future without diminution, decreed by their common counsel and that of good men the form noted below for bachelors in arts determining in Lent, as is the custom. In the first place the proctor, touching the Bible, shall select two persons whom he believes qualified to choose examiners of those determining, who, touching the Bible, shall swear that without hate or love of any person or any part of their nation, they will choose three masters, whom they know to be strict and qualified in examining faithfully, more intent on the promotion and advantage of the university, less susceptible to prayer or bribe. These three when chosen shall similarly swear on the Bible that they will faithfully examine and proceed with rigor of examination, licentiating the worthy and conducting themselves without hate of any person or group of their nation, also without envy or any rancor of mind or other sinister perturbation. Moreover, those who have insufficient standing in the examination and are unworthy to pass they shall fail, sparing no one, moved neither by prayer nor bribe nor fear nor love or any other occasion or indirect favor of persons.

The masters presenting candidates, moreover, and the bachelors themselves shall give personal security that they will make no entreaties on behalf of bachelors nor seek favor from the examiners or from the nation or from the university, either by themselves or through others, but will accept the simple statement of the examiners. By the same token, if it happens that bachelors are failed, that they will not bring contumely or complaints or threats or other evils against the examiners, either by themselves or through others, because they ought to suppose that the examiners have acted according to their consciences and good faith for the honor of the university and the nation.

Moreover, a bachelor coming up for the licentiate in arts at Paris should be twenty years old or at least in his twentieth year, and of honorable life and laudable conversation. He should not have a cope without a hood of the same cloth, nor a hood with knots. He should not wear a mitre on his head in the classrooms while he is determining. If he has the right to the tonsure, he may have the tonsure, nor may he or should he be blamed on this account. Also before he is admitted to examination he shall give personal security that he has his own classroom of a master qualified to teach in it throughout Lent, and has his own master under whom he seeks the license of determining, or a bachelor about to incept in arts at the latest before Lent, in whose classroom he will determine. Further, that he has attended lectures in arts for five years or four at least at Paris continuously or elsewhere in a university of arts. Further, that he has heard the books of Aristotle on the Old Logic, namely, the *Praedicamenta* and *Periarmeniae* at least twice in ordinary lectures and once cursorily, the *Six Principles* at least once in ordinary lectures and once cursorily, the three first books of the *Topics* and the *Divisions* once in ordinary lectures or at least cursorily, the *Topics* of Aristotle and *Elenci* twice in ordinary lectures and once at least cursorily or if not cursorily at least thrice in ordinary, the *Prior Analytics* once in ordinary lectures and once cursorily, or, if he is now attending, so that he has heard at least half before Lent and is to continue, the *Posterior Analytics* once in ordinary lectures completely. Also that he shall have heard *Priscian minor* (books 17-18) and the *Barbarismus* twice in ordinary lectures and at least once cursorily, *Priscian major* (books 1-16) once cursorily. Also he shall have heard *De anima* once or be hearing it as aforesaid. Also he shall give satisfaction that he has diligently attended the disputations of masters in a recognized university for two years and for the same length of time has answered as required concerning sophisms in class. Also he shall promise that he will respond to question for a full year from the beginning of one Lent to the beginning of the next.

If, moreover, a bachelor shall be found sufficiently qualified in knowledge according to the examiners and shall not have completed the required number of years or books or lectures, the nation reserves to itself the power to dispense with these, as shall seem expedient to it. And in such case only it shall be permissible for his master to petition the nation for him.

Also if, after the exercise of cursory lectures has been made and finally completed, he shall have transgressed in the said exercise in any way, he shall in no case be admitted to the examination for determination. Nor similarly shall a master, whether now teaching or not, who, after the said exercise has been made as stated and finally confirmed by the masters, shall have transgressed in the said exercise, be accepted as presenting a bachelor, until full satisfaction shall have been made to the rector or proctors for the university by the master or the bachelor who has transgressed.

Also the bachelor licensed to determine shall begin to determine at the latest on the next day after Brandons. If he shall not have begun to determine then, he shall not be allowed to do so during Lent. And from the said Monday he shall determine continuously till the middle of Lent, unless he shall have lawful cause excusing him. And then let it be licit for no one to determine for him as substitute, unless such substitute has the license to teach in arts at Paris or has determined elsewhere through Lent or is licensed to determine in that present Lent, always providing that the same shall have determined continuously from the said Monday following Brandons until the middle of Lent. Also if a bachelor shall have been licensed to determine in the arts at Paris in one year and from a legitimate cause shall have failed to determine in that Lent in which he was licensed, which sometimes happens, he may afterwards determine in some subsequent Lent, regularly however and as others do, but he shall not substitute for others unless he shall have first determined during Lent in a fixed place. Also, until he shall have paid for the university a sum such and so great as he offered for personal security, and another for the nation, he shall not be given license to determine. Also if at the latest he shall not have been licensed before the last Sunday before Lent, he shall not be admitted later that year to the examination for determination.

Also, it shall be enjoined on him that all through Lent, and thereafter so long as he shall belong to the faculty of arts as student or teacher, he shall obey the mandate of rector and proctor in lawful and honorable matters. Also he shall not give drinks except on the first day he begins to determine and the last, unless this is done by the permission of the rector or the proctor of his nation, who can give him a dispensation in this regard as shall seem expedient to them, considering nevertheless the many factors about the determiners which are here involved.

Also, the examiners shall diligently collect from the bachelors the money to be paid to the university and nation and faithfully keep what is collected, and at the summons of the rector and proctors of the four nations deposit it at the day set in the common chest of the university of artists. Also the money received for the nation they shall deposit in the common chest before the Sunday after Ash Wednesday. Also none of the said examiners can by himself, without his associates deputed with him for determinations, license anyone or presume alone to examine.

Also, in addition to the aforesaid, after the candidates shall have been licensed, let them be present every Friday at the Vespers of the blessed Virgin and at mass the Saturday following, until Palm Sunday, under the penalty by which masters are bound.

But inasmuch as by this form it is not right nor will be for rich or poor, noble or ignoble, to put it off later, if they do not appear to seek license of determining in the aforesaid manner, therefore, to notify them it is provided by the masters that the present form be twice announced in classes each year, so that the first time it shall be read in the classrooms of masters between Purification and Lent, and the other time between the feast of St. Remy and All Saints or thereabouts, when there shall be a general meeting. Moreover, individual masters shall be bound on their honor to observe this ordinance. Also, however, if anyone is found acting contrary to the said ordinance, he shall be suspended from lecturing for a month.

COURSES IN ARTS, PARIS, 1255

Chartularium universitatis Parisiensis, I, 277-79.

In the year of the Lord 1254. Let all know that we, all and each, masters of arts by our common assent, no one contradicting, because of the new and incalculable peril which threatens in our faculty—some masters hurrying to finish their lectures sooner than the length and difficulty of the texts permits, for which reason both masters in lecturing and scholars in hearing make less progress—worrying over the ruin of our faculty and wishing to provide for our status, have decreed and ordained for the common utility and the reparation of our university to the honor of God and the church universal that all and single masters of our faculty in the future shall be required to finish the texts which they shall have begun on the feast of St. Remy at the times below noted, not before.

The Old Logic, namely the book of Porphyry, the *Praedicamenta, Periarmeniae, Divisions* and *Topics* of Boethius, except the fourth, on the feast of the Annunciation of the blessed Virgin or the last day for lectures preceding. *Priscian minor* and *major, Topics* and *Elenchi, Prior* and *Posterior Analytics* they must finish in the said or equal time. The *Ethics* through four books in twelve weeks, if they are read with another text; if *per se,* not with another, in half that time. Three short texts, namely *Sex principia, Barbarismus,* Priscian on accent, if read together and nothing else with them, in six weeks. The *Physics* of Aristotle, *Metaphysics,* and *De animalibus* on the feast of St. John the Baptist; *De celo et mundo,* first book of *Meteor-*

ology with the fourth, on Ascension day; *De anima,* if read with the books on nature, on the feast of the Ascension, if with the logical texts, on the feast of the Annunciation of the blessed Virgin; *De generatione* on the feast of the Chair of St. Peter; *De causis* in seven weeks; *De sensu et sensato* in six weeks; *De sompno et vigilia* in five weeks; *De plantis* in five weeks; *De memoria et reminiscentia* in two weeks; *De differentia spiritus et animae* in two weeks; *De morte et vita* in one week. Moreover, if masters begin to read the said books at another time than the feast of St. Remy, they shall allow as much time for lecturing on them as is indicated above. Moreover, each of the said texts, if read by itself, not with another text, can be finished in half the time of lecturing assigned above. It will not be permitted anyone to finish the said texts in less time, but anyone may take more time. Moreover, if anyone reads some portion of a text, so that he does not wish, or is unable, to complete the whole of it, he shall read that portion in a corresponding amount of time.

If a bachelor shall incept before the feast of St. Denis, he may end his lectures with those resuming on the feast of the blessed Remy. Those who begin after the feast of St. Denis shall finish their texts by as much later as they began later than others. Each in good faith shall according to his estimate portion out his text proportionally to the time allowed for his lectures. Further, no one shall be allowed to give more than two ordinary lectures, nor to make them extraordinary, nor to give them except at the ordinary hour and in ordinary wise.

Moreover, from the feast of St. John the Baptist till the feast of St. Remy each shall arrange his lectures as shall seem most convenient for himself and his auditors. Also no one shall presume to give more than two cursory lectures on any day when lectures are held, nor more than three on a day when there are not regular lectures, nor to begin any course until he has finished the preceding course, unless he shall have been detained by serious illness over fifteen days or shall have been out of town for good reason more than fifteen days, or if the scholars do not want to hear him further. Also, no one shall be permitted to deliver any lectures on the days of the apostles and evangelists or on the three days immediately following Christmas, Easter, and Pentecost, or after the third hour on the eve of those three days. These things, moreover, we have decreed and ordained to be observed inviolate. Let no one, therefore, infringe this page of our ordinance or rashly go against it. But should anyone presume to attempt this, let him know that he will incur the wrath of the whole university and suspension of lectures for a year. In testimony and support of which thing we have decreed that the present letter be sealed with the seals of the four nations by their consent. Given in the year 1254 on the Friday before Palm Sunday.

❁

CRIMINAL CLERKS AT PARIS, 1269

PROCLAMATION OF THE OFFICIAL OF THE EPISCOPAL COURT OF PARIS AGAINST CLERKS AND SCHOLARS WHO GO ABOUT PARIS ARMED BY DAY AND NIGHT AND COMMIT CRIMES: JANUARY 11, 1269

Chartularium universitatis Parisiensis, I, 481-82.

The official of the court of Paris to all the rectors of churches, masters and scholars residing in the city and suburb of Paris, to whom the present letters may come, greeting in the Lord. A frequent and continual complaint has gone the rounds that there are in Paris some clerks and scholars, likewise their servants, trusting in the folly of the same clerks, unmindful of their salvation, not having God before their eyes, who, under pretense of leading the scholastic life, more and more often perpetrate unlawful and criminal acts, relying on their arms: namely, that by day and night they atrociously wound or kill many persons, rape women, oppress virgins, break into inns, also repeatedly committing robberies and many other enormities hateful to God. And since they attempt these and other crimes relying on their arms, we, having in mind the decree of the supreme pontiff in which it is warned that clerks bearing arms will be excommunicated, also having in mind that our predecessors sometimes excommunicated those who went about thus, and in view of the fact that this is so notorious and manifest that it cannot be concealed by any evasion and that their proclamation was not revoked, wishing to meet so great evils and to provide for the peace and tranquility of students and others who wish to live at peace, at the instance of many good men and by their advice do excommunicate in writing clerks and scholars and their servants who go about Paris by day or night armed, unless by permission of the reverend bishop of Paris or ourself. We also excommunicate in writing those who rape women, break into inns, oppress virgins, likewise all those who have banded together for this purpose. No less do we excommunicate all those who have known anything about the aforesaid, unless within seven days from the time of their information, after the proclamation issued against the aforesaid has come to their notice, they shall have revealed what they know to the said reverend bishop or ourselves and have submitted to fitting emendation. Nevertheless we specially reserve to the lord bishop or ourselves the right to absolve clerks excommunicated for the aforesaid reasons.

But inasmuch as some clerks and scholars and their servants have borne arms in Paris, coming there from their parts or returning to their parts, and likewise certain others, knowing that clerks, scholars and their servants have borne arms in Paris, fear that for the said reasons they have incurred the said penalty of excommunication, we do declare herewith that it neither is nor was our intention that those clerks, scholars and their servants should be liable to the said sentence who, coming to Paris for study and bearing arms on the way, on first entering the city bear the same to their lodgings, nor, further, those, wishing to return home or setting out on useful and honest business more than one day's journey from the city of Paris, who have borne such arms going and returning while they were outside the city. We further declare that in the clause in which it is said, "We excommunicate all those who have known anything about the aforesaid," etc., we do not understand that word, *aforesaid,* to refer to all and each of the aforesaid but to the clauses immediately preceding, namely, concerning those who rape women, break into inns, oppress virgins and those who band together for these ends. Moreover, you shall so observe the present mandate that you cannot be charged with or punished for disobedience. Given in the year 1268 A.D., the Friday following Epiphany.

EARLY STATUTES OF THE SORBONNE

Chartularium universitatis Parisiensis, I, 505-14.

In the first part, where the first personal pronoun is used, Robert de Sorbonne (1201-1274), the founder of the college about 1257, appears to be speaking and the statutes seem therefore to date before 1274. At first merely a college for students of theology, the Sorbonne in the sixteenth and seventeenth centuries came to be a designation for the faculty of theology, while since the nineteenth century the name has been applied to the entire university. The following regulations furnish a detailed picture of how such an institution was run, except that it should be kept in mind that the fellows were theological students and so older and maturer than the average residents in colleges at Paris.

I wish that the custom which was instituted from the beginning in this house by the counsel of good men may be kept, and if anyone ever has transgressed it, that henceforth he shall not presume to do so.

No one therefore shall eat meat in the house on Advent, nor on Monday or Tuesday of Lent, nor from Ascension day to Pentecost.

Also, I will that the community be not charged for meals taken in rooms. If there cannot be equality, it is better that the fellow eating in his room be charged than the entire community.

Also, no one shall eat in his room except for cause. If anyone has a guest, he shall eat in hall. If, moreover, it shall not seem expedient to the fellow to bring that guest to hall, let him eat in his room and he shall have the usual portion for himself, not for the guest. If, moreover, he wants more for himself or his guest, he should pay for it himself. But if in the judgment of the fellow who introduces him the guest be a person of consequence or one through whom the house might be aided or the fellow promoted, then the said fellow may invite one or two others to entertain the guest and do him honor. These shall similarly have the portions due them from the community but always without loss to the community.

Also, no one resident in town shall eat in the house except in hall, and if he eats in a private room for cause, he shall scrupulously give his excuse before the bearer of the roll.

Also, if three or less were bled, they may have one associate who has not been bled. If they number more than three and less than eight, they may have two who have not been bled. If eight or more have been bled, then they may have three who have not been bled and who shall have their portions. If, however, more were not bled than as has been said, they shall have nothing from the common table.

Also, those who have been bled may eat in a private room for three days if they will, for as is said in the thirty-third chapter of *Genesis,* "On the third day the pain of a wound is worse."

Also, when fellows eat in private rooms, the fragments are collected lest they be lost and are returned to the dispenser who puts them in the common repository for poor clerks.

Also, the fellows should be warned by the bearer of the roll that those eating in private rooms conduct themselves quietly and abstain from too much noise, lest those passing through the court and street be scandalized and lest the fellows in rooms adjoining be hindered in their studies.

Also, those eating in private rooms shall provide themselves with what they need in season as best they can, so that the service of the community may be disturbed as little as possible. But if there are any infringers of this statute who are accustomed to eat in private rooms without cause, they shall be warned by the bearer of the roll to desist, which if they will not do, he shall report it to the master. If, moreover, other reasons arise for which anyone can eat in a private room, it shall be left to the discretion of the roll-bearer and proctors until otherwise ordered.

Also, the rule does not apply to the sick. If anyone eats in a private room because of sickness, he may have a fellow with him, if he wishes, to entertain and wait on him, who also shall have his due portion. What shall be the portion of a fellow, shall be left to the discretion of the dispenser. If a fellow shall come late to lunch, if he comes from classes or a sermon or business of the community, he shall have his full portion, but if from his own affairs, he shall have bread only.

Also, if a fellow eats in pension five days or less, he shall be a guest; but if he eats in town, he shall pay no less than if he had eaten in the house.

Also, whenever a fellow eats in town, whether he informs the household or not, he shall pay the whole pension and extras, and this in order that fellows may be discouraged from frequent eating in town.

Also, all shall wear closed outer garments, nor shall they have trimmings of vair or grise or of red or green silk on the outer garment or hood.

Also, no one shall have loud shoes or clothing by which scandal might be generated in any way.

Also, no one shall be received in the house unless he shall be willing to leave off such and to observe the aforesaid rules.

Also, no one shall be received in the house unless he pledges faith that, if he happens to receive books from the common store, he will treat them carefully as if his own and on no condition remove or lend them out of the house, and return them in good condition whenever required or whenever he leaves town.

Also, let every fellow have his own mark on his clothes and one only and different from the others. And let all the marks be written on a schedule and over each mark the name of whose it is. And let that schedule be given to the servant so that he may learn to recognize the mark of each one. And the servant shall not receive clothes from any fellow unless he sees the mark. And then the servant can return his clothes to each fellow.

Also, no outsider shall be placed on pension without permission of the master, nor shall he eat or sleep in the house as a guest more than three or four days without his permission.

Also, it is ordained that those who have lived in the house at the expense of the house until they could provide for themselves shall within a short time prepare and dispose themselves to progress in public sermons through the parishes, in disputations and lectures in the schools; otherwise they shall be totally deprived of the benefits of the house. And it may be they were able to do this by virtue of privilege: nevertheless I give them warning in all charity. Moreover, concerning those who are newly received or about to be admitted it is ordained that unless they have made progress in sermons, disputations and lectures as aforesaid within seven years from the time of their admission, they shall similarly be deprived. And if it should by chance happen that someone from fear of losing his pension should try to undertake to lecture on some text incautiously, unprepared, incompetent or unworthy, that he shall not be permitted to do so because of the scandal to others, unless by the judgment and testimony of the more advanced students in the house he be deemed competent and fitted to lecture.

Also, I wish, counsel, and decree that on fast days from All Saints to Lent those on pension in the house shall not eat except at Vespers and after all the day's lectures are over.

Also, for peace and utility we propound that no secular person living in town—scribe, corrector or anyone else—unless for great cause eat, sleep in a room, or remain with the fellows when they eat, or have frequent conversation in the gardens or hall or other parts of the house, lest the secrets of the house and the remarks of the fellows be spread abroad.

Also, no outsider shall come to accountings or the special

meetings of the fellows, and he whose guest he is shall see to this.

Also, no fellow shall bring in outsiders frequently to drink at commons, and if he does, he shall pay according to the estimate of the dispenser.

Also, no fellow shall have a key to the kitchen.

Also, no fellow shall presume to sleep outside the house in town, and if he did so for reason, he shall take pains to submit his excuse to the bearer of the roll.

Also, no fellow in the presence of outsiders shall propose in hall anything pertaining to the society except the word of God, which no one shall presume to impede but all shall hear in silence him who proposes it.

Also, no women of any sort shall eat in the private rooms. If anyone violates this rule, he shall pay the assessed penalty, namely, sixpence.

Also, no fellow shall send any dish outside the house, except by the consent of the person who has charge of them.

Also, if anyone has spoken opprobrious words or shameful to a fellow, provided it is established by two fellows of the house, he shall pay a purse which ought to belong to the society.

Also, if one of the fellows shall have insulted, jostled or severely beaten one of the servants, he shall pay a sextarium of wine to the fellows, and this wine ought to be *vin supérieur* to boot.

Also, no one shall presume to take a dish or tray either at lunch or dinner except as it is passed to him by the provost and his helpers or the servants. Moreover, he who has done otherwise shall be penalized two quarts of wine. And therefore each provost should be diligent in serving the fellows well.

Also, at the deliberations of the fellows each shall peacefully remain silent until he has been called upon by the prior, and after he has had his say, he shall listen to the others calmly.

Also, no one shall form the habit of talking too loudly at table. Whoever after he has been warned about this by the prior shall have offended by speaking too loudly, provided this is established afterwards by testimony of several fellows to the prior, shall be held to the usual house penalty, namely, two quarts of wine.

The penalty for transgression of statutes which do not fall under an oath is twopence, if the offenders are not reported by someone, or if they were, the penalty becomes sixpence in the case of fines. I understand not reported to mean that, if before the matter has come to the attention of the prior, the offender accuses himself to the prior or has told the clerk to write down twopence against him for such an offense, for it is not enough to say to the fellows, "I accuse myself."

In all these and other good customs let the roll-bearer of the house be careful; but if he shall be remiss, he shall be held to the penalty assessed in the house which transgressors incur.

PART II

For the peace and utility of the community we ordain thus as to electing petty proctors and concerning those things which pertain to the exercise of their office. First, that each fellow in entering the office of proctor be required to swear according to the form of oath which fellows usually take on their admission, namely, that he will exercise the office well and faithfully and diligently.

Also, that before they leave office they ought to choose and nominate proctors to succeed themselves a fortnight before the times hitherto observed. The times are these: feast of St. Bartholomew, Christmas, and Easter. Those named are required to answer to the society the same day, if they were named at dinner; if in the afternoon, next day at dinner under penalty of twelve pence so far as answering is concerned, if they have received notice of their election which ought to be given them by the electors. Moreover, if they have accepted at that time, they may straightway receive accounts, if they wish, and their predecessors shall be prepared to render accounts. But if they wish, they may wait till the limit, unless they or one of them wishes or intends to leave the house.

Concerning those leaving we ordain as follows, that if any

one of those elected wishes to leave the house within the fortnight mentioned, if he shall have accepted office he shall receive account before he leaves and his co-elect shall be required to receive the account with him and to exercise the functions pertaining to the office. Nor after they have accepted the office can they refuse it except because of a complete withdrawal from the house, without prospect of return within the term of the proctorship, or on account of grave infirmity or a lectureship, so that it cannot be fulfilled by themselves or by a suitable substitute. Because if one should allege complete withdrawal and then return within the term of the proctorship, he would be held to pay the same penalty as if he had not accepted the office. If, moreover, those chosen and nominated shall have refused the office, they shall pay the specified penalty, namely, ten solidi within a day after their nomination, which, if they fail to pay, for each day of delinquency each shall be charged sixpence and the proctors-electors shall keep choosing others until new proctors are had, in order that the utility of the society may not be retarded.

Moreover, this arrangement shall be observed in those who have held office before, that those shall be first chosen who are farthest removed from the time of office-holding, unless by the society or a majority thereof they be deemed unfit. If, moreover, of those older ones two held office before or paid the fine at the same time, it shall be at the discretion of the electors to choose this or that. Those, moreover, who were not proctors before, if they performed minor offices, namely, reading in hall, provostship, and office in chapel, can be elected indifferently at the electors' will and discretion.

To these functions, moreover, are held generally all petty proctors, forsooth to correct servants and to conduct themselves as follows: that they at any time with the persons here named, namely, the weekly reader, provost, clerk of the chapel and priest, without further deliberation of the other fellows can, or the majority of the said persons can, expel servants with or without salary on their conscience for the good of the fellows. And the proctors shall be held to provide other fit servants.

Also, all petty proctors generally shall be required at the beginning of their proctorship to receive and record a complete number of vessels and furniture from the preceding proctors and servants and to hand on to their successors a similar inventory. But if any are broken or lost, they ought first to repair these in order that the number of vessels may always remain certain and complete.

Besides, all vessels which are brought to table they should return clear, pure and whole at the end of their proctorship.

Also, they should attend to cleaning the chapel, hall, and court and cutting the grass at due seasons, and about all matters appertaining thereto.

Also, they should provide sufficiently concerning napkins and towels that the napkins be washed fresh and clean at least twice a week and the towels thrice.

Once a month they should propose what need to be provided for the fellows and, after deliberation by the greater and better part of the fellows who have remained in congregation, they should proceed in accordance with their deliberation. If no deliberation could be held, they should nevertheless provide for the needs of the society as shall seem to them expedient.

Also, they shall provide enough wine so that at least two hogsheads full are left at the close of their proctorship.

Also, the wines bought shall not be appraised by themselves but together with three or four fellows summoned for this and so precisely appraised according to the market where they are bought that equality shall be observed so far as possible.

Also, they shall call their rolls during octave in the accustomed manner and, when the time is up, they shall name the deficient for fines unless they wish to pay for them with their own money. But if they wish to pay for them, they should expunge them from the roll before the time expires. If they do not, they or the others shall be held to fines. The accustomed fine in the house is this, sixpence for absence for one day and a penny for each succeeding day of absence.

Also, they may use the money of the society for the personal utility of no one that results in damage or grievance to the society. Nay more, at the close of their proctorship they shall refund it all in cold cash or exchange, which if they do not do, they shall be charged ten solidi a day. But if they do not pay both fine and principal, for each day's delinquency each shall be penalized sixpence. If, moreover, they contumaciously delay in the said payments for a fortnight, then they shall be deprived of the fare of the society, the service of the domestics, and everything else in our power, without holding any further deliberation.

Moreover, if in some makings of change something has been lost and in others gained, the gain shall not be taken to distribute, unless first the lost has been restored.

Also, if any bad investment has been made in any debts through some unexpected cause and in some exchanges something has been made which ought to be distributed, let that bad debt be reckoned in the distribution and made up from the gain which was taken from the money of the society, and this in order that the fellows to whom the distribution ought to be made shall be more concerned about the recovery of the debt and that the money which is designated for the use of the society may always remain intact.

Along with these general requirements for all petty proctors are some special ones for certain of them, namely those who were elected at Easter: to provide concerning servants at the feast of St. John or concerning the preceding if they were fit, and to receive pledges anew, and to inquire into, to reduce to writing, and to leave to their successors the names of their sureties, the streets in which they dwell, and their standing. If they bring in new ones, they are required to do the same. And before they are hired outright and in full, they are tested for eight or fifteen days as is customary and those approved by the whole society or at least a majority are kept. Moreover, in accordance with the custom of Paris their sureties go surety for them with this added or specified that, if the servants for whom they swear contract debts which were credited to them from reverence for the house and society without the consent or knowledge of the fellows, if the servants should leave the house without paying, the sureties will be held for those debts. Moreover, those servants who are engaged shall take oath according to the form given them.

Also, the said proctors should provide wood for the hall and kitchen for a year, unless by vote of the fellows the time shall be extended after the feast of St. Bartholomew.

Also, to provide for all needs of the society which fall within the time of their proctorship.

Moreover, those of the feast of St. Bartholomew[1] are required to provide wood unless it has been provided by others and for the making of verjuice unless their predecessors have attended to it, and especially to do what should be done in vintages of *salinato, rapeto* and other wines as far as the money will go.

Those, moreover, of Christmas are required to make provision for Lent of peas, beans, spices and other things as the time requires.

Also, the same are required to make in the accustomed way a collection for common expenses, namely, wood for the hall, the service of domestics, sheets, towels and other things of the sort, having summoned four or five discreet fellows a little after Christmas, in order that the collection may be fully attended to before Brandons at least. Moreover, the fellows residing for the year personally in the house or the absent who have those answering for them in the house shall alone contribute to the collection. If, however, others who were absent through the year wish for some reason to contribute to the collections and if they have property in the house, they may contribute in this way, that the amount be beyond the sum to be placed in the collection, so that always without debts the money assigned to the society in the accounts of the proctors remain an integral whole, both in annual income and cold cash, lest by lack of cash money and reason of debts the utility of the society be retarded. Those not paying the col-

[1] The proctors would seem to have been elected thrice a year, at Easter, on St. Bartholomew's (August 24), and at Christmas.

lection shall be held at the stated term to the customary fine which we estimate at twelve pence for delinquency of one day, and one penny for each subsequent day of default.

In what we have said about fines for those not paying the rolls and collections and all other dues, in which particular fellows are bound to the society, we intend to bind both absent and present by the same law, so that they may be careful before they leave to inquire what obligations they have and to pay them, or at least leave other fellows in their place to answer for them and give satisfaction as carefully as they would for themselves.

PART III

These are the duties of the janitor. First he is required to reply courteously to every comer, and, if such a person asks for some fellow of the house, he is required to seek him and call him, unless the caller be some scholar for whom some fellow of the house has specially told him that he may have free access to his room.

When, moreover, the janitor goes to find some fellow in his room or elsewhere, he shall close the door after him. If the caller is a man of note, he shall allow him to wait in the court. If not, he shall remain between the two gates.

Also, the janitor is required to keep clean the entire court within and without and all the street so far as our house extends, and the walks and steps and all the rooms of the fellows and also the common passage to the private rooms, to provide water for the lavatory and keep the lavatory clean inside and out.

Also, he shall serve no one eating or drinking in a private room, unless after curfew when the gate is locked with a key, which key he is to carry with him.

Also, under no circumstances shall he go to town for anyone. But if for some urgent need of his own he has to go to town, he is required to have someone of the house to guard the gate, which if he does not do and the gate is found unguarded, he shall forfeit sixpence from his salary as penalty.

Also, he shall under no circumstances linger in the kitchen nor shall he do anything there.

Also, after curfew he must close the great gate and at the sign of St. James always open it and always keep the keys with him. If anyone of the house has to leave before the hour, he must rise and close the gate after him. If, moreover, any persons are accustomed to enter after the aforesaid hour or anyone to go out before, he is required by his oath to report this to the prior. Similarly, if he sees any faults in the domestics, or any of the goods of the house carried outside by anyone, he is required to reveal this. Also, if he sees any outsider carrying anything out of the house under his garment, he shall not permit him to leave, unless someone from the house accompanies him to the gate.

Also, at lunch he shall have the portion of a fellow without wine; at dinner however he shall have bread and soup as much as is deemed enough for him once, and a half trayful of the fragments remaining after the fellows are served and the domestics have their share. Also each day he shall have a pint of wine.

Moreover, he ought always to eat these at the gate while the fellows are at table. Moreover, he should reserve nothing in his room but return the fragments for the common benefit of clerics. If he shall have transgressed these provisions, let the prior himself correct him. If, by the testimony of the fellows or the majority of them he is found incorrigible, the prior may freely expel him.

His salary is twelve solidi.

REGULATION OF BOOKSELLERS, PARIS, 1275

Chartularium universitatis Parisiensis, I, 532-34.

The university of masters and students at Paris as a perpetual reminder. Since that field is known to bring forth rich fruit, for which the care of the farmer *colonus* provides painstakingly in all respects, lest we, laboring in the field of the Lord to bring forth fruit a hundredfold in virtues and science, the Lord disposing, should be molested or impeded, especially by those who by a bad custom hang about the university of Paris for the sake of gain, which they make in mercenary works and assistance, we ordain by decree and decree by ordinance that the stationers who vulgarly are called booksellers (*librarii*), shall each year or every second year or whenever they shall be required by the university, give personal oath that, in receiving books to sell, storing, showing, and selling the same and in their other functions in connection with the university, they will conduct themselves faithfully and legitimately.

Also, since some of the aforesaid booksellers, given to insatiable cupidity, are in a way ungrateful and burdensome to the university itself, when they put obstacles in the way of procuring books whose use is essential to the students and by buying too cheaply and selling too dearly and thinking up other frauds make the same books too costly, although as those who hold an office of trust they ought to act openly and in good faith in this matter, which they would better observe if they would not simultaneously act as buyer and seller, we have decreed that the same booksellers swear, as has been stated above, that within a month from the day on which they receive books to sell they will neither make nor pretend any contract concerning those books to keep them for themselves, nor will they suppress or conceal them in order later to buy or retain them, but in good faith, immediately they have received the books or other things, they will offer them for sale at an opportune place and time. And if they shall be asked by the sellers, they shall estimate and state in good faith at how much they really believe the books offered for sale can be sold at a just and legitimate price, and they shall also put the price of the book and the name of the seller somewhere on the book so that it can be seen by one looking at it. They shall also swear that, when they sell the books, they will not assign or transfer them entirely to the purchasers nor receive the price for them until they have communicated to the seller or his representative what price he is going to receive, and that concerning the price offered for the book they will tell the pure and simple truth without fraud and deceit, nor otherwise in any way shall they attempt anything about their office by cupidity or fraud, whence any detriment could come to the university or the students.

Also, while the laborer is worthy of his hire, which too he licitly seeks by civil law (*Proxenetica*), since nevertheless the standard which should be maintained in such matters is frequently exceeded by the booksellers, we have decreed that the stationers swear that they will not demand for books sold beyond four pence in the pound and a smaller quantity *pro rata* as their commission, and these they shall demand not from the seller but the purchaser.

Also, since many damages come from corrupt and faulty exemplars, we have decreed that the said booksellers swear that they will apply care and pains with all diligence and toil to have true and correct exemplars, and that for exemplars they shall not demand from anyone anything beyond the just and moderate rent or gain or beyond that which shall have been assessed by the university or its deputies.

Also, we have decreed that, if perchance the said booksellers shall be unwilling to swear to the aforesaid or any of the aforesaid, or after having sworn shall have committed fraud in connection with them, or shall not have diligently observed them all and each, not only shall they be utterly ousted from the grace and favor of the university but also henceforth they shall not have the liberty of exercising the office which they exercised before on behalf of the university. So that no master or scholar shall presume to have any business or contract whatever with the said booksellers, after it has been established that the said booksellers have committed a violation of the aforesaid rules or any one of them. But if any master or scholar shall presume to contravene this, he shall be deprived of the society of the masters and scholars until he shall have been reinstated by the university itself. Acted on after deliberation and decreed are these in the general congregation at Paris in the convent of the Friars Preachers and sealed with the seal of the university on December 8, 1275 A.D.

MASTERS TO KEEP A RECORD OF THEIR SCHOLARS, PARIS, 1289

Chartularium universitatis Parisiensis, II, 35-36.

To all who shall see the present letters the rector of the university of Paris and the masters, one and all, of the faculty of arts send greeting in the Son of the glorious Virgin. Noticing that because of the multitude of scholars of our faculty we do not know the names of many and cannot discern who are good and legitimate or factitious, and some pretend to be scholars of our faculty in order to enjoy the privileges and liberties of the same and of the university and be defended, who as putrid members should be separated from such a body or association (for both on account of such the faculty is often defamed and belittled by many, and the masters of the said faculty are in various ways impeded from study and contemplation, and good scholars because of the association and influence of such persons withdraw from the university so that they are unable to acquire the precious pearl of science): we, wishing to apply a wholesome remedy for this, decree and also ordain that the masters of the said faculty, one and all, and also those who are about to incept in the said faculty, shall be required by oath, all fraud aside, to write down the names of their own scholars, that they may have knowledge of the good ones and be able to give lawful testimony about them in place and time and on any necessary occasion, so that only those attending the university and conducting themselves towards masters as is customary and statutory with respect to both ordinary and cursory lectures and making due compensation for the same, if they are so required by their own masters, and if the masters shall be content with them, shall enjoy the privileges and liberties of the faculty and university and may be promoted to particular functions in the said faculty. But fictitious scholars and hangers-on of the university shall not be written down with the good, but as useless shall be removed from the bosom and association of the faculty, so that without dispensation from the faculty they may not be promoted to any standing in the faculty nor enjoy the privileges and liberties of the university but shall be held for non-scholars by each of the masters by their oaths. Moreover, we will and ordain that every rector upon his institution shall be bound by oath that he will cause the present ordinance to be circulated annually through the classes of the masters by a sworn servitor. Nevertheless, we wish that, these things notwithstanding, all statutes and privileges of the university be inviolably observed in all and by all. And that these may have firm validity, the seals of the four nations are affixed to the present schedule. Given in the year of the Lord 1289, at St. Julien le Pauvre, the Friday following the feast of St. Denis.

HAZING OF FRESHMEN FORBIDDEN, PARIS, 1340

Chartularium universitatis Parisiensis, II, 496.

This is the ordinance made by the deputies of the university as to the punishment of those hazing Freshmen. First, that no one, of whatever faculty he be, shall take any money from a Freshman because of his class or anything else, except from roommates with whom he lives or as a voluntary gift, under penalty of deprivation of any honor now held or to be held from the university, which deprivation from now as from then the said university brings upon any offending thus.

. . .

Fourth, the said university bids the said Freshmen, under penalty of deprivation of any honor from the said university, that if anyone does any wrong to them by word or deed on account of their class, they shall straightway secretly reveal this to the proctors and deans of the faculties who in general congregation shall be required to reveal the names of the offenders by their oaths.

Fifth, the said university enjoins all those renting lodgings to students that, as soon as they know that any corporal violence or threats have been made to a Freshman because of his class, they immediately reveal this, as above directed.

Sixth, the said university enjoins all who have taken its oaths that, if they know any person or persons to have inflicted bodily violence or insult, threats and any injury upon Freshmen because of their class, they reveal this by their oaths as quickly as they can, as has been said above.

❁

METHOD OF LECTURING IN THE LIBERAL ARTS PRESCRIBED, PARIS, DECEMBER 10, 1355

Chartularium universitatis Parisiensis, III, 39-40.

In the name of the Lord, amen. Two methods of lecturing on books in the liberal arts having been tried, the former masters of philosophy uttering their words rapidly so that the mind of the hearer can take them in but the hand cannot keep up with them, the latter speaking slowly until their listeners can catch up with them with the pen; having compared these by diligent examination, the former method is found the better.

Wherefore, the consensus of opinion warns us that we imitate it in our lectures. We, therefore, all and each, masters of the faculty of arts, teaching and not teaching, convoked for this specially by the venerable man, master Albert of Bohemia, then rector of the university, at St. Julien-le-Pauvre, have decreed in this wise, that all lecturers, whether masters or scholars of the same faculty, whenever and wherever they chance to lecture on any text ordinarily or cursorily in the same faculty, or to dispute any question concerning it, or anything else by way of exposition, shall observe the former method of lecturing to the best of their ability, so speaking forsooth as if no one was taking notes before them, in the way that sermons and recommendations are made in the university and which the lectures in other faculties follow. Moreover, transgressors of this statute, if the lecturers are masters or scholars, we now deprive henceforth for a year from lecturing, honors, offices and other advantages of our faculty. Which if anyone violates, for the first relapse we double the penalty, for the second we quadruple it, and so on. Moreover, listeners who oppose the execution of this our statute by clamor, hissing, noise, throwing stones by themselves or by their servants and accomplices, or in any other way, we deprive of and cut off from our society for a year, and for each relapse we increase the penalty double and quadruple as above.

We further ordain for the stricter observance of this statute that each rector at his creation shall swear and make his successor swear to proceed to the punishment of such transgressors.

Those incepting and determining shall similarly swear to observe the statute, otherwise they shall not be admitted to the degree of bachelor and of master. Moreover, we do not mean by this statute to exclude dictation of any determination, notable treatise, or exposition which youths sometimes write in the street of Straw on feast days, provided nevertheless that it is not done at the time of the university sermon. Nor shall anyone venture to give dictation of this sort outside the classrooms of the said faculty, otherwise he will incur the same penalty to which we have subjected auditors. Neither by this do we mean to derogate from the ancient statutes as to the method of lecturing, but these shall remain in force.

In testimony of which we have thought fit to append to the present statute the seal of the rector together with the seals of the four nations, namely, the Gallican, of Picardy, Normandy, and England and their consent together with the mark and subscription of the undersigned notary. Given and enacted in the congregation of our faculty, non-teachers as well as teachers, specially convoked for this at St. Julien-le-Pauvre in Paris, 1355 A.D., the tenth day of the month of December, ninth indiction, the third year of the pontificate of our most holy father in Christ and lord, Innocent by divine providence the sixth, pope, there being present for this the discreet men, Jacobus de Pavillione, John Candellus, Peter Guerardus, Conrad Almannus, serving the university of Paris in the said faculty of arts and many other witnesses called together specially for this.

And I, Simon called Quinimo, a clerk of the diocese of Tulle, public notary by apostolic and imperial authority, etc.

Suggestions for Further Reading

Rashdall, H. H. *The Universities of Europe in the Middle Ages.* 3 vols. Oxford, 1942; Rait, R. S. *Life in the Mediaeval University.* Cambridge, 1912; Kibre, P. *The Nations in the Mediaeval University.* Cambridge, 1948; *FCC* vol. II, Ch. XXII; *EG* 246-250.

Robert Grosseteste

Robert Grosseteste was born around 1175 at Stradbroke, in Suffolk, England. He studied law, medicine, and theology at Oxford, and quite possibly at Paris, as well. After completing his studies, Grosseteste joined the teaching faculty at Oxford, and there organized the philosophy curriculum. Sometime around 1221 he was made Chancellor of Oxford, the first to hold that post. Throughout his life, Grosseteste remained a member of the secular clergy; nonetheless, he served as first reader in theology at the Franciscan House of Studies at Oxford from 1229 to 1235. In this capacity Grosseteste exerted tremendous influence upon the subsequent development of Franciscan thought.

In the year 1235, Grosseteste was made Bishop of Lincoln, then the largest single diocese in England. From this date, until his death eighteen years later, he worked energetically not only in the affairs of his diocese, but as well in the cause of church and state reform. Grosseteste had been present at Runnymede in 1215 at the historic signing of *Magna Charta* by King John. Later, in his office as Bishop of Lincoln, he was to come into conflict on a number of occasions with King John's successor, Henry III.

Despite his intensely demanding academic, political, and ecclesiastical commitments, Grosseteste managed to compose an immense number of writings. In addition to many original scientific and philosophical works—most of which display very clearly a strong Augustinian influence—Grosseteste made important contributions to the learning of his time through his numerous translations of Greek writers into Latin. He translated Aristotle's *Ethics,* portions of *On The Heavens and the Earth,* and the works of several other writers as well.

We present below, in its entirety, Grosseteste's important and influential little tract, *On Light.* It is a typical example of the philosophic-scientific synthesis which came to characterize the Oxford thinkers of this period. Further, this tract was to serve as an important source of the "light metaphysics" of the Middle Ages.

ROBERT GROSSETESTE ON LIGHT*

The first bodily form (*forma*), which some call corporeity, I judge to be light. For light (*lux*) of itself diffuses itself in every direction, so that a sphere of light as great as you please is engendered instantaneously (*subito*) from a point of light, unless something opaque stands in the way. But corporeity is that upon which of necessity there follows the extension of matter into three dimensions, although nevertheless each of them, namely corporeity and matter, is a substance which in itself is simple and has no dimensions at all. But it was impossible for form which in itself is simple and without dimensions to bring in everywhere dimensions into matter which is similarly simple and without dimensions, except by plurifying itself and by diffusing itself instantaneously in every direction and, in its diffusion of itself, extending matter, since form cannot abandon matter, because it (form) is not separable, and because matter cannot be emptied of form. Still, I have put forward light as being that which of itself has this operation, namely to plurify itself and to diffuse itself instantaneously in every direction. Therefore whatever does this work either is light itself or is a doer of this work insofar as it participates in light, which does this of itself. Therefore corporeity either is

---

* Reprinted by permission from *On Light, or The Incoming of Forms,* translated by C. G. Wallis and published by the St. John's Bookstore, Annapolis, 1939.

light itself or is the doer of the said work and the bringer of dimensions into matter, insofar as it (corporeity) participates in light itself and acts through the virtue of the light itself. But it is impossible for the first form to bring dimensions into matter through the virtue of a form which follows upon it (the first form). Therefore light is not a form which follows upon corporeity, but is corporeity itself.

Further: men of good sense judge that the first bodily form is more worthy than all the later forms and of a more excellent and noble essence and more like the forms which stand separate. But light is of a more worthy and more noble and more excellent essence than all bodily things; and it is more like the forms which stand separate—and they are the intelligences—than all bodies are. Therefore light is the first bodily form.

Therefore as light, which is the first form created in first matter and which of itself plurifies itself everywhere infinitely and stretches out equally in every direction, could not abandon matter, it drew out matter, along with itself, into a mass as great as the world-machine (*machina mundi*) and in the beginning of time extended matter. Nor could the extension of matter occur through a finite plurification of light, because a simple which is plurified a finite number of times does not engender a quantum (*simplex finities replicatum quantum non generat*), as Aristotle shows in the DE COELO ET MUNDO. But if a simple is plurified an infinite number of times, it necessarily engenders a finite quantum, because the product of the infinite plurification of something exceeds infinitely that by the plurification of which it was produced. Yet a simple is not exceeded infinitely by a simple, but a finite quantum alone exceeds a simple (thing) infinitely. For an infinite quantum exceeds a simple (thing) infinitely an infinite number of times. Therefore, if light, which in itself is simple, is plurified an infinite number of times, it necessarily extends matter, which is similarly simple, into dimensions of finite magnitude.

But it is possible than an infinite sum of number be related to an infinite sum (of number) in every numeric ratio and also in every non-numeric ratio. And there are infinites which are greater (*plura*) than other infinites; and infinites which are smaller (*pauciora*) than other infinites. For the sum of all numbers both even and odd is infinite; and so it is greater than the sum of all even numbers, which nevertheless is infinite. For (the sum of the even and odd) exceeds the sum of the even by the sum of all the odd numbers. Moreover the sum of the numbers doubled continuously from unity is infinite; and similarly the sum of all the halves corresponding to these doubles is infinite. And the sum of these halves is necessarily half of the sum of their doubles. Similarly the sum of all numbers tripled from unity is three times the sum of all the thirds corresponding to the triples. And the same thing is clear in all species of numeric ratio, since the infinite can be proportioned to the infinite in any of these ratios.

But if there are posited the infinite sum of all the doubles continuously from unity and the infinite sum of all the halves corresponding to those doubles and if unity or any finite number you please be taken away from the sum of the halves; then, after the subtraction has been made, the ratio of two to one will no longer hold between the first sum and the remainder of the second sum. Nor does any numeric ratio hold any longer; because, if, in the case of a numeric ratio after a subtraction has been made from the lesser sum, some other numeric ratio still holds, it is necessary that what has been subtracted be an aliquot part or the aliquot parts of an aliquot part of that from which it has been subtracted. But a finite number cannot be an aliquot part or the aliquot parts of an aliquot part of an infinite number. Therefore, if a number is subtracted from the infinite sum of halves, a numeric ratio no longer holds between the infinite sum of doubles and the remainder of the infinite sum of halves.

Therefore, since this is the case, it is manifest that light, by its infinite plurification, extends matter into lesser finite dimensions and into greater finite dimensions according to any ratios you please, that is, numeric and non-numeric ratios. For if light by an infinite plurification of itself extends matter to a dimension of two cubits, then by twice this same infinite plurification it extends matter to a dimension of four cubits, and by half of that same plurification it extends matter to the dimension of one cubit; and so on according to the other numeric and non-numeric ratios.

This, I presume, was the concept (*intellectus*) of the philosophers who lay down that all things are composed of atoms and who say that bodies are composed of surfaces, and surfaces of lines, and lines of points.—And this opinion does not contradict the one which lays down that magnitude is composed only of magnitudes; because "whole" is said in as many senses as "part" is. For in one sense "half" is said to be "part" of the "whole," because, if taken twice, it gives the whole: and in another sense the side is part of the diameter, not because, if taken an aliquot number of times, it gives the diameter; but because, if taken an aliquot number of times, it is exceeded by the diameter. And in another sense the angle of tangency is said to be part of a right angle, into which it goes an infinite number of times, and nevertheless, if subtracted from it a finite number of times, lessens it; and in still another sense a point is part of a line, into which it goes an infinite number of times, and, if substracted from it a finite number of times, does not lessen it.

Accordingly, returning to my discourse, I say that by the infinite plurification of itself equally in every direction light extends matter everywhere equally into the form of a sphere; and it follows of necessity that in this extension the outmost parts of matter are more extended and more rarefied than the inmost parts near the center. And since the outmost parts will have been rarefied to the utmost, the inner parts will still be susceptible of greater rarefaction.

Therefore light in the aforesaid way, extending matter into the form of a sphere and rarefying the outmost parts to the utmost, has in the farthest sphere fulfilled the possibility of matter and has not left matter susceptible of any further impression. And so the first body is perfected in the boundary of the sphere and is called the "firmament," having nothing in its composition except first matter and first form. And accordingly it is the most simple body as regards the parts constituting its essence and greatest quantity, and it does not differ from the genus body except that in it (the most simple body) matter has been fulfilled merely by the first form. But the genus body, which is in this and in other bodies and which has first matter and first form in its essence, abstracts from the fulfillment of matter by the first form and from the diminishing of matter by the first form.

And so, when the first body, which is the firmament, has been fulfilled in this way, it spreads out its lumière (*lumen*) from every part of itself to the center of the whole. For since light (*lux*) is the perfection of the first body and plurifies itself from the first body naturally, then of necessity light is diffused to the center of the whole. And since light is the whole which is not separable from matter in the diffusion of itself (light) from the first body, it extends the spirituality of the matter of the first body. And thus there proceeds from the first body "lumière," which is a spiritual body or, as you may prefer to say, bodily spirit. And this lumière in its passage does not divide the body through which it passes; and accordingly it passes instantaneously (*subito*) from the first body of the heavens down to the center. And its passage is not as if you were to understand that something one in number passes instantaneously from the heaven to the center—for that is quite impossible; but its passage occurs through the infinite plurification of itself and the infinite engendering of lumière. Therefore the lumière itself, which has been spread out from the first body to the center and gathered together, has assembled the mass (*molem*) existing within the first body. And since the first body, as being fulfilled and invariable, could not now be diminished, and since no place could become void, it was necessary in the very assembling that the outmost parts of the mass should be extended and dispersed. And thus a greater density came about in the inmost parts of the said mass, and the rarity was increased in the outmost parts. And the power of the lumière which was doing the assembling and the power of the lumière which in the very assembling was doing the separating were so great that they subtilized and rarefied to the utmost the outmost parts of the mass contained within the first body. And so there came to be in the outmost parts of the said mass "the second sphere," which is fulfilled and not receptive of any further impression. And thus there is the fulfillment and perfection of the second sphere: for lumière is engendered from the first sphere, and light, which in the first sphere is simple, is twofold in the second sphere.

But just as the lumière engendered by the first body has fulfilled the second sphere and within the second sphere has left the mass denser, so the lumière engendered from the second sphere has perfected the "third sphere" and within the third sphere has left the mass still denser by the assembling. And this assembling which disperses (*congregatio disgregans*) proceeded in this order, until the "nine celestial spheres" were fulfilled, and until the most dense mass—which was matter for the four elements, was assembled within the ninth and lowest sphere. But the lowest sphere, which is the sphere of the "moon," also engenders lumière from itself, and by its lumière it has assembled the mass contained within itself, and by this assembling it has subtilized and dispersed its outmost parts. Nevertheless the power of this lumière was not so great that by its assembling it dispersed its outmost parts to the utmost. On that account imperfection and the possibility of the reception of assembling and dispersal has remained in every part of this mass. And the highest part of this mass was not dispersed to the utmost but by its dispersal was made to be fire, and it still remained matter for the elements. And this element, engendering lumière from itself and assembling the mass contained within itself, has dispersed its outmost parts, but with a smaller dispersal of the fire itself; and thus it has brought forth "fire." But fire, engendering lumière from itself and assembling the mass contained within, has dispersed its outmost parts, but with a smaller dispersal of itself. And thus it has brought forth air. Air also, engendering from itself a spiritual body or bodily spirit and assembling that which is contained within itself and by this assembling dispersing its outer parts, has brought forth "water" and "earth." But because more of this assembling virtue than of the dispersing has remained in water, the water together with the earth has remained weighty.

So in this way the thirteen spheres of this sensible world were brought into being; namely the nine celestial, which cannot be altered, increased, generated, or corrupted, because fulfilled; and the four spheres which exist in the contrary manner and can be altered, increased, generated, and corrupted, because unfulfilled. And that is clear, since every higher body by reason of the lumière engendered from itself is the form (*species*) and perfection of the body following. And just as unity is potentially every number which follows, so the first body by the plurification of its own lumière is every body which follows.

The earth however is all the higher bodies because the higher lumières are summed up in itself; on that account the earth is called Pan by the poets—that is, All; and it is named Cybele, as if *cubile,* from the cube, that is, from solidity; because the earth is the most greatly compressed of all bodies, that is, Cybele the mother of all the gods; because, though the higher lumières are gathered together in the earth, nevertheless they are not arisen in the earth by their own operations, but it is possible for the lumière of any sphere you please to be drawn forth from the earth into act and operation; and so whatever god you wish will be born of the earth as if of some mother. But the middle bodies have two relations. For indeed they are related to the lower bodies as the first heaven is to all the remaining; and to the higher bodies, as the earth is to all the other bodies. And thus in some certain modes all the remaining bodies are in any one of them.

And the form (*species*) and perfection of all bodies is light (*lux*): but the light of the higher bodies is more spiritual and simple, while the light of the lower bodies is more bodily and plurified. Nor are all bodies of the same form or species, though they have originated from a simple or plurified light; just as all numbers are not of the same form or species, though nevertheless they are produced by the greater or lesser plurification from unity.

And in this discourse it is quite clear what the meaning is of those who say, "all things are one by the perfection of one light," and the meaning of those who say, "those things which are many are many by the diverse plurification of the very light."

But since the lower bodies participate in the form (*formam*) of the higher bodies, the lower bodies, by its participation in the same form as the higher body, is receptive of movement from the same bodiless motor virtue, by which motor virtue the higher body is moved. Wherefore the bodiless virtue of intelligence or soul, which moves the first and highest sphere by the daily movement, moves all the lower celestial spheres by the same daily movement. But insofar as they are lower, they receive this movement more weakly, because insofar as a sphere is lower, the first and bodily light in it is less pure and more weak.

But though the elements do participate in the form of the first heaven, nevertheless they are not moved in a daily movement by the mover of the first heaven. Although they participate in that first light, nevertheless they do not yield to the first motor virtue, since they have that light as impure, weak, and distant from its purity in the first body, and since they have density of matter too, which is the beginning (*principium*) of resistance and unyieldingness. Nevertheless some think that the sphere of fire wheels around in the daily movement, and they take the wheeling around of comets as a sign of that, and they say moreover that this movement continues as far as the waters of the sea, so that the tides of the sea may come from it. But nevertheless all who rightly philosophize say that the earth is exempt from this movement.

Moreover, in the same way because the spheres after the second sphere—usually named the eighth in the upward reckoning—participate in its form, all share in its movement which they have as their own in addition to the daily movement.

But because the celestial spheres are fulfilled and are not receptive of rarefaction or condensation, the light in them does not bend the parts of matter away from the center, in order to rarefy them, or toward the center, in order to condense them. And on that account the celestial spheres themselves are not receptive of movement upward or downward, but only of circular movement from the intellectual motor virtue, which turns back its glance toward itself in a bodily fashion (*in sese aspectum corporaliter reverberans*) and makes the spheres themselves resolve in a circular bodily movement. But because the elements themselves are unfulfilled, rarefiable, and condensable, the lumière which is in them either bends away from the center, in order to rarefy them, or toward the center in order to condense them. And on that account they are naturally movable either upward or downward.

But in the highest body, which is the most simple of bodies, there are four things to be found, namely, form, matter, composition, and the composite. Now the form, as being most simple, has the place of unity. But on account of the twofold power of the matter, namely its ability to receive impressions and to retain them, and also on account of density, which has its roots in matter—and this twofold power belongs first principally to the number two—matter is duly allotted the nature of the number two. But the composition holds the number three in itself, because in the composition there are evident the formed matter and the materialized form and the thing about the composition which is its very own (*proprietos*) and found in any composite whatever as a third thing other than the matter and the form. And that which besides these three is properly the composite is comprehended under the number four. Therefore the number four is in the first body, wherein all the other bodies are virtually; and accordingly at the roots (*radicaliter*) the number of the other bodies is not found to be beyond ten. For when the number one of the form, and the number two of the matter and the number three of the composition and the number four of the composite are added together, they make up the number ten. On this account ten is the number of the bodies of the spheres of the world, because, although the sphere of the elements is divided into four, nevertheless it is one by participation in the terrestrial and corruptible nature.

From this it is clear that ten is the full number of the universe, because every whole and perfect thing has something in itself like form and unity, and something like matter and the number two and something like composition and the number three, and something like the composite and the number four. And it is not possible to add a fifth beyond these four. Wherefore every whole and perfect thing is a ten.

But from this it is evident that only the five ratios found between the four numbers one, two, three, and four, are fitted to the composition and to the concord which makes every composite steadfast. Wherefore only those five concordant ratios exist in musical measures, in dances, and in rhythmic times.

Suggestions for Further Reading

Crombie, A. C. *Grosseteste and Experimental Science.* Oxford, 1953; Sharp, D. E. *Franciscan Philosophy at Oxford.* Oxford, 1930; *FCC* vol. II, ch. XXIV; *EG* 261-265; *AAM* 118-124; *RMcK* vol. I, 259-287.

Albert the Great

Albert the Great was born at Lauingen in Swabia, Germany, in 1206. He pursued his higher studies at the University of Padua, famed for its liberal-arts program. While at Padua, he entered the Dominican Order in 1223. After completing his studies at Padua, Albert returned to Germany where he taught at Hildesheim, Freiburg, Ratisbon, Strasburg, and Cologne. From Cologne, Albert was sent to the University of Paris, where he received the doctoral degree in 1245. It was at Paris, from 1245 to 1248, that he had St. Thomas Aquinas as his student. In 1248, Albert returned to Cologne to organize the *studium generale* and he took Aquinas with him to serve as second professor and *magister studentium.* Starting a few years later, Albert's studies and work were to be interrupted intermittently because of ecclesiastical assignments. From 1254 to 1257 he served as Provincial of Teutonia, the German province of the Dominican Order. During this period, in 1256, he was ordered by Pope Alexander IV to attend the papal court at Anangi in order to defend the Mendicants against the secular clergy professors of the University of Paris. In 1260, the same Pope ordered him to become the Bishop of Regensburg, a position which he hastened to resign as soon as the Pope died in 1261. Thereafter, he returned to the Dominican Order. Due to the fact that he had once been a bishop, Albert was exempted in part from the control of the Order, leaving him free to use his time and his revenues as he saw fit. In 1263 his activities were again curtailed by appointment as a papal legate to preach a crusade in Germany and Bohemia. Subsequently, he lectured at Wurzburg and Strasburg. In 1270, he settled in Cologne, where—as also in 1252 and 1258—he made peace between the Archbishop of Cologne and the city. Four years later, 1274, he attended the Council of Lyons where he advocated the acknowledgment of Rudolph of Hapsburg as king of Germany. Thomas Aquinas had also been summoned to this Council, but died on the way—an event that was to have a marked effect upon the remainder of Albert's career. Albert was so attached to the memory of Aquinas that in 1277 when it was announced that Etienne Tempier, and others, desired to condemn the writings of Aquinas as too favorable to philosophers not of the faith, Albert—despite his advanced years—traveled all the way to Paris to defend the writings. After this, Albert returned to Cologne, where he died on November 15, 1280. Beatified by Pope Gregory XV in 1622, Albert was canonized by Pope Pius XI.

It was Albert's stated purpose to make intelligible to the Latins the major parts and instruments of philosophy by writing a book for every book that Aristotle had written, had planned to write, or should have written. The work which we shall present below clearly belongs to the latter class. Aristotle, in the *Categories* (or the *Predicaments,* as the work is sometimes called), lists ten categories: substance or essence, quantity, quality, relation, place, time, position, state, action or activity, affection or passivity. Of the ten listed, Aristotle treated only four at any length: substance, quantity, quality, and relation. Inasmuch as the *Categories* was a basic textbook in the medieval schools, the deficiency as regards extended treatment of the last six categories was bound to be corrected. The first writer to attend this task was Gilbert de la Porrée, whose *Book on the Six Principles* was adopted as a text-supplement to Aristotle's *Categories.* Reprinted below in its entirety is Albert's *Commentary* on Gilbert's influential and remarkable little tract.

❁

ALBERT THE GREAT ON THE SIX PRINCIPLES *

TREATISE I. CONCERNING FORM

Chapter 1. What is treated of, when a Book on the Six Principles is composed.

Although certainly the order of the predictables has been determined sufficiently in the *Predicaments,* as far as it belongs to the intention of the logician, nevertheless for easier instruction—in order that one may know concerning each, what they predicate, and how what is predicable generically and specifically and individually of each is ordered to one universal which is the first principle of all of them—we shall again determine particularly concerning the six, on which it was touched only briefly and by way of example in the book on the *Predicaments.* But just as in the book on the *Predicaments,* we have followed the theory of Aristotle, so in this book we follow Gilbert de la Porrée, who discovered those things which are treated concerning the six principles and who brought them together for an easier understanding of those things which were seen to have been stated succinctly in the book on the *Predicaments.* Although these things could have been omitted, nevertheless we have assumed this task because of the usefulness to students. For this account therefore we expound these things for the information of students—these things along with others.

Many indeed have assigned many reasons why contrariwise these six are called "principles," although the other four, which have been treated, have been called "predicaments."

---

* Translated especially for this volume by Professor J. P. Mullally, Queens College, New York, from the critical edition of P. B. Sulzbacher published at Freiburg under the title: *Albertus Magnus, Liber Sex Principiorum,* in 1954.

Certainly according to the teaching of Porphyry the ten primary genera are the ten principles of things, upon which every resolution of things depends, and which are the primary essences, constituting by their essentiality and containing in the ambit of their universality all the things which are objects capable of being ordered to a determination of a predicate or a subject. Their coordination, as we have said, must be treated of in the first part of logic, by virtue of the fact that reason only joins together that which previously it has compared, nor does it compare except what it has previously classified according to the nature of the comparables. Wherefore the way in which the ordination happens was first taught in the theory of Porphyry. But the ordination, according as it exists in the ordered, is taught in the theory of the book of the *Predicaments* and in the theory of the Six Principles and in the theory on Divisions.

But since every ordination of subjects and supposita happens in relation to a unit and depends on a unit, that on which the ordination depends in the greatest [degree], is first and the principle of all others. But it is called a genus insofar as it is the first formable subject in relation to the determination of everything contained in the form of a species and of an individual. Moreover it is called a principle insofar as it is the first [thing] constituting and essentiating all the things which belong to its coordination, in which from the point of view of act and understanding it is contained as the originating principle of their essences.

But although all the supreme genera are called principles in this way, nevertheless some are more and more properly called genera, and some rather principles. For substance, quantity and quality are rather called genera, by virtue of the fact that they are contained absolutely in their contents in act and understanding, which is a property of a genus, according to which it is a genus, to which a species is subject. In fact they are called principles from a consequent because they are not originating causes absolutely and as regards being, but rather conversely as regards being they are related to their inferiors as principled. But relation is a genus in the way in which the others are; but not so properly as the others can be or be called a principle because as regards being it is always founded on some other and, frequently, it is founded on other genera and the things belonging to the other genera.

But the remaining six are not properly called genera, because they do not affirm something contained in others absolutely as regards act and understanding, as is the case with relation to the nature of those things, as is obvious in the induction of each. For action does not affirm a nature [*quid*] contained in the substance of others, nor passion nor place nor time nor position nor habit; rather they affirm in some way that they are like a principle of that to which they belong. For action, because it is in "that which is acted," affirms a principle of that which is effected by the action. And as far as action is in the agent, it affirms a principle by which the agent effects that which he does. Similarly passion, because it is in the patient, affirms that by which the patient is moved in consequence of the form of the agent, but it does not affirm a nature [*quid*] which is part of the nature and substance of something. Therefore certainly passion by its very name does not affirm a genus; but rather a principle. Place [*ubi*] is a similar case, because this results from a locus, nor is locus a principle except of that which is in a locus. On the contrary the located is related to a locus, when it is in place [*ubi*]. And therefore place, since it has to do with what is extrinsic, whereas genus has to do with what is intrinsic to substance, is named a principle rather than a genus. It is all the very same way with regard to when [*quando*], which results from time. But time is the measure of motion. But motion is the act of that which is moved, moving it toward the form of the moving. And therefore when [*quando*], which is in that which is in time through a relation to time certainly does not name something which belongs to substance as a genus, rather it names a principle, through the motion of which, it [*quando*] is a measure. But position, which affirms an arrangement of parts in a locus and in a whole, also affirms a principle rather than a genus, because motion and action and passion changing those things to which they are related, are a cause of the order of parts in relation to the form of a whole. Therefore position does not affirm the nature [*quid*] of a thing in position, but in accordance with its name, that is "position," affirms a principle of existence of the whole, which is originated from the position of the parts in the whole and in the locus. Habit, relative to that of which it is a habit, affirms nothing which belongs to the nature of the habited according to which the genus is the nature [*quid*] belonging to that of which it is the genus, rather it affirms a principle of conservation of the habited. And on account of this, although the others affirm principles relative to the being of those [things] to which they belong, this last affirms a principle of conservation. And again they are called principles rather than genera. On this account also they are more forms, that is, remaining outside, than they are essences.

But these can be understood as follows: for either they are principles relative to being, or to well being. If relative to being: either from the point of view of the agent, and in this way there will be action, or from the point of view of that which is done, and this in two ways: namely, according to that which is recipient of the act of the agent, or according to the effect, which results from the act of the agent. If in the first way: either according to the action itself, which the patient receives, and in this way there is passion; or according to a measure extrinsically added. If according to a measure extrinsically added: either it is according to a measure of an action or a passion as such, and thus there is when [*quando*]; or according to a measure of the passive or of that which suffers, and thus there is where [*ubi*]. But if it is according to an effect, which the agent causes in the patient itself, then there is position. Because from the action of an agent and the passion of a patient the parts are situated in the passive relative to the reception of the form, which the agent impresses, and one part effectuated above and another below, and one right and another left, according to that which the power of the agent works in it. On the contrary, if one affirms a principle not relative to being, but to well being, then there is habit.

But although in this way by their names they affirm principles, nevertheless for their coordination, insofar as being is signified by the names, predicated and contained in act and understanding in that of which they are predicated, they affirm genera. And therefore by their names they affirm principles, and the things, which they signify, are genera.

But if anybody asks how this science, which treats of six, is one, it must be answered that these six are united in the intention of principle, and in this way nothing prevents there being one science of six.

Just as in the case of the others, so also in this case the method of Philosophy must be retained. For it is characteristic of a philosopher, as Aristotle says, only to accept a demonstrated statement, that is to say, passions and differentiae must be demonstrated as belonging to a subject and the parts of a subject so as to cause perfect knowledge of the things which are explained. Therefore the definitions of each of these must be posited, from which as from middle terms everything which must be taught is proved. For in this way the soul is perfected as regards the contemplative part, which is the ultimate of happiness itself, as Aristotle teaches in Book X of the *Ethics*.

But that which some say concerning art, whether philosophy evidently progresses after the fashion of an art, is foolish, because art only exists in the factive concerning external matter, since Aristotle says, that art is a factive principle with reason. In this way to make is not to do.

Chapter 2. Concerning form, what it is and how it is treated of here.

Therefore wishing to determine concerning the six principles, all of which are forms and as it were extrinsic to these things of which they are [the forms], by virtue of the fact that they do not belong to the being and substance of those things of which they are [the forms]—and form is spoken of, as Plato says, as if remaining without—it is necessary for us to begin with the determination of form, in order that it may be known, from what as from a primary genus they take [their] origin. For Boethius states in the beginning of the *De Trinitate,* that only those things are properly called forms which are separate. But those, which are in matter, are properly called images, by virtue of the fact that they have been produced in accordance with them by assimilation and imitation. But these which we call principles, are all outside the substance of those of which they are [the principles], just as action is outside the substance of the agent, and passion constitutes nothing of the substance of the patient. Also with relation to when [*quando*] and where [*ubi*], neither of which constitutes anything of the substance of those things which are in place and in time. Moreover, position is extrinsic on account of this, because it affirms an arrangement of the parts in place, and this is outside the substance of the parts and of the whole. But concerning habit there is no doubt that it is taken from what is extrinsic. Therefore, since all these remain extrinsic, all these share the predication of form in accordance with the name of form, and just as they are called principles, so also they are called forms.

But the form meant cannot be determined in this way, unless form is defined universally and through the definition the intention of form which is the object of our present attention is arrived at. Speaking generally therefore about form, we state, in accordance with that which the logician ought to state about the form, that the form is contingent relative to composition, consisting of a simple and immutable essence.

For here we are defining form in a logical definition. For speaking logically form is the intention, which fixes the formal being of the whole, and the very concept of the whole, as was stated in the theory Concerning the Universals (*De Universalibus*). But I say, that it fixes the formal being of the whole, whether this being be substantial, or accidental, whether it be potential being, or actual, just as "animal" affirms the potential being of the whole man, and "rational" affirms the actual being of the whole man. But "man" affirms the whole being composed of both. However, "white" affirms the accidental being of a whole, and the "risible" affirms the accidental being of the whole of an actuated nature and species.

But such being as this is only contingent in relation to composition, that is, to the composite or with respect to composition. Because if it happened to a part of a composition or a composite, it would not be predicable of the whole: nor could the concept be affirmed of the whole being. And I say "contingent," not that this form always happens, or *per accidens* comes to the composite in accordance with that which is the form; because thus it is species or accident or property or genus or differentia. And therefore it does not always happen to, rather sometimes it is substance. Rather therefore I say "happens" because the mode of receiving it, inasmuch as it is a concept of a whole, is always *per accidens* and always contingent. For there is a universal which is prior to a thing (*universale ante rem*), and this is a cause of a thing essentially or accidentally. And there is a universal which is in a thing (*in re*) and this is the substance of a thing or an accident disposed toward a substance. And there is a universal which is subsequent to a thing (*post rem*), and this is the universal separated from the thing itself by the intellect, and this happens to a thing and is accidental to a thing. For this is nothing if not the acceptance of a universal or of a form without the here and without the now, which is the acceptance of the thing simple and separate from the particular and the particulars. And in this way the form meant is the universal, which the intellect classifies in a genus and a species, and whose coordination it reduces to a predicament or to a principle. And in this way the form constitutes the formal being of a whole, accepted by the intellect, which it does not happen to accept in the nature of the form, which is the form of a part; for this form belongs to matter in the particular, and it is not predicable of a whole. Thus therefore the universal form, accepted for the substantial or accidental being of a whole, predicable of a whole and not of a part, is the form, which is contingent relative to composition.

But that which is added, that it exists "consisting of a simple essence," is [added] on this account, because such being, although it belongs to the composite whole, nevertheless has been grasped with a view to the form and not with a view to the matter. But it is not grasped with a view to the form, as a part of the composite, rather it is grasped with a view to form, according as it is the cause of the being of the whole, encompassing the whole and determining to being. And because that form is nothing if not the form, albeit it is of the whole, it therefore has in itself no principle of composition, rather it is a simple essence, although it is not an essence of the simple, but of the composite. For in this way matter is not a simple essence, because matter at least in potency has a part and a part. But form, neither in potency nor in act has a part and a part. Therefore this is proper to form but not to matter.

But if it is objected that species is a form, but yet has a part and a part, because it has a genus and a differentia, we answer that these parts are not divided in the species, because the very same thing which is in the genus as confused and indeterminate, is in the species specified and determined. Rather the genus affirms as confused and indeterminate, but the differentia as determining and the species as determined. But these do not differ in formal being, although they differ as the nature of the determinable differs from the nature of the determining and from the nature of the determined. For the determining differentia only determines through the formal, which is act, and determines the formal, which is potency. And the determined species only affirms the formal so determined. But if it affirmed something different, the genus would not be predicated of the species, nor would the differentia be predicated of the species. And therefore it is certain, that these three affirm what is formally the same. And because a differentia is in its genus as a capacity—and to be in another as a capacity according to the capacity of a formal cause is to be in it as regards inchoation; and inchoation of form and perfection are the same in the substance of the form, diverse in being—it [i.e. the differentia] is therefore one and the same in potency and act. Therefore that definition is one and not many. And according to what has been said, species is substantially a simple essence, although there are in it those [things] which differ in nature according to being. And therefore it is said, that form consists of a simple essence.

Moreover, it certainly is immutable, because nothing is changed from the point of view of mutation except matter, or a subject composed of matter and form. But form, according as it is a universal form, is neither of these, and therefore the essence is essentially immutable. Nevertheless it is changed accidentally, insofar as sometimes it is generated or corrupted according to the being which is in this or in that. But we are not speaking here of the change which is accidental. It is proved in another way, that the form which is a universal, whether it be accidental or substantial, is contingent relative to composition and it is not a composite. For such a form is not a composition or a composite, because each and every composite coming to another composite causes something greater either according to essence or according to quantity. But a form coming to composition does not cause something greater; therefore form is not a composite, but contingent to the composite or to composition.

Moreover that the form coming to the composite does not cause something greater, is proven both in the case of accidental form, and in the case of substantial form. Indeed in the case of the accidental, because the body in virtue of the fact that it is white, is not said to have been made greater or less, than if it were not white; but when it is white, it is said to be only altered. Also in the case of substantial [forms], because of the fact that the body and the soul joined together constitute a man, it is not stated that greater or less has been caused but the perfect in the form of the species.

Nevertheless this causes doubt, because the universal form coming to is a certain essence, and therefore that to which it comes, seems to have been increased from the point of view of the essence. To this one must answer, that the universal is posterior to that of which it is the universal, although the universal nature itself is prior to that of which it is predicated. And insofar as it is universal, it has only intentional being or, as Boethius says, conceptual, and this is not natural being. And therefore it adds nothing essential, rather it is a concept of that which is natural. But this is clear to understand from those things which have been stated more frequently in the theory of the Universals.

But because indeed the same thing happens to be mentioned concerning certain other things, which are not universal forms, that they evidently are simple essences in virtue of the fact that they are not composed of matter and form, as in the case of the soul of man, which is not composite in this way, therefore we stated in the definition: "consisting of an immutable essence." For in the soul of man according to the sensible part, which is in it, the alteration of contrariety according to the movements of the passions is found, for example, of sorrow and of joy. For although the movements of the passions of joy and of sorrow belong to the composite and not to the soul as subject, as Aristotle states in [Book] I of the *De Anima,* nevertheless, as Averroes states, in the case of these the soul coexperiences with the body, and thus is changed in some way. And therefore it is not form, as we are speaking here of form.

But still since, as some say, it is something which is subject to simplicity and is subject to no change, inasmuch as they affirm being in the case of that which is the soul of the world, which they say is simple and unchangeable, therefore in order that I might divide and distinguish this form concerning which we are speaking here, from all others, I have added: "contingent relative to composition." For it is a long and difficult [task] to determine concerning the soul of the world, what it is and how, and it belongs to the first philosopher according to the part in which a determination is made of the primary and universal causes. Nevertheless we state briefly, that it is not the first cause, nor is it any intelligence, rather [it is] the mover of the first mobile, the principle of life and of spatial movement for it. And according to this motion it is the cause of life and motion in everything, as is stated in the *Book on Causes* [*Liber de Causis*]. And this soul is not contingent relative to composition or to the composite, rather it is the form of one thing, that which is the first mobile. Wherefore it cannot be the form, which is the universal, because the universal is a form contingent relative to the composite, and it is not the form of a part, as has been stated very frequently. Therefore, the previously cited definition of the form will be a term. For that definition is called a term, which includes all the terms regarding the being of the thing defined. For this definition will be seen to contain neither anything superfluous nor less than suffices for to state the being of the form, if anyone would want to investigate subtly and not superstructively.

However, this must be noted, that those things which have been said, neither are true concerning the substantial form nor the accidental form, rather they are true concerning the form which is the universal, whether it be substance or accident, according as it is predicable as a genus or a differentia or a property or an accident in any genus whatsoever or in a principle of the predicables.

Chapter 3. Concerning a doubt, whether the form is immutable.

However, one experiences a doubt which is caused by what has been induced previously: for speaking about the form, inasmuch as it is common to accidental and substantial [form], and inasmuch as it is universal, predicable either essentially (*in quid*) or accidentally (*in quale*), because the form is indeed signified as the concept of the whole being of a thing, according to the manner in which the discourse also is a form, and whiteness predicated of that whiteness, and according to the manner in which formal reason and opinion are forms of the soul, predicated of this or that reason or opinion, hence in saying of such a form, that it is immutable, we come face to face with a number of objections. For one sees that many forms are changeable or mutable into contraries. For the same statement is susceptive of truth and falsity. For the statement that I am sitting is true while I am sitting and the same statement is false while I am not sitting. Similarly exactly the same whiteness is susceptive of clarity and obscurity. Also a formal reason or opinion is one susceptive of that truth which is in the thing and of the falsity which is not in the thing, although all these nevertheless are forms, concepts of a whole being and predicable of a whole, and yet they are contingents relative to composition.

But to this one answers that, just as was stated, the form exists consisting of an immutable essence. And that which is asserted of whiteness, is not as stated. For it is not the same whiteness which, as far as form is concerned, is susceptive of clarity and obscurity. Rather two whitenesses as regards being succeed each other in the subject, one of which is clearer and the other obscurer on account of the opacity and clarity of the subject. For there is no difference between saying that the whiteness is clear and saying that the subject or recipient is clear, since whiteness as regards one and the same being of whiteness is in the same way. For it is obscured and it is clarified by reason of the obscurity or clarity of the subject. And that which is more obscure is not the same in quantity of whiteness to that which is clearer. And similar to this is that which is said in Book V of the *Physics,* that health is not the same in the morning and in the evening, by virtue of the fact that the same equality of animal humours does not remain, although the susceptive of health is the same in the morning and in the evening, yet not under the same form of health.

Moreover similarly an argument or opinion numerically the same and a discourse numerically one are not susceptive of the truth or falsity, which is or is not in reality, by changing themselves, but rather, as the Philosopher says in the *Perihermeneias,* the statement, which is vocal, is a note and a sign of the passions, which are in the soul, passions which are caused in the soul by the received forms of them. And therefore truth in reason or in mind or in opinion is an adequation of things or of opinions or of concepts. Or falsity in mind or in opinion is an inequality of mind and things. Similarly truth in a statement is an adequation of a sign signifying the thing in a word and of the thing signified. Therefore as regards the true it is changed into the false not according to a mutation of itself, but rather as the signs are changed through the mutation of those things to which they are referred. In virtue of this therefore, that the thing signified is or is not, in virtue of this the mind or an opinion and a discourse are true or false without any change of the opinion or of the statement. And Boethius gives an example of this: If someone remains immobile and someone else, passing to the opposite side, is found at his right after having been at his left, without any change on his part, from only the movement of the other, he is referable to him, positionwise, as being to the right or to the left. But we have discussed these matters in other places.

However, here we must understand that the truth in a statement is twofold. For there is the truth of the sign, according as the sign is simply related to the act of the sign, and not related to signifying this or that, as that is called a true sign which does not deceive in the act of signifying. And, as Anselm proves, a statement does not lose this truth because of a change of the thing signified. For the statement that I sit is a true sign of the fact that I sit, whether I am sitting or I am not sitting; for it always signifies that I sit. And in this it does not deceive, by not signifying that rightly and truly, for, insofar as it is a sign, it has been made to signify that. For a true sign is that which signifies rightly that which it has to signify and does not deceive in this. But there is another truth in a sign related to signifying this and adequated to that, as the statement: "I sit" is adequated to the thing, while I am sitting. But this is changed by the mutation of the thing itself, and we are speaking here of this [truth], and not of the first; for the first remains unchangeable, as long as the sign remains as is. Indeed on account of this some thought the first truth to be one and the same for all true signs, although this may be doubtful, since the sign is right and true, when it signifies that which it has been made to signify by the first truth, establishing and ordering all. And thus, as regards the sign, the correctness of the sign is caused by its being related to its first exemplary cause. Nevertheless this relation can be reckoned by beginning from the first truth, and so it is one. Also it can be considered from the point of view of the related signs, and so it falls into a multitude, and thus is considered absolutely. Therefore absolutely it is many, and relatively it is one.

Chapter 4. What is the substantial and consequently what is the accidental.

But because every form, which is a whole and the concept of a whole being, which is predicated of something, either is substantial or accidental, it is necessary to speak here of the substantial, what it is, and consequently also to determine what the accidental is. Therefore we say that the substantial according to its name is that which has the mode of substance in being substantial; and this sometimes is a substance, and sometimes not a substance by nature, it nevertheless has the mode of substance. Indeed it is substance, when it is in the genus of substance, for example animal both is substance and substantial to man, and man both substance and substantial to Socrates. Similarly, rational is substantial to man and to Socrates. But sometimes it is not substance, yet having the mode of substance, as color is related to whiteness, and as quality is related to color, or a disgregated object of sight is related to whiteness, and as the extremity of brightness is related to color. For genus is substantial as matter, and differentia is substantial as form. Nevertheless substantial is spoken of in another way, namely, that which is in something as in an essential cause, as risible is called substantial to man, because it is in the nature of man as in an essential cause. And that neither is substance nor has the mode of substance in determining substance, but it has the mode of substance to the extent of belonging inseparably. Still the substantial is spoken of in a fourth way, that which belongs to the definitive nature in place of the differentia, although it constitutes nothing of the essence and the being of it, just as the nose is substantial to the pug-nosed, and the eye to the blind, and the tibia to the lame, and the back to a hump, and generally [speaking] a subject to its proper accident.

And because in this way that is sometimes called substantial which is not substance, yet having a certain mode of substance, Boethius affirmed as a consequence, that the substantial is a mean between substance and accident. But it is not a mean through a denial of each of the extremes, having been stated in accordance with the nature and being proper to itself, for such a mean cannot exist, by virtue of the fact that everything which is, is a substance or an accident according to the nature of its being. Rather it is a mean by virtue of this fact, that it shares something of each, as we have said; for it has the nature of an accident and the mode of a substance.

But the accidental is spoken of in opposite ways, namely that a nature is sometimes a substance and has the mode of an accident, as the extraneous which belongs to or fits on account of something else, as a sixth finger, which, although it be a substance, nevertheless because it is not caused by the form of the hand, but by an abundance of matter, is accidental as a consequence. Also the accidental is that which has the nature and mode of an accident, as the whiteness of Socrates, or that which does not belong in the definition and in whose definition a subject does not belong, and that which does not belong through an essential and proper cause. Therefore since the substantial and the accidental is spoken of in these ways, we say, that the substantial is that which confers being on composition, that is, on the composed from some composition. Moreover I say "that which confers being" as genus and matter, and as differentia or form on the composite, which is composed of genus and differentia or of matter and form. And I say "from some composition," because true composition for certain exists from matter and form, which are mutually distinct as to nature, and neither is a principle of the other. But a certain kind of composition and not composition absolutely exists from genus and differentia, for the differentia is in the genus essentially after the fashion of the imperfect, and the genus is a principle of it, from which it is educed by the active intellect, and for this reason it does not cause absolute composition. Therefore the defined by genus and differentia is one and not multiple. For it is the same in potency and act, and no other essence is a differentia unless it is contained in the formal potency of the genus. Therefore this substantial is present as in many, and it is impossible for this to be absent from that thing to which it is substantial.

But this is obvious in the case of what is formal, as reason belongs to man and sense to animal, or similes of these in other cases. And indeed an example exists in the case of accidents, for instance, a continuum exists in continua (a line, a surface and a body) and the discrete exists in the discrete (to be sure in a statement and in a number). But if that which was stated, is substantial, that which confers being on a thing, and that which cannot be absent from the being of a thing, then among the substantial principles one is like matter and the other like form. Just as indeed the body is substantial to man as matter, the soul is substantial to man as form; and in this way the body will be substantial to man and the soul likewise. And because logical or rational composition corresponds to natural composition, therefore also reason or the rational will be substantial to man and the genus animal likewise. But these and similars to these have been explained through treatment in the theory of the book which is entitled *On the Categories* [*De Categoriis*].

But it was necessary to say something about these here, because through these principles we grasp how certain things have to be classified in the six principles and certain things [have] to be excluded from the coordination of such. For whatever things depend upon any principle in such a way that the principle confers being on them, and that their being cannot exist without that principle, without doubt these are related to the coordination of such principles. But those which do not have reference to them except *per accidens,* are ordered to another as to a genus and a principle, or perhaps they are in one thing according to something and in another thing according to something. For nothing prevents one and the same thing from being in different predicaments according to the diversity of those things which are in it, of which one by chance is substantial, but the other accidental. As, for example, a bicubital white body, which in virtue of the fact that it is a body, is in substance; but in virtue of the fact that it is white, is in the quale of quality, and in virtue of the fact that it is bicubital, is in the quantum of quantity. But this has already been determined more often in other [works], both in the *Isagoge* and in the *Categories*. Consequently we introduced the substantial and the accidental here for this reason.

Chapter 5. Concerning the origin of forms, whether they exist by nature or from the operation of art.

Now a certain kind of form, whether it be substantial or accidental, which was understood as universal—and so is identical with the whole of which it is predicated—seems to be produced by nature, but another kind by an act or operation of an art. For reason or the rational is a form produced by nature in the rational itself. The same is also the case with accidental forms. For heat is a natural form produced by nature. Similarly also a different passion in the genus of quality, as color and odor and taste and such like, and health and sickness. For in all such it is clear that these forms, both substantial and accidental, exist by nature. On the contrary, other forms exist by an act or by our operation, as a house and a goblet and a couch and such like. But in the case of some things doubt exists, whether they begin by nature or by an act or by a work of art, as in the form of an incision, as when Esculapius or Hector is sculptured. The reason for the doubt in such cases is because it is seen from the fact that such forms are by nature, that art adds nothing to matter in such cases, and therefore that which belonged by nature, remains. For that which art produces in such, consists wholly in removing and separating certain parts from a subject. And because [what art produces] adds nothing to a work of art, it does not belong, it seems, to the work of art in what is molded. And therefore such forms seem to be by nature and not by art.

However to this one must say, that in such cases the subject of the form and the matter of the forms is not by an act or by a work of art. But that the forms be seen and appear is by an act or by an operation of art. For that which is in matter, is wholly by nature, to which nothing has been added by art, rather something has been separated from it. And if, from those things which are wholly natural, some things are separated and nothing is added to them, those things which are left, are natural and by nature. Therefore such a form according to all the things which are in it, seems to be by nature. But that [such a form] is perceived by sight as determined in such or such a way by lines, can only be by an act and operation of art, because nature has not produced such a determination of lines. But what is said has the same value as if one were to say, that the matter of a form exists by nature, but the form itself, according as the form is the determination of a quantum, exists by an act or an operation of art. And this is the truth, because although art adds nothing material, nevertheless by separating it contributes to the being of the form, in relation to whose formal being the separation of the parts contributes more than the addition of any matter. For we do not say that the form is such a nature [*quid*], that it has matter, from which it comes to be, but only in relation to which it comes to be. Moreover in relation to the formal being of the form the ablation or the separation of the parts confers more than the collation of any material parts.

But although we may speak in this way about the form of an incision which consists in the separation of parts of the subject, nevertheless it is certain, that whichever of such forms depends upon a conjunction and not only a separation, as the form of a house or a couch or a tripod and such like—because in them something artistic is made by means of an addition—those exist by an act and an operation of art and not of nature. Therefore one must speak in this way concerning the form of an incision, which form alone is actually produced by an incision of the parts. In this way therefore it is clear what things exist as the form of an incision. And an account of this Empedocles said that, in the case of all things which exist by art, nature is the matter, but form is an accident. For if the wood of a couch is planted, the couch will not sprout, rather the wood. Therefore since it is the nature from which the sprouting will sprout, the nature will be the wood, and not the form of art, which exists in the couch.

However, such a determination is not valid in the case of generals or universals, which are in many and belong to many, which are predicated of them. The general or universal essence of those things which are in many, predicated of them, cannot exist by an operation of art, because it is impossible for such an essence to exist by an operation of art, by virtue of the fact that every form of art is an accident and accidental. But such a form is substantial and belongs essentially [*per se*] to those things whose form it is. But still such a universal form does not seem to be caused by nature, for the reason that those things which are produced by the power of nature, seem to be caused by an act of creating and generating and they derive [their] origin from the creating or generating. But the end of creating or generating is always the particular and not the universal; therefore it is not by a work of nature, as it seems. Moreover, if one were to say, that creatures are universal and general forms of such a kind, it can be immediately evident to anyone, that this is not true, for since the end of creation or generation is not the universal but the particular, no reason or example can be assigned, how the general may be created or generated. Therefore, it is necessary to say, that forms of such a kind are natural and perfected by nature and not by an operation of art or by design.

But it seems that it must be said, that nature works secretly in such cases, and this is the particular nature. Indeed it intends and produces this in the agent and in the patient. But the universal, which orders this relative to divine being, intends the simple and the universal. And because the universal nature works in the particular, therefore, when a particular nature produces this, and because this is a man, the universal nature produces this in a man, and so on. And in this way as a consequence that which is universal is produced. And indeed this existing in that is a universal, although it is not a universal, insofar as it is in that, as was said in the theory Concerning the Universal (*De Universalibus*). But it is universal because of the natural capacity for existing in many or in the plural. But when matter is divided actually during generation, it is effected actually in many, and nature does this secretly.

However, nature is said to work secretly in these for two reasons, one of which is that acts always belong to particulars. And on account of that the particular nature operating is manifest. But when a particular nature operates, it only operates by virtue of the universal nature, which is hidden in it, and considered only by the intellect; and in this way the universal nature operates secretly. But the second reason is that what is operated by nature is the particular manifest to the senses. But that by which that having the form of a species and a nature exists, is hidden and as a consequence generated, and therefore here it generates this, and this is evident. But because here the generating is man, on this account also here man has been generated, because otherwise generation would not be univocal. And this is hidden as far as we are concerned, grasped by the intellect alone. And therefore we say that nature operates secretly in such cases. For just as from the conjunction of many having one reason for unity—as for example many horses or many men—a certain determination of distinction is effected, which is brought about with respect to the first things from which that conjunction happens, which goes beyond the discrete quantity of each and every one of those, so that all simultaneously are of a greater quantity than [that] of each one of those, so from the separation of the singulars, which are one in species and in genus, when they are compared to each other according to the form according to which they are essentially similar, one common to all is understood, which, however, is wholly in each one, which goes beyond the predication of each of the first things in this respect, that anything belonging to each one alone [is predicated] of one only, but that which constitutes the similarity of these, is predicated of many. Because of this all such universality is natural, because it proceeds from singularity, that is, from the essential similarity of singulars. And in this way singularity in one is the similar cause of universality. Moreover nature is the cause of such a singular. And therefore nature is the cause of universality—because whatever is a cause of a cause, is a cause of the caused—from that cause in some way. But singularity is coequated to creation or generation, because the end of creation and generation, is the singular.

However, speculating subtly in this way we discover that nature operates in the operations or actions of art, by virtue of the fact that even in the case of animals, deprived of reason, we discover nature managing works of art, as for example in the case of the hives of the bees and the nests of swallows. And nature causes this, insofar as it is a work and an instrument of intelligence. Certainly in this way we discover the first creator of all creatures operating in the creature, and we perceive this from the very act of the creator. For we see, that he has stabilized the whole of nature according to a certain number and proportion, which proportion does not exist except for the wisdom of the creator. For intelligence, insofar as it is intelligence, does not possess as a quality that intelligence works in nature proportionate to this or that nature, rather it possesses this quality insofar as it is divine. For "this" depends upon the wisdom of the one who disposes and produces and orders the whole in its proper proportions. But what we have said up to this point suffices for an explanation of what was stated. For these matters belong to another and a more profound investigation; for they belong to the part of First philosophy, which is concerned with the universal and primary causes.

Chapter 6. Concerning the division of the predicable forms and concerning which of these we have in mind here.

But these things having been thus determined regarding the predicable forms, the division of forms must be understood in order to know to which forms attention is directed in this book. Therefore let us state that one form, which is universal, whether substantial or accidental, is indeed in the subject as accident, but another is affirmed or is predicated essentially [*in quid*] of the subject, because it is a subjective part of it. For example, knowledge in a subject is indeed in the soul in the way in which an accident is in a subject; and it is affirmed of a subject, for example, of grammar, which is a species of knowledge and a subjective part. And such a form is a universal accident, related essentially to the subject in which it exists, in the category of quality, and to the species which is subjected to it. Certainly some form is in a subject as accident, and it is affirmed or is predicated of a subject or of no subjective part, for example, whiteness of Socrates. And the same holds for whatever forms are individual. For these are indeed related to the subject, in which they exist, and are predicated of that according to the category of quality, but they cannot be related to that which underlies them because nothing underlies the individual, by virtue of the fact that it is the ultimate subject. But certain such forms are indeed affirmed of a subject but are in no subject, for example, substantial forms, which are not in a subject as accident, because they contribute to the being, and they are a part of that which constitutes the being of a thing. Moreover, they are affirmed of the subject itself, because they are predicated according to substantial quality, as differentia, or essentially [*in quid*], as genus. And an example of this form is such as rational and mortal and other substantial differentiae.

But with regard to those forms, which indeed are in the subject as accidents but are unaffirmable of the subject—by virtue of the fact that they contain nothing under themselves subject to themselves, as accidental individual forms—some indeed are sensibles, that is, perceptibles to a proper or the common sense, others [are] insensibles, which are perceptibles to no proper or common sense. For a sensible is that which is perceived by some sense, for example, the whiteness of Socrates, or the taste of this, or heat, or even a stroke—these are perceived by the sense of touch—or a percussion, which is a sound here and now, or sweetness, or odor, or [anything whatever] of such kinds that it is perceived by a proper or the common sense, as magnitude, or figure, or motion, or rest, or number, or something of such kinds. But the insensibles are those things which are not perceived by a sense, but by simple reason or the intellect, for example, doctrine and science, which are in the soul by the intellect. Similarly also virtue, whether intellectual, or moral or even heroic. For none such is perceptible to a sense. Moreover absolutely or universally nothing which is included in the number of things which are affirmed of a subject, or the universal, inasmuch as it is the universal, is sensible. For the universal, according to that which it abstracts from this and from that, only exists in the intellect. And therefore Boethius says, that the particular exists, while one is perceiving, the universal, while one is understanding. But all these things have to be determined amongst those things which are *De Anima*.

But from the things which have already been posited here by division, it is clear that some which are included among the number of particular forms, are situated somewhere in a determinate part of the subject, in which they exist, as blackness in the pupil of the eye. But some of such particular forms are such, that it is difficult to assign the part of the subject in which they are situated, for example, knowledge, paternity and filiation, and others similar to these, unless perchance it be said that they are situated in the complexion of the generating and the composing. For paternity for certain is a form of relation which belongs to the whole and not to a part of that of which it is the cause, because it arises from the act of active generation by the generating. But it is an act of the whole and not of a part. But similarly filiation belongs to the whole of the one who is born, on account of the passive generation, which belongs to the whole. Still these are posited in the complexion of the generating according to cause but not according to subject, which complexion is the cause of the complexion of the seed. And according to cause they are posited in the composition of the things generating, which composition is attended to in the position and arrangement of the members in which the seed is maturated to generation, as are the members, which are called seminal vessels.

However, knowledge, understood indeed as act, does not have position; but understood as an aptitude, is posited in the complexion of the knowing, because as regards subtle humours and spirits they are more fit for to know. Certainly on account of this Alexander said that the possible intellect is a kind of preparation in the body. However, some say that knowledge is situated in the whole and not in a part, because in its case there is both the passive intellect and the light of intelligence and the phantasm from which it receives, and in this way that which pertains to understanding is said to be in the whole, because neither does it exist without the soul nor without the body nor without the intelligence. But we must not pay much attention to these things here, because they are not relevant to what has been proposed.

However, this must be adverted to, because in the case of each of the things which has been mentioned, some notation or annotation or name has to do with the incomplexity, which belongs to the word. For each of these is a sign of an incomplex word, and it is not signified in a complex statement. But in this way that denoted by an incomplex word either will be a subsisting thing, that is, a substance, or contingent to another, that is, an accident.

But of those things, which are contingent, that is, happen to substance, each comes to substance either extrinsically, that is, through an extrinsic cause, or it is considered absolutely according to being and cause within substance. As for example, a line, a surface and a body, which is a third dimension, is considered according to being and cause within the substance to which it belongs. For quantity is caused by matter, and is about measurings intrinsically. It is certainly similar in the case of qualities which are caused by form and dispose a substance intrinsically. In fact with regard to those things which extrinsic as regards cause befall or come to substance, they are either an act which is to do, or to experience or passion, or disposition or position or place, or to be somewhere or where [*ubi*], or in a space of time or when [*quando*]—for example, once upon a time, yesterday, today, because, as Priscian says, time is a pause in a march of mutable things; and in this way when [*quando*] is caused by time—or they are according to habit. For there are not many accidents extrinsic to substance, and therefore there are only six principles. But this has already been proved in what was previously considered in this book.

However, it has been sufficiently argued or determined in that book which is entitled *On the Categories* [*De Categoriis*] concerning those predicables, which subsist, as substance and those things which are contained in the genus of substance, and likewise concerning those things which do not advene extrinsically, but only exist according to cause and being in those things, in which they are through existence. Also similarly regarding relation, which arises, as frequently, through the intrinsic. But we shall have to speak continuously in what follows concerning the rest, which come more frequently to substance through the extrinsic, which also on account of this do not have the name of predicables but of principles, by virtue of the fact that they do not predicate something simply inhering, but rather that something is related in some other way to another.

Chapter 7. Concerning the intention in regard to the understanding of what has been said.

For the understanding of everything which has been said, it must be known, that the Stoics first lit upon the name and nature of "form," and prior to them, those philosophers who were followers of Epicurus, referred every cause to matter. For seeing that there is nothing in matter by which that which is formable, can be formed, and that formable matter cannot be the cause of the forming of the form itself, they have affirmed that forms are separated from matter by virtue of the fact that whatever forms are in matter, have been introduced into matter; and therefore they cannot be the causes of the formation of matter. For that which essentially and substantially and by itself is the cause of formation, is not the formed, but rather the forming by itself. And therefore they have posited such forms unfailingly forming to exist outside of matter, and existing as separated in the light of the first active intellects, from which they have to be produced as from some image of the form of all things which are formed.

But they have said that these forms, in this way remaining outside and forming all things, are expanded with the very light of the active intellects over the things which have to be formed. And therefore they have said that such forms are incorruptible formal principles by which a true knowledge and conception of things is caused, just as a color is exposed by the light of the sun or is poured forth over colored visibles, according to those who say—and in fact it is true—that colors do not exist in the darkness, rather they are diffused upon the advent of light over determined bodies. Certainly on account of this have the Pythagoreans called color "an appearance" [*epiphanium*], that is, "a becoming visible from above" [*desuper eminentem*]. Therefore in this way they have said that material forms are poured forth from the separated forms by the light of the active intellect, and that therefore material forms are not truly called forms, but rather the images of true forms, but both the separated and their images are predicated of things: the separated indeed by virtue of the fact that in the case of matter they are infused into all by the light of the intellect which is penetrative of things, and they cause the being, and are the principles of cognition of them; the images [are predicated of things] because they are likenesses of [the forms], and are in matter according to being and are mutable in accordance with the mutation of matter. But that the images are principles of knowing those things whose forms they are, they have this from the separated forms, which are the stable and certain causes of them.

Therefore some say that such a form is the form which happens in composition, by virtue of the fact that it is poured forth on the composite by the light of the intellect, and that this is what consists of a simple and invariable essence, because that is simple which exists in the light of the intellect. And that is invariable which is not varied by a variation of matter, because although matter is varied under that form, nevertheless it depends only upon the light of the intellect, and therefore it is not varied. Just as we see that colors are not varied by art and variated colored objects, by virtue of the fact that they depend only upon the light, which is in the transparent, not insofar as it is an element or compounded of elements or a body mutable according to form, but rather according to the fact that the transparent communicates with the perpetual body above. However, the composition of these does not have to do with what has been intended, because such a form is not divisible into the substantial and the accidental, nor into the universal and the particular.

Therefore others say, that the form which is a contingent to composition, is an accidental form. For an accident is that which is in something, which is perfect as regards being, as Avicenna says. And therefore an accident exists by means of a whole being and follows the perfect as a consequence. And because that which exists perfectly is the composite, they therefore say, that this form only happens to composition according to substance, so that composition forsooth according to accident always presupposes to itself composition according to substance. But it is not easy to prove how this form consists of a simple and invariable essence, since an accident, as Aristotle proves in Book IX of *First philosophy,* is not an essence according to being. Nor is the essence altogether simple, in whose essence there is always a subject; nor can that be altogether invariable which always depends as regards being on that which continuously is varied. For on account of this Aristotle says, that health is not the same in the morning and in the evening, because health depends upon the complexion of the animal, which is varied continuously due to the continuous action and passion of agents and patients. But still this accidental form does not admit universally the divisions of form, which have been introduced.

Therefore it must be said, that the form concerning which we have spoken is the form which is the universal. For this form is the form of a whole and not of a part, and the very composition in the composite is material to that, just as the composite of the rational soul and the body is material to man. For otherwise it would not be predicable, unless the intention were not of a part, but of a whole. And this is the form of reason and logic. The form, which is a principle in physics, is a form of a part and not of a whole. And because this form is of the whole, therefore the definition which states the quiddity of such a form, contains within itself both the potential and the actual, and both the material related to form and the formal related to matter, as when one says: "mortal rational animal." For animal is potential and material, whereas the others are actual or formal. This therefore is contingent to composition in the way in which it was discussed, at least to the composition of the "that which is and by which it is," concerning which it has to be determined fully in the *Book on Causes* [*Libro de causis*]. And this form is fixed and it is an essence depending upon the light of the intellect, being formed of the essentially and through its own proper being invariable, varied *per accidens* according to the being which it has in this or in that. Also this form is divisible by division to every form which is determined. And this is the form by whose nature everything which is ordered in genus or species, receives the reason for its coordination. With regard to this, therefore, one must understand everything which has been said here concerning form.

Suggestions for Further Reading

Reilly, G. C. *Psychology of St. Albert the Great compared with that of St. Thomas.* Washington, 1934; Albert, S. *Albert the Great.* Oxford, 1948; Schwertner, Thos. M. *St. Albert the Great.* New York, 1932; *FCC* vol. II, ch. XXX; *EG* 277-294; *AAM* 153-162; *RMcK* vol. I, 315-375.

Peter of Spain

Peter of Spain, born Petrus Juliani, first saw the light of day sometime during the second decade of the thirteenth century. After completing his preliminary studies at the Cathedral school of Lisbon, he attended the University of Paris, where he studied logic, physics, and metaphysics under Albert the Great, and medicine and theology under John of Parma. In 1245 Peter went to the University of Siena, where he was active as a member of the Faculty of Medicine from 1246 to 1250. His activities between 1250 and 1261 are unknown. In 1261 Peter became Dean of the Cathedral of Lisbon. Subsequently, he became an archdeacon in the diocese of Braga, where he probably met Teobaldi Visconti, who, after becoming Pope Gregory X, made Peter Physician-in-Ordinary in 1272. The following year, Peter became the Archbishop of Braga and the Cardinal of Tusculum. Along with other great figures of the Church, such as Albert the Great, Peter attended the second Council of Lyons in 1273. Pope Gregory X, who had summoned the Council, died in January of the year 1276, and was succeeded by Popes Innocent V and Hadrian V, both of whom died in the same year. On September 13, 1276, Peter of Spain was elected Pope. He took the name John XXI. Less than a year later, on May 20, 1277, Peter died, after having been fatally injured when the roof of a private study collapsed on him.

No student of medieval thought can be ignorant of the prestige and influence of Peter's *Summulae Logicales*—his famous text on logic. From the middle of the thirteenth century this text was studied by all students, all philosophers, and all theologians as a foundation for the study of science and the art of dialectic. The *Summulae* is divided into seven tracts. The selection presented below in its entirety—*The Treatise on Supposition*—is one of the treatises contained in Tract VII. A full grasp of the material it sets forth is fundamental to any understanding of the developments in logic which occurred in the later Middle Ages.

PETER OF SPAIN ON SUPPOSITION*

TREATISE ON SUPPOSITIONS

Some linguistic expressions are *complex,* for example, "The man is running," "white man." But others [are] *incomplex,* for example, "man" by itself, which is an incomplex term. Moreover, each and every incomplex term either signifies substance, or quality or quantity, or relation, and so on, in accordance with the other ten predicaments. *Term,* as it is taken here, is a word which signifies the universal or the singular, for example, "man" or "Socrates." The *signification* of a term, as it is taken here, is the conventional representation of a thing by a word. But because every thing is universal or singular, it is necessary that words which do not signify a universal or a particular do not signify anything according as signification of a term is taken here; and thus it is not a term as term is taken here; and therefore neither signified universals, nor particulars, are terms.

With regard to signification, one is substantival and this is accomplished through a substantive noun, for example, "man"; another [is] adjectival and this is accomplished through an adjective or through a verb, for example, "white" or "running." But with regard to these there is not substantival or adjectival signification in a proper sense, rather something is signified substantively or adjectivally, because adjectivity or substantiv-

* Translated especially for this volume by J. P. Mullally of Queens College, New York, from the edition of I. M. Bochenski, Torino, 1947.

ity are modes of the things which are signified but are not significations. In fact, substantive nouns are said *to stand for* or to denote, where as adjectives and also verbs are said *to characterize.*

But *supposition* is the acceptance of a substantive term for something. However, supposition and signification differ, because signification exists through the imposition of a word for to signify a thing, but supposition is the acceptance of the term itself which already signifies a thing for something, for example, when one says "Man runs," the term "man" stands for Socrates or Plato and the rest of men. Wherefore, signification is prior to supposition and they are not the same, because to signify is characteristic of the word, but to denote is characteristic of the term already composed of the word and signification. Therefore supposition is not signification. Furthermore, signification is the relation of a sign to the signified, whereas supposition is not the relation of a sign to the signified but of the substituted to the denoted, hence signification and supposition differ. *Characterization* is the acceptance of an adjectival term for something.

One kind of supposition is general, another discrete. *General supposition* is that which is accomplished by means of a general term, for example, "man." *Discrete supposition* is that which is accomplished by means of a discrete term. In like manner with regard to general suppositions, one type is natural, another accidental. *Natural supposition* is the acceptance of a general term for all those things of which it was born fit to be predicated, for example, "man" taken by itself of its very nature possesses as a quality the denotation of all men who are and who have been and who will be. *Accidental supposition* is the acceptance of a general term for all those things which its adjunct determines, for example, "Man exists"; the term "man" here denotes those who exist at the present time. But when one says "Man existed," it denotes those who existed in the past. Then when one says "Man will exist," it denotes those who will exist, and so it has different suppositional values depending upon the diversity of those terms which are added to it.

With regard to accidental suppositions, one type is simple, another personal. *Simple supposition* is the acceptance of a general term for the universal thing specified by it, for example, when one says "Man is a species" or "Animal is a genus," the term "man" denotes man in general and not any inferior, and it is similar in the case of any general term whatsoever, for example, "Risible is a property," "Rational is a differentia."

With regard to simple suppositions, one type is that of a general term *functioning as the subject,* for example, "Man is a species"; another type is that of a general term *functioning as predicate* in an affirmative, for example, "Every man is an animal"; the term "animal" functioning as predicate has simple supposition, because it denotes only the nature of the genus; indeed another type is that of a general term *placed after an exceptive word,* for example, "Every animal, other than man, is irrational." The term "man" has simple supposition. Hence the following is not a valid inference: "Every animal, other than man, is irrational, hence every animal other than this man," rather there is in this case a fallacy of figure of speech, in proceeding from simple to personal supposition. Similarly here: "Man is a species, hence some man"; and here: "Every man is animal, hence this animal": in all these cases an inference is made from simple supposition to personal.

But that a general term, functioning as predicate, is understood simply, is obvious when one says: "There is the same science of all opposites," for unless the term "science" should have simple supposition, there would be a fallacy. For there is no particular science of all contraries, for medicine is not a science of all contraries, but only of the healthy and the ill, and grammar of the grammatically proper and improper, and so on.

Personal supposition is the acceptance of a general term for its inferiors, for example, when one says: "Man runs," the term "man" stands for its inferiors, namely, for Socrates and for Plato and so on.

Further, with regard to personal supposition, one type is determinate, another indeterminate. *Determinate supposition* is the acceptance of a general term taken indefinitely or with a sign of particularity, for example, "A man is running" or "Some man is running," and each is called determinate, because, although in each of these statements the term "man" may denote any man, both one running and one not running, nevertheless they are true of only one man who is running. For it is one thing to denote and another to cause a statement to be true of something in the case of the above statements. In fact, as was stated, the term "man" denotes every man, both those running and those not running, yet it causes the statement to be true only for a running man. However, it is clear that there is determinate supposition in each of these statements, because when one says: "An animal is Socrates, an animal is Plato and so on, hence every animal is every man," there is in this case a fallacy of figure of speech in proceeding from a determinate many to one; and so the general term, taken indefinitely, has determinate supposition and it is similar with a particular sign.

However, *indeterminate supposition* is the acceptance of a general term for many by means of a universal sign; for example, when one says: "Every man is an animal," the term "man" is understood for many by means of the universal sign, because it is understood for any one whatsoever of the things it denotes.

Further, with regard to personal suppositions, one type is *indeterminate by the necessity of the sign or mode,* another *by the necessity of the thing* [signified], for example, when one says: "Every man is an animal," the term "man" is made indeterminate or is distributed for any one whatsoever of the things it denotes by the necessity of the sign, and since each and every man has his own essence, the verb "is" is understood by the necessity of the thing [signified] for as many essences as "man" is understood for men; and since his own animality belongs to each and every man, "animal" as a consequence is understood in this case by the necessity of the thing signified for as many animals as "man" is understood for men and the verb "is" is understood for essences. Whence the term "man" is said to denote indeterminately, inconstantly and distributively, but it is understood indeterminately and distributively because it denotes every man; however, it is understood *inconstantly,* because a valid inference can be made to any one whatsoever of its inferiors, for example, "Every man is an animal, hence Socrates or Plato." But the term "animal" is said *to be inconstantly immobile* because a valid inference cannot be made [to its inferiors], for example, "Every man is an animal, hence every man is this animal"; nay rather an inference is made here from simple supposition to personal just as in this case: "Man is the noblest of creatures, hence any man"; also "The rose is the most beautiful of flowers, hence any rose." But they differ in this, because in the latter there is simple supposition on the part of the subject, whereas in the other the simple supposition is on the part of the predicate.

But does not what was said seem to be contradicted because in the proposition: "Every man is an animal," the term "animal," functioning as predicate, has simple supposition, although previously it were said that it should have indeterminate supposition inconstantly. To this it must be replied, that, according to some people the genus animal is predicated in this case of many species and the term "animal" is understood for itself in general because it is a genus and has simple supposition. But insofar as that common nature of the genus itself is multiplied by reason of the things denoted by man, it is said in this way to have indeterminate supposition, not inconstantly but constantly. For inconstantly indeterminate supposition cannot exist simultaneously with simple, neither in the same respect nor in different respects, nay rather constantly indeterminate supposition can exist simultaneously with the simple, not in the same respect but in different respects, as was said. And in this way it is necessary to solve the contrariety which was obvious to those maintaining that a term functioning as predicate should have simple supposition and should be made constantly indeterminate by an affirmative universal sign being in the subject, for example, "Every man is an animal."

But I believe that it is impossible for a general term functioning as predicate to be made indeterminate, constantly or inconstantly, by an affirmative universal sign being in the subject, for example, "Every man is an animal" and in other similar propositions. For, as Porphyry indicates, everything which is predicated of another either is greater than it or equal to the very thing of which it is predicated; and he had essential predication in mind. But in this proposition: "Every man is an animal," the predication is essential and it is not of equal extension; therefore the greater is predicated, but not the accidental; therefore the substantial or the essential; therefore the genus or the differentia; but not the differentia; therefore the genus. But the nature of the genus, when it is distributed inconstantly or constantly, is not a genus; therefore when one says: "Every man is an animal," since the genus is there predicated, it is impossible for the general term to be distributed inconstantly or constantly, because it signifies the nature of the genus; for indeed it would not be a genus, just as if man be distributed inconstantly or constantly, it will not be a species.

Again, this same conclusion is evident from what Aristotle says in the Book of the *Topics*. For he says that it is necessary that everything which is predicated of another either is predicated convertibly of it or not; and if convertibly, it is a differentia or a property; if it is not predicated convertibly of the thing, either it falls into the definition of the thing or it does not; if it does not fall, it is an accident, if it falls into the definition, either it is a genus or a differentia. And here Aristotle had in mind the case of direct predication and of the species as such functioning as subject or distributed. But in this proposition, "Every man is an animal," there is direct predication and "man" is the subject, the equal or an accident is not predicated, therefore a genus or a differentia is predicated; but not the differentia; therefore the genus. And so the conclusion is the same as before, for it is not possible for a general term functioning as predicate to be made indeterminate inconstantly or constantly.

Futhermore, the universal whole which is a genus and the quantitative whole are related to each other in an opposite manner. For the universal whole is a general term taken without a universal sign, for example, "animal." But the quantitative whole is a general term taken with a universal sign, for example, "every man." But the quantitative whole is twofold: for one kind is complete, for example, wherever a general term is made inconstantly indeterminate; the other kind of quantitative whole is incomplete or limited, for example, wherever a general term is made constantly indeterminate; for example, "every man" is a quantitative whole, for if it be distributed a simple general term becomes a quantitative whole. And so in a certain way it is and in a certain way it is not; therefore it is impossible for a quantitative whole to be a genus in as far as it is of such a kind; therefore it is not possible for a general term, functioning as predicate, to be made indeterminate, as was stated.

Also, that composition by which the inferiors are reduced to the more general is opposed to that composition by which the more general is reduced to its inferiors. In the first case, general is taken in the sense of that which is common, for in this way the general itself contains in itself all the individuals which are under it. But in the other case general is taken distributively or as indeterminate for all or for some. If therefore a genus is essentially fixed in the nature of genus or in the nature of the general, it is not possible for it to be distributed insofar as it is of such a kind. And all these arguments are conceded.

But the reason which prompted these arguments is easy to solve. For they state, that at the time one says: "Every man is an animal," since each man has his own essence and his own animality, by virtue of the fact that it is not possible to be a man without being an animal, therefore the term "animal" is understood for as many animals as the term "man" is understood for men. Certainly, one sees that there is no force in this argument. For when I say: "Every man is white," "Every man is black," since it is impossible to be a man without being an animal, it is necessary that as many animals or animalities are understood in the subject as there are men for which the term "man" is understood.

However, it is foolish to say that the multiplicity of animalities is there from the multiplicity of the predicate since "white" or "black" is the predicate in this case. Whence it must be said that man consists, logically speaking but not naturally, of rational animal and it is on this account that man in himself possesses animal. For when man is multiplied, he has in himself a multitude of those animalities, for example, when I say: "Every man is white," "Every man is black," in no way does he have these animalities from the predicate.

It is similar in the matter under discussion, when a genus is predicated, for example, "Every man is an animal"; for in this proposition "man" under which is understood the multiplicity of those animalities, is subject, as was stated, and this genus, namely "animal," which is not distributed in any way, neither inconstantly nor constantly, is the predicate, but in this case it denotes the very essence of the universal genus which is predicable of many. Whence "animal" is the predicate and "animal" is understood in the subject just as when one says: "Every mortal rational animal is an animal."

Similarly, I say that the verb "is" neither is distributed inconstantly nor constantly, because the fact that an animal might be or might exist in a man was implied in the subject itself before it became subject in a proposition to an essential or accidental predicate. And for this reason we destroy a certain antecedent division of suppositions, namely, of indeterminate suppositions: one type is *indeterminate by the necessity of the sign* or of the mode, another *by the necessity of the thing.*

For we assert that all indeterminacy exists by the necessity of the mode; just as in this case: "Every rational animal is mortal," the term "animal" is understood by the power of the sign for every animal that is a man. Similarly in this case: "Every man is an animal," the term "man" is understood not only for every man but also for every animal that is a man. And it is on account of this that there are as many animalities there as there are humanities in the same place, naturally speaking (because the humanity in each individual man is the same, speaking of course according to the view point of logic, not naturally); in this way man in general is the same. Whence the fact that this animality and that exists, is by reason of matter.

For in the natural order my humanity is essentially other than your humanity, just as my animality, through which my humanity exists in me, is other than your animality, through which your humanity happens to you; and because of this the sign or mode, in distributing man does not distribute animal, rather it limits animal generally to man through his differentiae. Whence all indeterminacy exists by the necessity of the mode or sign. And these remarks concerning suppositions suffice.

Suggestions for Further Reading

J. P. Mullally. *The Summulae Logicales of Peter of Spain.* Notre Dame, Ind., 1945; P. Boehner. *Medieval Logic.* Manchester, 1952; E. A. Moody. *Truth and Consequences in Mediaeval Logic.* Amsterdam, 1953; *EG* 319-323; *AAM* 245-250.

Roger Bacon

Roger Bacon was one of the most colorful personalities of the entire medieval period. Irascible, stubborn, imaginative, and utterly convinced of the rectitude and value of his own views, he did not hesitate to attack many of the outstanding men of his time—among them no less respected a figure than Albert the Great. Though he charged the bulk of his contemporaries, among other things, with obscurantism in philosophy, faulty scriptural exegesis, ignorance of languages, and undue veneration for theological commentaries even to the point of preferring these to the Bible itself, Bacon's principle attacks were leveled against what he considered to be their abysmal ignorance and neglect of the sciences. It is precisely his own display of the scientific outlook—an emphasis upon the value and utility of experimental science—which characterizes Bacon's thought and distinguishes it most sharply from that of his fellow philosophers. As has often been remarked, no great violence would be committed by those who construed the phrase, "the Baconian reform of science," as referring to the labors of the obscure thirteenth-century monk, Roger, rather than the esteemed seventeenth-century philosopher of science, Francis.

Our knowledge of the circumstances surrounding Bacon's life is quite scanty and not undisputed. He was definitely born in England, possibly at Ilchester, sometime around 1212. He pursued his education at Oxford, where it is quite likely that he studied under Robert Grosseteste, for whose scientific activities and capabilities he always entertained the liveliest admiration. After leaving Oxford, at an unknown date, Bacon went to Paris, where it is assumed that he taught for a while. Although at Paris he met with a certain Peter of Maricourt whose scientific experiments won his most profound respect, Bacon, on the whole, considered his Parisian colleagues as intellectually inferior to the Oxonians.

Upon returning to England, sometime around 1250, Bacon entered the Franciscan Order. He then commenced teaching at Oxford until, in 1257, he was obliged to retire, apparently having incurred the displeasure of his superiors. In 1278 Bacon, having been accused by the General of his own order of teaching certain unspecified "novelties," was tried, convicted, and jailed. His confinement seems to have lasted until 1292; and it was either in this year, or shortly thereafter, that Bacon died. He was laid to rest in the Franciscan church at Oxford.

Despite his erratic and stormy career, Bacon managed to turn out an impressive number of writings. A selection from Part Six of his chief work, the *Opus Maius,* is given below.

ROGER BACON ON EXPERIMENTAL SCIENCE *

CHAPTER I

Having laid down fundamental principles of the wisdom of the Latins so far as they are found in language, mathematics, and optics, I now wish to unfold the principles of experimental science, since without experience nothing can be sufficiently known. For there are two modes of acquiring knowledge, namely, by reasoning and experience. Reasoning draws a conclusion and makes us grant the conclusion, but does not make the conclusion certain, nor does it remove doubt so that the mind may rest on the intuition of truth, unless the mind discovers it by the path of experience; since many have the arguments relating to what can be known, but because they lack experience they neglect the arguments, and neither avoid what

* Reprinted by permission of the University of Pennsylvania Press from *The Opus Maius of Roger Bacon*, 1928, vol. 2.

is harmful nor follow what is good. For if a man who has never seen fire should prove by adequate reasoning that fire burns and injures things and destroys them, his mind would not be satisfied thereby, nor would he avoid fire, until he placed his hand or some combustible substance in the fire, so that he might prove by experience that which reasoning taught. But when he has had actual experience of combustion his mind is made certain and rests in the full light of truth. Therefore reasoning does not suffice, but experience does.

This is also evident in mathematics, where proof is most convincing. But the mind of one who has the most convincing proof in regard to the equilateral triangle will never cleave to the conclusion without experience, nor will he heed it, but will disregard it until experience is offered him by the intersection of two circles, from either intersection of which two lines may be drawn to the extremities of the given line; but then the man accepts the conclusion without any question. Aristotle's statement, then, that proof is reasoning that causes us to know is to be understood with the proviso that the proof is accompanied by its appropriate experience, and is not to be understood of the bare proof. His statement also in the first book of the *Metaphysics* that those who understand the reason and the cause are wiser than those who have empiric knowledge of a fact, is spoken of such as know only the bare truth without the cause. But I am here speaking of the man who knows the reason and the cause through experience. These men are perfect in their wisdom, as Aristotle maintains in the sixth book of the *Ethics,* whose simple statements must be accepted as if they offered proof, as he states in the same place.

He therefore who wishes to rejoice without doubt in regard to the truths underlying phenomena must know how to devote himself to experiment. For authors write many statements, and people believe them through reasoning which they formulate without experience. Their reasoning is wholly false. For it is generally believed that the diamond cannot be broken except by goat's blood, and philosophers and theologians misuse this idea. But fracture by means of blood of this kind has never been verified, although the effort has been made; and without that blood it can be broken easily. For I have seen this with my own eyes, and this is necessary, because gems cannot be carved except by fragments of this stone. Similarly it is generally believed that the castors employed by physicians are the testicles of the male animal. But this is not true, because the beaver has these under its breast, and both the male and female produce testicles of this kind. Besides these castors the male beaver has its testicles in their natural place; and therefore what is subjoined is a dreadful lie, namely, that when the hunters pursue the beaver, he himself knowing what they are seeking cuts out with his teeth these glands. Moreover, it is generally believed that hot water freezes more quickly than cold water in vessels, and the argument in support of this is advanced that contrary is excited by contrary, just like enemies meeting each other. But it is certain that cold water freezes more quickly for any one who makes the experiment. People attribute this to Aristotle in the second book of the *Meteorologics;* but he certainly does not make this statement, but he does make one like it, by which they have been deceived, namely, that if cold water and hot water are poured on a cold place, as upon ice, the hot water freezes more quickly, and this is true. But if hot water and cold are placed in two vessels, the cold will freeze more quickly. Therefore all things must be verified by experience.

But experience is of two kinds; one is gained through our external senses, and in this way we gain our experience of those things that are in the heavens by instruments made for this purpose, and of those things here below by means attested by our vision. Things that do not belong in our part of the world we know through other scientists who have had experience of them. As, for example, Aristotle on the authority of Alexander sent two thousand men through different parts of the world to gain experimental knowledge of all things that are on the surface of the earth, as Pliny bears witness in his *Natural History*. This experience is both human and philosophical, as far as man can act in accordance with the grace given him; but this experience does not suffice him, because it does not give full attestation in regard to things corporeal owing to its difficulty, and does not touch at all on things spiritual. It is necessary, therefore, that the intellect of man should be otherwise aided, and for this reason the holy patriarchs and prophets, who first gave sciences to the world, received illumination within and were not dependent on sense alone. The same is true of many believers since the time of Christ. For the grace of faith illuminates greatly, as also do divine inspirations, not only in things spiritual, but in things corporeal and in the sciences of philosophy; as Ptolemy states in the *Centilogium,* namely, that there are two roads by which we arrive at the knowledge of facts, one through the experience of philosophy, the other through divine inspiration, which is far the better way, as he says.

Moreover, there are seven stages of this internal knowledge, the first of which is reached through illuminations relating purely to the sciences. The second consists in the virtues. For the evil man is ignorant, as Aristotle says in the second book of the *Ethics.* Moreover, Algazel says in his *Logic* that the soul disfigured by sins is like a rusty mirror, in which the species of objects cannot be seen clearly; but the soul adorned with virtues is like a well-polished mirror, in which the forms of objects are clearly seen. For this reason true philosophers have labored more in morals for the honor of virtue, concluding in their own case that they cannot perceive the causes of things unless they have souls free from sins. Such is the statement of Augustine in regard to Socrates in the eighth book of the *City of God,* Chapter III. Wherefore the Scripture says, "in a malevolent soul, etc." For it is not possible that the soul should rest in the light of truth while it is stained with sins, but like a parrot or magpie it will repeat the words of another which it has learned by long practice. The proof of this is that the beauty of truth known in its splendor attracts men to the love of it, but the proof of love is the display of a work of love. Therefore he who acts contrary to the truth must necessarily be ignorant of it, although he may know how to compose very elegant phrases, and quote the opinions of other people, like an animal that imitates the words of human beings, and like an ape that relies on the aid of men to perform its part, although it does not understand their reason. Virtue, therefore, clarifies the mind, so that a man comprehends more easily not only moral but scientific truth. I have proved this carefully in the case of many pure young men, who because of innocency of soul have attained greater proficiency than can be stated, when they have had sane advice in regard to their study. Of this number is the bearer of this present treatise, whose fundamental knowledge very few of the Latins have acquired. For since he is quite young, about twenty years of age, and very poor, nor has he been able to have teachers, nor has he spent one year in learning his great store of knowledge, nor is he a man of great genius nor of a very retentive memory, there can be no other cause except the grace of God, which owing to the purity of his soul has granted to him those things that it has as a rule refused to show to all other students. For as a spotless virgin he has departed from me, nor have I found in him any kind of mortal sin, although I have examined him carefully, and he has, therefore, a soul so bright and clear that with very little instruction he has learned more than can be estimated. And I have striven to aid in bringing it about that these two young men should be useful vessels in God's Church, to the end that they may reform by the grace of God the whole course of study of the Latins.

The third stage consists in the seven gifts of the Holy Spirit, which Isaiah enumerates. The fourth consists in the beatitudes, which the Lord defines in the Gospels. The fifth consists in the spiritual senses. The sixth consists in fruits, of which is the peace of God which passes all understanding. The seventh consists in raptures and their states according to the different ways in which people are caught up to see many things of which it is not lawful for a man to speak. And he who has had diligent training in these experiences or in several of them is able to assure himself and others not only in regard to things spiritual, but also in regard to all human sciences. Therefore since all the divisions of speculative philosophy proceed by arguments, which are either based on a point from authority or on the other points of argumentation except this division which I am now examining, we find necessary the science that is called experimental. I wish to explain it, as it is useful not only to philosophy, but to the knowledge of God, and for the direction of the whole world; just as in the preceding divisions I showed the relationship of the languages and sciences to their end, which is the divine wisdom by which all things are disposed . . .

CHAPTER ON THE SECOND PREROGATIVE OF EXPERIMENTAL SCIENCE

This mistress of the speculative sciences alone is able to give us important truths within the confines of the other sciences, which those sciences can learn in no other way. Hence these truths are not connected with the discussion of principles but are wholly outside of these, although they are within the confines of these sciences, since they are neither conclusions nor principles. Clear examples in regard to these matters can be given; but in what follows the man without experience must not seek a reason in order that he may first understand, for he will never have this reason except after experiment. Hence in the first place there should be readiness to believe, until in the second place experiment follows, so that in the third reasoning may function. For if a man is without experience that a magnet attracts iron, and has not heard from others that it attracts, he will never discover this fact before an experiment. Therefore in the beginning he must believe those who have made the experiment, or who have reliable information from experimenters, nor should he reject the truth, because he is ignorant of it, and because he does not arrive at it by reasoning. I shall state, then, those things that I hold to have been proved by experiment.

Example I.

Mathematical science can easily produce the spherical astrolabe, on which all astronomical phenomena necessary for man may be described, according to precise longitudes and latitudes. The device of Ptolemy in the eighth book of the *Almagest* is used with reference to circles as well as stars, as I have stated, by means of a certain similitude, but the subject is not fully explained by that device, for more work is necessary. But that this body so made should move naturally with the daily motion is not within the power of mathematical science. But the trained experimenter can consider the ways of this motion, aroused to consider them by many things which follow the celestial motion, as, for example, the three elements which rotate circularly through the celestial influence, as Alpetragius states in his book on *Celestial Motions,* and Averroës in the first book on the *Heavens and the World;* so also comets, the seas and flowing streams, marrows and brains and the substances composing diseases. Plants also in their parts open and close in accordance with the motion of the sun. And many like things are found which, according to a local motion of the whole or of parts, are moved by the motion of the sun. The scientist, therefore, is aroused by the consideration of things of this kind, a consideration similar in import to that in which he is interested, in order that at length he may arrive at his goal. This instrument would be worth the treasure of a king, and would supersede all other astronomical instruments and clocks, and would be a most wonderful instrument of science. But few would know how in a clear and useful manner to conceive of such a miracle and of similar ones within the confines of mathematical science.

Example II.

Another example can be given in the field of medicine in regard to the prolongation of human life, for which the medical art has nothing to offer except the regimen of health. But a far longer extension of life is possible. At the beginning of the world there was a great prolongation of life, but now it has been shortened unduly. Many have thought that the reason for this prolongation and shortening of life is found in the influence of the heavens. For they considered that the arrangement of the heavens was best at the beginning, and that as the world grows old all things decay. They think that the stars were created in more advantageous positions, in which stars have their dignities, which are called house, exaltation, triplicity, face, and boundary; and in a better relationship of these to one another in accordance with the diversity of aspects or the invisible projection of rays. They also think that they have gradually receded from this position, and that in accordance with this recession they impose a shortened span of life up to some fixed boundary, at which there will be a state of rest. But this idea has many contradictions and difficulties, of which I must now speak.

Whether this shall prove to be true or not, another reason must be given, which is ready at hand for us and is plain, which cannot be contradicted, and which we know by experience. Therefore in regard to this we must strive, that the wonderful and ineffable utility and splendor of experimental science may appear and the pathway may be opened to the greatest secret of secrets, which Aristotle has hidden in his book on the *Regimen of Life*. For although the regimen of health should be observed in food and drink, in sleep and in wakefulness, in motion and in rest, in evacuation and retention, in the nature of the air and in the passions of the mind, so that these matters should be properly cared for from infancy, no one wishes to take thought in regard to them, not even physicians, since we see that scarcely one physician in a thousand will give this matter even slight attention. Very rarely does it happen that any one pays sufficient heed to the rules of health. No one does so in his youth, but sometimes one in three thousand thinks of these matters when he is old and approaching death, for at that time he fears for himself and thinks of his health. But he cannot then apply a remedy because of his weakened powers and senses and his lack of experience. Therefore fathers are weakened and beget weak sons with a liability to premature death. Then by neglect of the rules of health the sons weaken themselves, and thus the son's son has a doubly weakened constitution, and in his turn weakens himself by a disregard of these rules. Thus a weakened constitution passes from father to sons, until a final shortening of life has been reached, as is the case in these days.

Not only is there this accidental cause, but there is also another, consisting in the disregard of morals. For sins weaken the powers of the soul, so that it is incompetent for the natural control of the body; and therefore the powers of the body are weakened and life is shortened. This weakening passes from father to son, and so on. Therefore owing to these two natural causes the longevity of man of necessity has not retained its natural course from the beginning; but for these two reasons the longevity of man has been shortened contrary to nature. Moreover, it has been proved that this excessive shortening of the span of life has been retarded in many cases, and longevity prolonged for many years by secret experiments. Many authors write on this topic. Wherefore this excessive shortening of life must be accidental with a possible remedy.

Since I have shown that the cause of a shortening of life of this kind is accidental, and therefore that a remedy is possible, I now return to this example which I have decided to give in the field of medicine, in which the power of medical art fails. But the experimental art supplies the defect of medicine in this particular. For the art of medicine can give only the proper rules of health for all ages. For although noted authors have spoken inadequately concerning the proper regimen of the aged, it has been possible, however, for medicine to give such a regimen. This regimen consists in the proper use of food and drink, of motion and rest, of sleep and wakefulness, of elimination and retention, of the air, and in the control of the passions of the mind. But if from birth a man followed a proper regimen to the end of his life, he would reach the limit of life set by God and nature, in accordance with the possibility of a proper regimen. But since it is impossible for this regimen to be followed by any one, and since few, nay, scarcely any one at all, from youth pay any heed to this regimen, and very few old people observe it as it is possible, therefore the accidents of old age of necessity come before old age and senility, namely, in the period of the prime of life, which is the age of human beauty and strength. In these times this period of life does not continue beyond forty-five or fifty years.

All these accidents of old age and senility are white hair,

pallor, wrinkling of the skin, excess of mucus, foul phlegm, inflammation of the eyes, and general injury to the organs of sense, diminution of blood and of the spirits, weakness in motion and breathing and in the whole body, failure in both the animal and natural powers of the soul, sleeplessness, anger and disquietude of mind, and forgetfulness, of which the royal Hali says that old age is the home of forgetfulness; and Plato that it is the mother of lethargy. Because of the lack of a proper regimen of health all these accidents and many more come to men in the prime of life, that is, either in greater or lesser degree, in accordance with the better or worse control they have exercised over themselves in the matter of their health, and in accordance with a better and stronger constitution and a better or worse control exercised over their morals. But the medical art does not furnish remedies against this corruption that comes from lack of control and failure in regimen, just as all physicians expert in their own art know, although medical authors confess that remedies are possible, but they do not teach them. For these remedies have always been hidden not only from physicians, but from the whole rank and file of scientists, and have been revealed only to the most noted, whom Aristotle mentions in the first book of the *Topics* in the division of the probable. Not only are remedies possible against the conditions of old age coming at the time of one's prime and before the time of old age, but also if the regimen of old age should be completed, the conditions of old age and senility can still be retarded, so that they do not arrive at their ordinary time, and when they do come they can be mitigated and moderated, so that both by retarding and mitigating them life may be prolonged beyond the limit, which according to the full regimen of health depends on the six articles mentioned. And there is another farther limit, which has been set by God and nature, in accordance with the property of the remedies retarding the accidents of old age and senility and mitigating their evil. The first limit can be passed but the second cannot be.

Because of these two limits the Scripture says more than once, "Thou hast set its bounds which cannot be passed"; for it is impossible for the ultimate limit to be passed, but the first limit can be passed, although it is rarely passed; but the second limit cannot be passed. The proper regimen of health, therefore, as far as a man can possess it, would prolong life beyond its common accidental limit, which man because of his folly does not protect for his own interest; and thus some have lived for many years beyond the common limit of life. But a special regimen by means of remedies retarding the common limit mentioned, which the art of directing the health does not exceed, can prolong life much further. What is possible is shown by Dioscorides, who says that there may be some medicine to protect man from the swiftness of old age and from cold and from the drying up of his members, so that by its means the life of man may be prolonged. In the *Tegni* near the end Hali maintains this. Again he says, "Those who have lived a long time have used medicines by which their life has been prolonged." Avicenna, moreover, speaks in regard to such matters as follows in the second book of the *Canon,* "There is a medicine that settles and divides every constitution as it should be." But medical authorities have not given those medicines, nor have they been stated in their books, since these writers pay attention only to the art of caring for the health, and that, too, insufficiently as regards the elderly and the aged, as has been stated. But learned men devoted to experimental science have given thought to these matters, influenced thereto not only by their utility but by the action of animals which in many ways avoid a premature death, as, for example, the stag, the eagle, the snake, and many other animals that prolong their life by natural action, as authors state and experience has shown. Influenced by these examples they believed that God himself granted this power to brutes for the instruction of mortal man. Therefore they lay in wait for animals, in order that they might learn the powers of herbs, stones, metals, and other things, with which they improved their bodies in many apparently miraculous ways, just as we gather with the utmost certainty from the books of Pliny, Solinus, Avicenna on *Animals,* Tullius on the *Divine Nature,* from the philosophy of Artephius, and from other books and various authors, and many people have had experience in this matter. For in Paris lately there was a scientist who sought for snakes and took one and cut it into small portions, except that the skin of the belly on which it crept remained intact. This snake crept as it was able to a certain herb by the touch of which it was immediately cured. The experimenter collected the herb of wondrous virtue. Since human reason is superior to all the wisdom of animals, scientists thus encouraged by the examples of animals have thought out better and greater means.

And especially was the wisdom granted to the world through the first men, namely, through Adam and his sons, who received from God himself special knowledge on this subject, in order that they might prolong their life. We can learn the same through Aristotle in the book of *Secrets,* where he says that God most high and glorious has prepared a means and a remedy for tempering the humors and preserving health, and for acquiring many things with which to combat the ills of old age and to retard them, and to mitigate such evils; and has revealed these things to his saints and prophets and to certain others, as the patriarchs, whom he chose and enlightened with the spirit of divine wisdom, etc. And below he says that there is a medicine called the ineffable glory and treasure of philosophers, which completely rectifies the whole human body. This medicine is said to have been discovered by Adam or by Enoch and secured through a vision, as he himself states, although it has not been fully attested which of these first produced this medicine. But these matters and the most secret of secrets of this kind have always been hidden from the rank and file of philosophers, and particularly so after men began to abuse science, turning to evil what God granted in full measure for the safety and advantage of men.

Many examples, moreover, of these facts are written. Artephius, who traveled over all the regions of the East in his search for knowledge, found Tantalus, teacher of the king of India, seated on a golden throne and discoursing on nature and on the motions of the heavens. This same Tantalus humbled himself and became a pupil of Artephius, who is said in the book of his own philosophy to have lived actually for many centuries by means of secret experiments. Pliny, moreover, in the twenty-second book of the *Natural History* states that a man stood in the presence of Augustus, who had prolonged his life beyond a hundred years. To the astonishment of the bystanders he was strong, robust, and active to such a degree that the emperor in wonder asked him what he did so as to live in this way. The man replied in a riddle, as Pliny says, that he had applied oil on the outside and mead on the inside. Moreover, as stated in the book on the *Accidents of Old Age,* in the time of King William of Sicily a man was found who renewed the period of his youth in strength and sense and sagacity beyond all human calculation for about sixty years, and from a rustic ploughman became a messenger of the king. While ploughing he found a golden vessel in the fields hidden in the earth, which contained an excellent liquor. Thinking the liquor was dew from the sky he drank it and washed his face, and was renewed in mind and body beyond measure. And in the book just mentioned it is recorded that a man anointed with an excellent unguent the whole surface of his body with the exception of the soles of his feet, and lived for several centuries without decay except in his soles, which he had neglected to anoint, and for this reason he nearly always rode. Moreover, the author of this book bore witness that he had seen a man, and had talked with him, who had lived for several centuries, because he took a medicine prepared by scientists for a great king, who lost hope for himself and wished the medicine to be tried on an ignorant person. Thus the man's life was prolonged, and he had official letters from the Pope of that time and from others in regard to this fact.

Therefore the excellent experimenter in the book on the *Regimen of the Aged* says that if what is tempered in the fourth degree, and what swims in the sea, and what grows in the air, and what is cast up by the sea, and a plant of India, and what is found in the vitals of a long-lived animal, and the two snakes which are the food of Tyrians and Aethiopians, be prepared and used in the proper way, and the *minera*[1] of the noble ani-

[1] Old French word meaning mine used here probably in the sense of blood.

mal be present, the life of man could be greatly prolonged and the conditions of old age and senility could be retarded and mitigated. But that which is tempered in the fourth degree is gold, as is stated in the book on *Spirits and Bodies*,[2] which among all things is most friendly to nature. And if by a certain experiment gold should be made the best possible, or at any rate far better than nature and the art of alchemy can make it, as was the vessel found by the rustic, and it should be dissolved in such water as the ploughman drank, it would then produce a wonderful action on the body of man. And if there is added that which swims in the sea, namely, the pearl, which is a thing most efficacious for preserving life, and there is added also the thing that grows in the air.[3] This last is an *anthos* [flower] and is the flower of seadew, which possesses an ineffable virtue against the condition of old age. But the *dianthos* that is put in an electuary is not a flower, but is a mixture of leaves and fragments of wood and a small portion of flower. For the pure flower should be gathered in its proper season, and in many ways it is used in foods and drinks and electuaries. To these must be added what is cast up by the sea. This last is ambergris, which is spermaceti, a thing of wondrous virtue in this matter. The plant of India is similar to these, and is the excellent wood of the aloe, fresh and not seasoned. To these ingredients there is added that which is in the heart of a long-lived animal, namely, the stag. This is a bone growing in the stag's heart, which possesses great power against premature old age. The snake which is the food of the Tyrians is the Tyrian snake from which Tyriaca[4] is made, and whose flesh is properly prepared and eaten with spices. This is an excellent remedy for the condition of old age and for all the corruptions of the constitution, if it is taken with things suitable to one's constitution and condition, as we are taught in the book on the *Regimen of the Aged*. Aristotle, moreover, in the book of *Secrets* recommends strongly the flesh of the

---

[2] *I.e.*, gases and solids.

[3] Bacon does not complete these sentences, but the sense is clear enough.

[4] Antidote against poisonous bites.

Tyrian snake for our ills. The snake that is the food of the Aethiopians is the dragon, as David says in the psalm, "Thou hast given it as food to the tribes of the Aethiopians." For it is certain that wise men of Aethiopia have come to Italy, Spain, France, England, and those lands of the Christians in which there are good flying dragons, and by the secret art they possess lure the dragons from their caverns. They have saddles and bridles in readiness, and they ride on these dragons and drive them in the air at high speed, so that the rigidity of their flesh may be overcome and its hardness tempered, just as in the case of boars and bears and bulls that are driven about by dogs and beaten in various ways before they are killed for food. After they have domesticated them in this way they have the art of preparing their flesh, similar to the art of preparing the flesh of the Tyrian snake, and they use the flesh against the accidents of old age, and they prolong life and sharpen their intellect beyond all conception. For no instruction that can be given by man can produce such wisdom as the eating of this flesh, as we have learned through men of proved reliability on whose word no doubt can be cast.

If the elements should be prepared and purified in some mixture, so that there would be no action of one element on another, but so that they would be reduced to pure simplicity, the wisest have judged that they would have the most perfect medicine. For in this way the elements would be equal. Averroës, moreover, asserts in opposition to Galienus in the tenth book of the *Metaphysics* that if the mixture was made with an equality of the miscibles, the elements would not act or be acted on, nor would they be corrupted. Aristotle also maintains this view in the fifth book of the *Metaphysics,* where he has stated definitely that no corruption occurs when the active potencies are equal; and this is an assured fact.

For this condition will exist in our bodies after the resurrection. For an equality of elements in those bodies excludes corruption for ever. For this equality is the ultimate end of the natural matter in mixed bodies, because it is the noblest state, and therefore in it the appetite of matter would cease, and would desire nothing beyond. The body of Adam did not possess elements in full equality, and therefore the contrary elements in him acted and were acted on, and consequently there was waste, and he required nourishment. For this reason he was commanded not to eat of the fruit of life. But since the elements in him approached equality, there was very little waste in him; and hence he was fit for immortality, which he could have secured if he had eaten always of the fruit of the tree of life. For this fruit is thought to have elements approaching equality; and therefore it was able to continue incorruption in Adam, which would have happened if he had not sinned. Scientists, therefore, have striven to reduce the elements in some form of food or drink to an equality or nearly so, and have taught the means to this end. But owing to the difficulty of this very great experiment, and because few take an interest in experiments, since the labor involved is complicated and the expense very great, and because men pay no heed to the secrets of nature and the possibilities of art, it happens that very few have labored on this very great secret of science, and still fewer have reached a laudable end.

Those men, however, of whom mention has been made, who prolonged their life for centuries, had a medicine of this kind prepared with more or less skill. For Artephius, who, it is stated, lived a thousand and twenty-five years, had a better medicine than the aged ploughman, in whom his youth was renewed for sixty years. That liquor which the rustic drank is thought to have approached an equality of elements far beyond ordinary foods and drinks; but yet it was far from possessing full equality. For there are many degrees in the approach to final equality, which the medicine of Artephius failed to secure, as well as that which caused the man to live for five hundred years who had the papal letter in attestation of so great a miracle, of whom mention was made above. Nor is it strange if Aristotle did not live so long, nor Plato, nor many other famous philosophers; since in the *Categories* Aristotle says he was ignorant of the quadrature of the circle, which bears no comparison to a secret of this kind. Avicenna, moreover, says in the third book of the *Physics* that he did not yet know the category of habit; and now I judge that this is easily learned, and we wonder that these men were ignorant of matters so evident. For all wisdom is from the Lord God; and therefore sometimes to the simple are granted things that the most learned and famous cannot know. But medicine cannot give us these things nor does it mention them; but the greatness of the secret belonging to an experimental science of this kind has proved them. What, then, the remedies are and what things they contain, are discovered especially in the book of the *Secrets of Aristotle* and in the philosophy of Artephius, and in the book on the *Conditions of Old Age,* and in the treatise on the *Regimen of the Elderly and the Aged,* and in the books of Pliny, and elsewhere in many ways.

Example III.

In the third place, the dignity of this science can be exemplified in alchemy. For that whole art is scarcely so perfected that the greater metals may be produced from the lighter ones, as gold from lead, and silver from copper. But that art never suffices to show the natural and artificial grades of gold and the modes of its grades. For experimental science has brought both to light, since it has discovered both the four natural grades and their seventeen modes and the artificial ones. By experiment it can be produced beyond twenty-four. Thus the vessel in which the liquor was contained, by means of which the ploughman became the messenger of the king, had a purity of gold far beyond the twenty-four, as its test and worth showed. But when those twenty-four degrees are found in a mass of gold, the gold is the best that can be produced by nature. But when there are twenty-four degrees of gold and one part of silver or one degree, the gold is inferior to the former, and thus the diminution of the degrees of the gold goes as far as sixteen, so that there are eight grades of gold with an admixture of silver. But the mineral power in the belly of the earth is not able sometimes to digest matter into the nature of gold, and does what it can by digesting it into the form of silver. And that I am not led astray in this matter by my imagination is proved by the fact that men are found in several parts of the world who are clever at producing those sixteen modes, and have discovered pieces and masses of gold in those seventeen modes. They then made a mixture of silver and air with gold in the aforesaid modes, so that they might have seventeen lumps of gold made artificially, by means of which they might learn the natural modes of gold. Since this art is not known to the majority of those who are eager for gold, many frauds consequently are perpetrated in this world. The art of alchemy not only omits these modes, but this gold of twenty-four degrees is very rarely found, and with the greatest difficulty. There have always been a few who during their life have known this secret of alchemy; and this science does not go beyond that. But experimental science by means of Aristotle's *Secrets of Secrets* knows how to produce gold not only of twenty-four degrees but of thirty and forty degrees and of as many degrees as we desire. For this reason Aristotle said to Alexander, "I wish to disclose the greatest secret"; and it really is the greatest secret, for not only would it procure an advantage for the state and for every one his desire because of the sufficiency of gold, but what is infinitely more, it would prolong life. For that medicine which would remove all the impurities and corruptions of a baser metal, so that it should become silver and purest gold, is thought by scientists to be able to remove the corruptions of the human body to such an extent that it would prolong life for many ages. This is the tempered body of elements, of which I spoke above.

CHAPTER ON THE THIRD PREROGATIVE OR THE DIGNITY OF THE EXPERIMENTAL ART

But there is a third dignity of this science. It arises from those properties through which it has no connection with the other sciences, but by its own power investigates the secrets of nature. This consists in two things; namely, in the knowledge of the future, the past, and the present, and in wonderful works by which it excels in the power of forming judgments the ordinary astronomy dealing with judgments. For Ptolemy in the book introductory to the *Almagest* says that there is a more certain road than that through the ordinary astronomy, and this is the pathway of experiment, which follows the course of nature, to which many of the philosophers who are believers are turning, just like Aristotle and a host of the authors of judgments formed from the stars, as he himself says, and as we know by proper practice, which cannot be gainsaid. This science was discovered as a complete remedy for human ignorance and inadvertence; for it is difficult to get accurate astronomical instruments, and it is more difficult to get verified tables, especially those in which the motion of the planets is equalized. The use, moreover, of these tables is difficult, but still more difficult is the use of the instruments. But this science has discovered the definitions and the means by which it can answer easily every question, as far as the power of a single branch of philosophy can do so, and by which it can show us the forms of the celestial forces, and the influences of the heavenly bodies on this world without the difficulty of the ordinary astronomy. This part of the science relating to judgments has four principal divisions or secret sciences.

Moreover, certain bear witness that activities of this science which display philosophy consist in changing the character of a region, so that the habits of its people are changed. One of such witnesses was Aristotle himself, the most learned of philosophers. When Alexander asked him in regard to the nations which he had discovered, whether he should exterminate them because of the ferocity of their character, or should permit them to live, he replied in the book of *Secrets,* "If you can alter the air of those nations, permit them to live; if you cannot, then kill them." For he maintained that the air of these nations could be changed advantageously, so that the complexions of their bodies would be changed, and then their minds influenced by their complexions would choose good morals in accordance with the freedom of the will. This is one of the secrets.

Moreover, certain assert that change is effected by the sun. There is, as an illustration, the example of Aristotle when he said to Alexander, "Give a hot drink from the seed of a plant to whomsoever you wish, and he will obey you for the rest of your life." Some maintain that an army may be stupefied and put to flight. Of this number is Aristotle, who says to Alexander, "Take such a stone, and every army will flee from you." They bear witness that these statements and innumerable others of this kind are true, not meaning that violence is done to the freedom of the will, since Aristotle, who maintains this view, says in the *Ethics* that the will cannot be coerced. The body, moreover, can be changed by the influence of things, and the minds of people are then aroused and influenced to desire voluntarily that to which they are directed; just as we see in the book of *Medicine* that through potions and many medicines people can be changed in body and in the passions of the soul and in the inclination of the will.

There are, moreover, other inventions belonging more to nature which do not have as their object a marvelous change in the will, and they are diversified in character. Some of these possess an excellence of wisdom with other advantages, as, for example, perpetual baths most suitable for human use that do not require any artificial renewal; and ever-burning lamps. For we see many things that cannot be impaired by fire, nay, that are purified by fire, like the skin of the salamander and many other things of this kind, which also can be so prepared that they are externally luminous of themselves, and retain the power of fire, and give forth flame and light. Moreover, against foes of the state they have discovered important arts, so that without a sword or any weapon requiring physical contact they could destroy all who offer resistance. There are many kinds of these inventions. Some of these are perceived by no one of the senses, or by smell alone, and of these inventions Aristotle's book explains that of altering the air, but not those of which I spoke above. These last are of a different character, since they act by means of an infection. There are others also that change some one of the senses, and they are diversified in accordance with all the senses.

Certain of these work a change by contact only and thus destroy life. For malta, which is a kind of bitumen and is plentiful in this world, when cast upon an armed man burns him up. The Romans suffered severe loss of life from this in their conquests, as Pliny states in the second book of the *Natural History,* and as the histories attest. Similarly yellow petroleum, that is, oil springing from the rock, burns up whatever it meets if it is properly prepared. For a consuming fire is produced by this which can be extinguished with difficulty; for water cannot put it out. Certain inventions disturb the hearing to such a degree that, if they are set off suddenly at night with sufficient skill, neither city nor army can endure them. No clap of thunder could compare with such noises. Certain of these strike such terror to the sight that the coruscations of the clouds disturb it incomparably less. Gideon is thought to have employed inventions similar to these in the camp of the Midianites. We have an example of this in that toy of children which is made in many parts of the world, namely, an instrument as large as the human thumb. From the force of the salt called saltpeter so horrible a sound is produced at the bursting of so small a thing, namely, a small piece of parchment, that we perceive it exceeds the roar of sharp thunder, and the flash exceeds the greatest brilliancy of the lightning accompanying the thunder.

There are also very many things that slay every poisonous animal by the gentlest touch, and if a circle is made around these animals with things of this kind the animals cannot get out, but die, although they are not touched. But if a man is bitten by a poisonous animal, by the application of the powder of such things he can be healed, as Bede states in his *Ecclesiastical History* and as we know by experience. And thus there are innumerable things that have strange virtues, whose potencies we are ignorant of solely from our neglect of experiment.

But there are other inventions which do not possess such advantage for the state, but are to be looked upon as miracles of nature, such as experiments with the magnet, not only on iron, but on gold and other metals. Moreover, if the experiment on iron were not known, it would be viewed as a great miracle. And surely in respect to the action of the magnet on iron there are phenomena unknown to those who use the magnet which show in a wonderful way the dissolutions of nature. Just as also from these the faithful experimenter knows how to experiment on the mutual attraction of other things, as, for example, the stone that passes to the acid, and bitumen that ignites from fire placed at a distance from it, as Pliny states in the second book of the *Natural History;* and certain other things that are mutually attracted although locally separated. This is truly wonderful beyond all that I have seen and heard. For after I saw this, there has been nothing difficult for my intellect to believe, provided it had a trustworthy authority. And that this fact may not be hidden from your Reverence, this phenomenon occurs in the parts of plants divided and locally separated. For if a sapling of one year's growth is taken, which springs forth beside the roots of the hazel, and is divided longitudinally, and the divided parts separated by the space of a palm or four fingers, and one person holds on one side the extremities of the two parts, and another similarly on the other side, always with an equal and gentle grasp, so that the parts are kept opposite each other in the same position they had before the division, within the space of half a mile[1] the parts of the twig begin to approach each other gradually, but with greater force at the end of the experiment, so that at length they meet and are united. The ends, however, remain apart, because they are prevented from meeting owing to the force exerted by those holding the parts. This is a very wonderful thing. For this reason magicians perform this experiment, repeating different incantations, and they believe that the phenomenon is caused by virtue of the incantations. I have disregarded the incantations and have discovered the wonderful action of nature, which is similar to that of the magnet on iron. For just as the one attracts the other because of the similar nature of the iron and the magnet, so do the parts in this case. Hence the natural force, which is similar in both parts of the twig, causes them to unite. If they were arranged in the required way, they would meet at the extremities just as in the middle and more quickly, as, for example, if the ends were

[1] Time taken to walk half a mile.

minutely pierced and threads passed through the ends, so that they could be suspended in the air without hindrance. This is true not only of hazel saplings but of many others, as in the case of willows and perhaps in that of all saplings if they were arranged in the required manner. But since in such matters the mind thinks more aptly than the pen writes, I forbear for the present. I am here merely writing down the statements of scientists and noting their achievements. The genius of these men I admire more than I understand.

Concluding thus the subject of this science experimental without restriction, I shall now show its advantage to theology, as I have done similarly in the case of the other sciences. Since I have now shown the intrinsic nature of this science, it is evident to all that next to moral philosophy this science is the most useful, and it is so in the first place to theology itself in its unrestricted sense because of the literal and spiritual meaning in which it consists. For I showed above that the literal meaning consists in expressing the truth in regard to created things by means of their definitions and descriptions, and I likewise showed that reasoning does not arrive at this truth, but that experiment does. Wherefore this science next to moral philosophy will present the literal truth of Scripture most effectively, so that through suitable adaptations and similitudes the spiritual sense may be derived, owing to the peculiar nature of the sacred Scripture and in accordance with the methods employed by the sacred writers and by all sages.

Then this science as regards the commonwealth of believers is useful, as we saw in its special knowledge of the future, present, and past, and in its display of wonderful works on behalf of Church and state, so that all useful activities are promoted and the opposite are hindered both in the few and in the multitude, as was explained. And if we proceed to the conversion of unbelievers, it is evidently of service in two main ways with numerous subdivisions, since a plea for the faith can be effectively made through this science, not by arguments but by works, which is the more effective way. For to the man who denies the truth of the faith because he cannot understand it I shall state the mutual attraction of things in nature, just as I described it. Likewise I shall tell him that a jar may be broken without human force, and the wine contained in it remain motionless and without flow for three days; and that gold and silver in a pouch, and a sword in its scabbard may be consumed without injury to their containers, as Seneca states in the book of *Natural Questions*. I shall tell him, moreover, that the birds called kingfisher in the depth of winter compel the stormy sea to be calm and restrain itself until they have laid their eggs and brought forth their young, as Basil and Ambrose in the *Hexaemeron* and philosophers and poets state. For these facts and similar ones ought to influence a man and urge him to accept the divine verities. Since if in the vilest creatures verities are found by which the pride of the human intellect ought to be subdued so that it may believe them although it does not understand them, conviction should follow, or injury will be done to infallible truth, since a man ought rather to humble his mind to the glorious truths of God. Surely there is no comparison.

But there is still another very useful way; since the formation of judgments, as I have said, is a function of this science, in regard to what can happen by nature or be effected in art, and what not. This science, moreover, knows how to separate the illusions of magic and to detect all their errors in incantations, invocations, conjurations, sacrifices, and cults. But unbelievers busy themselves in these mad acts and trust in them, and have believed that the Christians used such means in working their miracles. Wherefore this science is of the greatest advantage in persuading men to accept the faith, since this branch alone of philosophy happens to proceed in this way, because this is the only branch that considers matters of this kind, and is able to overcome all falsehood and superstition and error of unbelievers in regard to magic, such as incantations and the like already mentioned. How far, moreover, it may serve to reprobate obstinate unbelievers is already shown by the violent means that have just been touched upon, and therefore I pass on.

We must consider, however, that although other sciences do many wonders, as in the case of practical geometry, which produces mirrors that burn up every opposing object, and so too in the other sciences, yet all things of such wonderful utility in the state belong chiefly to this science. For this science has the same relation to the other sciences as the science of navigation to the carpenter's art and the military art to that of the engineer. For this science teaches how wonderful instruments may be made, and uses them when made, and also considers all secret things owing to the advantages they may possess for the state and for individuals; and it directs other sciences as its handmaids, and therefore the whole power of speculative science is attributed especially to this science. And now the wonderful advantage derived from these three sciences in this world on behalf of the Church of God against the enemies of the faith is manifest, who should be destroyed rather by the discoveries of science than by the warlike arms of combatants. Antichrist will use these means freely and effectively, in order that he may crush and confound the power of this world; and by these means tyrants in times past brought the world under their sway. This has been shown by examples without end.

But I now cite the one example of Alexander the Great in place of all other examples that might be cited, who when he set out for Greece to conquer the world had only 32,000 foot soldiers and 4500 horsemen, as Orosius states to Augustine in his book *Ormesta Mundi,* bringing war with so small a force upon the whole world. It is uncertain which is the more wonderful, that he conquered or that he ventured the attack. In his first battle with King Darius he overcame 600,000 Persians with a loss in his army of 20 horsemen and nine foot soldiers. In the second battle he conquered 400,000 men, and of his own army 130 foot soldiers and 150 horsemen fell. After this he easily subdued the rest of the world, which had become terrified. But Orosius says that he conquered not less by skill than by the valor of the Macedonians. Nor is it to be wondered at, since Aristotle was with him in these wars, as we read in the life of Aristotle. Seneca, moreover, states in the *Natural Questions* that Alexander conquered the world under the guidance of Aristotle and Callisthenes, who were his teachers in all knowledge. But Aristotle was his chief teacher; and it is easily apparent from what has been said how by the paths of knowledge Aristotle was able to hand over the world to Alexander. Moreover, the Church should consider the employment of these inventions against unbelievers and rebels, in order that it may spare Christian blood, and especially should it do so because of future perils in the times of Antichrist, which with the grace of God it would be easy to meet, if prelates and princes promoted study and investigated the secrets of nature and of art.

Suggestions for Further Reading

Little, A. G. (ed.). *Roger Bacon Essays,* Oxford, 1914; Bridges, J. H. *The Life and Work of Roger Bacon,* London, 1914; *FCC* vol. II, 442-448; *EG* 294-312; *AAM* 127-136; *RMcK* vol. II, 3-110.

St. Thomas Aquinas

St. Thomas Aquinas was born at Roccasacca Castle, near Naples, the youngest son of Landulf, Count of Aquino. His earliest studies were pursued at the Benedictine monastery of Monte Cassino, and at Naples. In spite of determined opposition from his family, who had other plans for his future, Thomas, in 1244, entered the Dominican Order. The next year he entered the University of Paris. Thomas was so quiet, and so preoccupied by his studies, that he was dubbed "the dumb ox" by his fellow students. In 1248 he accompanied his teacher, Albert the Great, to Cologne in order to found a Dominican House of Studies. By 1252 he was back at Paris, where he pursued his higher studies, completing them in 1256. Thomas then taught at Paris until 1259. In this year he traveled to Italy to accept a teaching assignment connected with the Papal Court. In this capacity he was to teach at Anagni under Pope Alexander IV, from 1259 to 1261; at Orvieto and Rome under Urban IV, from 1261 to 1267; and at Viterbo under Clement IV, from 1267 to 1268.

In 1268 Thomas returned to his teaching post at the University of Paris, where he remained until 1272. His next assignment was to Naples, to found a new Dominican House of Studies. Thomas remained there, teaching and writing, until 1274, at which time Pope Gregory X called him to Lyons to participate in the Church Council. His health, however, had been seriously undermined by overwork and study and he was taken ill on the journey. The saint died at the Cistercian monastery of Fossanuova, between Naples and Rome.

Writing as he did in the controversial days following on the reintroduction of the Aristotelian corpus in the west, Thomas produced a philosophical system which has been called by many of its admirers "the supreme synthesis." This system, very far indeed from being the merest potpourri of disparate ideas suggested by the term "synthesis," was the product of a daring and original mind which could envision how elements of Platonism, Augustinianism, Aristotelianism, and even Averroism, could be utilized to expound a total point of view which remained faithful at once to the brute facts of everyday experience and to the orthodox teachings of Catholicism.

St. Thomas was a most prolific writer. From among his many works we have chosen to present below the opening chapters of his massive and astonishingly fertile *Summa Contra Gentiles.*

ST. THOMAS ON THE TRUTH OF THE CATHOLIC FAITH *

CHAPTER 1

THE OFFICE OF THE WISE MAN

"My mouth shall meditate truth, and my lips shall hate impiety" (*Prov.* 8:7).

1. The usage of the multitude, which according to the Philosopher is to be followed in giving names to things,[1] has commonly held that they are to be called wise who order things rightly and govern them well. Hence, among other things that men have conceived about the wise man, the Philosopher in-

* Reprinted by permission of Doubleday and Company from *On the Truth of the Catholic Faith* (*Summa Contra Gentiles*), Book I: God, translated by A. C. Pegis. Published as an Image Book Original, New York, 1955.

[1] Aristotle, *Topics*, II, 1 (102a 30).

cludes the notion that "it belongs to the wise man to order." [2] Now, the rule of government and order for all things directed to an end must be taken from the end. For, since the end of each thing is its good, a thing is then best disposed when it is fittingly ordered to its end. And so we see among the arts that one functions as the governor and the ruler of another because it controls its end. Thus, the art of medicine rules and orders the art of the chemist because health, with which medicine is concerned, is the end of all the medications prepared by the art of the chemist. A similar situation obtains in the art of ship navigation in relation to shipbuilding, and in the military art with respect to the equestrian art and the equipment of war. The arts that rule other arts are called architectonic, as being the ruling arts. That is why the artisans devoted to these arts, who are called master artisans, appropriate to themselves the name of wise men. But, since these artisans are concerned, in each case, with the ends of certain particular things, they do not reach to the universal end of all things. They are therefore said to be wise with respect to this or that thing; in which sense it is said that "as a wise architect, I have laid the foundation" (I Cor. 3:10). The name of the absolutely wise man, however, is reserved for him whose consideration is directed to the end of the universe, which is also the origin of the universe. That is why, according to the Philosopher, it belongs to the wise man to consider the highest causes.[3]

2. Now, the end of each thing is that which is intended by its first author or mover. But the first author and mover of the universe is an intellect, as will be later shown.[4] The ultimate end of the universe must, therefore, be the good of an intellect. This good is truth. Truth must consequently be the ultimate end of the whole universe, and the consideration of the wise man aims principally at truth. So it is that, according to His own statement, divine Wisdom testifies that He has assumed flesh and come into the world in order to make the truth known: "For this was I born, and for this came I into

---

[2] Aristotle, *Metaphysics*, I, 2 (982a 18).
[3] Aristotle, *Metaphysics*, I, 1 (981b 28).
[4] See below, ch. 44; also *SCG*, II, ch. 24.

the world, that I should give testimony to the truth" (John 18:37). The Philosopher himself establishes that first philosophy is the science of truth, not of any truth, but of that truth which is the origin of all truth, namely, which belongs to the first principle whereby all things are. The truth belonging to such a principle is, clearly, the source of all truth; for things have the same disposition in truth as in being.[5]

3. It belongs to one and the same science, however, both to pursue one of two contraries and to oppose the other. Medicine, for example, seeks to effect health and to eliminate illness. Hence, just as it belongs to the wise man to meditate especially on the truth belonging to the first principle and to teach it to others, so it belongs to him to refute the opposing falsehood.

4. Appropriately, therefore, is the twofold office of the wise man shown from the mouth of Wisdom in our opening words: to meditate and speak forth of the divine truth, which is truth in person (Wisdom touches on this in the words *my mouth shall meditate truth*), and to refute the opposing error (which Wisdom touches on in the words *and my lips shall hate impiety*). By *impiety* is here meant falsehood against the divine truth. This falsehood is contrary to religion, which is likewise named *piety*. Hence, the falsehood contrary to it is called *impiety*.[6]

CHAPTER 2

THE AUTHOR'S INTENTION IN THE PRESENT WORK

1. Among all human pursuits, the pursuit of wisdom is more perfect, more noble, more useful, and more full of joy.

It is more perfect because, in so far as a man gives himself to the pursuit of wisdom, so far does he even now have some share in true beatitude. And so a wise man has said: "Blessed is the man that shall continue in wisdom" (Ecclus. 14:22).

---

[5] Aristotle, *Metaphysics*, Iα, 1 (993b 30).

[6] In the present chapter, I have changed *wickedness* in the Douay text to *impiety*, since this is demanded by the sense.

It is more noble because through this pursuit man especially approaches to a likeness to God Who "made all things in wisdom" (Ps. 103:24). And since likeness is the cause of love, the pursuit of wisdom especially joins man to God in friendship. That is why it is said of wisdom that "she is an infinite treasure to men! which they that use become the friends of God" (Wis. 7:14).

It is more useful because through wisdom we arrive at the kingdom of immortality. For "the desire of wisdom bringeth to the everlasting kingdom" (Wis. 6:21).

It is more full of joy because "her conversation hath no bitterness, nor her company any tediousness, but joy and gladness" (Wis. 7:16).

2. And so, in the name of the divine Mercy, I have the confidence to embark upon the work of a wise man, even though this may surpass my powers, and I have set myself the task of making known, as far as my limited powers will allow, the truth that the Catholic faith professes, and of setting aside the errors that are opposed to it. To use the words of Hilary: "I am aware that I owe this to God as the chief duty of my life, that my every word and sense may speak of Him." [1]

3. To proceed against individual errors, however, is a difficult business, and this for two reasons. In the first place, it is difficult because the sacrilegious remarks of individual men who have erred are not so well known to us so that we may use what they say as the basis of proceeding to a refutation of their errors. This is, indeed, the method that the ancient Doctors of the Church used in the refutation of the errors of the Gentiles. For they could know the positions taken by the Gentiles since they themselves had been Gentiles, or at least had lived among the Gentiles and had been instructed in their teaching. In the second place, it is difficult because some of them, such as the Mohammedans and the pagans, do not agree with us in accepting the authority of any Scripture, by which they may be convinced of their error. Thus, against the Jews we are able to argue by means of the Old Testament, while

[1] St. Hilary, *De Trinitate*, I, 37 (*PL*, 10, 48).

against heretics we are able to argue by means of the New Testament. But the Mohammedans and the pagans accept neither the one nor the other. We must, therefore, have recourse to the natural reason, to which all men are forced to give their assent. However, it is true, in divine matters the natural reason has its failings.

4. Now, while we are investigating some given truth, we shall also show what errors are set aside by it; and we shall likewise show how the truth that we come to know by demonstration is in accord with the Christian religion.

CHAPTER 3

ON THE WAY IN WHICH DIVINE TRUTH IS TO BE MADE KNOWN

1. The way of making truth known is not always the same, and, as the Philosopher has very well said, "it belongs to an educated man to seek such certitude in each thing as the nature of that thing allows." [1] The remark is also introduced by Boethius.[2] But, since such is the case, we must first show what way is open to us in order that we may make known the truth which is our object.

2. There is a twofold mode of truth in what we profess about God. Some truths about God exceed all the ability of the human reason. Such is the truth that God is triune. But there are some truths which the natural reason also is able to reach. Such are that God exists, that He is one, and the like. In fact, such truths about God have been proved demonstratively by the philosophers, guided by the light of the natural reason.

3. That there are certain truths about God that totally surpass man's ability appears with the greatest evidence. Since, indeed, the principle of all knowledge that the reason perceives about some thing is the understanding of the very substance of that being (for according to Aristotle "what a thing is" is the

---

1 Aristotle, *Nicomachean Ethics*, I, 3 (1094b 24).
2 Boethius, *De Trinitate*, II (*PL*, 64, col. 1250).

principle of demonstration),[3] it is necessary that the way in which we understand the substance of a thing determines the way in which we know what belongs to it. Hence, if the human intellect comprehends the substance of some thing, for example, that of a stone or of a triangle, no intelligible characteristic belonging to that thing surpasses the grasp of the human reason. But this does not happen to us in the case of God. For the human intellect is not able to reach a comprehension of the divine substance through its natural power. For, according to its manner of knowing in the present life, the intellect depends on the sense for the origin of knowledge; and so those things that do not fall under the senses cannot be grasped by the human intellect except in so far as the knowledge of them is gathered from sensible things. Now, sensible things cannot lead the human intellect to the point of seeing in them the nature of the divine substance; for sensible things are effects that fall short of the power of their cause. Yet, beginning with sensible things, our intellect is led to the point of knowing about God that He exists, and other such characteristics that must be attributed to the First Principle. There are, consequently, some intelligible truths about God that are open to the human reason; but there are others that absolutely surpass its power.

4. We may easily see the same point from the gradation of intellects. Consider the case of two persons of whom one has a more penetrating grasp of a thing by his intellect than does the other. He who has the superior intellect understands many things that the other cannot grasp at all. Such is the case with a very simple person who cannot at all grasp the subtle speculations of philosophy. But the intellect of an angel surpasses the human intellect much more than the intellect of the greatest philosopher surpasses the intellect of the most uncultivated simple person; for the distance between the best philosopher and a simple person is contained within the limits of the human species, which the angelic intellect surpasses. For the angel knows God on the basis of a more noble effect than does man; and this by as much as the substance of an angel,

---

[3] Aristotle, *Posterior Analytics*, II, 3 (90b 31).

through which the angel in his natural knowledge is led to the knowledge of God, is nobler than sensible things and even than the soul itself, through which the human intellect mounts to the knowledge of God. The divine intellect surpasses the angelic intellect much more than the angelic surpasses the human. For the divine intellect is in its capacity equal to its substance, and therefore it understands fully what it is, including all its intelligible attributes. But by his natural knowledge the angel does not know what God is, since the substance itself of the angel, through which he is led to the knowledge of God, is an effect that is not equal to the power of its cause. Hence, the angel is not able, by means of his natural knowledge, to grasp all the things that God understands in Himself; nor is the human reason sufficient to grasp all the things that the angel understands through his own natural power. Just as, therefore, it would be the height of folly for a simple person to assert that what a philosopher proposes is false on the ground that he himself cannot understand it, so (and even more so) it is the acme of stupidity for a man to suspect as false what is divinely revealed through the ministry of the angels simply because it cannot be investigated by reason.

5. The same thing, moreover, appears quite clearly from the defect that we experience every day in our knowledge of things. We do not know a great many of the properties of sensible things, and in most cases we are not able to discover fully the natures of those properties that we apprehend by the sense. Much more is it the case, therefore, that the human reason is not equal to the task of investigating all the intelligible characteristics of that most excellent substance.

6. The remark of Aristotle likewise agrees with this conclusion. He says that "our intellect is related to the prime beings, which are most evident in their nature, as the eye of an owl is related to the sun." [4]

7. Sacred Scripture also gives testimony to this truth. We read in Job: "Peradventure thou wilt comprehend the steps of God, and wilt find out the Almighty perfectly?" (11:7). And

---

[4] Aristotle, *Metaphysics*, Iα, 1 (993b 9).

again: "Behold, God is great, exceeding our knowledge" (Job 36:26). And St. Paul: "We know in part" (I Cor. 13:9).

8. We should not, therefore, immediately reject as false, following the opinion of the Manicheans and many unbelievers, everything that is said about God even though it cannot be investigated by reason.

CHAPTER 4

THAT THE TRUTH ABOUT GOD TO WHICH THE NATURAL REASON REACHES IS FITTINGLY PROPOSED TO MEN FOR BELIEF

1. Since, therefore, there exists a twofold truth concerning the divine being, one to which the inquiry of the reason can reach, the other which surpasses the whole ability of the human reason, it is fitting that both of these truths be proposed to man divinely for belief. This point must first be shown concerning the truth that is open to the inquiry of the reason; otherwise, it might perhaps seem to someone that, since such a truth can be known by the reason, it was uselessly given to men through a supernatural inspiration as an object of belief.

2. Yet, if this truth were left solely as a matter of inquiry for the human reason, three awkward consequences would follow.

3. The first is that few men would possess the knowledge of God. For there are three reasons why most men are cut off from the fruit of diligent inquiry which is the discovery of truth. Some do not have the physical disposition of such work. As a result, there are many who are naturally not fitted to pursue knowledge; and so, however much they tried, they would be unable to reach the highest level of human knowledge which consists in knowing God. Others are cut off from pursuing this truth by the necessities imposed upon them by their daily lives. For some men must devote themselves to taking care of temporal matters. Such men would not be able to give so much time to the leisure of contemplative inquiry as to reach the

highest peak at which human investigation can arrive, namely, the knowledge of God. Finally, there are some who are cut off by indolence. In order to know the things that the reason can investigate concerning God, a knowledge of many things must already be possessed. For almost all of philosophy is directed toward the knowledge of God, and that is why metaphysics, which deals with divine things, is the last part of philosophy to be learned. This means that we are able to arrive at the inquiry concerning the aforementioned truth only on the basis of a great deal of labor spent in study. Now, those who wish to undergo such a labor for the mere love of knowledge are few, even though God has inserted into the minds of men a natural appetite for knowledge.

4. The second awkward effect is that those who would come to discover the above-mentioned truth would barely reach it after a great deal of time. The reasons are several. There is the profundity of this truth, which the human intellect is made capable of grasping by natural inquiry only after a long training. Then, there are many things that must be presupposed, as we have said. There is also the fact that, in youth, when the soul is swayed by the various movements of the passions, it is not in a suitable state for the knowledge of such lofty truth. On the contrary, "one becomes wise and knowing in repose," as it is said in the *Physics*.[1] The result is this. If the only way open to us for the knowledge of God were solely that of the reason, the human race would remain in the blackest shadows of ignorance. For then the knowledge of God, which especially renders men perfect and good, would come to be possessed only by a few, and these few would require a great deal of time in order to reach it.

5. The third awkward effect is this. The investigation of the human reason for the most part has falsity present within it, and this is due partly to the weakness of our intellect in judgment, and partly to the admixture of images. The result is that many, remaining ignorant of the power of demonstration, would hold in doubt those things that have been most

---

[1] Aristotle, *Physics*, VII, 3 (247b 9).

truly demonstrated. This would be particularly the case since they see that, among those who are reputed to be wise men, each one teaches his own brand of doctrine. Futhermore, with the many truths that are demonstrated, there sometimes is mingled something that is false, which is not demonstrated but rather asserted on the basis of some probable or sophistical argument, which yet has the credit of being a demonstration. That is why it was necessary that the unshakeable certitude and pure truth concerning divine things should be presented to men by way of faith.[2]

6. Beneficially, therefore, did the divine Mercy provide that it should instruct us to hold by faith even those truths that the human reason is able to investigate. In this way, all men would easily be able to have a share in the knowledge of God, and this without uncertainty and error.

7. Hence it is written: "Henceforward you walk not as also the Gentiles walk in the vanity of their mind, having their understanding darkened" (Eph. 4:17-18). And again: "All thy children shall be taught of the Lord" (Isa. 54:13).

CHAPTER 5

THAT THE TRUTHS THE HUMAN REASON IS NOT ABLE TO INVESTIGATE ARE FITTINGLY PROPOSED TO MEN FOR BELIEF

1. Now, perhaps some will think that men should not be asked to believe what the reason is not adequate to investigate, since the divine Wisdom provides in the case of each

---

[2] Although St. Thomas does not name Maimonides or his *Guide for the Perplexed* (*Dux neutrorum*), there are evident points of contact between the Catholic and the Jewish theologian. On the reasons for revelation given here, on our knowledge of God, on creation and the eternity of the world, and on Aristotelianism in general, St. Thomas has Maimonides in mind both to agree and to disagree with him. By way of background for *SCG*, I, the reader can usefully consult the references to Maimonides in E. Gilson, *History of Christian Philosophy in the Middle Ages* (New York, 1955), pp. 649-651.

thing according to the mode of its nature. We must therefore prove that it is necessary for man to receive from God as objects of belief even those truths that are above the human reason.

2. No one tends with desire and zeal toward something that is not already known to him. But, as we shall examine later on in this work, men are ordained by the divine Providence toward a higher good than human fragility can experience in the present life.[1] That is why it was necessary for the human mind to be called to something higher than the human reason here and now can reach, so that it would thus learn to desire something and with zeal tend toward something that surpasses the whole state of the present life. This belongs especially to the Christian religion, which in a unique way promises spiritual and eternal goods. And so there are many things proposed to men in it that transcend human sense. The Old Law, on the other hand, whose promises were of a temporal character, contained very few proposals that transcended the inquiry of the human reason. Following this same direction, the philosophers themselves, in order that they might lead men from the pleasure of sensible things to virtue, were concerned to show that there were in existence other goods of a higher nature than these things of sense, and that those who gave themselves to the active or contemplative virtues would find much sweeter enjoyment in the taste of these higher goods.

3. It is also necessary that such truth be proposed to men for belief so that they may have a truer knowledge of God. For then only do we know God truly when we believe Him to be above everything that it is possible for man to think about Him; for, as we have shown,[2] the divine substance surpasses the natural knowledge of which man is capable. Hence, by the fact that some things about God are proposed to man that surpass his reason, there is strengthened in man the view that God is something above what he can think.

4. Another benefit that comes from the revelation to men

---

[1] *SCG*, III, ch. 48.

[2] See above, ch. 3.

of truths that exceed the reason is the curbing of presumption, which is the mother of error. For there are some who have such a presumptuous opinion of their own ability that they deem themselves able to measure the nature of everything; I mean to say that, in their estimation, everything is true that seems to them so, and everything is false that does not. So that the human mind, therefore, might be freed from this presumption and come to a humble inquiry after truth, it was necessary that some things should be proposed to man by God that would completely surpass his intellect.

5. A still further benefit may also be seen in what Aristotle says in the *Ethics*.[3] There was a certain Simonides who exhorted people to put aside the knowledge of divine things and to apply their talents to human occupations. He said that "he who is a man should know human things, and he who is mortal, things that are mortal." Against Simonides Aristotle says that "man should draw himself toward what is immortal and divine as much as he can." And so he says in the *De animalibus* that, although what we know of the higher substances is very little, yet that little is loved and desired more than all the knowledge that we have about less noble substances.[4] He also says in the *De caelo et mundo* that when questions about the heavenly bodies can be given even a modest and merely plausible solution, he who hears this experiences intense joy.[5] From all these considerations it is clear that even the most imperfect knowledge about the most noble realities brings the greatest perfection to the soul. Therefore, although the human reason cannot grasp fully the truths that are above it, yet, if it somehow holds these truths at least by faith, it acquires great perfection for itself.

6. Therefore it is written: "For many things are shown to thee above the understanding of men" (Ecclus. 3:25). Again: "So the things that are of God no man knoweth but the Spirit of God. But to us God hath revealed them by His Spirit" (I Cor. 2:11, 10).

---

3 Aristotle, *Nicomachean Ethics*, X, 7 (1177b 31).
4 Aristotle, *De partibus animalium*, I, 5 (644b 32).
5 Aristotle, *De caelo et mundo*, II, 12 (291b 26).

CHAPTER 6

THAT TO GIVE ASSENT TO THE TRUTHS OF FAITH IS NOT FOOLISHNESS EVEN THOUGH THEY ARE ABOVE REASON

1. Those who place their faith in this truth, however, "for which the human reason offers no experimental evidence,"[1] do not believe foolishly, as though "following artificial fables" (II Peter 1:16). For these "secrets of divine Wisdom" (Job 11:6) the divine Wisdom itself, which knows all things to the full, has deigned to reveal to men. It reveals its own presence, as well as the truth of its teaching and inspiration, by fitting arguments; and in order to confirm those truths that exceed natural knowledge, it gives visible manifestation to works that surpass the ability of all nature. Thus, there are the wonderful cures of illnesses, there is the raising of the dead, and the wonderful immutation in the heavenly bodies; and what is more wonderful, there is the inspiration given to human minds, so that simple and untutored persons, filled with the gift of the Holy Spirit, come to possess instantaneously the highest wisdom and the readiest eloquence. When these arguments were examined, through the efficacy of the above-mentioned proof, and not the violent assault of arms or the promise of pleasures, and (what is most wonderful of all) in the midst of the tyranny of the persecutors, an innumerable throng of people, both simple and most learned, flocked to the Christian faith. In this faith there are truths preached that surpass every human intellect; the pleasures of the flesh are curbed; it is taught that the things of the world should be spurned. Now, for the minds of mortal men to assent these things is the greatest of miracles, just as it is a manifest work of divine inspiration that, spurning visible things, men should seek only what is invisible. Now, that this has happened neither without preparation nor by chance,

[1] St. Gregory, *Homiliae in evangelia*, II, hom. 26, i (*PL*, 76, col. 1197).

but as a result of the disposition of God, is clear from the fact that through many pronouncements of the ancient prophets God had foretold that He would do this. The books of these prophets are held in veneration among us Christians, since they give witness to our faith.

2. The manner of this confirmation is touched on by St. Paul: "Which," that is, human salvation, "having begun to be declared by the Lord, was confirmed unto us by them that hear Him: God also bearing them witness of signs, and wonders, and divers miracles, and distributions of the Holy Ghost" (Heb. 2:3-4).

3. This wonderful conversion of the world to the Christian faith is the clearest witness of the signs given in the past; so that it is not necessary that they should be further repeated, since they appear most clearly in their effect. For it would be truly more wonderful than all signs if the world had been led by simple and humble men to believe such lofty truths, to accomplish such difficult actions, and to have such high hopes. Yet it is also a fact that, even in our own time, God does not cease to work miracles through His saints for the confirmation of the faith.

4. On the other hand, those who founded sects committed to erroneous doctrines proceeded in a way that is opposite to this. The point is clear in the case of Mohammed. He seduced the people by promises of carnal pleasure to which the concupiscence of the flesh goads us. His teaching also contained precepts that were in conformity with his promises, and he gave free rein to carnal pleasure. In all this, as is not unexpected, he was obeyed by carnal men. As for proofs of the truth of his doctrine, he brought forward only such as could be grasped by the natural ability of anyone with a very modest wisdom. Indeed, the truths that he taught he mingled with many fables and with doctrines of the greatest falsity. He did not bring forth any signs produced in a supernatural way, which alone fittingly gives witness to divine inspiration; for a visible action that can be only divine reveals an invisibly inspired teacher of truth. On the contrary, Mohammed said that he was sent in the power of his arms—which are signs

not lacking even to robbers and tyrants. What is more, no wise men, men trained in things divine and human, believed in him from the beginning. Those who believed in him were brutal men and desert wanderers, utterly ignorant of all divine teaching, through whose numbers Mohammed forced others to become his followers by the violence of his arms. Nor do divine pronouncements on the part of preceding prophets offer him any witness. On the contrary, he perverts almost all the testimonies of the Old and New Testaments by making them into fabrications of his own, as can be seen by anyone who examines his law. It was, therefore, a shrewd decision on his part to forbid his followers to read the Old and New Testaments, lest these books convict him of falsity. It is thus clear that those who place any faith in his words believe foolishly.

CHAPTER 7

THAT THE TRUTH OF REASON IS NOT OPPOSED TO THE TRUTH OF THE CHRISTIAN FAITH

1. Now, although the truth of the Christian faith which we have discussed surpasses the capacity of the reason, nevertheless that truth that the human reason is naturally endowed to know cannot be opposed to the truth of the Christian faith. For that with which the human reason is naturally endowed is clearly most true; so much so, that it is impossible for us to think of such truths as false. Nor is it permissible to believe as false that which we hold by faith, since this is confirmed in a way that is so clearly divine. Since, therefore, only the false is opposed to the true, as is clearly evident from an examination of their definitions, it is impossible that the truth of faith should be opposed to those principles that the human reason knows naturally.

2. Furthermore, that which is introduced into the soul of the student by the teacher is contained in the knowledge of the teacher—unless his teaching is fictitious, which it is im-

proper to say of God. Now, the knowledge of the principles that are known to us naturally has been implanted in us by God; for God is the Author of our nature. These principles, therefore, are also contained by the divine Wisdom. Hence, whatever is opposed to them is opposed to the divine Wisdom, and, therefore, cannot come from God. That which we hold by faith as divinely revealed, therefore, cannot be contrary to our natural knowledge.

3. Again. In the presence of contrary arguments our intellect is chained, so that it cannot proceed to the knowledge of the truth. If, therefore, contrary knowledges were implanted in us by God, our intellect would be hindered from knowing truth by this very fact. Now, such an effect cannot come from God.

4. And again. What is natural cannot change as long as nature does not. Now, it is impossible that contrary opinions should exist in the same knowing subject at the same time. No opinion or belief, therefore, is implanted in man by God which is contrary to man's natural knowledge.

5. Therefore, the Apostle says: "The word is nigh thee, even in thy mouth and in thy heart. This is the word of faith, which we preach" (Rom. 10:8). But because it overcomes reason, there are some who think that it is opposed to it: which is impossible.

6. The authority of St. Augustine also agrees with this. He writes as follows: "That which truth will reveal cannot in any way be opposed to the sacred books of the Old and the New Testament." [1]

7. From this we evidently gather the following conclusion: whatever arguments are brought forward against the doctrines of faith are conclusions incorrectly derived from the first and self-evident principles imbedded in nature. Such conclusions do not have the force of demonstration; they are arguments that are either probable or sophistical. And so, there exists the possibility to answer them.

[1] St. Augustine, *De genesi ad litteram*, II, c. 18 (*PL*, 34, col. 280).

CHAPTER 8

HOW THE HUMAN REASON IS RELATED TO THE TRUTH OF FAITH

1. There is also a further consideration. Sensible things, from which the human reason takes the origin of its knowledge, retain within themselves some sort of trace of a likeness to God. This is so imperfect, however, that it is absolutely inadequate to manifest the substance of God. For effects bear within themselves, in their own way, the likeness of their causes, since an agent produces its like; yet an effect does not always reach to the full likeness of its cause. Now, the human reason is related to the knowledge of the truth of faith (a truth which can be most evident only to those who see the divine substance) in such a way that it can gather certain likenesses of it, which are yet not sufficient so that the truth of faith may be comprehended as being understood demonstratively or through itself. Yet it is useful for the human reason to exercise itself in such arguments, however weak they may be, provided only that there be present no presumption to comprehend or to demonstrate. For to be able to see something of the loftiest realities, however thin and weak the sight may be, is, as our previous remarks indicate, a cause of the greatest joy.

2. The testimony of Hilary agrees with this. Speaking of this same truth, he writes as follows in his *De Trinitate:* "Enter these truths by believing, press forward, persevere. And though I may know that you will not arrive at an end, yet I will congratulate you in your progress. For, though he who pursues the infinite with reverence will never finally reach the end, yet he will always progress by pressing onward. But do not intrude yourself into the divine secret, do not, presuming to comprehend the sum total of intelligence, plunge yourself into the mystery of the unending nativity; rather, understand that these things are incomprehensible."[1]

[1] St. Hilary, *De Trinitate*, II, 10, ii (*PL*, 10, coll. 58-59).

CHAPTER 9

THE ORDER AND MANNER OF PROCEDURE IN THE PRESENT WORK

1. It is clearly apparent, from what has been said, that the intention of the wise man ought to be directed toward the twofold truth of divine things, and toward the destruction of the errors that are contrary to this truth. One kind of divine truth the investigation of the reason is competent to reach, whereas the other surpasses every effort of the reason. I am speaking of a "twofold truth of divine things," not on the part of God Himself, Who is truth one and simple, but from the point of view of our knowledge, which is variously related to the knowledge of divine things.

2. Now, to make the first kind of divine truth known, we must proceed through demonstrative arguments, by which our adversary may become convinced. However, since such arguments are not available for the second kind of divine truth, our intention should not be to convince our adversary by arguments: it should be to answer his arguments against the truth; for, as we have shown,[1] the natural reason cannot be contrary to the truth of faith. The sole way to overcome an adversary of divine truth is from the authority of Scripture—an authority divinely confirmed by miracles. For that which is above the human reason we believe only because God has revealed it. Nevertheless, there are certain likely arguments that should be brought forth in order to make divine truth known. This should be done for the training and consolation of the faithful, and not with any idea of refuting those who are adversaries. For the very inadequacy of the arguments would rather strengthen them in their error, since they would imagine that our acceptance of the truth of faith was based on such weak arguments.

3. This, then, is the manner of procedure we intend to follow. We shall first seek to make known that truth which

---

[1] See above, ch. 7.

faith professes and reason investigates.[2] This we shall do by bringing forward both demonstrative and probable arguments, some of which were drawn from the books of the philosophers and of the saints, through which truth is strengthened and its adversary overcome. Then, in order to follow a development from the more manifest to the less manifest, we shall proceed to make known that truth which surpasses reason, answering the objections of its adversaries and setting forth the truth of faith by probable arguments and by authorities, to the best of our ability.[3]

4. We are aiming, then, to set out following the way of the reason and to inquire into what the human reason can investigate about God. In this aim the first consideration that confronts us is of that which belongs to God in Himself.[4] The second consideration concerns the coming forth of creatures from God.[5] The third concerns the ordering of creatures to God as to their end.[6]

5. Now, among the inquiries that we must undertake concerning God in Himself, we must set down in the beginning that whereby His Existence is demonstrated, as the necessary foundation of the whole work. For, if we do not demonstrate that God exists, all consideration of divine things is necessarily suppressed.

CHAPTER 10

THE OPINION OF THOSE WHO SAY THAT THE EXISTENCE OF GOD, BEING SELF-EVIDENT, CANNOT BE DEMONSTRATED

1. There are some persons to whom the inquiry seeking to demonstrate that God exists may perhaps appear super-

---

[2] This effort occupies St. Thomas through Books I-III of the present work.

[3] The transition of Books I-III to Book IV may be clearly seen from the last two paragraphs of the first chapter of Book IV.

[4] This is the subject of Book I.

[5] This is the subject of Book II.

[6] This is the subject of Book III.

fluous. These are the persons who assert that the existence of God is self-evident, in such wise that its contrary cannot be entertained in the mind. It thus appears that the existence of God cannot be demonstrated, as may be seen from the following arguments.

2. Those propositions are said to be self-evident that are known immediately upon the knowledge of their terms. Thus, as soon as you know the nature of a *whole* and the nature of a *part,* you know immediately that every whole is greater than its part. The proposition *God exists* is of this sort. For by the name *God* we understand something than which a greater cannot be thought. This notion is formed in the intellect by one who hears and understands the name *God.* As a result, God must exist already at least in the intellect. But He cannot exist solely in the intellect, since that which exists both in the intellect and in reality is greater than that which exists in the intellect alone. Now, as the very definition of the name points out, nothing can be greater than God. Consequently, the proposition that God exists is self-evident, as being evident from the very meaning of the name God.

3. Again, it is possible to think that something exists whose non-existence cannot be thought. Clearly, such a being is greater than the being whose non-existence can be thought. Consequently, if God Himself could be thought not to be, then something greater than God could be thought. This, however, is contrary to the definition of the name God. Hence, the proposition that God exists is self-evident.

4. Furthermore, those propositions ought to be the most evident in which the same thing is predicated of itself, for example, *man is man,* or whose predicates are included in the definition of their subjects, for example, *man is an animal.* Now, in God, as will be shown in a later chapter,[1] it is pre-eminently the case that His being is His essence, so that to the question *what is He?* and to the question *is He?* the answer is one and the same. Thus, in the proposition *God*

---

1 See below, ch. 22.

exists, the predicate is consequently either identical with the subject or at least included in the definition of the subject. Hence, that God exists is self-evident.

5. What is naturally known is known through itself, for we do not come to such propositions through an effort of inquiry. But the proposition that God exists is naturally known since, as will be shown later on,[2] the desire of man naturally tends toward God as toward the ultimate end. The proposition that God exists is, therefore, self-evident.

6. There is also the consideration that that through which all the rest are known ought itself to be self-evident. Now, God is of this sort. For just as the light of the sun is the principle of all visible perception, so the divine light is the principle of all intelligible knowledge; since the divine light is that in which intelligible illumination is found first and in its highest degree. That God exists, therefore, must be self-evident.

7. These, then, and others like them are the arguments by which some think that the proposition *God exists* is so self-evident that its contrary cannot be entertained by the mind.

CHAPTER 11

A REFUTATION OF THE ABOVE-MENTIONED OPINION AND A SOLUTION OF THE ARGUMENTS

1. In part, the above opinion arises from the custom by which from their earliest days people are brought up to hear and to call upon the name of God. Custom, and especially custom in a child, comes to have the force of nature. As a result, what the mind is steeped in from childhood it clings to very firmly, as something known naturally and self-evidently.

2. In part, however, the above opinion comes about be-

2 *SCG*, III, ch. 25.

cause of a failure to distinguish between that which is self-evident in an absolute sense and that which is self-evident in relation to us. For assuredly that God exists is, absolutely speaking, self-evident, since what God is is His own being. Yet, because we are not able to conceive in our minds that which God is, that God exists remains unknown in relation to us. So, too, that every whole is greater than its part is, absolutely speaking, self-evident; but it would perforce be unknown to one who could not conceive the nature of a whole. Hence it comes about, as it is said in *Metaphysics* II, that "our intellect is related to the most knowable things in reality as the eye of an owl is related to the sun." [1]

3. And, contrary to the point made by the *first* argument, it does not follow immediately that, as soon as we know the meaning of the name *God,* the existence of God is known. It does not follow first because it is not known to all, even including those who admit that God exists, that God is that than which a greater cannot be thought. After all, many ancients said that this world itself was God. Furthermore, no such inference can be drawn from the interpretations of the name *God* to be found in Damascene.[2] What is more, granted that everyone should understand by the name *God* something than which a greater cannot be thought, it will still not be necessary that there exist in reality something than which a greater cannot be thought. For a thing and the definition of a name are posited in the same way. Now, from the fact that that which is indicated by the name *God* is conceived by the mind, it does not follow that God exists save only in the intellect. Hence, that than which a greater cannot be thought will likewise not have to exist save only in the intellect. From this it does not follow that there exists in reality something than which a greater cannot be thought. No difficulty, consequently, befalls anyone who posits that God does not exist. For that something greater can be

---

1 Aristotle, *Metaphysics*, Iα, 1 (993b 9).

2 St. John Damascene, *De fide orthodoxa*, I, 9 (*PG*, 94, coll. 836B-837B).

thought than anything given in reality or in the intellect is a difficulty only to him who admits that there is something than which a greater cannot be thought in reality.

4. Nor, again, is it necessary, as the *second* argument advanced, that something greater than God can be thought if God can be thought not to be. For that He can be thought not to be does not arise either from the imperfection or the uncertainty of His own being, since this is in itself most manifest. It arises, rather, from the weakness of our intellect, which cannot behold God Himself except through His effects and which is thus led to know His existence through reasoning.

5. This enables us to solve the *third* argument as well. For just as it is evident to us that a whole is greater than a part of itself, so to those seeing the divine essence in itself it is supremely self-evident that God exists because His essence is His being. But, because we are not able to see His essence, we arrive at the knowledge of His being, not through God Himself, but through His effects.

6. The answer to the *fourth* argument is likewise clear. For man naturally knows God in the same way as he naturally desires God. Now, man naturally desires God in so far as he naturally desires beatitude, which is a certain likeness of the divine goodness. On this basis, it is not necessary that God considered in Himself be naturally known to man, but only a likeness of God. It remains, therefore, that man is to reach the knowledge of God through reasoning by way of the likenesses of God found in His effects.

7. So, too, with the *fifth* argument, an easy solution is available. For God is indeed that by which all things are known, not in the sense that they are not known unless He is known (as obtains among self-evident principles), but because all our knowledge is caused in us through His influence.

CHAPTER 12

THE OPINION OF THOSE WHO SAY THAT THE EXISTENCE OF GOD CANNOT BE DEMONSTRATED BUT IS HELD BY FAITH ALONE

1. There are others who hold a certain opinion, contrary to the position mentioned above, through which the efforts of those seeking to prove the existence of God would likewise be rendered futile. For they say that we cannot arrive at the existence of God through the reason; it is received by way of faith and revelation alone.

2. What led some persons to hold this view was the weakness of the arguments which had been brought forth by others to prove that God exists.

3. Nevertheless, the present error might erroneously find support in its behalf in the words of some philosophers who show that in God essence and being are identical, that is, that that which answers to the question *what is it?* is identical with that which answers to the question *is it?* Now, following the way of the reason we cannot arrive at a knowledge of what God is. Hence, it seems likewise impossible to demonstrate by the reason that God exists.

4. Furthermore, according to the logic of the Philosopher, as a principle to demonstrate whether a thing is we must take the signification of the name of that thing;[1] and, again according to the Philosopher, the meaning signified by a name is its definition.[2] If this be so, if we set aside a knowledge of the divine essence or quiddity, no means will be available whereby to demonstrate that God exists.

5. Again, if, as if shown in the *Posterior Analytics*,[3] the knowledge of the principles of demonstration takes its origin from sense, whatever transcends all sense and sensibles

1 Aristotle, *Posterior Analytics*, II, 9 (93b 23).
2 Aristotle, *Metaphysics*, IV, 7 (1012a 23-24).
3 Aristotle, *Posterior Analytics*, I, 18 (81a 38).

seems to be indemonstrable. That God exists appears to be a proposition of this sort and is therefore indemonstrable.

6. The falsity of this opinion is shown to us, first, from the art of demonstration which teaches us to arrive at causes from their effects. Then, it is shown to us from the order of the sciences. For, as it is said in the *Metaphysics,*[4] if there is no knowable substance higher than sensible substance, there will be no science higher than physics. It is shown, thirdly, from the pursuit of the philosophers, who have striven to demonstrate that God exists. Finally, it is shown to us by the truth in the words of the Apostle Paul: "For the invisible things of God . . . are clearly seen, being understood by the things that are made" (Rom. 1:20).

7. Nor, contrary to the *first* argument, is there any problem in the fact that in God essence and being are identical. For this is understood of the being by which God subsists in Himself. But we do not know of what sort this being is, just as we do not know the divine essence. The reference is not to the being that signifies the composition of intellect. For thus the existence of God does fall under demonstration; this happens when our mind is led from demonstrative arguments to form such a proposition of God whereby it expresses that He exists.

8. Now, in arguments proving the existence of God, it is not necessary to assume the divine essence or quiddity as the middle term of the demonstration. This was the second view proposed above. In place of the quiddity, an effect is taken as the middle term, as in demonstrations *quia.*[5] It is from such effects that the meaning of the name *God* is taken. For all divine names are imposed either by removing the effects of God from Him or by relating God in some way to His effects.

9. It is thereby likewise evident that, although God transcends all sensible things and the sense itself, His effects, on which the demonstration proving His existence is based, are

---

[4] Aristotle, *Metaphysics*, IV, 3 (1005a 18).

[5] That is, demonstrations proving *that* something is so—for example, *that* God exists.

nevertheless sensible things. And thus, the origin of our knowledge in the sense applies also to those things that transcend the sense.

CHAPTER 13

ARGUMENTS IN PROOF OF THE EXISTENCE OF GOD

1. We have now shown that the effort to demonstrate the existence of God is not a vain one. We shall therefore proceed to set forth the arguments by which both philosophers and Catholic teachers have proved that God exists.

2. We shall first set forth the arguments by which Aristotle proceeds to prove that God exists. The aim of Aristotle is to do this in two ways, beginning with motion.

3. Of these ways the first is as follows.[1] Everything that is moved is moved by another. That some things are in motion—for example, the sun—is evident from sense. Therefore, it is moved by something else that moves it. This mover is itself either moved or not moved. If it is not, we have reached our conclusion—namely, that we must posit some unmoved mover. This we call God. If it is moved, it is moved by another mover. We must, consequently, either proceed to infinity, or we must arrive at some unmoved mover. Now, it is not possible to proceed to infinity. Hence, we must posit some prime unmoved mover.

4. In this proof, there are two propositions that need to be proved, namely, that *everything that is moved is moved by another*, and that *in movers and things moved one cannot proceed to infinity.*

5. The first of these propositions Aristotle proves in three ways. The *first* way is as follows. If something moves itself, it must have within itself the principle of its own motion; otherwise, it is clearly moved by another. Furthermore, it must be primarily moved. This means that it must be moved

---

1 Aristotle, *Physics*, VII, 1 (241b 24).

by reason of itself, and not by reason of a part of itself, as happens when an animal is moved by the motion of its foot. For, in this sense, a whole would not be moved by itself, but a part, and one part would be moved by another. It is also necessary that a self-moving being be divisible and have parts, since, as it is proved in the *Physics*,[2] whatever is moved is divisible.

6. On the basis of these suppositions Aristotle argues as follows. That which is held to be moved by itself is primarily moved. Hence, when one of its parts is at rest, the whole is then at rest. For if, while one part was at rest, another part in it were moved, then the whole itself would not be primarily moved; it would be that part in it which is moved while another part is at rest. But nothing that is at rest because something else is at rest is moved by itself; for that being whose rest follows upon the rest of another must have its motion follow upon the motion of another. It is thus not moved by itself. Therefore, that which was posited as being moved by itself is not moved by itself. Consequently, everything that is moved must be moved by another.

7. Nor is it an objection to this argument if one might say that, when something is held to move itself, a part of it cannot be at rest; or, again, if one might say that a part is not subject to rest or motion except accidentally, which is the unfounded argument of Avicenna.[3] For, indeed, the force of Aristotle's argument lies in this: *if* something moves itself primarily and through itself, rather than through its parts, that it is moved cannot depend on another. But the moving of the divisible itself, like its being, depends on its parts; it cannot therefore move itself primarily and through itself. Hence, for the truth of the inferred conclusion it is not necessary to assume as an absolute truth that a part of a being moving itself is at rest. What must rather be true is this conditional proposition: *if the part were at rest, the whole would be at rest*. Now, this proposition would be true even though its antecedent be impossible. In the same way, the following

[2] Aristotle, *Physics*, VI, 4 (234b 10).
[3] Aristotle, *Posterior Analytics*, I, 18 (81a 38).

conditional proposition is true: *if man is an ass, he is irrational.*

8. In the *second* way, Aristotle proves the proposition by induction.[4] Whatever is moved by accident is not moved by itself, since it is moved upon the motion of another. So, too, as is evident, what is moved by violence is not moved by itself. Nor are those beings moved by themselves that are moved by their nature as being moved from within; such is the case with animals, which evidently are moved by the soul. Nor, again, is this true of those beings, such as heavy and light bodies, which are moved through nature. For such beings are moved by the generating cause and the cause removing impediments. Now, whatever is moved is moved through itself or by accident. If it is moved through itself, then it is moved either violently or by nature; if by nature, then either through itself, as the animal, or not through itself, as heavy and light bodies. Therefore, everything that is moved is moved by another.

9. In the *third* way, Aristotle proves the proposition as follows.[5] The same thing cannot be at once in act and in potency with respect to the same thing. But everything that is moved is, as such, in potency. For motion is *the act of something that is in potency inasmuch as it is in potency.*[6] That which moves, however, is as such in act, for nothing acts except according as it is in act. Therefore, with respect to the same motion, nothing is both mover and moved. Thus, nothing moves itself.

10. It is to be noted, however, that Plato, who held that every mover is moved,[7] understood the name *motion* in a wider sense than did Aristotle. For Aristotle understood motion strictly, according as it is the act of what exists in potency inasmuch as it is such. So understood, motion belongs only to divisible bodies, as it is proved in the *Physics.*[8] According to Plato, however, that which moves itself is not a body.

---

4 Aristotle, *Physics*, VIII, 4 (254b 8).
5 Aristotle, *Physics*, VIII, 5 (257a 39).
6 Aristotle, *Physics*, III, 1 (201a 10).
7 Plato, *Phaedrus*, p. 247C.
8 Aristotle, *Physics*, VI, 4 (234b 10).

Plato understood by motion any given operation, so that *to understand* and *to judge* are a kind of motion. Aristotle likewise touches upon this manner of speaking in the *De anima*.[9] Plato accordingly said that the first mover moves himself because he knows himself and wills or loves himself. In a way, this is not opposed to the reasons of Aristotle. There is no difference between reaching a first being that moves himself, as understood by Plato, and reaching a first being that is absolutely unmoved, as understood by Aristotle.

11. The second proposition, namely, *that there is no procession to infinity among movers and things moved*, Aristotle proves in three ways.

12. The *first* is as follows.[10] If among movers and things moved we proceed to infinity, all these infinite beings must be bodies. For whatever is moved is divisible and a body, as is proved in the *Physics*.[11] But every body that moves some thing moved is itself moved while moving it. Therefore, all these infinites are moved together while one of them is moved. But one of them, being finite, is moved in a finite time. Therefore, all those infinites are moved in a finite time. This, however, is impossible. It is, therefore, impossible that among movers and things moved one can proceed to infinity.

13. Furthermore, that it is impossible for the above-mentioned infinites to be moved in a finite time Aristotle proves as follows. The mover and the thing moved must exist simultaneously. This Aristotle proves by induction in the various species of motion. But bodies cannot be simultaneous except through continuity or contiguity. Now, since, as has been proved, all the afore-mentioned movers and things moved are bodies, they must constitute by continuity or contiguity a sort of single mobile. In this way, one infinite is moved in a finite time. This is impossible, as is proved in the *Physics*.[12]

14. The *second* argument proving the same conclusion is

---

9 Aristotle, *De anima*, III, 7 (431a 6).
10 Aristotle, *Physics*, VII, 1 (241b 24).
11 Aristotle, *Physics*, VI, 4 (234b 10).
12 Aristotle, *Physics*, VII, 1 (241b 12); VI, 7 (237b 23ff.).

the following.[13] In an ordered series of movers and things moved (this is a series in which one is moved by another according to an order), it is necessarily the fact that, when the first mover is removed or ceases to move, no other mover will move or be moved. For the first mover is the cause of motion for all the others. But, if there are movers and things moved following an order to infinity, there will be no first mover, but all would be as intermediate movers. Therefore, none of the others will be able to be moved, and thus nothing in the world will be moved.

15. The *third* proof comes to the same conclusion, except that, by beginning with the superior, it has a reversed order. It is as follows. That which moves as an instrumental cause cannot move unless there be a principal moving cause. But, if we proceed to infinity among movers and things moved, all movers will be as instrumental causes, because they will be moved movers and there will be nothing as a principal mover. Therefore, nothing will be moved.

16. Such, then, is the proof of both propositions assumed by Aristotle in the first demonstrative way by which he proved that a first unmoved mover exists.

17. The second way is this. If every mover is moved, this proposition is true either by itself or by accident. If by accident, then it is not necessary, since what is true by accident is not necessary. It is something possible, therefore, that no mover is moved. But, if a mover is not moved, it does not move: as the adversary says. It is therefore possible that nothing is moved. For, if nothing moves, nothing is moved. This, however, Aristotle considers to be impossible—namely, that at any time there be no motion.[14] Therefore, the first proposition was not possible, since from a false possible, a false impossible does not follow. Hence, this proposition, *every mover is moved by another,* was not true by accident.

18. Again, if two things are accidentally joined in some being, and one of them is found without the other, it is probable that the other can be found without it. For example, if

---

[13] Aristotle, *Physics*, VIII, 5 (256a 12).
[14] Aristotle, *Physics*, VIII, 5 (256b 4-13).

white and *musical* are found in Socrates, and in Plato we find *musical* but not *white,* it is probable that in some other being we can find the *white* without the *musical.* Therefore, if mover and thing moved are accidentally joined in some being, and the thing moved be found without the mover in some being, it is probable that the mover is found without that which is moved. Nor can the example of two things, of which one depends on the other, be brought as an objection against this. For the union we are speaking of is not essential, but accidental.

19. But, if the proposition that every mover is moved is true by itself, something impossible or awkward likewise follows. For the mover must be moved either by the same kind of motion as that by which he moves, or by another. If the same, a cause of alteration must itself be altered, and further, a healing cause must itself be healed, and a teacher must himself be taught and this with respect to the same knowledge. Now, this is impossible. A teacher must have science, whereas he who is a learner of necessity does not have it. So that, if the proposition were true, the same thing would be possessed and not possessed by the same being—which is impossible. If, however, the mover is moved by another species of motion, so that (namely) the altering cause is moved according to place, and the cause moving according to place is increased, and so forth, since the genera and species of motion are finite in number, it will follow that we cannot proceed to infinity. There will thus be a first mover, which is not moved by another. Will someone say that there will be a recurrence, so that when all the genera and species of motion have been completed the series will be repeated and return to the first motion? This would involve saying, for example, that a mover according to place would be altered, the altering cause would be increased, and the increasing cause would be moved according to place. Yet this whole view would arrive at the same conclusion as before: whatever moves according to a certain species of motion is itself moved according to the same species of motion, though mediately and not immediately.

20. It remains, therefore, that we must posit *some first mover that is not moved by any exterior moving cause.*

21. Granted this conclusion—namely, that there is a first mover that is not moved by an exterior moving cause—it yet does not follow that this mover is absolutely unmoved. That is why Aristotle goes on to say that the condition of the first mover may be twofold.[15] The first mover can be absolutely unmoved. If so, we have the conclusion we are seeking: there is a first unmoved mover. On the other hand, the first mover can be self-moved. This may be argued, because that which is through itself is prior to what is through another. Hence, among things moved as well, it seems reasonable that the first moved is moved through itself and not by another.

22. But, on this basis, the same conclusion again follows.[16] For it cannot be said that, when a mover moves himself, the whole is moved by the whole. Otherwise, the same difficulties would follow as before: one person would both teach and be taught, and the same would be true among other motions. It would also follow that a being would be both in potency and in act; for a mover is, as such, in act, whereas the thing moved is in potency. Consequently, one part of the self-moved mover is solely moving, and the other part solely moved. We thus reach the same conclusion as before: there exists an unmoved mover.

23. Nor can it be held that both parts of the self-moved mover are moved, so that one is moved by the other, or that one moves both itself and the other, or that the whole moves a part, or that a part moves the whole. All this would involve the return of the afore-mentioned difficulties: something would both move and be moved according to the same species of motion; something would be at once in potency and in act; and, furthermore, the whole would not be primarily moving itself, it would move through the motion of a part. The conclusion thus stands: one part of a self-moved mover must be unmoved and moving the other part.

24. But there is another point to consider. Among self-

---

15 Aristotle, *Physics*, VIII, 5 (256a 13).
16 Aristotle, *Physics*, VIII, 5 (257b 2).

moved beings known to us, namely, animals, although the moving part, which is to say the soul, is unmoved through itself, it is yet moved by accident. That is why Aristotle further shows that the moving part of the first self-moving being is not moved either through itself or by accident.[17] For, since self-moving beings known to us, namely, animals, are corruptible, the moving part in them is moved by accident. But corruptible self-moving beings must be reduced to some first self-moving being that is everlasting. Therefore, some self-moving being must have a mover that is moved neither through itself nor by accident.

25. It is further evident that, according to the position of Aristotle, some self-moved being must be everlasting. For if, as Aristotle supposes, motion is everlasting, the generation of self-moving beings (this means beings that are generable and corruptible) must be endless. But the cause of this endlessness cannot be one of the self-moving beings, since it does not always exist. Nor can the cause be all the self-moving beings together, both because they would be infinite and because they would not be simultaneous. There must therefore be some endlessly self-moving being, causing the endlessness of generation among these sublunary self-movers. Thus, the mover of the self-moving being is not moved, either through itself or by accident.

26. Again, we see that among beings that move themselves some initiate a new motion as a result of some motion. This new motion is other than the motion by which an animal moves itself, for example, digested food or altered air. By such a motion the self-moving mover is moved by accident. From this we may infer that no self-moved being is moved everlastingly whose mover is moved either by itself or by accident. But the first self-mover is everlastingly in motion; otherwise, motion could not be everlasting, since every other motion is caused by the motion of the self-moving first mover. The first self-moving being, therefore, is moved by a mover who is himself moved neither through himself nor by accident.

---

[17] Aristotle, *Physics*, VIII, 6 (258b 15).

27. Nor is it against this argument that the movers of the lower spheres produce an everlasting motion and yet are said to be moved by accident. For they are said to be moved by accident, not on their own account, but on account of their movable subjects, which follow the motion of the higher sphere.

28. Now, God is not part of any self-moving mover. In his *Metaphysics,* therefore, Aristotle goes on from the mover who is a part of the self-moved mover to seek another mover —God—who is absolutely separate.[18] For, since everything moving itself is moved through appetite, the mover who is part of the self-moving being moves because of the appetite of some appetible object. This object is higher, in the order of motion, than the mover desiring it; for the one desiring is in a manner a moved mover, whereas an appetible object is an absolutely unmoved mover. There must, therefore, be an absolutely unmoved separate first mover. This is God.

29. Two considerations seem to invalidate these arguments. The first consideration is that, as arguments, they presuppose the eternity of motion, which Catholics consider to be false.

30. To this consideration the reply is as follows. The most efficacious way to prove that God exists is on the supposition that the world is eternal. Granted this supposition, that God exists is less manifest. For, if the world and motion have a first beginning, some cause must clearly be posited to account for this origin of the world and of motion. That which comes to be anew must take its origin from some innovating cause; since nothing brings itself from potency to act, or from non-being to being.

31. The second consideration is that the demonstrations given above presuppose that the first moved being, namely, a heavenly body, is self-moved. This means that it is animated, which many do not admit.

32. The reply to this consideration is that, if the prime mover is not held to be self-moved, then it must be moved immediately by something absolutely unmoved. Hence, even

---

18 Aristotle, *Metaphysics*, XII, 7 (1072a 23).

Aristotle himself proposed this conclusion as a disjunction: it is necessary either to arrive immediately at an unmoved separate first mover, or to arrive at a self-moved mover from whom, in turn, an unmoved separate first mover is reached.[19]

33. In *Metaphysics* II Aristotle also uses another argument to show that there is no infinite regress in efficient causes and that we must reach one first cause—God.[20] This way is as follows. In all ordered efficient causes, the first is the cause of the intermediate cause, whether one or many, and this is the cause of the last cause. But, when you suppress a cause, you suppress its effect. Therefore, if you suppress the first cause, the intermediate cause cannot be a cause. Now, if there were an infinite regress among efficient causes, no cause would be first. Therefore, all the other causes, which are intermediate, will be suppressed. But this is manifestly false. We must, therefore, posit that there exists a first efficient cause. This is God.

34. Another argument may also be gathered from the words of Aristotle. In *Metaphysics* II he shows that what is most true is also most a being.[21] But in *Metaphysics* IV he shows the existence of something supremely true from the observed fact that of two false things one is more false than the other, which means that one is more true than the other.[22] This comparison is based on the nearness to that which is absolutely and supremely true. From these Aristotelian texts we may further infer that there is something that is supremely being. This we call God.

35. Damascene proposes another argument for the same conclusion taken from the government of the world.[23] Averroës likewise hints at it.[24] The argument runs thus. Contrary and discordant things cannot, always or for the most part, be parts of one order except under someone's government, which enables all and each to tend to a definite end. But in

19 Aristotle, *Physics*, VIII, 5 (258a 1; b 4).
20 Aristotle, *Metaphysics*, Iα, 2 (994a 1).
21 Aristotle, *Metaphysics*, Iα, 1 (993b 30).
22 Aristotle, *Metaphysics*, IV, 4 (1008b 37).
23 St. John Damascene, *De fide orthodoxa*, I, 3 (*PG*, 94, col. 796CD).
24 Averroës, *In II Physicorum*, t.c. 75 (fol. 75v-76r).

the world we find that things of diverse natures come together under one order, and this not rarely or by chance, but always or for the most part. There must therefore be some being by whose providence the world is governed. This we call God.

Suggestions for Further Reading

Pegis, A. C. (ed.). *Basic Writings of St. Thomas Aquinas.* 2 vols. New York, 1954; Gilson, E. *The Christian Philosophy of St. Thomas Aquinas.* New York, 1956; D'Arcy, M. C. *Thomas Aquinas.* London, 1930; Maritain, J. *St. Thomas Aquinas.* London, 1946; *FCC* vol. II, 302-423; *EG* 361-387; *AAM* 163-191; *RMcK* vol. II, 149-239.

St. Bonaventure

St. Bonaventure, christened Johannes Fidanza, was born in 1221 at Bagnora, Italy. He entered the Franciscan Order as a young man, sometime around 1240. At Paris, where he went to study, he was initiated into the Augustinian philosophy, and his own thought developed entirely within the Augustinian mold. Bonaventure taught for a time at Paris, but was excluded from the University in 1255 because the faculty was loath to admit members of the mendicant orders as doctors and professors. It was only through the intercession of the Pope that Bonaventure, and the Dominican St. Thomas, were finally received as doctors on the same day. In 1257, Bonaventure left the University to become Minister General of the Franciscan Order, and in this capacity devoted the greater portion of his remaining life to the administration of Franciscan affairs. He was appointed Bishop of Albano and Cardinal in 1273, and died in 1274—the very same year as St. Thomas. Bonaventure was buried at Lyons in the presence of Pope Gregory X.

St. Bonaventure's thought represents the high point in the long tradition of Christian mysticism which stemmed from St. Augustine. As such, Bonaventure's philosophy, along with that of St. Thomas, is an essential part of the Christian tradition. The Thomist philosophy, with its devotion to the ideal of intellectual contemplation, is perfectly complemented by the philosophy of Bonaventure, with its devotion to the attainment of union with God through mystic love.

It was during the thirteenth century that philosophy was separated from the liberal arts; and though at the time of St. Bonaventure it constituted a science properly so-called, still the term "philosophy" was often used to denote the sum total of secular knowledge—the "arts." It is in this broad sense that St. Bonaventure uses the term in his little work, *Retracing the Arts to Theology,* reprinted below in its entirety.

ST. BONAVENTURE ON RETRACING THE ARTS TO THEOLOGY*

1. *Every good gift and every perfect gift is from above, coming down from the Father of Lights,* says James in the first chapter of his epistle. These words of Sacred Scripture not only indicate the source of all illumination but they likewise point out the generous flow of the manifold rays which issue from that Fount of light. Notwithstanding the fact that every illumination of knowledge is within, still we can with reason distinguish what we may call the *external* light, or the light of mechanical art; the *lower* light, or the light of sense perception; the *inner* light, or the light of philosophical knowledge; and the *higher* light, or the light of grace and of Sacred Scripture. The first light illumines in regard to structure of *artifacts;* the second, in regard to *natural forms;* the third, in regard to *intellectual truth;* the fourth and last, in regard to *saving truth.*

2. The first light, then, since it enlightens the mind in reference to structure of *artifacts,* which are, as it were, exterior to man and intended to supply the needs of the body, is called the light of *mechanical art.* Being, in a certain sense, servile and of a lower nature than philosophical knowledge, this light can rightly be termed *external.* It has seven divisions corresponding to the seven mechanical arts enumer-

* Translated by Sr. Emma Therese Healy and appearing as Vol. I of *The Works of St. Bonaventure* published by The Franciscan Institute, St. Bonaventure, New York, 1955. Reprinted by permission.

ated by Hugh in his *Didascalicon,* namely, weaving, armour-making, agriculture, hunting, navigation, medicine, and the dramatic art. That the above-mentioned arts *suffice* (for us) is shown in the following way. Every mechanical art is intended for man's *consolation* or for his comfort; its purpose, therefore, is to banish either *sorrow* or *want;* it either *benefits* or *delights,* according to the words of Horace:

> Either to serve or to please is the wish of the poets.

And again:

> He hath gained universal applause who hath combined the profitable with the pleasing.

If its aim is to afford *consolation* and amusement, it is *dramatic art,* or the art of exhibiting plays, which embraces every form of entertainment, be it song, music, poetry, or pantomime. If, however, it is intended for the *comfort* or betterment of the exterior man, it can accomplish its purpose by providing either *covering* or *food,* or by *serving as an aid in the acquisition of either.* In the matter of *covering,* if it provides a soft and light material, it is *weaving;* if a strong and hard material, it is *armour-making* or metal-working, an art which extends to every tool or implement fashioned either of iron or of any metal whatsoever, or of stone, or of wood.

In the matter of *food,* mechanical art may benefit us in two ways, for we derive our sustenance from *vegetables* and from *animals.* As regards *vegetables,* it is *farming;* as regards *flesh meats,* it is *hunting.* Or again, as regards *food,* mechanical art has a twofold advantage: it aids either in the *production* and multiplication of crops, in which case it is agriculture, or in the various ways of preparing food, under which aspect it is hunting, an art which extends to every conceivable way of preparing foods, drinks, and delicacies—a task with which bakers, cooks, and innkeepers are concerned. The term "hunting" (*venatio*), however, is used for all these things because it has a certain excellence and courtliness.

Furthermore, as an aid in the acquisition of each (clothing

and food), the mechanical arts contribute to the welfare of man in two ways: either by *supplying a want,* and in this case it is *navigation,* which includes all *commerce of articles* of covering or of food; or by *removing impediments* and ills of the body, under which aspect it is *medicine,* whether it is concerned with the preparation of drugs, potions, or ointments, with the healing of wounds, or with the amputation of members, in which latter case it is called surgery. Dramatic art, on the other hand, is the only one of its kind. Thus the sufficiency (of the mechanical arts) is evident.

3. The second light, which enables us to discern *natural forms,* is the light of *sense perception.* Rightly is it called the *lower* light because sense perception begins with a material object and takes place by the aid of corporeal light. It has five divisions corresponding to the five senses. In his *Third Book on Genesis,* Saint Augustine bases the *adequacy* of the senses on the nature of the light present in the elements in the following way. If the light or brightness which makes possible the discernment of things corporeal exists in a *high degree of its own property* and in a certain purity, it is the sense of *sight; commingled with the air,* it is *hearing; with vapor,* it is *smell; with fluid,* it is *taste; with solidity of earth,* it is *touch.* Now the sensitive life of the body partakes of the nature of light for which reason it thrives in the nerves, which are naturally unobstructed and capable of transmitting impressions, and in these five senses it possesses more or less vigor according to the greater or less soundness of the nerves. And so, since there are in the world five simple substances, namely, the four elements and the fifth essence, man has for the perception of all these corporeal forms five senses well adapted to these substances, because, on account of the well-defined nature of each sense, apprehension can take place only when there is a certain conformity and fitness between the organ and the object. There is another way of determining the adequacy of the senses, but Saint Augustine sanctions this method and it seems reasonable, since corresponding elements on the part of the organ, the medium, and the object lend joint support to the proof.

4. The third light, which enlightens man in the investigation of *intelligible truths,* is the light of *philosophical knowledge.* It is called *inner* because it inquires into inner and hidden causes through principles of learning and natural truth, which are inherent in man. There is a triple diffusion of this light in *rational, natural,* and *moral* philosophy, which seems adequate, since it covers the three aspects of truth—truth of *speech,* truth of *things,* and truth of *morals. Rational* philosophy considers the truth of *speech; natural* philosophy, the truth of *things;* and *moral* philosophy, the truth of *conduct.* Or we may consider it in a different light. Just as we find in the Most High God efficient, formal or exemplary, and final causality, since "He is the Cause of being, the Principle of knowledge, and the Pattern of human life," so do we find it in the illumination of philosophy, which enlightens the mind to discern the *causes of being,* in which case it is *physics;* or to grasp the *principles of understanding,* in which case it is *logic;* or to learn the *right way of living,* in which case it is *moral* or practical philosophy. We are now considering it under its third aspect. The light of philosophical knowledge illumines the intellectual faculty itself and this enlightenment may be threefold: if it governs the *motive power,* it is *moral* philosophy; if it *rules itself,* it is *natural* philosophy; if it directs *interpretation,* it is *discursive* philosophy. As a result, man is enlightened as regards the truth of life, the truth of knowledge, and the truth of doctrine.

And since one may, through the medium of *speech,* give expression to what he has in mind with a threefold purpose in view: namely, to manifest his thought, to induce someone to believe, or to arouse love or hatred, for this reason, *discursive* or rational philosophy has three sub-divisions: *grammar, logic,* and *rhetoric.* Of these sciences the first aims to express; the second, to teach; the third, to persuade. The first considers the reasoning faculty as *apprehending;* the second, as *judging;* the third, as *persuading.* Since the mind apprehends by means of *correct* speech, judges by means of *true* speech, and persuades by means of *embellished* speech, with good reason does this triple science consider these three qualities in speech.

Again, since our intellect must be guided in its judgment by formal principles, these principles, likewise, can be considered under three aspects: in relation to *matter,* they are termed *formal;* in relation to the *mind,* they are termed *intellectual;* and in relation to *Divine Wisdom,* they are called *ideal. Natural* philosophy, therefore, is subdivided into *physics* proper, *mathematics,* and *metaphysics.* Thus *physics* treats of the generation and corruption of things according to natural powers and seminal causes; *mathematics* considers forms that can be abstracted in their pure intelligibility; *metaphysics* treats of the cognition of all beings, which it leads back to one first Principle from which they proceeded according to the *ideal causes,* that is, to God, since He is the *Beginning,* the *End*, and the *Exemplar.* Concerning these ideal causes, however, there has been some controversy among metaphysicians.

Since the government of the motive power is to be considered in a threefold way, namely, as regards the *individual,* the *family*, and the *state,* so there are three corresponding divisions of *moral* philosophy: namely, *ethical, economic,* and *political,* the content of each being clearly indicated by its name.

5. Now the fourth light, which illumines the mind for the understanding of *saving truth,* is the light of *Sacred Scripture.* This light is called *higher* because it leads to things above by the manifestation of truths which are beyond reason and also because it is not acquired by human research, but comes down by inspiration from the *"Father of Lights."* Although in its *literal* sense it is *one,* still, in its spiritual and *mystical* sense, it is *threefold,* for in all the books of Sacred Scripture, in addition to the *literal* meaning which the words outwardly express, there is understood a threefold *spiritual* meaning: namely, the *allegorical,* by which we are taught what to believe concerning the Divinity and humanity; the *moral,* by which we are taught how to live; and the *anagogical,* by

which we are taught how to be united to God. Hence all Sacred Scripture teaches these three truths: namely, the eternal generation and Incarnation of Christ, the pattern of human life, and the union of the soul with God. The first regards *faith;* the second, *morals;* and the third, the *ultimate end of both.* The doctors should labor at the study of the first; the preachers, at the study of the second; the contemplatives, at the study of the third. The first is taught chiefly by Augustine; the second, by Gregory; the third, by Dionysius. Anselm follows Augustine; Bernard follows Gregory; Richard (of Saint Victor) follows Dionysius. For Anselm excels in reasoning; Bernard, in preaching; Richard, in contemplating; but Hugh (of Saint Victor) in all three.

6. From the foregoing statements it can be inferred that, although according to our first classification the light coming down from above is *fourfold,* it still admits of *six* modifications: namely, the light of *Sacred Scripture,* the light of *sense perception,* the light of *mechanical art,* the light of *rational philosophy,* the light of *natural philosophy,* and the light of *moral philosophy.* And for that reason there are in this life six illuminations, and they have their twilight, for all *knowledge will be destroyed;* for that reason too there follows a seventh day of rest, a day which knows no evening, *the illumination of glory.*

7. Wherefore, very fittingly may these six illuminations be related to the six days of creation or illumination in which the world was made, the knowledge of Sacred Scripture corresponding to the creation of the first day, that is, to the creation of light, and so on, one after the other in order. Moreover, just as all those creations had their origin in one light, so too are all these branches of knowledge ordained for the knowledge of Sacred Scripture; they are contained in it; they are perfected by it; and by means of it they are ordained for eternal illumination. Wherefore, all our knowledge should end in the knowledge of Sacred Scripture, and especially is this true of the *anagogical* knowledge through which the illumination is reflected back to God whence it came. And there

the cycle ends; the number six is complete and consequently there is rest.

8. Let us see, therefore, how the other illuminations of knowledge are to be brought back to the light of Sacred Scripture. First of all, let us consider the illumination of *sense perception,* which is concerned exclusively with the cognition of sense objects, a process in which there are three phases to be considered: namely, the *medium* of perception, the *exercise* of perception, and the *delight* of perception. If we consider the *medium* of perception, we shall see therein the Word begotten from all eternity and made man in time. Indeed, a sense object can stimulate a cognitive faculty only through the medium of a similitude which proceeds from the object as an offspring from its parent, and this by generation, by reality, or by exemplarity, for every sense. This similitude, however, does not complete the act of perception unless it is brought into contact with the sense organ and the sense faculty, and once that contact is established, there results a new percept. Through this percept the mind is led back to the object by means of the similitude. And even though the object is not always present to the senses, still the fact remains that the object by itself, when in its finished state, begets a similitude. In like manner, know that from the mind of the Most High, Who is knowable by the interior senses of our mind, from all eternity there emanated a Similitude, an Image, and an Offspring; and afterwards, when "the fulness of time came," He was united to a mind and a body and assumed the form of man, which had never been before. Through Him the minds of all of us which receive that Similitude of the Father through faith in our hearts, are brought back to God.

9. If we consider the *exercise* of sense perception, we shall see therein *the pattern of human life,* for each sense applies itself to its proper object, shrinks from what may harm it, and does not usurp what does not belong to it. In like manner, the *spiritual sense* lives in an orderly way when it exercises itself for its own purpose, against *negligence;* when it refrains from what is harmful, against *concupiscence;* and when it refrains

from usurping what does not belong to it, against *pride*. Of a truth, every disorder springs from negligence, from concupiscence, or from pride. Surely then, he who lives a prudent, temperate, and submissive life leads a well-ordered life, for thereby he avoids negligence in things to be done, concupiscence in things to be desired, and pride in things that are excellent.

10. Furthermore, if we consider the *delight* of sense perception, we shall see therein the union of God and the soul. Indeed every sense seeks its proper sense object with longing, finds it with delight, and never wearied, seeks it again and again, because "the eye is not filled with seeing, neither is the ear filled with hearing." In the same way, our spiritual senses must seek with longing, find with joy, and time and again experience the beautiful, the harmonious, the fragrant, the sweet, or the delightful to the touch. Behold how the Divine Wisdom lies hidden in sense perception and how wonderful is the contemplation of the five spiritual senses in the light of their conformity to the senses of the body.

11. By the same process of reasoning is Divine Wisdom to be found in the illumination of the *mechanical arts*, the sole purpose of which is the *production of artifacts*. In this illumination we can see the *eternal generation and Incarnation of the Word*, the *pattern of human life*, and the *union of the soul with God*. And this is true if we consider the *production*, the *effect*, and the *fruit* of a work, or if we consider the *skill of the artist*, the *quality of the effect produced*, and the *utility of the product derived therefrom*.

12. If we consider the *production*, we shall see that the work of art proceeds from the artificer according to a similitude existing in his mind; this pattern or model the artificer studies carefully before he produces and then he produces as he has predetermined. The artificer, moreover, produces an exterior work bearing the closest possible resemblance to the interior exemplar, and if it were in his power to produce an effect which would know and love him, this he would assuredly do; and if that effect could know its maker, it would be

by means of the similitude according to which it came from the hands of the artificer; and if the eyes of the understanding were so darkened that it could not elevate itself to things above itself in order to bring itself to a knowledge of its maker, it would be necessary for the similitude according to which the effect was produced to lower itself even to that nature which the effect could grasp and know. In like manner, understand that no creature has proceeded from the Most High Creator except through the Eternal Word, "in Whom He ordered all things," and by which Word He produced creatures bearing not only the nature of His *vestige* but also of His *image* so that through knowledge they might become like unto Him. And since by sin the rational creature had dimmed the eye of contemplation, it was most fitting that the Eternal and Invisible should become visible and take flesh that He might lead us back to the Father. Indeed, this is what is related in the fourteenth chapter of Saint John: "No one comes to the Father but through Me," and in the eleventh chapter of Saint Matthew: "No one knows the Son except the Father; nor does anyone know the Father except the Son, and him to whom the Son chooses to reveal him." For that reason, then, it is said, "the Word was made flesh." Therefore, considering the illumination of mechanical art as regards the production of the work, we shall see therein the Word begotten and made incarnate, that is, the Divinity and the Humanity and the integrity of all faith.

13. If we consider the *effect,* we shall see therein the *pattern of human life,* for every artificer, indeed, aims to produce a work that is beautiful, useful, and enduring, and only when it possesses these three qualities is the work highly valued and acceptable. Corresponding to the above-mentioned qualities, in the pattern of life there must be found three elements: *"knowledge, will,* and *unaltering* and *persevering toil."* *Knowledge* renders the work beautiful; the *will* renders it useful; *perseverance* renders it lasting. The first resides in the rational, the second in the concupiscible, and the third in the irascible appetite.

14. If we consider the *fruit,* we shall find therein *the union of the soul with God,* for every artificer who fashions a work does so that he may derive *praise, benefit,* or *delight* therefrom—a threefold purpose which corresponds to the three formal objects of the appetites: namely, a *noble* good, a *useful* good, and an *agreeable* good. It was for this threefold reason that God made the soul rational, namely, that of its own accord, it might *praise* Him, *serve* Him, *find delight* in Him, and be at rest; and this takes place through charity. "He who abides in it, abides in God, and God in him," in such a way that there is found therein a kind of wondrous union and from that union comes a wondrous delight, for in the Book of Proverbs it is written, "My delights were to be with the children of men." Behold how the illumination of mechanical art is the path to the illumination of Sacred Scripture. There is nothing therein which does not bespeak true wisdom and for this reason Sacred Scripture quite rightly makes frequent use of such similitudes.

15. In like manner is Divine Wisdom to be found in the illumination of *rational philosophy,* the main concern of which is *speech.* Here are to be considered three elements corresponding to the three aspects of speech itself: namely, the *person speaking,* the *delivery* of the speech, and its final purpose or its effect upon the *hearer.*

16. Considering speech in the light of the *speaker,* we see that all speech signifies a *mental concept.* That inner concept is the word of the mind and its offspring which is known to the person conceiving it; but that it may become known to the hearer, it assumes the form of the voice, and clothed therein, the intelligible word becomes sensible and is heard without; it is received into the ear of the person listening and still it does not depart from the mind of the person uttering it. Practically the same procedure is seen in the begetting of the Eternal Word, because the Father conceived Him, begetting Him from all eternity, as it is written in the eighth chapter of the Book of Proverbs, "The depths were not as yet, and I was already conceived." But that He might be known by man who is endowed with senses, He assumed the nature of flesh, and

"the Word was made flesh and dwelt amongst us," and yet He remained "in the bosom of the Father."

17. Considering speech in the light of its *delivery,* we shall see therein the pattern of *human life,* for three essential qualities work together for the perfection of speech: namely, *suitability, truth,* and *ornament.* Corresponding to these three qualities, every act of ours should be characterized by *measure, beauty,* and *order* so that it may be *controlled* by its proper measure in its external work, *rendered beautiful* by purity of affection, and *regulated* and adorned by uprightness of intention. For then truly does one live an upright and well-ordered life when his intention is upright, his affection pure, and his activity within its proper limit.

18. Considering speech in the light of its *purpose,* we find that it aims to *express,* to *instruct,* and to *persuade;* but it never *expresses* except by means of a likeness; it never *teaches* except by means of a clear light; it never *persuades* except by power; and it is evident that these effects are accomplished only by means of an inherent likeness, light, and power intrinsically *united to the soul.* Therefore, Saint Augustine concludes that he alone is a true teacher who can impress a likeness, shed light, and grant power to the heart of his hearer. Hence it is that "he who teaches within hearts has his Chair in heaven." Now as perfection of speech requires the union of power, light, and a likeness within the soul, so, too, for the instruction of the soul in the knowledge of God by interior conversation with Him, there is required a union with Him who is "the brightness of his glory and the image of his substance, and upholding all things by the word of his power." Hence we see how wondrous is this contemplation by which Saint Augustine in his many writings leads souls to Divine Wisdom.

19. By the same mode of reasoning is the Wisdom of God to be found in the illumination of *natural philosophy,* which is concerned chiefly with the *formal causes* in *matter,* in the *soul,* and in the *Divine Wisdom.* These formal causes it is fitting to consider under three aspects: namely, as regards the *relation of proportion,* the *effect of causality,* and their

medium of union; and in these three can be accordingly found the three (central ideas of the three senses of Holy Scripture) mentioned above.

20. Considering the formal causes according to their *relation of proportion,* we shall see therein the *Word Eternal* and the *Word Incarnate.* The *intellectual* and abstract causes are, as it were, midway between the *seminal* and the *ideal* causes. But *seminal* causes cannot exist in *matter* without the generation and production of form; neither can *intellectual* causes exist in the *soul* without the generation of the word in the mind. Therefore, *ideal* causes cannot exist *in God* without the generation of the Word from the Father in due proportion. Truly, this is a mark of dignity, and if it becomes the creature, how much more so the Creator. It was for this reason that Saint Augustine said the Son of God is the "art of the Father." Again, the natural tendency in matter is so ordained toward intellectual causes that the generation is in no way perfect unless the rational soul be united to the material body. By similar reasoning, therefore, we come to the conclusion that the highest and noblest perfection can exist in this world only if a nature in which there are the seminal causes, and a nature in which there are the intellectual causes, and a nature in which there are the ideal causes are simultaneously combined in the unity of one person, as was done in the Incarnation of the Son of God. Therefore all natural philosophy, by reason of the relation of proportion, predicates the Word of God begotten and become Incarnate so that He is the *Alpha* and the *Omega,* that is, He was begotten in the beginning and before all time but became Incarnate in the fullness of time.

21. Now if we think of these causes according to the *effect of causality,* we shall be considering the *pattern of human life,* since generation by seminal causes can take place in generative and corruptible matter only by the beneficent light of the heavenly bodies which are far removed from generation and corruption, that is, by the *sun,* the *moon,* and the *stars.* So too the soul can perform no living works unless it receive from the sun, that is, from Christ, the aid of His gratuitous light; unless it seek the protection of the moon, that is, of the

Virgin Mary, Mother of Christ; and unless it imitate the example of the other saints. When all these concur, there is accomplished in the soul a living and perfect work; therefore the right order of living depends upon this threefold cooperation.

22. Moreover, if we consider these formal causes as regards their *medium of union,* we shall understand how *union of the soul with God* takes place, for the corporeal nature can be united to the soul only through the medium of moisture, (vital) spirit, and warmth—three conditions which dispose the body to receive life from the soul. So too we may understand that God gives life to the soul and is united to it only on the condition that it be *moistened* with tears of compunction and filial love, made *spiritual* by contempt of every earthly thing, and *be warmed* by desire for its heavenly home and its Beloved. Behold how in natural philosophy lies hidden the Wisdom of God.

23. In the same way is the light of *Sacred Scripture* to be found in the illumination of *moral philosophy.* Since moral philosophy is concerned principally with rectitude, it treats of general justice which Saint Anselm calls the "rectitude of the will." The term "right" has a threefold signification and accordingly, in the consideration of rectitude are revealed the three central ideas (of the senses of Sacred Scripture) previously mentioned. In one sense of the word, that is called *"right,* the middle of which is not out of line with its extreme points." If then God is perfect rectitude and that by His very nature since He is the Beginning and the End of all things, it follows that in God there must be an intermediary *of His own nature* so that there may be one Person who only produces, another who is only produced, but an intermediary who both produces and is produced. There is likewise need of an intermediary in the *going forth* and in the *return* of things: in the *going forth,* an intermediary which will be more on the part of the one producing; in the *return,* one which will be more on the part of the one returning. Therefore, as creatures went forth from God by the Word of God, so for a perfect return, it was necessary that the Mediator *between God and man* be

not only God but also man so that He might lead men back to God.

24. In another sense, that is called *"right"* which is conformed to rule. Accordingly, in the consideration of rectitude there is seen the *rule of life.* For he indeed lives rightly who is guided by the regulations of the divine law, as is the case when the will of man accepts necessary *precepts,* salutary *warnings,* and *counsels* of perfection that he may thereby prove *the good* and *acceptable and perfect will of God.* And then is the rule of life right when no obliquity can be found therein.

25. In the third sense, that is called *"right"* the summit of which is raised upward, as for instance, we say that man has an upright posture. And in this sense, in the consideration of rectitude there is manifested the *union of the soul with God;* for since God is above, it necessarily follows that the apex of the mind itself must be raised aloft. And indeed this is what actually happens when man's *rational nature* assents to the First Truth for His own sake and above all things, when his *irascible nature* strives after the Highest Bounty, and when his *concupiscible nature* clings to the Greatest Good. He who thus keeps close to God *is one spirit with him.*

26. And so it is evident how the *manifold Wisdom of God,* which is clearly revealed in Sacred Scripture, lies hidden in all knowledge and in all nature. It is evident too how all divisions of knowledge are handmaids of theology, and it is for this reason that theology makes use of illustrations and terms pertaining to every branch of knowledge. It is likewise evident how wide is the illuminative way and how in everything which is perceived or known God Himself lies hidden within. And this is the fruit of all sciences, that in all, faith may be strengthened, *God may be honored,* character may be formed, and consolation may be derived from union of the Spouse with His beloved, a union which takes place through charity, to the attainment of which the whole purpose of Sacred Scripture, and consequently, every illumination descending from above, is directed—a charity without which all knowledge is vain because no one comes to the Son except

through the Holy Ghost who teaches us *all the truth, who is blessed forever. Amen.*

Suggestions for Further Reading

Gilson, E. *The Philosophy of St. Bonaventure.* London, 1938; De Benedictis, M. M. *The Social Thought of St. Bonaventure.* Washington, 1946; O'Donnell, C. M. *The Psychology of St. Bonaventure and St. Thomas Aquinas.* Washington, 1937; *FCC* vol. II, 240-293; *EG* 331-340; *AAM* 137-152; *RMcK* vol. II, 111-148.

Giles of Rome

For roughly six hundred years the western Church faced no problem of having to defend its doctrines against rival philosophical claims. This situation changed abruptly when, in the latter half of the twelfth century, the works of Aristotle, Avicenna, Averroës, Maimonides, and other pagan, Arabic, and Jewish thinkers finally entered the Christian cultural orbit. At first these systems of thought which claimed competence in philosophical domains long considered the exclusive preserve of Christian thinkers were received with great reverence and candor. But as it began to appear that many of these importations contained powerfully structured arguments leading to conclusions diametrically opposed to approved teachings, the Church began to take steps accordingly. At the University of Paris in 1210, and again in 1215, students were forbidden to read the works of the new philosophers, except those on formal logic, and masters were forbidden to lecture on them. Still, as seems always to be the case with prohibited writings, these works continued to circulate. Only gradually, as the Christian thinkers themselves undertook to master the contents of the proscribed writings in order to get themselves into a better position to defend the Faith, did a critical spirit begin to manifest itself among the Christian scholars. Giles of Rome's tract, *The Errors of the Philosophers,* which is presented below in its entirety, is one of the first such analyses undertaken to examine the new literature in its relation to Christian views.

Born in 1247, Giles entered the Order of the Hermits of St.

Augustine about 1260. From 1269 to 1272 he was a student at the University of Paris, where he studied under St. Thomas Aquinas. Giles composed the *Errors* about 1270: the very year that Etienne Tempier, Bishop of Paris, formally condemned some of the very theses which Giles himself cites as dangerous to orthodoxy. In 1278 Giles aroused the displeasure of his superiors by coming out rather strongly against a philosophical doctrine which had many important adherents. For this, and other such offenses, he was directed to make a formal retraction. Giles refused to comply; and as a consequence was barred from pursuing his higher studies in theology at the University. In the year 1285, however, having finally decided to make the required public retraction, Giles returned to the University and completed his studies. He then taught at Paris until 1292, when he was elected General of his order. In 1295 he was made Archbishop of Bourges. Giles died, in 1316, at Avignon.

GILES OF ROME ON THE ERRORS OF THE PHILOSOPHERS*

HERE BEGIN THE ERRORS OF THE PHILOSOPHERS ARISTOTLE, AVERROËS, AVICENNA, ALGAZEL, ALKINDI, AND RABBI MOSES (MAIMONIDES), COMPILED BY BROTHER GILES OF THE ORDER OF ST. AUGUSTINE

And a compilation of Aristotle's errors is placed first.

CHAPTER I

As it is the case that many wrong conclusions follow from one faulty statement, so the Philosopher has drawn many errors from one faulty principle.

1. For he believed nothing to be disposed in some condition in which it previously was not, except it came to be that way through a preceding motion. He held, moreover, that there is no novelty except where there is change, taken properly. Because, therefore, every change taken properly is a terminus of motion, there can be no novelty without a preceding motion. Now from this principle he concluded that motion never began to be; since if motion began, the motion was new. But nothing is new except through some preceding motion. Therefore there was motion before the first motion, which is a contradiction.

2. Further: he erred because he posited time never to have

---

* Translated especially for this volume by H. Shapiro from the edition of J. Koch, published by Marquette University Press in 1944 under the title *Giles of Rome Errores Philosophorum.*

begun. Now time always follows on motion, if, therefore, motion never began, neither did time. Moreover, it seemed to him that the principle of time involved a special difficulty. For since an instant is always the end of the past and the beginning of the future, a first instant cannot be given, because there was a time before every instant, and before any assigned time there was an instant. Time, therefore, did not begin, but is eternal.

3. Further: because of what has already been stated, he was forced to posit a mobile to be eternal and the world to be eternal. For as one cannot give a time without motion, and motion without a mobile, if time and motion are eternal, the mobile will be eternal, and so the world would never begin. All of this is clear from Book VIII of the *Physics*.

4. Further: he was forced to posit the heavens to be ungenerated and incorruptible, and never to have been made but always to have been. For since among the varieties of motion only the circular is continuous—as is clear from Book VIII of the *Physics*—if any motion is eternal, the circular will be eternal. And since circular motion is proper to the heavens—as is shown in Book I *On the Heavens and the Earth*—it then follows that the heavens are uncreated and that they were never made. Moreover, he had a special reason why the heavens never began: because whatever has the power to be forever in the future, always had the power to be in the past. And since the heavens will never cease to be, they did not begin to be.

5. Further: since, according to him, whatever comes about comes from pre-existent matter, he concluded that there could not be another world. Hence, God could not make another world, since this one is constructed from all the matter there is. This error also is found in Book I, *On the Heavens and the Earth*.

6. He held further that generation in this sublunary world would never end, and that it never began. For corruption precedes and follows every generation, and generation precedes and follows every corruption. Because of this, since a corruption has preceded any generation, while some generation has

preceded a corruption, it is impossible for generation and corruption to have had a beginning; nor is it possible for them to cease to be, since a corruption follows any generation, and a generation follows any corruption. If, therefore, either generation or corruption were to cease, there would be a generation after the final generation, and a corruption after the final corruption. Moreover, that a corruption precedes and follows generation, he proved by way of motion. For something is not generated except because something is corrupted; and so corruption precedes generation and also follows it, since every generable is corruptible, and every corruptible will be corrupted of necessity. Thus also generation precedes corruption, because nothing is corrupted except it was previously generated; and generation follows because the corruption of one thing is the generation of another. However, this error—that generation and corruption neither begin nor end—can be found in Book I, and more expressly in Book II, *On Generation and Corruption.*

7. Further: since generation in this sublunary world is brought about through the sun, he was forced to maintain that the sun—to quote him—"will never cease to generate plants and animals." This is clear from Book I, *On Plants.*

8. Further: since, according to his posited principle, there is no novelty without a preceding motion, he erred in maintaining that something new could not proceed immediately from God. This is clear in Book II of his *On Generation and Corruption,* where he says that "the same thing, remaining the same, always makes the same."

9. Further: he was constrained to deny the resurrection of the dead. That he held it as erroneous that the dead should rise again, is clear from Book I, *On the Soul.* Also, in Book VIII of the *Metaphysics* he held that the dead cannot return to life except through many intermediaries; and if one does return, it does not return numerically the same, because things which have lost substance do not return numerically the same, as is said at the end of Book II, *On Generation and Corruption.*

Now if someone were to wish to excuse Aristotle on the

ground that he is speaking in a naturalistic sense, this would not do: because he believed that nothing new could proceed from God immediately, but that every novelty comes about by way of motion and natural operation.

10. Further: since he believed that nothing new could occur except by way of motion and through the operation of nature, he believed—as appears in Book I of the *Physics* where he argues against Anaxagoras—that an intellect which wants to separate passions and accidents from substance is, to quote him, "an intellect seeking the impossible." On this account it seems to follow that God cannot make an accident without a subject.

11. Further: since by way of motion the generation of one thing never occurs unless there is the corruption of another; and since one substantial form is never introduced unless another is expelled; and since the matter of all things possessing matter is the same; it follows that there are not more substantial forms in one composite than there are in another. Indeed, to one who would consistently pursue this line of reasoning, it would appear that there is but one substantial form in every composite; and this seems to be the Philosopher's view. Hence, in Book VII of the *Metaphysics,* in the chapter "On the Unity of Definition," he holds the parts of a definition not to be one, as he says, "because they are *in* one," but rather because they *define* one nature.

Now if he means here one composite nature consisting in many forms, then his view can be maintained; but if he means one simple nature, and that there is only one form in such a composite, it is false.

12. Further: he posited that where there is still water, or a sea, at some time it was there dry, and conversely; because time does not cease but is eternal, as is clear from Book I of *Meteors*. Hence, he also had to say, necessarily, that one cannot posit a first man or a first rainfall.

13. Further: since an intelligence is unable to move something unless it is itself actually moving; and since intelligences are posited to be in the best state when they are moving something; he said there were as many angels, or as many intelli-

gences, as there are orbs. This is quite clear from Book XII of the *Metaphysics*.

Divine Scripture, however, contradicts this, saying: "thousands of thousands tended to Him, and ten-thousand times a hundred-thousand stood before Him."

CHAPTER II
IN WHICH THE ERRORS OF ARISTOTLE ARE RESTATED IN SUM

These, therefore, are all of his errors in sum, namely:

1. That motion did not begin.
2. That time is eternal.
3. That the world did not begin.
4. That the heavens are not created.
5. That God could not make another world.
6. That generation and corruption neither began nor will end.
7. That the sun will always cause generation and corruption in this sublunary world.
8. That nothing new can proceed immediately from God.
9. That the resurrection of the dead is impossible.
10. That God cannot make an accident without a subject.
11. That there is but one substantial form in any composite.
12. That one cannot posit a first man or a first rainfall.
13. That there is no way in which two bodies can be in the same place.
14. That there are as many angels as there are orbs—because from this it follows that there are only 55 or 57.

Now certain men wanted to excuse the Philosopher's position on the eternity of the world. But this attempt cannot hold up, since he insists upon the aforesaid principle so as to demonstrate philosophical truths. Indeed, he almost never wrote a book of philosophy where he did not employ this principle.

Again, aside from the above-mentioned errors, some men

wanted to impute to him the view that God knows nothing outside Himself, so that this sublunary world is not known to Him—citing as reason for this view the words which are found in Book XII of the *Metaphysics*, in the chapter "The Opinion of the Fathers." But that they do not understand the Philosopher, and that this is not his intention, is clear from what is said in the chapter "On Good Fortune," where he says that God, known through Himself, is the past and the future. Moreover, other errors, with which we are not concerned as they arise from an improper understanding of Aristotle, are attributed to him.

CHAPTER III

IN WHICH IS REFUTED THE STATEMENT WHICH IS FUNDAMENTAL FOR ALL THE PHILOSOPHER'S ERRORS

Now all of his errors, if one investigates subtly, follow from this position: that *nothing new comes into being except there be a preceding motion.* This is, therefore, false: because God is the First Agent, and being a non-instrumental agent, He will be able to produce a thing without a preceding motion. Now an agent by nature is an instrumental agent; but because it is of the nature of an instrument that it move the moved, motion is of necessity presupposed in its action. The making, therefore, in the production of a first agent can be without such motion. Creation, therefore, is not motion, because motion presupposes a mobile. Creation, in truth, presupposes nothing; nor is creation properly a change, because all change is a terminus of motion; but, as is commonly held, it is a simple procession of things from the first agent. Therefore, whatever is argued by way of motion against the beginning of the world, or against that which is held by faith, is wholly sophistical.

CHAPTER IV

A COMPILATION OF THE ERRORS OF AVERROËS

Now the Commentator agrees in all the errors of the Philosopher. Indeed, he spoke even more ironically and with greater pertinacity than the Philosopher against those who posited the world to have begun. He is to be argued against incomparably more than against the Philosopher, because he more directly impugns our faith, holding to be false that which could not contain falsity as it is based upon the First Truth.

1. He went beyond the Philosopher's errors because he scorned all law, as is clear from Book II and XI of the *Metaphysics*, where he mocks the law of the Christians, or our Catholic law, and even the Saracen law, because they too posit the creation of things and that something can be created from nothing. He mocks also in the beginning of Book III of the *Physics*, where he holds that some men, because of the contrary assertion of the laws, are led to deny self-evident principles—as when they deny that nothing can be created out of nothing. Indeed, what is worse, he derisively calls us, and others who hold the law, "talkers," as if we were babblers and irrational wanderers. And also in Book VIII of the *Physics* he scorns the laws; while the "talkers" in law he calls "willers," because they assert that something can have being after wholly non-being. Indeed, he calls this dictum "a will," as if it were arbitrarily established only, and completely lacking in reason. And not only once or twice, but many times in the same Book VIII he exclaims in a similar manner against the laws asserting the creation.

2. He erred further, saying in Book VII of the *Metaphysics* that no immaterial thing transmutes a material thing except through the mediation of an intransmutable body. Because of this, it follows that an angel cannot move one stone here in the sublunary world. In a certain sense this does fol-

low from the Philosopher's position, however the Philosopher did not himself expressly take this position.

3. He erred further, saying in Book XII of the *Metaphysics* that the potency in the production of something could not be in the agent alone, scorning John the Christian who maintained this view. Indeed, Averroës' view is opposed to truth and the Saints, because in made things the whole principle of the made thing lies in the potency of the maker.

4. Further: he erred by saying in the same Book XII that no agent can immediately produce diverse and contrary things. And by saying this he scorns the speakers in the three laws: namely, the law of the Christians, Saracens and Moors—because they all asserted this.

5. Further: he erred, saying in Book XII that all intellectual substances are eternal and pure acts, having no admitted potency. But he was himself constrained by truth to contradict this opinion in Book III of *On the Soul,* where he says that "no form is absolutely free from potency except the first form"; for, as he himself adds, all "other forms are diversified in essence and quiddity."

6. Further: he erred saying in Book XII that God is neither solicitous, nor does He have care, nor does He provide for individuals existing in the sublunary world. For, as he says, "this is neither permissible to, nor consonant with, Divine Goodness."

7. He erred further, denying a Trinity to be in God, saying in Book XII that some men "held a Trinity to be in God, but they sought by this device to be evasive and to really say that there are three Gods and one God; still, they don't even know how to be evasive properly, because when substance is numbered, the aggregate will still be one through the one added intention."

Because of this, according to him, if God were three and one, it would follow that He would be a composite, which is contradictory.

8. Further: he erred because he said that God did not know particulars since they are infinite. This is clear from his comment in the chapter "The Opinion of the Fathers."

9. Further: he erred because he denied that all which occurs in the sublunary world is guided by Divine Solicitude or Divine Providence. For according to him, some things, as he puts it "occur owing to the necessity of matter" and without the guidance of such Providence.

But this is opposed to the Saints; because nothing that occurs here is completely independent of the aforesaid Guidance, since all that we see here is either brought about, or permitted, by Divine Providence.

10. Further: he erred because he posited that there was numerically one intellect in all. This is clear from Book III of *On the Soul.*

11. Further: since it follows from the position just stated that the intellect is not the form of the body, Averroës therefore concluded in the same Book III that the term "act" is applied equivocally to the intellect and to other forms. Because of this, he was constrained to say that man is not placed in a species through his possession of an intellective soul, but rather through his possession of a sensitive soul.

12. Further: reasoning from this principle, he concluded that from the union of the intellective soul and the body there is not constituted some third thing; and that from such a soul and body there no more arises a unity, than there arises such a unity from the union of the mover of the heavens and the heavens.

CHAPTER V
IN WHICH THE AFORESAID ERRORS ARE RESTATED IN SUM

These are all the errors in which the Commentator goes beyond those of the Philosopher:

1. That no law is true, although it may be useful.
2. That an angel can move nothing immediately except it be a heavenly body.
3. That an angel is a pure act.

4. That in no made thing does the whole principle of the making lie in the potency of the maker.

5. That from no agent can there proceed diverse things simultaneously.

6. That God has no providence over some particulars.

7. That there is no trinity in God.

8. That God does not know singulars.

9. That something can proceed from the necessity of matter without the guidance of Divine Providence.

10. That the intellective soul is not multiplied with the multiplication of bodies, but is numerically one.

11. That man is placed in a species by his possession of a sensitive soul.

12. That a thing no more becomes one through the union of the intellective soul and the body, than does such a unity arise from the conjoining of the mover of the heavens and the heavens.

CHAPTER VI
A COMPILATION OF THE ERRORS OF AVICENNA

1. Now Avicenna also seems to have erred in that he posited but one form in a composite. This is clear from section II of his *Metaphysics,* in the chapter "Concerning the Division of Corporeal Substances," where he maintains that the generic form is not made specific by some extrinsic agency—through which is implied that the specific form is not any essence beyond the essence of the generic form.

2. Further: he erred in positing the eternity of motion. Indeed, he held motion to be eternal. Hence, he says in Book IX of his *Metaphysics,* in the chapter "Concerning the Active Property of the First Principle," that: "it is clear that motion does not become after having not been, except through something that was; and that which was, did not begin to be except through a motion contingent upon that other motion." Hence,

affirming the Philosopher's fundamental position that nothing is in a new state except through a preceding motion, he held that motion did not begin, because then there would be motion before the first motion.

3. He erred further, maintaining that matter is presupposed in every new production. For this reason he says in the same chapter that "that which was not, cannot be, except it be preceded by receptive matter." Hence, he denies that something new could begin to be after nothingness, since—as he says himself—in nothingness there can be no "hour of ending, and hour of beginning," nor indeed, any temporal distinction whatsoever.

4. Further: he maintained that nothing contingent could proceed from a non-contingent God. Hence, he says in the same chapter that if something contingent proceeded immediately from God through His nature, He would be changed in nature; if through His intention, His intention would be changed; and if through His will, His will would be changed. Indeed, what is worse, he calls heretics all those who say that God precedes creation by a priority of duration, because by saying this, according to him, they deny freedom of will to God, since if God did not immediately produce the creation, He would not have full freedom of action, but rather He was compelled to await the time and the hour to act.

5. Further: he erred in positing the eternity of time. Indeed, motion could not be eternal unless time were eternal. He says, indeed, in the already-cited chapter, that the motion of the heavens has no beginning as respects duration, but rather as respects their having a principal agent. Now as motion of this kind is caused by a soul, as he himself says, and because a soul and a body make an animal, he concluded "that the heavens were an animal obedient to God."

Now all of the aforesaid errors took their origin in that he did not clearly see the mode in which God acts according to the order of His wisdom. God, indeed, could have made the world prior to when He made it; but that He did not do this was not caused by His awaiting something in the future upon which to initiate His action, but rather because He had arranged it that way according to His wisdom. Nor is it proper for motion to precede in order that something proceed immediately from God, as has been pointed out above in the place where the Philosopher's views were set forth.

6. Further: he erred in respect of the process of things from the first principle. For not only did he posit the products of the first principle to have eternally proceeded from it, but he also held that from the first principle nothing proceeds immediately except it be numerically one—as the first intelligence. This is clear from Book IX of his *Metaphysics* in the chapter, "Concerning the Order of Intelligences and Souls." Hence, in the same chapter, he posits that "neither bodies, nor the forms which are the perfection of bodies, are the first effects of the first principle itself."

7. Further: reasoning from the above, he continued in error, in that he says that the souls of the celestial bodies were produced by intelligences or by angels, and that one intelligence was produced by another.

8. He said further, that the celestial bodies were produced by souls and that they were produced through the mediation of their forms. From this position, it follows that the intelligences are the creators of the celestial souls, and the celestial souls are the creators of bodies, and that the higher intelligence is the creator of the lower intelligence.

9. Further: he held that our souls were produced by the last intelligence, upon which depends the governance of our souls and, consequently, our beatitude. Now this is clearly stated in the afore-mentioned chapter of the above-cited book.

10. He erred further with regard to the animation of the heavens. For he held the heavens to be animated. The soul of the heavens, he said, is not only an appropriate mover, as the Philosopher and the Commentator maintain, but that one thing is produced by the union of the soul of the heavens and the heavens, just as one thing is produced by the union of our soul and our body.

But this is in opposition to Damascene, who says in Book II, Chapter VI, that the heavens are inanimate and insensible.

11. He erred further as regards the giving of forms. For he

posited all forms to be from the giver of forms, as from the lowest intelligence. This is clear from that which is said in Book IX of his *Metaphysics,* in the chapter "Concerning the Disposition of Generation of the Elements."

But this is opposed to Augustine, who held the angels to induce no forms except through the furnishing of semen.

Moreover, he also held that our souls direct matter with respect to the reception of forms, as is clear from what he says in Book VI, *On Natural Things.* He believed enchantment to be true, in that the soul can be active not only in its own body, but also in an alien body.

12. Further: he erred in holding that there could be no evil in the intelligences, contradicting Scripture, where it is written that "in His angels He found depravity." But that this was his position is clear from what is said in Book IX of his *Metaphysics,* in the chapter, "On Showing how Things Are Contained under Divine Judgment."

13. He erred further as concerns the Divine Cognition, holding God could not know singulars in their proper form. This is clear from the last chapter in Book VIII of his *Metaphysics.*

14. Further: he erred concerning the Divine Attributes, holding that God's knowledge, and other of His perfections, are not something to be attributed positively to Him, but are rather to be attributed to Him only by negation.

But this is opposed to the Saint's way, according to whom such perfections are more truly in God than in us, and that God truly is whatever it is better to be than not to be.

15. He erred further with respect to the number of intelligences, positing there to be as many angels as there are orbs. Hence, he agrees with the Philosopher's dictum that the angels are about forty in number, since he believed that there were that many orbs. This position is set forth by him in Book IX of the *Metaphysics,* in the chapter, "How Actions Proceed from Higher Principles."

16. He erred further regarding prophecy. Now he spoke correctly with reference to prophecy when he said that a prophet is nobler than a non-prophet, because the prophet

hears Divine Words, and because he sees, or at least can see, "angels transfigured before him in a form which can be seen." But he spoke badly when he held prophecy to be natural, and because he maintained that prophecy is delivered to us according to the order which our soul has with respect to supercelestial souls and the last intelligence.

17. He erred further with respect to orisons, alms and litanies. He spoke correctly when he maintained such to be of efficacy to man in that God has concern for things; but he strayed badly when he held such things to be subsumed under the order of nature.

This is false, since such things as direct us to supernatural beatitude are subsumed under the order of grace. That this error was deliberate on Avicenna's part, is clear from Book X of his *Metaphysics* in the chapter "Concerning Aspirations and Orisons."

18. Further: he erred concerning our beatitude, holding it to depend upon our works. Now from his position it follows that our beatitude consists in the contemplation of the last intelligence, as is clear from Book X of his *Metaphysics,* in the chapter "Concerning the Cult of God and its Utility."

Still other errors can be imputed to him, but either they take their origin from those cited above, or they are reducible to them.

CHAPTER VII

IN WHICH THE AFORE-MENTIONED ERRORS OF AVICENNA ARE RESTATED IN SUM

These are all the errors of Avicenna:

1. That there is but one substantial form in a composite.
2. That motion is eternal.
3. That nothing comes from nothing.
4. That contingency cannot proceed immediately from the non-contingent.
5. That time never had a beginning.

6. That a plurality of things cannot proceed immediately from the first principle.

7. That from one intelligence, another intelligence either proceeds or is created.

8. That from the intelligences, the souls of the heavens either proceed or are created.

9. That from the soul of the heavens there proceeds the supercelestial bodies.

10. That from the last intelligence, our souls proceed.

11. That a single entity comes about from the union of the soul of the heavens and the heavens, just as from the union of our soul and body.

12. That the forms in this world are induced by the last intelligence and not by proper agents.

13. That bewitchment is something beyond the mere apprehension of the soul.

14. That the soul, through its imagination, is operative in alien bodies.

15. That there cannot be evil in the angels.

16. That God does not know singulars in their proper form.

17. That the attributes of God do not correspond positively to anything.

18. That there are as many intelligences as there are orbs.

19. That prophecy is natural.

20. That alms, litanies and orisons are subsumed under the natural order. On this account Avicenna appears to hold that whatever occurs here in this world, occurs necessarily; and also that he who fully knows the motion of the supercelestial beings, and the order of the spiritual substances, can foretell the future.

21. That our beatitude depends upon our works.

22. That our beatitude consists in the cognition of the last intelligence.

CHAPTER VIII

A COLLECTION OF ALGAZEL'S ERRORS

1. Now Algazel, being, for the most part, the summarizer and follower of Avicenna, erred in positing the motion of the heavens to be eternal. This is clear from his *Metaphysics,* in the chapter, "The Manner in which the Supercelestial Bodies Are Movable by the Soul."

2. Further: he erred in positing every intelligence, and whatever does not have matter, to be eternal.

3. He erred further, positing the supercelestial bodies not to have begun, and that there is in them no potency to be, other than with respect to place. All of this is clear from the same book and chapter cited above.

4. Further: he posited that a plurality of things could not proceed immediately from the first principle. On this account he held that nothing but a single thing could proceed immediately from God—as the first intelligence, or the first angel.

5. He posited further that the second angel and the first heaven proceed from the first angel; and that the third angel and the second heaven proceed from the second angel; and so on, until the last heaven and the last intelligence. He held also that there are ten intelligences and nine heavens, all of which took their origin in the aforesaid manner. Moreover, he says that there are no more than ten intelligences unless we were to posit that there are more than nine orbs. Also, he held one intelligence to be responsible for this sublunary world; holding, indeed, that this sublunary world constituted one sphere. Thereafter he posited ten spheres in the universe, namely: the prime mobile; the circle of the signs; the seven spheres of the planets; and the sphere of active and passive things. And since he held any sphere to be responsible to a certain intelligence, he concluded that there were ten intelligences. Since, therefore, according to this position, not all the spheres are heavenly, but only nine are heavenly while the tenth, truly, is the sphere of active and passive

things, it was consistent for Algazel to say that there were nine heavens and ten intelligences.

6. He erred further because he held that illuminations not only come down to us from God through the angels, but also that no goodness is derived immediately from God in this sublunary world, but that all goodness comes to us from God through the angels.

7. Further: he erred in maintaining that everything occurs of necessity, in a certain manner, and that nothing else can happen in this sublunary world except what does in fact happen, since God does not act, according to him, in a manner which is counter to the predispositions of matter. For, as he says, "if the matter from which flies come to be *could* receive a more perfect form, undoubtedly it would be given to it by the giver" of forms.

8. Further: he erred concerning Divine Providence, positing evil not to be permitted by Divine Providence even insofar as good is elicited from it. He held, rather, that evil owes to the necessity of matter. Indeed, he held that Saturn, Mars, fire and water, could not have proceeded from God without some evil proceeding from them.

This is false: because at the world's end such things will remain and yet there will be no evil from them, because generation and corruption will cease. Indeed, God can halt evil by conserving a thing in its being. Still, He does not permit evil to occur unless it be because He elicits a greater good from it. Now all these errors are found in Algazel's *Metaphysics,* in the section "Concerning the Properties of the First Principle," which section was called "The Flower of Divine Things" by Algazel.

9. Further: he erred concerning the first principle's cognition, positing it not to know particulars in their proper form, but rather to know them as universals; just as if someone, in knowing all the distances of the orbs and their motions would know all eclipses. This opinion is found in his *Metaphysics,* in the section "Concerning the Diversity of Predication."

10. He erred further, positing the soul of man to proceed

from the giver of forms, and that all the forms in this world proceed from that giver who is the last intelligence. This is clear from what he says in *The Science of Natural Things,* Section IV.

11. Further: he erred, positing all of our science to come to us from an intelligence, and saying that this intelligence is the last. For according to him, all of our science proceeds from the last, which is the tenth, intelligence.

12. He erred further, positing our soul to be beatified in that it understands the last intelligence.

13. He erred further, positing our final beatitude to be natural. Indeed, he held that such beatitude ought naturally to belong to the soul.

14. Further: he erred concerning the punishment of the soul, positing such punishment to consist only in that it is separated from the agent intelligence. Hence, in the separated soul he did not posit a sensible punishment except insofar as it suffers the punishment of damnation. In truth, in the soul that is conjoined to the body, sensible punishment could not proceed from the punishment of damnation; for he said that a soul conjoined to the body would not suffer and would not feel pain because of its separation from the agent intelligence, on account of the preoccupation which it has with the body.

15. Further: he erred concerning prophecy, positing prophecy, and the cognition of future events, to be in us naturally.

16. He erred further as regards the action of our soul, positing the soul to be operative in an alien body through imagination, and that "the impression of the soul passes over to another body so that it can kill a man and destroy the spirit through its thinking, and this is said to be 'bewitchment.' " On this account, as he sees it, the following is a true proverb: "that the eye sends a man into a ditch and a camel into a hot pool." These errors are all clear from what he says in Section V of his *Natural Science.*

CHAPTER IX

IN WHICH THE AFORESAID ERRORS ARE RESTATED IN SUM

1. That the motion of the heavens is eternal.
2. That no angel begins to be.
3. That the supercelestial bodies are eternal.
4. That a plurality of beings cannot proceed immediately from God.
5. That the first angel created the second angel, and the second angel created the third, and so on.
6. That the first angel created the first heaven, and the second angel created the second heaven, and so on.
7. That there are as many intelligences as there are orbs.
8. That no goodness is in us immediately from God.
9. That God cannot make anything other than He made it.
10. That Divine Providence cannot halt evil.
11. That God does not know particulars in their proper form.
12. That our soul is created by the last intelligence.
13. That the whole of our science comes to us from the last intelligence.
14. That our soul will be beatified by knowing the last intelligence.
15. That the final beatitude of our soul can follow naturally.
16. That the entire punishment of a separated soul lies in this: that it senses itself as separated from the last angel, upon whom its beatitude depends.
17. That prophecy and the cognition of future events can be in us naturally.
18. That our soul, by thought alone, can affect an alien body; while by imagination alone, it can kill a man.

CHAPTER X

A COLLECTION OF ALKINDI'S ERRORS

Now Alkindi, in the book *On the Theory of the Magical Arts,* sets forth many errors.

1. He erred indeed, because he held the future to depend, absolutely and unconditionally, upon the state of the supercelestial bodies. Hence, in the above-cited book, in the chapter "On the Rays of the Stars," he says that "one who knew the total state of the celestial harmony would have full knowledge of both the past and the future."

2. Further: he erred because he believed the effects of all the causes of the world to extend to any individual. From this it follows that every cause and caused has, as it were, infinite power, so that the power of any cause extends to every effect. Hence, in the book already cited, in the chapter "On the Rays of the Elements," he says that we should assert as true that "every actual entity having existence in this world emits the rays of elements into every part, so that they fill the whole world." It is in this way that every place in the world contains rays of all the things actually existing in it.

3. Further: he strayed into another error, maintaining that anything in this world which was fully known would yield full knowledge of the entire world. This is what he says in the chapter "On the Rays of the Stars," because, as he puts it: "the conditions under which one individual in the world is fully known represent, as in a mirror, the entire condition of the celestial harmony."

4. He erred further, believing everything to occur of necessity. For if all things are fully controlled by the motion of the supercelestial bodies, since such motion is necessary, everything occurs of necessity. And he writes as follows in the chapter "On the Theory of Possibles": "all things which are, and come to be, and occur, in the world of elements, are caused and created by the celestial harmony." And it is thus, because of their relation to this harmony, that the things of this world occur of necessity. In this way he held

men to be ignorant, in that they had hopes and desires and fears, since such states would be significant only where contingencies could properly obtain.

5. Further: he erred because he deprived the elements of this world, and individuals existing in the sphere of actions and passions, their proper actions. Indeed, he believed that such things do not act properly by their own power, but only through the power of the heavens. Hence, he says in the afore-mentioned chapter "On the Theory of Possibles," that: "according to the common belief, one element acts upon another through its rays and its power; while according to the precise truth, it does not act," for only the totality of the celestial harmony acts.

6. He erred further, believing that a spiritual substance could induce true forms by mental images alone. Augustine maintains the contrary of this in Chapters VI and VII of Book III *On the Trinity,* where he holds that whatever the angels effect, they effect through the application of semen. But the contrary is said by the same Alkindi in the chapter "On the Things which Bring the Effects of Motion to Pass," on the ground that the image of something conceived in the mind emits rays similar to that thing, having an action similar to the thing itself.

7. Further: he erred because he held that not only the imagined form had causal efficacy over the extramental thing, but also that matter itself was obedient to the desire of a spiritual substance as regards the reception of form. All this is clear from the chapter "On the Things which Bring the Effect of Motion to Pass."

8. Further: he erred, as is clear from the same chapter, because he believed that prayers directed to God and to spiritual creatures had efficacy for "causing good and excluding evil" naturally, and not because such prayers addressed to God brought us the goodness from Him. For he believed that when we pray to God, from the words themselves and from the desire itself, there are derived certain rays which naturally bring about that which we desire.

9. Further: he erred because he believed the motion of the will to be present in corporeal creatures as, say, the supercelestial bodies. This is clear from the chapter "On the Power of Words and the Effect of Orisons."

10. Further: he erred with reference to the Divine Attributes, believing such to apply abusively to God, holding that it was inconvenient for God to be called "The Creator," and "The First Principle," and "The Lord of Lords."

11. He erred further, maintaining characters to have action naturally with respect to that for which they are ordered. This is clear from the chapter "On the Theory of Figures."

12. Further: he erred concerning sacrifices, believing sacrifices made in the magical arts to effect naturally that for which they are performed.

13. Further: he erred, holding that sacrifices offered to spirits or to God accomplish nothing as regards our getting something through Him, but rather to have natural efficacy in attaining that for which they are performed.

14. Further: he erred because he denied that God and the spiritual substances are placated by our prayers and sacrifices. All of this is clear from the chapter "On Sacrifices."

15. He erred further, believing the supercelestial bodies, and their dispositions, to direct our operations from beginning to end whenever we undertake to do something, so that that constellation in which the task is undertaken dominates that task from beginning to end, however voluntary such task may be.

16. He erred further, believing some sacrifices to have such power naturally, that if some voluntary task is undertaken under their auspices, these sacrifices will dominate the task from beginning to end.

17. He erred further, believing oaths and curses can naturally dominate our states of being.

18. Further: he erred in believing characters to have such dominion over our affects, that if some voluntary task is begun under their auspices, that task would be directed from

beginning to end by those characters. But this is all evident from the beginning of the work, *Theory,* which the same Alkindi wrote.

CHAPTER XI
IN WHICH THE AFORESAID ERRORS ARE RESTATED IN SUM

These, therefore, are all the errors of Alkindi:

1. That every future event depends absolutely upon the condition of the supercelestial bodies.

2. That everything, by acting, extends to every part of the universe.

3. That any completely known thing in the universe will yield full knowledge of the order of the universe.

4. That everything occurs of necessity.

5. That existents in the sphere of actions and passions are lacking in actions of their own.

6. That a spiritual substance through imagination alone can induce true forms.

7. That a spiritual substance, by desire alone, can induce forms.

8. That God, and the spiritual substances, do nothing for us consequent upon our prayers and requests; but that if something comes about on account of these, it is because the prayers and requests naturally bring it about.

9. That the motions of the will are controlled by the supercelestial bodies.

10. That the perfections attributed to God do not denote anything in Him positively.

11. That characters attain naturally that to which they are directed.

12. That the sacrifices offered to God naturally bring about that for which they are offered.

13. That as a result of sacrifices offered to God and the spiritual substances nothing is conferred upon us.

14. That the supercelestial bodies direct our voluntary operations from beginning to end.

15. That the sacrifices, oaths and characters, under whose aegis our voluntary works begin, can direct such works from beginning to end.

CHAPTER XII

A COLLECTION OF THE ERRORS OF RABBI MOSES (MAIMONIDES)

Now Rabbi Moses, holding to the letter of the Old Testament, disagreed with the Philosopher regarding the eternity of motion. Indeed, he posited the world to have begun, as is clear from what he says in Chapters XV and XVI, Book II, *On the Exposition of the Law*. Hence, he compares Aristotle—who believes that he is demonstrating the eternity of the world, and who wishes to judge the nature of things after their productions with the nature of these things in the hour of their creation—to a boy who wishes to judge the conditions of men outside the womb with their condition in the womb. This is clear in Chapter XVII of the same book. Thus, Maimonides did not err in this matter; but he deviated from the solid truth and the Catholic faith in many other matters.

1. He held, indeed, that there was no multiplicity in God, either in things or in reason, as is clear in Chapter LI of Book I, *On the Exposition of the Law*. On this account it follows that there is no Trinity in God, since three persons are three things. Hence, in Chapter LXXI of the same book, he speaks almost derisively of Christian wise men laboring and seeking the principle of the Trinity, just as though it were ludicrous to believe in the Trinity.

2. Further: he erred concerning the Divine Attributes, believing wisdom and goodness to be equivocally in God and in us. This is evident from Chapter LVI of Book I, *On the Exposition of the Law*. In another place he also cites the

Prophets in support of his position, quoting: "To whom have ye likened Me?"

But this does not hold up, since our perfections are derived from the Divine Perfections; and since an agent always assimilates that which it acts upon, there cannot be a pure equivocation between them.

3. Further: he erred concerning such perfections, not believing them to exist truly in God. On this account, in Chapter LVII of Book I, *On the Exposition of the Law,* he says that God is, but not in essence; that He lives, but not in life; and that He is potent, but not in potential. Now all such things, according to Maimonides, are said of God either by way of negation, as he implies in the same chapter and book, or else these things are said of Him by causality—as God is said to live not because life is in Him, but because He causes life. This is clear from Chapter LXI of the same book.

4. He erred further concerning the proper attributes of the Persons, believing the Word and the Spirit of God to be attributed only essentially to the Divinity. Hence, in Book I, *On the Exposition of the Law,* expounding this Psalm: "by the Word of God the heavens were instituted; and by the Spirit of His Mouth, all of their power," Maimonides says that in the Divinity the terms "Word," and "Spirit," are used only for the Divine Will or the Divine Essence by which the heavens were made, even though these terms are used personally.

5. He erred further, concerning the supercelestial bodies, positing them to be animate and holding them to be rational animals. To support this view, he quoted the Psalm: "the heavens announce the glory of God"; and Job: "when the morning stars praised Me together." All of these are clear from Chapter V, Book III, *On the Exposition of the Law.*

6. Further: he erred concerning the motion of the supercelestial bodies and their innovation. For although he believed motion to have begun, he nevertheless believed that it would never end. Hence, he believed that the world would never be innovated universally, and that the Prophet's say-

ing: "there will be a new heaven and a new earth," means that these new heavens are already in existence. Now in explaining the following statement of Joel: "the sun shall be changed into darkness and the moon into blood, before the great and terrible day of the Lord shall come," he holds that this is a reference to the death of Gog and Magog and Sennacherib, and not to the day of judgment. All of this is clear from Chapter XXIX, Book II, *On the Exposition of the Law,* where he plainly holds that time and motion will never end, which is even more clear from another translation.

7. Further: he erred with respect to prophecy, believing that a man of himself could be sufficiently disposed toward the grace of prophecy, and that God does not elect any particular man for prophesying, but rather one who adapts himself for such things. Whence, he appears to hold Divine Grace to depend upon our works. But all of this is clear from what he says in Chapter XXXII of Book II, *On the Exposition of the Law.*

8. He erred further concerning Divine Power, holding some things to be possible to God, and some not. He holds, among the impossibles, that it is impossible for an accident to exist without a subject. Also certain men, whom he calls "separatists" because they said that God could do this, he held to be ignorant of the method of scientific discipline. However, this is clear from Chapter XV, Book II, *On the Exposition of the Law.*

9. Further: he erred concerning Divine Providence. Indeed, he believed God to have providence over men both with respect to the species and with respect to the individuals. Of things other than men, however, he said that God had providence only with respect to the species and not with respect to the individuals. Thus, in the case of the falling of leaves from the trees, and other such things which happen to individuals, he did not hold these as falling under the Divine Order of Providence, but he felt rather, that all such events occurred by accident, as is clear from Chapter XVII, Book III, *On the Exposition of the Law.*

10. Further: he erred concerning human nature and voli-

tion, holding that although such things may be changed by God, they are, however, never changed, because then the admonition of the Prophets would be pointless. He believed also that man without special aid from God could, by himself, vitiate all sins and implement all of the Prophets' injunctions.

From this position it appears to follow that Divine Grace is utterly superfluous. It is on this account that his position is worse than that of Pelagius; for according to Pelagius, even though we could live righteously without grace, still grace is not superfluous because by its possession we can live righteously more easily. That the foregoing, however, are Rabbi Moses' views is clear from what he writes in Chapter XXXII of Book III, *On the Exposition of the Law.*

11. He erred further concerning human acts, holding simple fornication not to be, in any sense, a sin according to natural law. He holds it to be a sin only by reason of its prohibition. This, however, is false; since matrimony is in the natural law. Hence, as he says, before that law was given, fornication was permitted. It is on this account that he says Judah did not sin with Thamar, because this occurred before the time of the law. But all this is clear from Chapter XLIX, Book III, *On the Exposition of the Law.*

CHAPTER XIII

IN WHICH THE AFORESAID ERRORS ARE RESTATED IN SUM

These are all the foregoing errors:

1. That in God there is no multiplicity either in things or in reason.
2. That there is no Trinity in God.
3. That perfections are attributed to God and to us purely equivocally.
4. That the Divine Attributes do not attribute anything to God positively.
5. That the Word is attributed to God only essentially.

6. That the supercelestial bodies are animate.

7. That although time began, it will never cease.

8. That the supercelestial bodies will always be in motion.

9. That the world will never be completely innovated.

10. That man can adequately dispose himself to receive the grace of prophecy.

11. That God cannot make an accident without a subject.

12. That Divine Providence, in things other than man, extends only to the species and not to the individuals; and that whatever happens to such individuals is accidental and unpredictable.

13. That God never changes the will of man.

14. That man, of himself, can live righteously and implement the warnings of the Prophets.

15. That simple fornication was not a mortal sin before the giving of the law.

O good Jesus, to Thy praise and out of reverence for Thy name, and also out of detestation for Thy contradictors, with Thy aid, in the first part of this treatise I have restated in summary form the passages in which Aristotle, Averroës, Avicenna, Algazel, Alkindi and Rabbi Moses write in contradiction to the faith bequeathed by Thee—which faith alone I consider to be true and Catholic. In this work I have simply collected all the errors of the above-cited philosophers; or have included herein those to which the diligent inquirer can reduce all others. Inasmuch as this could not have been accomplished without Thee, to Thee be honor and glory forever and ever. Amen.

Suggestions for Further Reading

FCC vol. II, 460-465; *EG* 418-423; *AAM* 205, 211 *et passim.*

Siger of Brabant

Siger was born about 1240 in the Duchy of Brabant (Belgium). He studied at the University of Paris from about 1255 to 1260, and attained the degree of Master of Arts between 1260 and 1265. Right from the beginning of his academic career Siger defended various doctrines considered dangerous to the faith, and together with an impressive group of his colleagues and students displayed an independence of spirit and an attachment to pagan and infidel philosophy which aroused considerable indignation in powerful quarters. St. Bonaventure attacked Siger in his sermons of 1267 and 1268; in 1270, St. Thomas directed a treatise, *On the Unity of the Intellect,* against him; and on December 10 of the same year, 1270, Etienne Tempier, Bishop of Paris, condemned thirteen propositions taken from the writings of Siger and his coterie. Despite these moves the crisis continued and the struggle between the unorthodox minority represented by Siger and the defenders of Christian orthodoxy became even more heated. Albert the Great, Giles of Rome, and others plunged into the controversy. Finally, on March 7, 1277, Tempier condemned 219 propositions representing the unorthodox teachings of the Arts faculty at the University, as well as certain theses professed by highly respected theologians of hitherto unquestioned orthodoxy.

Eventually, Siger, together with two of his colleagues, was commanded to appear before the court of the Inquisitor for France. Siger, however, fled the kingdom, and although we do not know with certainty where he went, it is quite probable that he turned himself over to the papal court, which was reputed to be milder than the court of the Inquisitor. Although the records are not clear on this point, it appears that Siger was not condemned as a heretic, but was merely detained at the papal court and kept under surveillance by some cleric underling. Unhappily, this cleric seems suddenly to have gone mad, and before he could be restrained he stabbed Siger to death. This incident occurred at Orvieto, between 1281 and 1284, in the pontificate of Martin IV. Twenty years later Dante placed Siger next to Thomas Aquinas in the "Heaven" of his *Divine Comedy* and devoted six mysterious lines to the unfortunate master of the University of Paris.

Reprinted below in its entirety is Siger's controversial work *On the Necessity and Contingency of Causes.*

SIGER DE BRABANT ON THE NECESSITY AND CONTINGENCY OF CAUSES *

[Here] begins a difficult question resolved by Master Siger of Brabant.

Your question is justly debatable: whether it is necessary that all future things be going to be before they are, and with regard to present and past things also: whether it was necessary for them to be going to be before they came to be.

And it seems that this is the case. 1. Every effect which comes to pass, results from a cause in relation to which its existence is necessary, as Avicenna[1] says and as can be proved also. For if some effect results from a cause which when posited, the effect is able to be posited and not to be posited, then that cause is being-in-potency-to-producing-an-effect, and it will require something educing it from potency

* Translated especially for this volume by J. P. Mullally and W. Quinn from the edition of J. J. Duin published in his *La doctrine de la Providence dans les écrits de Siger de Brabant*, Louvain, 1954.

1 *Metaph.*, VI, tr. 3 (ed. 1508, fol. 92rb, text A).

to act, which would make it a cause in act; wherefore it is necessary that every cause causing an effect be such that when posited, the effect is necessarily posited; and if that cause is [itself] the effect of another, the same is argued for it. For this [caused-cause] would come to be from such a cause as when posited, the former of necessity is posited, and so on up even to the first cause of all. Wherefore all effects seem to proceed from their causes in such a way that it is necessary for them to be going to be before they should come to be.

2. Moreover. In the things of the present there is the cause of all things which afterwards will come to be, so that all future things will come to be from present things, either without a medium or with a medium: one or more than one, many or few. But if in present things there exists the necessary cause of those which will come to be, what was proposed is a consequence; but if not, [if] rather from things of the present, future things are able to be and not to be, then the cause of future things is not in present things, except as matter. Whence no element of those future things which do not have a necessary cause in present things will come to be; or if it comes to be, matter proceeds [from potency] to act by itself without any agent. It is necessary, therefore, that in present things there exist the necessary cause of all future things; and the argument would be the same should someone appeal to what happened in times past.

3. Moreover. Everything which comes to be, comes to be either from an essential cause necessary to an effect, one which cannot be impeded, or from an essential cause which works frequently and in most cases, which nevertheless can be impeded, or from an accidental cause. And with regard to future things arising from a cause in the first way, it is clear that their coming-to-be is necessary. The effect of a cause which works in most cases and exists in that disposition in which it is not impeded, is necessary, so that whenever that cause is posited in such disposition, it is also necessary that the effect be posited. The same is true also for an effect which results from an accidental cause. For an ac-

cidental cause, taken according to that disposition wherein it is a necessary cause of its effect, necessarily brings about its effect. But if someone should say that that accident through which it causes necessarily, cannot happen to that cause—because an accident is not necessary—it can be argued as before: because that accidental being or that accidental cause, since it is a certain effect, proceeds from a cause existing in some one of the three aforesaid ways, and thus the occurrence of that accident will be necessary as before.

4. Moreover. In the Sixth Book of the *Metaphysics*[2] Aristotle maintains—and his commentator[3] does also—that if there were no accidental being, all things would be necessary; and this is certainly clear for a cause-which-works-in-most-cases would be necessary unless something were to happen to it. Now the fact is, however, that nothing is accidental being absolutely; for although some effect, referred to some particular cause of it, results from this cause accidentally, as through the concurrence of another agent, either through the impediment of a contrary or from the indisposition of matter concurring with that agent, nevertheless those concurrences referred to a higher cause which extends itself to many, are brought together by it as by an essential cause with which neither of these concurs. But if all things were necessary, if there were no accidental being, as Aristotle says, as has been seen, and nothing is accidental being absolutely, as has been said and will be evident in solving the question, then, it would seem that all effects have some essential cause from which they necessarily follow, although in relation to some definite cause, some of them proceed from an accidental cause and some from a cause which works in most cases. But, as it seems, each of these is referred to some necessary cause.

5. Moreover. Every effect having a cause in the present or past from which it necessarily follows, necessarily comes to be, as Aristotle maintains in the Sixth Book of the *Meta-*

---

[2] 3, 1027a 29-33.

[3] Averroës, *Metaph.*, VI, text 7, ed. 1542, fol. 145v.

physics.[4] But every future effect has a cause in the present from which it necessarily follows; the proof of which is Divine providence. For if *a* will come to be, it has been foreseen by God that *a* will come to be, and this by an infallible providence; for Divine providence cannot err. Wherefore *a* necessarily follows from such a cause of it.

6. Moreover. From the same thing it can be argued even more efficaciously: whenever some conditional is true, the consequence is necessary from the supposition of the antecedent. But this consequence is true: if *a* is foreseen to come to be, *a* will come to be absolutely, no addition having been made in the consequent that it will come to be necessarily or contingently. But if the antecedent is already true, the consequent is necessarily going to be.

7. Moreover. Let it be said: how can there be an infallible providence about a fallible thing, since these do not seem to be compatible? For if the order of a thing or of a cause to some effect is fallible, then the knowledge (*ratio*) of the order of that cause to its effect, or providence, will be fallible. For if this situation: *b* to come to be from *a* or that *b* will come to be from *a*, is fallible, although it will not fail, then reason or intellect preconceiving that *b* will come to be from *a*, is fallible. And the same kind of deficiency exists and the argument is the same for divine foreknowledge of future things which precedes those future things. For in those three ways in which one argues for providence, one can argue for foreknowledge, as is clearly evident to anyone who tries. Divine foreknowledge of future things and providence are different, however; for divine foreknowledge of future things, under the aspect of foreknowledge, pertains to the divine intellect according as it contemplates them absolutely; however, since providence is the part of prudence being about future things—prudence however pertains to the practical intellect—providence about future things pertains to the divine intellect not only according as it contemplates them, but also according as it directs them; hence it belongs

---

[4] 3, 1027 a 29 ss.

to providence to follow foresight. However, providence and foreknowledge agree in this, that each is infallible.

To the contrary. Aristotle maintains in the Sixth Book of the *Metaphysics*[5] that not all things come to pass of necessity, and, *in the same place,* he maintains that some causes are such that when posited sometimes they cause their effects, sometimes they do not. Thus it is clearly his intention that not all things come to pass of necessity, since *in the same place* he says that not all future things come to pass, for example, that the living be going to die. For something is already a fact, as that contraries are found in a body, from which necessarily death will come about. But although someone ought to die from sickness or violence, yet it is not yet necessary that it be the fact nor that it be in the present that he ought necessarily to die in such a fashion, as is said *above.*

Moreover. This is also clearly Aristotle's intention in the *Perihermeneias,*[6] where he maintains that not all things come to pass of necessity, because then it would not be necessary to take counsel or to negotiate. Therefore, etc.

We have divided the solution of this question into four parts. For in the first place some things concerning the order of causes to effects must be considered. Secondly, how some people have erred because of that order, believing that all things come to pass necessarily on account of the connection of causes and the condition of the universe. Thirdly, in what those who err in this way were mistaken and how the question is answered. Fourthly and finally, from the determined truth the reasonings of the adversaries of the truth must be gotten rid of.

I

With respect to the first it must be known that five orders of causes-in-relation-to-the-caused are found in the universe, and this is according to the intention of the *Philoso-*

---

5 3, 1027 a 29.

6 *De Interpretatione*, 9, 18 b 31, and 19 a 6.

phers. The first is that the First Cause, cause of the whole of being (*totius esse*), is the essential, immediate, necessary cause of the first intelligence, and is such that when posited, its first caused is also simultaneously posited; and this I affirm in accordance with the intention of the *Philosophers.* I say that it is the essential cause of [the first intelligence]; for the First Cause causes nothing accidentally, since nothing is able to concur with it, for then it would not be the cause of the whole of being (*totius entis*); for there is no causal order among accidents in relation to each other. I say that it is the immediate cause of [the first intelligence], because that is its first caused. It is also necessary cause of [the first intelligence] by reason of the fact that an essential cause, to which an impediment cannot happen and which does not cause through an intermediate impedible cause, is a necessary cause of its effect. But this is the way the First Cause is related to the first caused, and I also say, that it is necessary that it always exist simultaneous with its caused effect. For nothing prevents some present causes from being necessary in relation to future effects, by virtue of the fact that they are the cause of those effects through an intermediate motion and through an order to that which is moved, which causes posteriority in duration. But since the First Cause does not cause the first caused through an order to that which is moved nor through an intermediate motion, and since it is a necessary cause in relation to that which is its caused, they will be simultaneous as regards duration.

The second order is that the First Cause is the cause of the separated intelligences, of the spheres and of their motions, and universally of the ingenerables. The essential and necessary cause, I say, which also has being (*esse*) simultaneously with caused things of this kind; and this will be made clear in the same way in which it was made clear about the First Cause in relation to the first caused. But this order falls short of the previous order in this, that the First Cause is not the cause of the afore-mentioned except according to a certain order, and it is not the immediate cause of all of them, since from something one and simple only one proceeds immediately and not many except in a certain order; however as regards the order according to which the aforesaid proceed, nothing [is clear] to reason. Moreover the First Cause is not only the essential cause of any one of the aforesaid taking causality in the way indicated but also of the conjunction which occurs among them, as that this should have being with that.

The third order is that the First Cause is the cause that the moon at one time be in such a place, the sun in such a place, and so on for the other stars. And the First Cause is the essential and necessary cause of these, but not the immediate [cause], nor one which when posited these effects are posited, for the First Cause does not cause the said positions except through an order to the moved, which causes posteriority. Nevertheless, from the existence of the First Cause it will necessarily come about that at one time the sun is in such a place, the moon in such a place, and similarly for the other stars. And that it is a necessary cause is proved as before. For it is the essential cause of this, since it is first, to which nothing can happen, because it is not its nature to be impeded nor does it cause the aforesaid effects through intermediate impedible causes. The proper mover of any one star, however, is the essential, immediate and necessary cause of the aforesaid, but not such that when posited, the effect is posited. The First Cause certainly is an essential, necessary but not immediate cause, nor one which when posited, the effect of any conjunction and of a division occurring among the celestial stars is posited, so that all these are going to come about in a time determined by the First Cause. And therefore Aristotle[7] well says that, although from the celestial bodies something can come to be by chance and accidentally, nevertheless among them nothing happens by chance, since whatever comes to pass among them comes to pass from essential and necessary causes, as has been seen; such however does come to pass by chance. Moreover, no proper mover is the cause of the conjunctions or divisions among

---

[7] *Phys.* II, 4, 196 b 2.

the celestial bodies, but rather a higher cause is what unites; for what does not fall under the order of an inferior cause, falls under the order of a higher cause, and under its causality as well. For the order of any cause extends just as far as its causality. Whence the First Cause, and not the proper movers, orders the conjunctions and divisions among the stars.

The fourth order of causes is that the celestial bodies cause something in these inferiors, but in different ways. For something of the revolutions of the celestial bodies causes something here below as an essential, necessary, immediate cause and one which when posited, the effect is posited; also [it causes] something as an essential and necessary cause, but not one which when posited, the effect is posited, since it causes through a mediating motion; and it causes something but not as an immediate cause; and a revolution certainly causes something here below as an essential cause which works in most cases, since the celestial revolutions are naturally constituted to be impeded by an incapacity of matter; and it also causes something accidentally. But that which a celestial body causes here below accidentally, and what is accidental to them offering an impediment according to that which is taken absolutely, since it is a certain disposition of matter, or something here below acting contrary, is reduced to something of the celestial bodies as to a cause, but the very concurrence of the accident with the celestial body is not; yet nevertheless this concurrence is reduced to a superior cause, for whatever happens among the celestial bodies, in whatever way they are connected, has a unifying cause, as has been seen. And since every disposition of matter is referred to something of the celestial bodies, then, indeed, so uniting the celestial bodies unites the disposition of matter, caused by one revolution, to that [caused] by another revolution, whether that disposition is simultaneous with its cause, or is caused later, or remains later than its cause. Therefore the celestial bodies have this defect with respect to inferiors in relation to the divine causes which cause something in celestial bodies, that celestial bodies cause something accidentally and are able to be impeded, while this is not true of those other causes.

The fifth and last order of causes however is that particular lower causes, whose causality extends to few, have to cause some effects essentially and necessarily, other [effects] essentially though working only in most cases, and [still] others accidentally; nevertheless of the essential causality which is in these, a greater quantity is non-necessary causing, but causing which is effective in most cases, since these causes are especially subject to change. Nevertheless accidents here below, whether they are two causes concurring, or an impeding contrary agent or some disposition of matter, are found to be ordered and to have an essential cause of their conjunction in higher causes. For these inferiors are caused by superiors; therefore these two concurrences are caused either by one among the celestial bodies, or by many. In the first way they have an essential ordering cause among celestial bodies; in the second way, among divine things, as is clear from what was said before. But these particular causes fall short of celestial bodies in this, that celestial causes, even if they are impeded from their effect on account of an indisposition of matter, nevertheless are not capable of suffering and are not movable in themselves as are inferiors; and accidents still lower, which do not have their conjoining cause in particular causes, are found sometimes to be joined by something in the celestial bodies, by reason of the fact that a celestial cause extends to more than a particular inferior cause.

II

From the aforesaid, the second member of what was proposed above is clear, namely, what led *some* into the error that it is necessary that all future things which will come to pass be going to be before they are; likewise for all present and past things, before they should come to be. For every effect, related to the First Cause, comes from it as from its essential cause, since to that cause nothing happens. Therefore it also comes from it as from a non-impedible cause. For no cause is impedible unless an impediment can happen to it. From which it is argued as follows: every effect which results from an essential, non-impedible cause, results necessarily; but everything which results, in relation to the first cause of its coming-to-be, results from it as from an essential, non-impedible cause, as has already been shown. Therefore it is necessary that everything which comes to be, before it is, be going to be from the existence of the First Cause, which is the essential and non-impedible cause of the futurity of every effect which comes to be in its own time. And this reasoning is manifested because *Aristotle*[8] maintains that there are two situations which prevent it being the case that all things happen necessarily. One is that some things come from an essential cause, but an impedible one, and those are not necessary; for example, if someone drinking a warm beverage dies, still it is not necessary that a warm beverage drinker dies. The other is that certain [things] are accidents which certainly according to Aristotle[9] are not necessary, as that someone digging out a grave find a treasure. But if effects which, in relation to some particular cause, result from it as from an impedible cause, yet in relation to the First Cause, result from it as from an essential cause to which no impediment of its effect in a determinate time happens, then effects of this kind, which come to be from a particular cause in most cases, nevertheless in relation to the First Cause will come to be necessarily. But if, in addition, those things which are accidents in themselves and in relation to some particular causes, are always found to have a unifying and ordering cause, as has been seen previously, so that accidents of this kind also come from an essential, non-impedible cause, then accidents notwithstanding, all things would result from their causes necessarily. And this was what moved certain *Parisian Doctors* speaking out against the doctrine of their master, Aristotle, others maintaining other opinions for other reasons: although, they say, certain future things, which we call contingent in comparison to some of their causes, do not come from these

---

8 *Metaph.* VI, 3, 1027 a 29 ss.
9 *Metaph.* VI, 2, 1027 a 9 ss.

necessarily, nor is it necessary for them to be going to be, before they are, from these causes, nevertheless when future things of this kind are related to the First Cause, from which all intermediate causes up to the effect are and act, or to the whole connection of causes or the whole relationship of existing things, all things which will come to be, before they are, necessarily will be from the existence of the First Cause, the connection of causes, or the relationship of existents, so that it is absolutely true to say that all things which will come to be, before they are, have something in the relationship of existents so that it is necessary for them to be going to be.

III

Now we must consider the third item proposed above, namely, in what those who think in the afore-mentioned way err. And it is this: that although the First Cause is not an impedible cause or one with which an accidental impediment concurs, nevertheless it does not produce inferior effects immediately but through intermediate causes; and although these intermediate causes owe it to the order of the First Cause that they produce an effect, and at that time that they are not impeded, nevertheless they are still in their very nature impedible; therefore, although the First Cause is not impedible, nevertheless it produces an effect through an impedible cause. For which reason that effect, even in relation to the First Cause, was not necessarily going to be beforehand. And although all concurrences have an ordaining and unifying cause, yet not such a cause (as is apparent and the reason for which will be seen) as makes all accidents be necessary, so that some among them would not be rare, but rather all of them would be frequent, indeed necessary. However, if all things were to come to be necessarily, it would be necessary, not so much that the first cause of future things be not impedible, but that future things which come to be not come to be from the First Cause through intermediate impedible causes. It would also be necessary that in beings there would be no accident but that would have an essential cause unifying and ordaining it, not just any sort but one which would prevent it from being rare, so that, when Aristotle[10] maintains that, if there were no accident, all things would be necessary, we must understand that the removal of accident in relation to the First Cause does not make all things necessary, rather it would be necessary to remove an accidental impediment in relation to particular causes, through which intermediate causes the First Cause acts. And therefore, if anyone should especially prize the truth, he would find Aristotle, in the Sixth Book of the *Metaphysics,*[11] maintaining two things: one is that, if all future things were to come to be necessarily, then all things would come to be from essential, non-impedible causes; the other is that there would be no rare accident; in fact the two aforesaid accompany each other.

From these, summarily with Aristotle,[12] we say, finishing the question, that only those future things will come to be necessarily which will come to be from an essential, non-impedible cause, and not only the first but also a proximate cause; and because not all future things are such, but some of them are accidents, some of them moreover will come to be from causes that are impedible, although not impeded, for that reason not all things will come to be necessarily. And this is clear in this way. If anyone directs his attention, something is said to be necessarily going to be not only because it will come to pass and will not be otherwise, but because it is not able to be otherwise than that it should come to pass. Moreover, a future thing is not said to be impossible to be otherwise than that it should come to be, unless because its already present cause is such, not only that it will not be otherwise than that this kind of effect result from it, but because in its very nature [it is] such that it is not possible [for it] to be otherwise than that the effect come from it. And because not all things which will come to be, will come to be in this way from their cause, therefore not all things will come to be necessarily. For it is necessary, if all things which will come

---

10 *Metaph.* VI, 2, 1027 a 13.
11 *Metaph.* VI, 2-3, 1027 a 55.
12 *Metaph.* VI, 3, 1027 a 29.

to be are necessarily going to be, that each and every thing would have in present things some cause which cannot be impeded, from which this kind of future effect would come to be immediately, or through intermediate future causes likewise not impedible; as in a living thing there is a present cause of future death, not impedible from that effect. And therefore we call many effects contingently future, and not necessarily [future], even referring them to the whole connection of causes or interrelationship of present things, or even to the First Cause. For although in the interrelationship of present things or the whole connection of causes there is contained a cause which is not impeded or which is deprived of any future contingent impediment, nevertheless there is not contained in them a necessary, immobile, non-impedible cause, which cannot be otherwise; it is not the case for, if in the interrelationship of present things and the connection of causes there does not exist what moves, or impedes, or makes to be otherwise the present cause of a future contingent, not for that reason is there contained in the interrelationship of present things and the connection of causes the immobile cause of that future thing. And the First Cause, even if it is a non-impedible cause, nevertheless causes through the medium of an impedible cause, as has been said; neither is it necessary for contingent future things to come to pass with respect to Divine Providence, because it has been seen from the order and connection of causes and the interrelationship of present things that it is not necessary that many things come to be which will come to be; wherefore neither [will they come to be necessarily] from the reason and understanding of this order and of the connection of causes to caused. But divine providence is nothing other than the reason of the said order and the making of the said connection.

But now three doubts arise concerning what has been said. The first is this. How can these simultaneously be the case: The First Cause is a non-impedible cause with respect to any future thing which will come to be, and yet that effect proceeds from it through impedible causes; for if the intermediaries and the instruments are impedible from the effect, then the First Cause will be impedible from its effect, through those intermediaries.

The second doubt exists because, although a cause, which is called "a cause which works in most cases," taken essentially and absolutely, is able to be otherwise than that it produce an effect, nevertheless the same cause taken as not impeded is not able to be otherwise than that it produce the effect. In this way however it is a cause producing an effect, insofar, namely, as [it is] not impeded. Therefore it seems that the effect of necessity proceeds from that [cause].

The third doubt is this, how is it that not all accidents have necessary concomitance, although all have an essential and ordering cause, as has been said before. For the flowering of this tree and of that, which, considered in themselves, are accidents, have necessary, or at least frequent, concomitance on account of the fact that they have an essential cause unifying and conjoining them. But if all accidents, which, considered in themselves and related to some particular causes, have the nature of accidents reduced to a higher cause, are found to be ordered, why will the concomitance of all not be necessary, as [it is] of the aforesaid? And we ask this, for let it be the case that there should be some impedible causes from which something would also come to be accidentally: if the impediment happening were some one of the things necessary from a unifying and ordering cause, the necessity of futurity in those things which result, inasmuch as they result, is not taken away, although some [of them] would also come to be from causes sometimes impeded, since the concurrence of impediments would come to be necessarily.

The first of these is solved: for these are not the case simultaneously—the First Cause is the necessary cause to some effect which will come to be, and, that effect is produced through intermediate impedible causes. But for the First Cause to be a non-impedible cause is not for it to be necessary to some effect which will come to be, but is for it to be a cause to which no impediment is able to happen outside its order, so that from the fact that the First Cause is not impedible, it follows that the coming-to-be of something future cannot happen outside Its order. And therefore if under the order of the First Cause only one part of the contradiction of a contingent future would fall, so that the other is not able to fall under its order, as happens in the case of particular causes, that future would necessarily result from the First Cause. Now however, since such is not the particular order of the First Cause to the caused, what has been said does not occur. Whence from a particular and proximate cause a contingent future does not result necessarily, because it is possible for the coming-to-be of that future to occur otherwise and outside the order of that cause. Nor does that future thing result necessarily from the First Cause, for although it is not possible for the coming-to-be of that future thing to occur otherwise than according to the order of the First Cause by reason of the fact that it is not an impedible cause, nevertheless since not only does that future thing fall under its order but also the possible opposite of that future thing, therefore the coming-to-be of that future thing is not necessary even with respect to the First Cause.

With regard to the second one must know that, as Aristotle says in the First Book of the *De Caelo et Mundo*,[13] he who is sitting, while he is sitting, has a potency to standing. But he who is sitting, while he is sitting does not have a potency-to-standing-while-he-is-sitting. And therefore it is said in the *Perihermeneias*[14] that being which is, when it is, necessarily is; not however: what is, necessarily is. So also a non-impeded cause-which-works-in-most-cases, even when it is not impeded, is able to be such that the effect not result from it, although it is not possible that from a non-impeded cause, when not impeded, the effect not result; and since necessity is a certain impossibility-to-being-otherwise, it appears that there is a certain necessity in the coming-to-be of an effect from an impedible cause, and clearly, because a cause-which-works-in-most-cases, existing in that disposition in which it has to cause the effect, and not impeded, is not, when it is this way, in potency to not-causing the effect. And unless there

13 I, 12, 281 b 13.
14 Aristotle, *De Interpretatione*, 9, 19 a 22.

were such necessity, nothing would result from such causes; and Avicenna[15] had this necessity in mind when he said that every effect is necessary with respect to its cause. However this is not necessity absolutely, no more than is the necessity of any present thing. For a cause-which-works-in-most-cases, at the very time when it is not impeded, is impedible and has a potency to be such that the effect not come to be from it, although it does not have a potency-to-be-impeded-while-not-impeded. Not seeing these aforesaid necessities, however, *some* have fallen into diverse errors. For *some*, paying attention to the fact that a cause not impeded and universally existing in that disposition in which it has to cause the effect, is not, when it is this way, in potency to not causing that very effect, have said that all things come to pass necessarily; and it is already apparent in what they have erred. *Others*, however, in order that they might avoid this error, have fallen into a different one saying that a cause, existing in that disposition in which it has to cause the effect, would in no way be a cause necessary to the effect, because then counsel and free choice would be destroyed. However the aforesaid distinction of the necessary solves their ignorance. If all things were to result necessarily, viz., from non-impedible causes, counsel to prevent certain future effects would be idle, as if the drinking of poison were a non-impedible cause of death, it would be idle to seek advice about medicine. This case: that the very cause producing the effect, be a non-impedible and necessary cause, would take away freedom of choice, because then all our willing would be caused by a cause which the will could not resist. But this case: that the drinking of poison, when not impeded, is not in-potency-not-to-cause-death-while-not-impeded, does not remove counsel about medicine. But one should not consult in order that the drinking of poison, which is not impeded, might not induce death; rather one should consult because the drinking of poison, which is not impeded, was impedible, so that at other times the aforesaid drinking may be impeded by the aid of medi-

---

[15] *Metaph.*, VI, tr. 3, ed. 1508, 92rb, text A.

cine and may not induce death. However this case: that the will is always moved to willing under a cause existing in that disposition in which it is naturally constituted to move the will, and with the will itself existing in that disposition in which it is naturally constituted to be moved by such, does not take away freedom of choice, by reason of the fact that nothing moves the will that is not impedible from the motion, even if it is not impeded when it does move the will. Whence one must consider that the freedom of the will in its works must not be understood in this way, that the will is the first cause of its act-of-willing and its operating, being able to move itself to opposites, not moved by anything prior. For the will is not moved to willing except by some apprehension. Nor is this freedom of the will, that, the will itself existing in that disposition in which it is naturally constituted to be moved to willing something, and the mover also existing in that disposition in which it is naturally constituted to move, the will sometimes may not have to be moved, or it may have the potency-not-to-be-moved-when-it-is-so-disposed, the agent likewise being so disposed; for this is impossible. Rather freedom of the will consists in this, that even if the will be sometimes found moved by certain things, when these kinds of movers of the will are not impeded, such is the nature of the will that any one of those which can move the will, can be impeded from its motion; which happens to the will as opposed to the sensitive appetite, because the will wills from the judgment of reason, the sensitive appetite however desires from the judgment of sense. Now the fact is that we are born with a determinate judgment of sense with respect to the pleasurable and the painful, perceiving this determinately [as] pleasurable, that with sorrow. And because of this the sensitive appetite does not freely desire or flee from anything. However we are not so born with a determinate judgment about good and evil, rather either is possible; on which account also [either is possible] in the case of the will.

To the third it must be said that accidents, which have one cause and which are such that one of them is not able to result except from a cause from which the other results, are necessary; indeed these are not properly accidents, as in the example posited before, that when this tree flowers, the other does also. But for those things which concur from a unifying cause, while it is still possible for them to result from diverse causes, and for one of them to result [but] not from the cause of the other, the concomitance of such things is not necessary. As for example with the creditor willing to go to the market-place, the debtor is also willing from a common cause, as the sterility of the oats and the failure of the cereal plant; because it is still possible for these to result from different causes, and one of them not from the cause of the other, so it is that it accidentally happens that they are from one cause: for this reason, it is not necessary that with the creditor willing to go to the forum the debtor also be willing. And because the accidental does not have a unifying proximate cause except accidentally, and the remote cause moreover, which is God, does not induce necessity into the concomitance of accidents, therefore Aristotle[16] has well said that the accidental is not truly being but as it were only in name, nor truly one, and that there is no cause of its generation. Thus when any two are accidentally concurrent in being, it is true that they have a unifying cause, but just as it accidentally happens that these are united, so it happens that these are from one cause, since it is possible for one of them to come to be from its proper cause without the other coming to be. Therefore the fact that being-which-exists-only-in-most-cases will not result of necessity, for example, that someone drinking a warm beverage die, and the fact that those things which are accidental are certainly not necessary, for example, that someone digging find a treasure, these make it true that not all things are necessarily going to be but only those things which result from non-impedible causes and which have in present things such a cause as future death has in the body of an animal now living.

---

16 *Metaph.*, VI, 2, 1026 b 13.

IV

To the first objection maintaining the opposite it must be said that a cause of an effect, which works in most cases, taken in itself, is not necessary to the effect; the same cause even taken as not impeded, while it remains impedible, is still not necessary to the effect. But it is true that a cause-which-works-in-most-cases, taken as not impeded and as in the disposition in which it is a cause, is not, while not impeded and being so disposed, in potency to not causing the effect; and thus Avicenna[17] thought that every effect is necessary with respect to its cause, which necessity, as has been seen before, is no other kind than this: everything which is, is necessary-when-it-is. And since a cause-which-works-in-most-cases, posited as not-impeded, although at that time it also be in potency to be impeded and to the effect not being produced, nevertheless that cause not impeded is not in potency such that the effect is able not to be posited, the cause not being impeded, therefore for a cause-which-works-in-most-cases to be a cause actually causing an effect, nothing is required but the removal of the impediment nor does it need something essentially educing it from potency to act, since the cause impeded is not a cause in potency except accidentally.

To the second it must be said similarly, that a future contingent effect, which will come to pass, does not have in the interrelationship of present things only a cause which is as matter, but also a cause in act, not however a cause from which necessarily that effect will be going to be; and this is clear in this way. For it is able to have in the interrelationship of present things a non-impeded cause without an intermediate, or with one or more intermediates. And, as has been seen, such a cause is not necessary to the effect, nor is it a cause only as matter, requiring something which makes it a cause actually. Thus the reasoning is defective in supposing that, if a future effect does not have in the interrelationship

---

[17] *Metaph.*, VI, 3 (ed. 1508, fol. 92rb, text A).

of present things a cause which is a cause only as matter, that therefore there already exists presently some non-impeded and necessary cause of that effect.

The third objection is answered the same way as is apparent to anyone examining it.

To the fourth objection it must be said that in order for everything to come to pass necessarily even with respect to the First Cause and the whole connection of causes and the interrelationship of present things, it would be required that nothing would be accidental being, not only with respect to the First Cause, and that not only the First Cause would be a non-impedible cause, but also that no impediment would be able to happen with respect to intermediate causes, through which the First Cause produces its effects, as has been said before.

With regard to the other objection based on providence, it must be known that *some* have stated: everything that will come to be, is necessarily going to be on account of what is touched upon in the three reasonings about divine providence mentioned above. But they are mistaken. For divine providence does not impose necessity on things; which is apparent in this way. Divine providence is nothing other than the reason or intellect directing the connection and order of causes to the things which they cause. But if the said order and connection does not impose necessity on all future things, but only on some, [namely], whose which come to be from non-impedible causes, then neither does the reason [directing] the said connection impose necessity, because if the causes which the master of the house pre-ordains to some end, do not induce that [end] necessarily, then neither does the reason or intellect or providence of the master of the house.

On account of this *others*[18] have said that through divine providence not only is it provided for some future thing that it will come to be, but also how it will come to be, as, according to the condition of the proximate cause, contingently

[18] *Cf.* St. Thomas, *Sum. theol.*, I, 22, 4 *in corp.* and *ad* 1; *In Metaph.*, VI, lect 3, Cathala n. 1220.

or necessarily; and therefore with regard to the coming-to-be of future contingents they say that it is necessary that such come to be, contingently however. But this statement can be understood in three ways. In one way so that it might mean not that future things of this kind come to be necessarily, but that in the coming-to-be of future things of this kind, contingency is necessary, such that if they come to be, it is necessary for them to come to be contingently; and this is true; but this is not what they intend, who say that it is necessary that future things of this kind come to be, contingently however, since their intention is to posit necessity and infallibility in the coming-to-be of future things of this kind, by reason of the fact that it has been foreseen that these come to be, by infallible providence. And therefore one can understand in a second way the statement which says that it is necessary that future things of this kind come to be, contingently however: namely, that future things of this kind come to be contingently in relation to some impedible cause of them, and that nevertheless it is necessary that they come to be, in relation to providence and the whole connection of causes. And this is to say that, simply they come to pass necessarily, although in relation to something they are contingent; but, as has been seen before, that all things are necessarily going to be, even in relation to the whole connection of causes, is false. In a third way one can understand that they wish to say that contingency is the case absolutely, even in relation to divine providence and the connection of causes, and not only in relation to some cause. But then opposites are implied in the said statement, opposites which cannot be the case simultaneously. For these cannot be the case simultaneously, that it is necessary that *a* come to be, and yet it come to be contingently. But they do not affirm such except as, on account of the infallibility of divine providence, they posit infallibility and necessity in the coming-to-be of all future things. But, as has been said before, if the connection, order, and interrelationship of present things does not impose necessity on all future things, then neither does the knowledge of that order and the directing of the interrelationship.

But it must be diligently noted that if it were foreknown with regard to any future thing which we call contingent, that it will come to be, and it was foreknown by that knowledge which was of that thing in itself and not in another, and through that thing's proper concept, and by an infallible knowledge, whether the knowledge was divine or some other kind, then that future thing would necessarily be going to be. Thus, because *some* liken the divine knowledge by which He knows of any future thing that it will come to be, to their own knowledge, also positing that divine knowledge to be infallible, it is necessary for them to say that all things are necessarily going to be, as *Averroës* also says in the Sixth Book of the *Metaphysics,*[19] that according to that which is said in the *Legal Examples,* because all things are written in the tablet and because that which is written ought necessarily to pass into act, all things are necessarily going to be. For the *Legal Examples* accept that in the divine intellect is a knowledge about all things which will come to be, that they will be, and a knowledge by which these are known in themselves and not in another, and through their proper concept. For thus does the *Legal Examples* take it that all things are written in the tablet: Averroës intending through "written in the tablet" that which *some* call divine foreknowledge, providence, or predestination which is part of providence, or the book of life.

But it must be noticed that neither present things nor future things or the coming-to-be of future things are known through the divine intellect by a knowledge which is of them in themselves, but by that kind of knowledge by which something is known in another. For the aforesaid enjoy no knowledge in God except a knowledge which is of God's own self and is his substance. However it is not necessary that such an infallible and always true knowledge of future things impose necessity on future things, so that it must be said of any future contingent thing that it has not been foreseen and foreknown by God that this will be, because nothing is fore-

---

[19] VI, text 7, ed. 1542, fol. 146r.

seen and foreknown by God unless it is true. Now however, as Aristotle maintains in the *Perihermeneias,*[20] although it is true that a naval battle will be or will not be, nevertheless divisively to assert either truly does not happen. For if it were true that a naval battle will be, then it would be necessary that a naval battle will be, as is treated *in the same book.* Or if it sounds serious to the ears of some, that this is not foreknown by God, then it must be said, as has been said before, that, although the fact that *a* will be, does not enjoy knowledge in God, except such a knowledge which is of the divine substance itself and is the divine substance itself, even such a knowledge of the very fact that *a* will be, which is of *a* but in some other immutable thing, although that *a* will come to be is mutable, does not impose necessity on that *a* relative to coming to be.

From which one must answer to the first objection by conceding the major: that "a future effect which has a present cause from which it necessarily follows, will of necessity come to be"; and by denying the minor which takes it that "all things which will come to be have a present cause from which they follow necessarily"; and when it is proved: "because it has been foreseen that these will come to be," it can be denied, as has been said; and that it is not foreseen that *a* will come to be, since this is not true: or one must say that, although it has been foreseen that *a* will come to be, and by an infallible providence, nevertheless that *a* will come to be is fallible, by reason of the fact that that providence and knowledge of *a* itself is not infallible about *a* in itself, but in something else which is immutable. For in the divine intellect mutable things have immutable science and fallible future things also have an infallible foreknowledge and providence.

To the second objection about providence one must speak similarly, either by denying the antecedent, namely that it has been foreseen that *a* will come to be, for the aforesaid reason; or by destroying the consequent by which it is said that if it has been foreseen that *a* will come to be, therefore

20 *De Interpretatione* 9, 19 a 29.

a will come to be. For if from the interrelationship of present things and the connection of causes it does not follow that *a* will come to pass—for then it would be necessarily going to be from these—then neither from the existence of the First Cause [does it follow], since the First Cause does not cause that except through intermediate causes; and, if from the aforesaid it does not follow that *a* will come to pass, then neither [does it follow] from the providence which God has, since the providence which God has, is God; and also for this reason, since from ordered causes it is not necessary for any effect to follow, then neither [is it necessary] from the reason directing that order. Moreover, this consequence lies hidden: that *a* be going to be, if it has been foreseen that *a* will come to be: this happens because providence in relation to that coming-to-be is understood by a similitude to our knowledge and our providence regarding any future thing, that it will come to be.

To the third objection about providence one must say that just as there can be in God an immutable science of any mutable thing, by reason of the fact that science is not understood as the kind which is of that thing in itself, but in something immutable, so also there can be an infallible providence about a fallible future thing. It must be noted, however, that, although it is fallible that *a* be going to be, nevertheless the coming-to-pass of that *a* cannot occur outside the order of the First Cause, but neither is *a's* being able not to be going to be not outside its order.

And what has been said about divine providence would similarly be said if one argued from divine foreknowledge of future things or predestination.

And with this are terminated six problems and one question, and it has been determined by master Siger of Brabant.

Suggestions for Further Reading

Van Steenberghen, F. *The Philosophical Movement in the Thirteenth Century*. T. Nelson and Sons, 1955; Gilson, E. *History of Christian Philosophy in the Middle Ages,* New York, 1954; *FCC* vol. II, 435-442; *EG* 389-399; *AAM* 194-199.

John Duns Scotus

John Duns Scotus was born around 1265 at Maxton, in Roxborough County, Scotland. Scotus entered the Franciscan Order around 1280, and was ordained a priest in 1291. Although the dates of his academic career are by no means certain, we know that he studied at Oxford sometime before his ordination, and at the University of Paris from roughly 1293 to 1296. After completing his studies at Paris, Scotus returned to England and taught at Oxford until 1301. In 1302 he returned to Paris in order to pursue higher studies in theology. At Paris, however, he became involved in the dispute then raging between the Pope and Philip the Fair of France, and having supported the papal party, Scotus was obliged to leave France. Where he spent his period of banishment is not known. We hear next of Scotus during the year 1303-04 when he once again joined the teaching faculty at Oxford. In 1304 he returned to Paris to continue his interrupted studies, finally receiving the degree of Doctor of Theology in 1305. In 1307 Scotus was sent to Cologne to teach, and he died in that year or shortly thereafter. He was buried in the Franciscan church at Cologne.

Philosophy represents one type of discipline, while theology represents another. The object of philosophy is to develop a body of general statements whose claim to acceptance is based upon no other ground than the kind of evidence that is open to public corroboration by all men through their natural cognitive powers; the object of theology is to systematize and elaborate the beliefs constitutive of religious faith. The Scholastics recognized this distinction and the corresponding difference in the function of faith and reason. Speaking generally, it was their final aim to coordinate the two. In the selection given below—the Prologue to the *Ordinatio* of John Duns Scotus—we see Scotus attempting to effect just such a reconciliation.

JOHN DUNS SCOTUS ON FAITH AND REASON *

PART I. THE NECESSITY OF REVEALED KNOWLEDGE. DOES MAN IN HIS PRESENT STATE NEED TO BE SUPERNATURALLY INSPIRED WITH SOME KNOWLEDGE?

1. The question is raised whether man in his present state needs to be supernaturally inspired with some special knowledge he could not attain by the natural light of the intellect.

[*The Pro and Con*]

That he needs none, I argue as follows:[1]

[Arg. 1] Every faculty which has something common as its primary object, is as competent by nature in regard to everything contained under this object as it is with regard to what is of itself the natural object. This is proved by the case of the primary object of vision and the other things contained under it. And thus we may proceed inductively with the other faculties and their primary objects. Reason also proves the same, for the primary object is that which is equal to the faculty in question. But if this notion, namely, of the primary object, were verified of something that is beyond the

---

* Translation by A. Wolter, O.F.M. Reprinted from *Franciscan Studies*, Vol. XI, No. 3-4, 1951. By permission.

[1] For the refutation of these arguments see par. 90-94.

natural competency of the faculty, the object would not be equal to, but would exceed the faculty. The major then is evident. The natural primary object of our intellect is being *qua* being. Therefore, our intellect is able to know naturally any being whatsoever and consequently also any intelligible nonentity, for "affirmation explains denial." [2] Therefore, etc. Proof of the minor: Avicenna in the first book of the *Metaphysics*[3] says: " 'Being' and 'thing' are impressed first upon the soul. Neither can they be revealed through other notions." But if the primary object of the intellect were anything other than these, then "being" and "thing" could be made known through this other notion. But this is impossible.

2. [Arg. 2] Furthermore, the sense needs no supernatural knowledge in its present state; therefore, neither does the intellect. The antecedent is evident. Proof of the consequence: "Nature leaves out nothing necessary" (*On the Soul,* III).[4] Now, if this is true of things that are imperfect, all the more does it hold for things that are perfect. Consequently, if the inferior faculties lack nothing necessary for their function and the attainment of their end, all the more is this true of the higher faculty. Therefore, etc.

3. [Arg. 3] Furthermore, if some such knowledge were necessary, it would be so only because the faculty with its purely natural endowments is disproportionate to an object knowable only under such conditions. Therefore, an additional factor is required that the faculty may be made equal to the object. Now this other factor is either natural or supernatural. If natural, then the two combined are still disproportionate to the primary object. If this factor is supernatural, then the faculty is disproportionate to it; and so on *ad infinitum.* But since we cannot proceed to infinity according to *Metaphysics* II,[5] it is necessary to stop with the first [*viz.* something natural], and admit that the intellective faculty is

---

2 Aristotle, *Posterior Analytics*, I, ch. 25 (86b 34-35).
3 *Metaphysica*, I, c. 6 (*Opera*, Venetiis, 1508), 72rb.
4 Aristotle, *On the Soul*, III, ch. 9 (432b 21-22).
5 Aristotle, *Meta.*, II, ch. 2 (994a 1-994b 31).

proportionate to everything that can be known and in any way in which it can be known. Therefore, etc.

4. *To the Contrary:*

"All doctrine divinely inspired is useful for arguing . . . etc." (*Tim.* 3).[6]

Furthermore, it is said of wisdom: "No one can know its way, but He who knows all things knows it" (*Bar.* 3).[7] Therefore, no other can have wisdom save from Him who knows all things. So much for the necessity of revelation. As to the fact thereof, he adds: "He [God] gave it to Jacob, His child, and to Israel, His beloved."—referring to the Old Testament—and the following: "After these things, He was seen on earth and talked with men."—referring to the New Testament.

[*I. Controversy between the Philosophers and Theologians*]

5. In this question we are faced with the controversy between the philosophers and theologians. The philosophers insist on the perfection of nature and deny supernatural perfection. The theologians, on the other hand, recognize the deficiency of nature and the need of grace and supernatural perfection.

[*A. Opinion of the Philosophers*]

The philosophers, then, would say that no supernatural knowledge is necessary for man in his present state, but that all the knowledge he needs could be acquired by the action of natural causes. In support of this, they cite from various places both the authority and the reasoning of the Philosopher.

6. [First argument] [8] The first is that passage in the third book *On the Soul*,[9] where he [Aristotle] says that "the agent

---

6 *II Timothy*, 3, 16.

7 *Baruch*, 3, 31.

8 Cf. par. 72.

9 *On the Soul*, III, ch. 5 (430a 14-15).

intellect is that by which [the intellect] makes all things; the possible intellect is that by which it becomes all things." From this I argue as follows. Once a natural agent and patient are put together and not impeded, action necessarily follows, for an action depends essentially only upon these factors as prior causes. But in regard to every intelligible object, the agent intellect is active and the possible intellect receptive. They are naturally in the soul and are not impeded. This is evident. By their natural power, then, an act of knowledge regarding any intelligible object whatsoever is possible.

7. [Second argument] [10] This is confirmed by reason. Every natural passive faculty has some corresponding natural agent. Otherwise the passive faculty would seem to have no purpose in nature, since nothing in the realm of nature could reduce it to act. But the possible intellect is a passive faculty with regard to any intelligible object whatsoever. Some natural active power, consequently, corresponds to it. The thesis therefore follows. The minor is evident, since the possible intellect naturally seeks to know whatever can be known. Also it is naturally perfected by such knowledge. By nature then it is capable of receiving any knowledge whatsoever.

8. [Third argument] [11] Furthermore, speculative science is divided into mathematics, physics and metaphysics according to the *Metaphysics,* VI.[12] And from the proof for this, which is given there,[13] no other speculative science seems possible, since in these sciences the whole of being is considered, both in itself and in all its divisions. Now just as a speculative science other than these three would not be possible, neither is any practical science possible other than those acquired sciences that have to do with functional and productive activity. Consequently, practical acquired sciences suffice to perfect the practical intellect and speculative acquired sciences, the speculative intellect.

---

[10] Cf. par. 73-78.
[11] Cf. par. 79-82.
[12] *Meta.*, VI, ch. 1 (1026a 18-19).
[13] *Ibid.* (1025b 3-1026a 19).

9. [Fourth argument] [14] Furthermore, anyone capable by nature of knowing a principle can know naturally the conclusions included in that principle. This I prove from the fact that the knowledge of the conclusions depends solely upon an understanding of the principle and the deduction of the conclusion from the principle, as is evident from the definition of "to know" in the *Posterior Analytics,* I.[15] Now, the deduction is manifest of itself, as is clear from the definition of the perfect syllogism in the *Prior Analytics.*[16] "Such a syllogism needs nothing either for being, or for appearing, evidently necessary." Consequently if the principles be known, everything needed for a knowledge of the conclusion is there. And so the major is clear.

10. Now we know naturally the first principles in which all conclusions are virtually contained. Hence, we can also know naturally all the conclusions that can be known.

Proof of the first part of the minor. Since the terms of the first principles are most common, it follows that they can be known naturally, for according to the first book of the *Physics,*[17] we know first what is most common. But according to *Posterior Analytics,* I:[18] "we know and understand principles in so far as we know their terms." We can know first principles then naturally.

11. Proof of the second part of the minor. Since the terms of the first principles are most common, when they are distributed, they are distributed in regard to all the concepts that fall under them. Now in first principles, such terms are taken universally and therefore they extend to all particular concepts. Consequently, they include the terms of all particular conclusions.

---

14 Cf. par. 83-89.
15 *Post. Anal.*, I, ch. 2 (71b 9-12).
16 *Prior Anal.*, ch. 1 (24b 22-24).
17 *Phys.*, I, ch. 3 (184a 21).
18 *Post. Anal.*, I, ch. 3 (72a 23-25).

[*B. Refutation of the Opinion of the Philosophers*]

12. Three arguments can be raised against this opinion.[19] (Note:[20] By natural reason nothing supernatural can be shown to exist in the wayfarer, nor can it be proved that anything supernatural is necessarily required for his perfection. Neither can one who has something supernatural know it is in him. Here then it is impossible to use natural reason against Aristotle. If one argues from beliefs, it is no argument against a philosopher since the latter does not concede a premise taken on faith. Hence, these reasons which are here urged against him have as one premise something believed or proved from something believed. Therefore, they are nothing more than theological persuasions from beliefs to a belief.)

13. [First principal argument] The first way is this. Every agent who acts knowingly needs a distinct knowledge of his destiny or end. I prove this, because every agent acting for the sake of an end, acts from a desire of the end. Now everything that is an agent in virtue of itself [21] acts for the sake of an end. Therefore, every such agent seeks its end in a way proper to itself. Just as an agent that acts by its nature must desire the end for which it must act, so also the agent that acts knowingly. For the latter is also an agent in virtue of itself, according to the second book of the *Physics*.[22] The major then is clear.

But man can have no definite knowledge of his end from what is natural; therefore, he needs some supernatural knowledge thereof.

14. The minor is evident, first, because the Philosopher, following natural reason, maintained that perfect happiness

---

[19] Five arguments are actually adduced, but Scotus accepts only the first three as valid.

[20] Marginal note added by Scotus.

[21] A *per se* cause in contradistinction to an incidental (*per accidens*) cause acts either by deliberate intention (if rational) or automatically (if irrational) in virtue of a nature destined to produce just this effect.

[22] *Phys.*, II, ch. 5 (196b 17-22).

consists in the acquired knowledge of the pure Spirits,[23] as he apparently wishes to say in the *Ethics,* book I [24] and book X.[25] Or if he does not categorically assert that this is our highest possible perfection, at least natural reason can argue to no other, so that on this basis alone, we will either err or be in doubt about our specific end. Hence, it is with some doubt in mind that he says in the first book of the *Ethics,*[26] "If there be any gift of the gods, it is reasonable that it be happiness."

15. Secondly, the same minor is proved by reason. For we know the proper end only of such substances whose manifest actions show us that such an end is in accord with such a nature. Now of all the actions that we experience or know to exist in our nature at present, there are none that reveal that the vision of the pure Spirits is in accord with our nature. Naturally then we are unable to know definitely that this end is befitting our nature.

16. So much at least is sure, we cannot know definitely by natural reason certain conditions that make the end more desirable and cause us to seek it more fervently. For even granting that reason could prove that the face-to-face vision and enjoyment of God are the end of man, it still could not be inferred that these will be his forever or that they pertain to him as a whole, namely in body and soul, as will be pointed out in book IV, distinction 43.[27] And yet the fact that such a good will never cease is something that renders the end more attractive than if it were something transient. Also, it is more desirable to possess this good with a complete [human] nature than with the soul apart from the body, as is clear from Augustine, *On Genesis,* XIII.[28] It is necessary to know these and similar conditions associated with our end, if we are to seek it efficaciously. Still natural reason is insufficient in this

---

[23] Literally "Separated Substances," that is, those spiritual substances that, unlike the human soul, are not united with a body. They are God and the Intelligences (angels) responsible for the movement of the stars and planets.

[24] *Nicomachean Ethics*, I, ch. 6 (1097b 22-1098a 20).

[25] *Ibid.*, X, ch. 7 (1177a 12-1177b 1).

[26] *Ibid.*, I, ch. 9 (1099b 11-13).

[27] *Ordinatio*, IV, dist. 43, q. 2.

[28] *On Genesis*, XII, ch. 35 (PL 34, 483-484).

regard. Therefore, supernaturally given knowledge is required.

17. [Second principal reason] The second argument runs in this fashion. Everyone who knowingly acts for the sake of an end, needs to know how and in what way such an end may be attained. In addition, he must know all that is necessary for this end. Thirdly, he must know that this is all that is required. The first is clear, because if one knows not how or in what way the end is to be attained, he is also ignorant of the way in which he must dispose himself in order to attain it. The second is proved, for if one does not know all that is necessary for the end, he could fail to reach it because he did not know that a certain action was necessary for its attainment. So also with the third. If these means were not known to be sufficient, the doubt that there might be some unknown yet necessary factor, would keep one from efficaciously doing what was necessary.

18. But by natural reason one in this life is unable to know these three points. Proof that the first cannot be known. Beatitude is granted as the reward of merits which God accepts as worthy of such a reward. In consequence, beatitude does not follow with natural necessity from any kind of acts we may be able to perform, but is something that is freely given by God, who accepts as meritorious certain acts directed toward Him. Now, this is not something that can be known naturally, as is clear from the fact that the philosophers erred in this matter when they claimed everything God does immediately He does with necessity. The two other points, at least, are clear enough. For the fact that the divine will accepts just such and such things as worthy of eternal life, as well as the fact that just these things suffice, is not something that natural reason can know. This acceptance of what is only contingently related to it depends solely upon the divine will. Therefore, etc.

19. [Objections to the first two principal reasons] Objections are raised against these two reasons. To the first: Every created nature depends essentially upon anything that in vir-

tue of itself causes such a nature. By reason of this dependence, it is possible to know and to demonstrate by a simple demonstration of fact[29] any such cause of a given effect, once the latter is known. Now, since the nature of man can be known naturally by man—for it is not disproportionate to his cognitive power—it follows that once this nature is known, its destiny also could be known naturally.

20. This reason is confirmed. For if the destiny of a less perfect nature can be known from a knowledge of that nature, this is no less possible in our case, since what is destined for an end depends upon that end no less in the present case than it does in the others.

21. For this same reason, too, the proposition assumed in the proof of the minor, namely "the end of a substance is known only through the actions of that substance," would also seem to be false, since, by a demonstration of simple fact, the end of a nature could be known from a knowledge of that nature in itself.

22. And if it be maintained that reason infers only that man could know naturally his natural goal but not that which is supernatural, against this is Augustine's statement: "To be able to have faith, just as to be able to possess charity, pertains to the nature of men, although to have faith, just as to have charity, is due to the grace that is given to the faithful" (*On the Predestination of the Saints*).[30] Now, if the nature of man can be known naturally by man, then this ability in so far as it pertains to this nature, can also be known naturally. Consequently, it is also possible to know that such a nature can be ordained to an end for which charity and faith dispose it.

23. Likewise, man naturally seeks this goal which you call supernatural. Therefore, he is naturally ordained to it. This destiny, then, could be inferred from such an ordination just

---

29 For the difference between a simple demonstration of fact (*demonstratio quia*) and a demonstration which gives the reason for the fact (*demonstratio propter quid*) see Aristotle, *Posterior Analytics*, I, ch. 13.

30 *On the Predestination of the Saints*, ch. 5, n. 10 (PL 44, 986).

as it could be inferred from a knowledge of the nature ordained to such an end.

24. Also, according to Avicenna, it can be known naturally that *being* is the primary object of the intellect.[31] And it is naturally knowable that this notion of being is verified most perfectly of God. The end of any power, however, is the very best of those things which come under its primary object, for only in such is there perfect rest and delight, according to the tenth book of the *Ethics*.[32] Therefore, it can be known naturally that man according to his intellect is ordained to God as an end.

25. This reason is confirmed. For whoever can know any power naturally, is also able naturally to know what its primary object is. In addition he can know wherein the notion of this object is verified, as well as the fact that the most perfect of such things is the goal or end of this power. Now the mind knows itself, according to Augustine (*On the Trinity*).[33] Therefore, it knows what its primary object is, and it knows that God does not fall outside its scope, for otherwise God would not be intelligible to this mind in any way. Consequently, the mind knows that God is the very best of those things in which the notion of its primary object is to be found, and thus it knows that God is the goal of this faculty.

26. Against the second reason the following argument is adduced. If one extreme is known through the other, the media are also known. But those things necessary for reaching the goal are media between the nature and the end to be attained. Now, since the end could be known from a knowledge of the nature, as has been proved above,[34] it seems that the media necessary to this end can also be known in a similar way.

27. This reason is confirmed. For just as is the case with other things, so here also there seems to be a necessary con-

---

[31] Avicenna, *Meta.*, I, c. 6 (72rb).
[32] *Nic. Ethics*, X, ch. 4 (1174b 14-23).
[33] *On the Trinity*, IX, chs. 11-12 (PL 42, 970).
[34] Cf. par. 19.

nection of things with this end. But in other cases such a connection with the end serves to make other things known, for instance, such and such things are inferred to be necessary for health from the notion of health. Therefore, etc.

28. [Reply to the Objections] To the first of these,[35] I say that even though the argument is based on the notion of an end which is a final cause and not that of an end to be attained through some action—a distinction of ends that will be treated later[36]—nevertheless, to this objection as well as to what follows according to Augustine,[37] and to the third objection regarding the power and its primary object,[38] a single reply can be given. All these assume that our nature or our intellective power can be known naturally by us. Now this is false, if understood of that proper and special aspect by reason of which our nature is ordered to such an end, and in virtue of which it is capable of [receiving] the highest grace and has God as its most perfect object. For neither our soul nor our nature are known by us in our present state except under some general notion that can be abstracted from what the senses can perceive, as will be made clear later in distinction 3.[39] And to be ordained to this end, or to be able to possess grace or to have God as its most perfect object is not something that pertains to our nature under such a general notion.

29. Now to the form.[40] It is stated that from the being which is ordained to this end, the end itself can be demonstrated by a demonstration of simple fact. Now I say this is true only if the being ordained to the end is known precisely according to that proper aspect in virtue of which it has such a destiny. And so the minor is false. And when they try to prove it on the grounds that there is no disproportion, I say that although the mind is identified with itself, nevertheless

---

35 Cf. par. 19-21.
36 *Ordinatio* I, dist. 1, part 1, q. 1.
37 Cf. par. 22.
38 Cf. par. 24.
39 *Ordinatio* I, dist. 3, part 1, q. 3.
40 Cf. par. 19.

it is not proportionate to itself as object, except according to general notions which can be abstracted from what can be pictured in the imagination.

30. As to the confirmation,[41] I say that even with other substances, their proper ends (namely, those which they have in virtue of their proper natures) remain unknown unless there be some manifest actions from which an ordination to such an end might be inferred.

31. And from this, the answer to what is added against the proof of the minor is clear.[42] The proposition: "The proper end of a substance is known to us only through its manifest actions," is not false. For this proposition does not mean that the end could not be known in some other way. Indeed, it is true that if the substance were known in its proper nature, from such knowledge one could ascertain what causes this substance in virtue of itself. But no substance is known to us at present in this way and therefore, in this life, we are unable to infer the proper end of any substance except through the evident actions of this substance, which substance is known only confusedly and in general. In our case, however, the end can be proved from a knowledge of neither the nature nor its acts. Although the proof of the minor touches but one way, namely our ignorance of its acts, it presupposes the other, namely, our ignorance of the nature in itself.

32. To the second argument based on Augustine[43] I say that this ability to possess charity, in so far as it disposes one to love God in himself under His proper nature, is something that pertains to man according to a special aspect and not as common to himself and to what is perceptible by the senses. In consequence, this ability is not something about man that can be known naturally in this life, even as man himself is not known under that peculiar aspect in virtue of which he possesses this ability. And in this way I reply to the objection in so far as it can be used to support the principal claim [of the philosophers], namely that the minor of the first argu-

---

[41] Cf. par. 20.
[42] Cf. par. 21.
[43] Cf. par. 22.

ment [of the theologians] [44] is false. But in so far as it is leveled against the reply regarding the natural and supernatural end,[45] I answer: I concede that God is the natural end of man, but an end that must be attained supernaturally and not naturally. And this is what the following reason concerning natural desire proves, which proof I concede.

33. As to the other argument,[46] what it assumed must be denied, namely that it can be known naturally that being is the primary object of the intellect and this in so far as no restriction is made regarding a being that can be perceived by the sense and one that cannot. It must also be denied that Avicenna says this is something that can be known naturally, for he has mixed his religion—that of Mohammed—with philosophical matters, and some things he states as philosophical and proved by reason; others as in accord with his religion. Wherefore, he expressly assumes in the ninth book of the *Metaphysics,* chapter 7,[47] that the disembodied soul knows immaterial substances in themselves, and therefore these have to be placed under the primary object of the intellect. But it was not so according to Aristotle. For him, the primary object of our intellect is, or seems to be, the quiddity of what can be perceived by the senses. And by this he means either what is in itself perceptible by the senses or what falls under this designation. The latter is the quiddity which can be abstracted from what is perceptible to the senses.

34. However, I reply to what is cited from Augustine in confirmation of the argument.[48] His statement, I say, should be understood of the first act which of itself is fully sufficient for the second act, but its activity is hindered at present.[49] On

---

44 Cf. par. 14-15.
45 Cf. par. 22.
46 Cf. par. 24.
47 Avicenna, *Meta.*, IX, c. 7 (107ra).
48 Cf. par. 25.
49 By first act the scholastics understood a thing constituted in its nature with its various powers. In this case, the soul (and the faculties, such as the intellect, which are really identical with it) is in first act by the very fact that it exists. When these faculties or powers are in actual operation, the soul is said to be in second act. When Scotus claims that Augustine's statement that the mind knows itself

account of this hindrance, the second act in the present life is not elicited from the first. But more of this later.[50]

35. Some may object to this answer on the grounds that man in the state of original justice could have known his nature, and therefore the destiny of this nature, as the argument for the first objection claims.[51] Therefore, this knowledge is not supernatural.

36. Also, the reply to the last reason might be questioned.[52] For if we are ignorant of what the primary object of the intellect is because the intellect is not known under each proper aspect according to which it regards such an object, it follows that we cannot know that any given thing is intelligible, because the power is not known under every proper aspect according to which it could consider any given thing as an intelligible object.

37. I reply: To the first.[53] It is necessary to point out what kind of knowledge man had in his original state, a topic which may be put off until later.[54] But at least so far as man in his present state is concerned, it is called supernatural knowledge, because it exceeds man's natural power—natural, I understand, according to his fallen state.

38. As to the second,[55] I concede that at present our knowledge of the soul or of some of its faculties is not so distinct that such knowledge could be used to ascertain that

---

must be understood of the first, he simply means that the soul or mind by the very fact that it exists is intelligible in itself (and hence is only potentially "known"). As an intelligible object it is fully capable of acting as partial cause with the human intellect to produce an actual knowledge of itself (second act). In the present life, however, because of the fact that God intended man to be a composite of body and soul, man's intellectual activity is curtailed in such a way that he knows only what can be abstracted or deduced from sense knowledge. In the next life this impediment will be removed and the soul or intellect will be able to elicit a direct and intuitive knowledge of its own substance. Cf. also our article in *New Scholasticism*, XXIII (1949), esp. pp. 290-294.

50 *Ordinatio* I, dist. 3, part 1, q. 3.

51 Cf. par. 19.

52 Cf. par. 33.

53 Cf. par. 35.

54 *Ordinatio*, IV, dist. 1, part 2, q. 2.

55 Cf. par. 36.

some intelligible object corresponds to it. But from the act which we experience, we conclude that the power and the nature to which this act belongs regards as its object that which we perceive to be attained through the act in question. Hence, we do not infer the object of the faculty from a knowledge of the faculty in itself, but from the knowledge of the act we experience. But of a supernatural object we have neither kind of knowledge, and in consequence neither method of knowing the proper end of this nature is to be had.

39. The answer to the objection against the second reason is clear.[56] For the argument assumes something that has already been denied.[57] To the confirmation of this argument[58] I say that when the end follows naturally those things that lead to the end, and demands them naturally as prerequisites, then, such things could be inferred from the end. But in this case, these things do not follow naturally, but only in virtue of a [voluntary] acceptance on the part of the divine will, which reckons these merits as worthy of such an end.

40. [Third principal reason] A third main argument is raised against the opinion of the philosophers. The knowledge of pure Spirits is the most noble, because it has to do with the noblest class (*Metaphysics,* IV).[59] Hence, the knowledge of their proper attributes is noblest and most necessary. For their proper attributes are more perfectly knowable than those attributes they have in common with objects perceptible to the senses. But these proper attributes cannot be known merely from what is purely natural. For, in the first place, if these properties were found to be treated in any science possible to us at present, it would be in metaphysics. But it is not possible for us naturally to have a science of the proper attributes of these pure Spirits, as is evident. And this is what the Philosopher maintains when he says in the first book of the *Metaphysics*[60] that it is necessary for the wise man to

---

[56] Cf. par. 26.
[57] Cf. par. 28-29.
[58] Cf. par. 27.
[59] *Meta.*, IV, ch. 1 (1026a 21-23).
[60] *Ibid.*, I, ch. 2 (982a 8-10).

know all things in some way, and not in particular. And he adds: "For he who knows universals, knows in a sense all things." Here he calls the metaphysician the "wise man," just as he calls philosophy "wisdom."

41. I prove the same thing in a second way. These properties are not known by a science or knowledge that gives the reason for the facts[61] unless their proper subjects are known, for only the subjects give the reason for such proper attributes. Now the proper subjects of these attributes cannot be known naturally by us. Therefore, etc.

Neither can we know these properties from their effects by a demonstration of the simple fact.[62] Proof: the effect leaves the intellect in doubt with regard to these properties or even leads it into error. This is clear with regard to the properties of the First Spiritual Substance itself, for it is a property of this [divine] Substance that it can be shared with three [Divine Persons]. But the effects [*viz.* creatures] do not reveal this property, because they are not from this Substance in so far as it is a Trinity. And if one were to argue from the effects to the cause, one would rather conclude the very opposite and so be in error. For in no effect is one nature associated with more than one *supposit*.[63] It is also a property of this nature, in its external relations, to cause [its effects] contingently. And the effects lead one to infer the opposite view and to fall into error, as is evident from the opinion of philosophers

[61] Science or knowledge based on a demonstration of the reasoned fact. Cf. note 29.

[62] In this case, the demonstration of simple fact (*demonstratio quia*) is an *a posteriori* demonstration from effect to cause.

[63] *Supposit* (Latin, *suppositum*) and *person* as used by the scholastics have a technical meaning. The attempt to clarify the mystery of the Bl. Trinity and the Incarnation led to the distinction between the nature and the person possessing the nature. In Christ we have two natures (human and divine) but only one person (Second Person of the Bl. Trinity). In the Trinity, there are three persons (Father, Son, and Holy Spirit) but only one divine nature or essence. Since only a rational being can be a person, the more general term of *supposit* is used to cover that which is said to possess a given nature or natures. Where the supposit is rational, it is called person. Practically, every nature is a supposit (or person) if it is complete in itself and is not assumed by a higher supposit or person.

who held that the First Cause causes necessarily whatever it produces. As to the properties of the other pure Spirits [*viz.* the angels or Intelligences], clearly the same holds. For effects rather lead one to conclude that they are necessary and everlasting beings, according to the philosophers, instead of contingent beings, which have come into existence after being non-existent. Again, these philosophers also seem to conclude on the basis of movement that the number of these pure Spirits corresponds with the number of movements of the heavenly bodies. Again, [they held that] these pure Spirits were naturally beatified and incapable of sin—all of which is absurd.

42. [Objection to the third principal reason] Against this reason I argue that whatever necessary knowledge regarding these pure Spirits we may have at present by faith or what is commonly revealed [64] could also be had by a knowledge that is natural. And I prove it in this way. We can comprehend naturally any necessary truths whose terms we can know naturally. Now we know naturally the terms of all necessary revealed truths. Therefore, etc.

43. Proof of the major. These necessary truths are either mediately or immediately [evident]. If immediately, then, they are known once the terms are known, according to the first book of the *Posterior Analytics*.[65] If they are mediate truths, then we can conceive the middle term between them, since we can know the extremes. By joining this middle term with the two extremes, we have either mediate or immediate premises. If immediate, we argue as before. If mediate, the process of conceiving the middle term between the extremes and joining it with the latter continues until we come to truths that are immediately evident. In the last analysis, then, we shall arrive at necessary and immediate propositions,

---

64 The "common law" or "common revelation" is that destined for mankind in general. It is contrasted with special revelation given to certain individuals for some specific purpose in the Providence of God. Nowadays the distinction of "public" and "private" revelation is used.

65 *Post. Anal.*, I, ch. 3 (72b 23-25).

which are known from their terms and from which all other necessary truths follow. Hence, these mediate truths could be known naturally by us through those which are immediate.

44. Proof of the minor. If one who has faith contradicts one who has no faith, the two do not contradict each other in word only but according to the conceptual meaning, as is evident when the philosopher and theologian contradict each other regarding the proposition: "God is triune." Here, one denies and the other affirms not only the same name but also the same concept. Consequently, every simple concept that the theologian has, the philosopher also has.

45. [Reply to the objection] To this, I reply. There are certain truths about the pure Spirits that are immediate. Now I take one such primary and immediate truth, let us call it "a." In it are included many mediate truths, for instance, all those which affirm in particular what is common to the predicate of those things which are common to the subject, let us call them "b" and "c." These mediate truths are evident only through some immediate truth. Therefore, the former cannot be known unless the immediate truth is understood. If therefore some intellect could grasp the terms of "b" and combine them with one another in a proposition, but could not understand the terms of "a" nor, in consequence, the proposition "a" itself, then so far as this intellect is concerned, "b" would be a neutral proposition.[66] It is known neither through itself, nor through the immediate proposition [*viz.* "a"], since in our assumption the latter remains unknown. And so it is with us. For we have certain concepts common to material and immaterial substances, and these we can put together into propositions. But these latter are not evident except through those immediate truths which concern the proper and special character of these quiddities.[67] Now we do not conceive these quiddities under this aspect and therefore, neither

---

[66] Neutral proposition is not taken in the modern sense of a three-valued logic, but refers to a proposition which objectively is either true or false but whose truth value is unknown to the intellect, which withholds its assent.

[67] Namely, the pure Spirits or immaterial substances.

do we know those general truths which involve the universal concepts.

46. For example: if someone were able to conceive a triangle not according to its proper notion as a triangle but only under the notion of "figure" abstracted from a quadrangle, it would be impossible for him to grasp that property by which a triangle is the first [of plane geometrical figures], because this property could be conceived only if it were abstracted from a triangle itself. He could, however, abstract the notion of "first" from other things that are first, e.g. of numbers. Although his intellect could form the proposition: "Some figure is first," because it could grasp the terms involved, still such a proposition would be neutral to him, because it is a mediate proposition included in this immediate proposition: "A triangle is first in this way." But he would be unable to know this immediate proposition because he cannot grasp its terms. Therefore, he is not able to understand the mediate proposition, which can be known from the immediate proposition alone.

47. Applying this to the argument,[68] I deny the major. To the proof, I say that these necessary truths are mediately evident propositions. And when you say, "Therefore, we can conceive a medium between these extremes," I deny the consequence, because the medium between the extremes is at times essentially ordered, for example, when it is the essence of the extreme or is a prior attribute with regard to one that is posterior. Now a middle term through which one extreme can universally be inferred from the other is of this kind. I concede, therefore, that whoever can grasp the extremes can grasp such a middle term between them, because its concept is included in, or is the same as, that of the other extreme. But if the middle term is particular, and is contained under the other extremes and is not essentially related to these extremes, then it is not necessary that one who can conceive universal extremes, could conceive a means which is particular in regard to these extremes. So it is here. For the quid-

[68] Cf. par. 42.

dity under its proper and particular aspect has some immediate attribute inhering in it, and is a middle term that is less universal than the common concept of which this attribute, conceived in general, is predicated. Therefore, it is not a medium for universally inferring the attribute of the common concept, but only in a particular case. This is evident in the above example,[69] because it is not necessary that one who can conceive a figure in general and the general notion of being first, can conceive a triangle in particular, for a triangle is a medium contained under figure—a medium, I say, for concluding that a particular figure is first.

48. ([Note] This third argument[70] holds above all of the first immaterial substance [*viz.* God], for it is especially necessary to know God as a beatific object. Now the reply to the objection brought against it supposes that we conceive God naturally in the present life only in a concept that is common to Him and to what can be perceived by the senses, which is explained later in the first question of the third distinction. But even if this assumption were denied, it would still be necessary to maintain that any concept of God we could derive from creatures is imperfect, whereas that which could be had in virtue of His essence in itself would be perfect. Hence, what was said regarding the universal and particular notions,[71] would also be valid for the perfect and imperfect notions in this other view.)[72]

49. [Fourth principal reason] A fourth argument is this. Whatever is ordered to some end toward which it is not disposed, must be gradually disposed for this end. Man is ordered to a supernatural end toward which he is of himself indisposed. Therefore he needs to be gradually disposed to possess this end. This takes place by reason of some imperfect supernatural knowledge, which is maintained to be necessary. Therefore, etc.

50. But if it be objected that a perfect agent can remove

---

69 Cf. par. 46.
70 Cf. par. 40.
71 Cf. par. 47.
72 Namely, that of Henry of Ghent, *Summa* a. 13, q. 3, ad 2.

any imperfection immediately and can act immediately, I reply that even if it could do so by its absolute power, still it is more perfect to make the creature active in attaining its perfection than to deprive it of any such activity. But man could have some activity in the attainment of his final perfection. Hence, it is more perfect that such be given him. But this could not be done without imparting some imperfect knowledge which precedes that perfect knowledge which he is ultimately destined to possess.

51. [Fifth principal argument] A fifth argument is this. Any agent that makes use of an instrument in acting, cannot in virtue of this instrument perform any action which exceeds [in perfection] the nature of the instrument. The light of the agent intellect, however, is an instrument which the soul at present uses to understand things naturally. In consequence, the soul, using this light, is not capable of any action that would exceed this light. Therefore, the soul is incapable of any knowledge that it does not attain in this way. But this light of itself is limited to knowledge by way of the senses. Now the knowledge of many other things, however, is necessary for us at present. Therefore, etc.

52. This reason seems to militate against the position of the one who advanced it.[73] For according to this line of reasoning, the Uncreated Light would be unable to make use of the agent intellect as an instrument in producing a knowledge of pure truth. For such truth, according to him, cannot be ours through the senses without some special illumination. And so it follows that in knowing pure truth the light of the agent intellect plays no part at all, which seems hardly possible inasmuch as this illumination [by the agent intellect] is the most perfect of all intellectual activity. Consequently, the most perfect intellectual power in the soul should in some way concur with this action.

53. [Evaluation of the fourth and fifth reasons] These last two reasons[74] do not seem to be very efficacious. For the first would hold, if it were proved that man was destined for

[73] Namely, Henry of Ghent, *Summa* a. 8, q. 2.
[74] Cf. par. 49-51.

supernatural beatitude (the proof of which pertains to the questions of beatitude),[75] and if, in addition, it were shown that natural knowledge does not dispose one sufficiently in our present state for the attainment of supernatural knowledge. The second reason begs two points, namely, that a knowledge of certain things unknowable by way of the senses, is necessary, and that the light of the agent intellect is limited to things that can be known by way of the senses.

54. The first three reasons appear to be more probable.

[C. *Objection to the opinion of the Theologians*]

That no such knowledge, however, is necessary for salvation, I prove:[76] Let us assume that someone is not baptized. When he grows up, he has no one to teach him. The affections [of his will], such as he is capable of, are good and in accord with what his natural reason tells him is right. What reason reveals to him as evil, he avoids.

Although God could visit such a one, teaching him the common law[77] by man or angel even as He visited Cornelius,[78] still let us assume that such an individual is taught by no one. Nevertheless, he will be saved. And even if he should be instructed later, before such instruction he is just and consequently, worthy of eternal life. For, by willing what is good, even before he is instructed, he merits grace which renders him just. And still he has no theology, not even in regard to the primary truths of faith. His is purely natural knowledge. Consequently, nothing that pertains to theology is, absolutely speaking, necessary for salvation.

55. [Reply] It could be said that such an individual, by willing what is good in general, merits *de congruo*[79] to be jus-

---

[75] *Ordinatio*, IV, suppl. d. 49, q. 7.

[76] Note by Scotus. Par. 54-55.

[77] See note 64.

[78] *Acts of the Apostles*, 10, 1-48.

[79] Theologians distinguish between that which merits a reward *de condigo*, *viz.* in strict justice, and that which merits it *de congruo*, that is, it is fitting that it be rewarded even though there is no strict obligation in justice.

tified from original sin, and God does not deprive such a one of this gift of His liberality. Hence, He gives him the first grace without using the sacrament,[80] because God is not constrained to make use of the sacraments. But grace is not [ordinarily] given without the habit of faith. Hence, such an individual actually possesses the habit of theology, even though this habit could not be reduced to act. Neither could such an individual be baptized unless first instructed. And even though it would not be a contradiction [for God] to give grace without faith, for these are distinct habits and reside in different faculties, nevertheless, just as in baptism these two are infused simultaneously, so, for the same reason, they could be given together in this case. For God is no less gracious toward one whom He justifies without the sacraments, because of merit *de congruo,* than He is toward one whom He justifies through the reception of the sacrament without any merit on this individual's part. And thus it is possible for God by his absolute power to save anyone, and to enable him to merit glory without infused faith—if God were to give grace without faith—for once such an individual possessed grace, he could use it properly to will what he knew by natural reason and acquired faith (or by natural reason alone without acquired faith, if no one were to teach him).[81] Nevertheless, according to God's usual way of acting, He does not give grace without first giving the habit of faith, for grace is not assumed to be infused unless faith is also infused. But this

---

80 Namely, of baptism.

81 Acquired faith is contrasted with the infused virtue of faith. The former is possible on purely natural grounds, as for instance, when we give credence to some historical event on the basis of reliable authority. It is possible, says Scotus (*Ordinatio*, III, suppl. d. 23, q. un. Cf. Vives edition, v. 15, 5-30) for one to assent to truths that have been divinely revealed even without the special theological virtue given directly by God (infused virtue) as is clear from the case of a heretic who has lost the latter by doubting one article of faith and yet retains his belief in the others by acquired faith. As the infused virtue does not actually impart knowledge as such (as is clear from the case of an infant which receives the three theological virtues of faith, hope and charity at baptism), instruction in the actual content of revelation is required and this involves acquired faith.

is not because of any necessity, as if grace without faith would not be sufficient, but because of the divine liberality which reforms the whole [soul, *viz.* intellect and will]. Then, too, many would be less perfectly inclined to assent to certain truths without infused faith.

56. Now, I say, there is a similar relation in the case of the habit of theology, which, when perfect, includes both an infused and an acquired faith of the articles [of the Creed] and of other things revealed by God in Scripture, so that there is not just infused faith, or just acquired faith, but both together. Hence, if we are speaking of the more fundamental or prior habit which theology includes, *viz.* infused faith, it is true, according to the usual way in which God acts,[82] that theology is necessary for all, as a general rule. But it is not true that theology is necessary for all, if we understand by theology the second habit which it includes, *viz.* acquired faith. But if we speak of the necessity based on God's usual way of acting, perhaps it [*viz.* theology in so far as it includes acquired faith] is necessary for an adult who could have and is able to understand a teacher, that he have an acquired faith with regard to certain general truths.

[*II. Solution to the Question*]

57. To the question, then, I reply first by distinguishing in what sense something may be called supernatural. For a capacity to receive may be compared to the act which it receives or to the agent from which it receives [this act]. Viewed in the first way, this potentiality is either natural or violent or neither natural nor violent. It is called natural, if it is naturally inclined toward the form it receives. It is violent, if what it suffers is against its natural inclination. It is neither the one nor the other, if it is inclined neither to the form which it receives nor to its opposite. Now from this

---

[82] That is, *de potentia ordinata*. Theologians distinguish between *de potentia Dei absoluta*, *viz.* what God can do absolutely speaking, and *de potentia Dei ordinata*, what God can do relative to His own decisions or eternal decrees.

viewpoint, there is no supernaturality. But when the recipient is compared to the agent from which it receives the form, then there is naturalness if the recipient is referred to an agent which is naturally ordained to impress such a form in such a recipient. Supernaturalness is had, however, when the recipient is referred to an agent which does not impress this form upon this recipient naturally.

58. Before[83] this distinction is applied to the case at hand, several arguments are brought to bear against it, first on the grounds that the distinction of "natural" and "violent" is based upon the recipient's relation to the agent and not merely to the form, and secondly on the count that the distinction of "natural" and "supernatural" is based upon the recipient's relation to the patient and not to the agent exclusively. I will not cite the arguments for these points here.

59. Nevertheless, the solution seems reasonable, because a cause which causes anything in virtue of itself is that cause whose presence is followed by the effect even when all other factors are excluded or varied. Now even though a form contrary to the inclination is induced only by means of some agent which does violence to the recipient, and even though a supernatural agent acts supernaturally only by inducing some form, still the precise character of "violent" arises by virtue of the relation of the recipient to the form, whereas that of "supernatural" arises precisely in virtue of the relation of the recipient to the agent. This is proved from the fact that as long as the recipient and form remain what they are (*viz.* that the form can be received, but only contrary to the inclination of the recipient), then no matter how the agent is varied, violence is still done to the recipient. Similarly, when the agent and recipient are so related to each other that the recipient is altered only by an agent that does not act naturally (I say "only" to exclude any preparation by a natural agent), whatever be the form such an agent induces, it will be supernatural with regard to the recipient.

A second proof that such is the case is based not only on

---

[83] Note by Scotus. Par. 58-59.

the induction [of the form] but on its permanency. A form which does violence to the recipient may remain in it without any external action, but not for a long time. Another remains naturally and for some time. [Hence, the external agent need not be taken into consideration.] Again, one form that endures is natural; another supernatural, but only by reason of the agent, so that if the latter were not taken into consideration, the form could not be called supernatural. But it might be called natural, because it perfects naturally, if the relation of the form to the recipient alone is considered.

60. Applying this to the question at issue, I say that if the possible intellect be compared to the knowledge that is actualized in it, no knowledge is supernatural to it, because the possible intellect is perfected by any knowledge whatsoever and is naturally inclined toward any kind of knowledge. But according to the second way of speaking, that knowledge is supernatural which is generated by some agent which by its very nature is not ordained to move the possible intellect in a natural manner.

61. In our present state, however, the possible intellect, according to the Philosopher, is ordained to be moved to knowledge by the agent intellect and the phantasm. Therefore, that knowledge alone is natural to it which is impressed by these agencies.

In virtue of these, however, all conceptual knowledge which one has in this life according to the common law, can be obtained, as is evident from the objections raised against the third principal reason.[84] Consequently, even though God by way of revelation could cause some special knowledge, as for instance, when one is rapt in ecstasy, still such supernatural knowledge is not necessary according to the common law.[85]

62. It is different, however, with the truth of propositions, because as has been shown by the three reasons adduced against the first opinion,[86] even when the agent intellect and

---

[84] Cf. par. 84.
[85] See note 64.
[86] Cf. par. 13ff.

sense image are fully active, many propositions we need to know remain unknown or neutral. The knowledge of such propositions must be given to us in a supernatural manner, because no one could naturally discover them and teach them to others, for on natural grounds alone, if they are neutral to one, they are to all. The question of whether it would be possible, once such knowledge was originally imparted, for another to assent to these propositions on purely natural grounds will be discussed in book III, distinction 23. The original transmission of such knowledge, however, is called revelation. It is supernatural, therefore, since it is due to an agent that does not naturally move our intellect in its present state.

63. Another way in which an action or knowledge could be called supernatural would be because it is from an agent which takes the place of a supernatural object. For that object which is able to cause such propositions as "God is triune" and the like, is the divine essence known in its proper nature. Knowable in this way, it is a supernatural object. Whatever agent, then, causes some knowledge of truths which such an object would be able to make evident when known in its own nature, such an agent [I say] takes the place of this object. And if this agent would cause as perfect a knowledge of those truths as the object would cause if known in itself, then such an agent would substitute perfectly for the object. But no matter how imperfect the knowledge caused by such an agent would be, it is still virtually contained in that perfect knowledge which the object would cause if known in itself.

64. And so it is in this case. For one who reveals that "God is triune" causes in the mind some knowledge of this truth, obscure though it be, a knowledge which concerns an object unknown in its proper nature. If this object were known properly, it would be able to produce a clear and perfect knowledge of this truth. In so far as this knowledge is obscure and is included eminently in the clear knowledge, as the imperfect is included eminently in the perfect, to that extent, then, the agent which reveals or causes the obscure

truth, takes the place of the object that could cause a clear knowledge of the same. This is true especially when the agent could cause a knowledge of a certain truth only by taking the place of a certain object, and when it would be unable to make known a truth about this object by taking the place of some less perfect object that could naturally move our intellect. For no such inferior object virtually includes any knowledge of these truths, be it clear or obscure knowledge. Hence, it is necessary that the agent somehow take the place of a supernatural object, even when causing this obscure knowledge.

65. The difference between these two ways in which revealed knowledge is called supernatural is apparent if we consider each separately. Thus, if a supernatural agent would cause a knowledge of some natural object, for example, if it infused the knowledge of geometry in someone, this would be supernatural in the first way but not in the second. What is supernatural in the second way, however, is supernatural in both ways, for the second way implies the first, but not vice versa. However, where there is only the first type of supernatural [e.g. infused geometry], it is not impossible that what is supernatural could have been produced naturally [under other conditions]. Where something is supernatural in the second way, however, it is necessary that it be produced supernaturally, since it could not possibly be produced naturally.

[*III. Concerning the three principal reasons against the philosophers*]

66. The three reasons upon which this solution is based are confirmed by arguments from authority. The first[87] is confirmed by the statement of Augustine in the *City of God*, XVIII, Chapter 41:[88] "The philosophers, not knowing to what end these things were to be referred, were able to see some truth among the false things they asserted."

---

[87] Cf. par. 13-16.
[88] *City of God*, XVIII, ch. 41 (PL 41, 602).

67. The second argument[89] is confirmed by Augustine in the *City of God,* XI, Chapter 2:[90] "What good is it to know where one must go if one does not know how to get there?" In this the philosophers erred, for even though they handed on some truths regarding virtues, still their teaching was tainted with error, as he points out in the text quoted above.[91] This is clear from their books. For Aristotle criticizes the polities devised by many another (*Politics* II),[92] and yet his own polity is not without reproach, since he teaches that the gods are to be honored. "It is fitting," he says (*Politics* VII, ch. 7),[93] "that honor be shown to the gods," and in the same book, Chapter 5:[94] "There ought to be a law . . . that no deformed child shall be nursed."

68. The third argument[95] is confirmed by Augustine in the *City of God,* XI, Chapter 3:[96] "We need the testimony of others concerning objects that lie beyond the reach of our own senses, since we cannot know them by our own testimony." And this confirms our main solution throughout,[97] for those propositions which the argument declares to be neutral so far as we are concerned,[98] cannot be believed by anyone on the basis of his own testimony, but he must needs have the testimony of someone who is above the whole of mankind.

69. It is doubtful just how this first revelation or imparting of such knowledge actually did or could have taken place. Was it by some interior or by some exterior communication, together with such signs as would suffice to cause assent? For the problem at hand, it is enough to point out that such knowledge could be supernaturally revealed in either way. But in neither way could it be imparted without error by man right from the beginning.

---

89 Cf. par. 17-18.
90 *City of God*, XI, ch. 2 (PL 41, 318).
91 Cf. par. 66.
92 *Politics*, II, chs. 1-12.
93 *Ibid.*, VII, ch. 9 (1329a 29-32).
94 *Ibid.*, ch. 16 (1335b 19-25).
95 Cf. par. 40-41.
96 *City of God*, XI, ch. 3 (PL 41, 318).
97 Cf. par. 57-65.
98 Cf. par. 40-41.

70. The objection is raised that these three reasons[99] refute themselves, for whatever they reveal as necessary to know is something that is true, since we can really know only what is true. Consequently, whatever these arguments reveal to be necessary for us to know—for example, that the end of man is the enjoyment of God in himself (first argument); that the manner of reaching Him is by way of merits which God accepts as worthy of such a reward (second argument); that God is triune and causes things contingently, etc. (third argument)—all these are shown to be true. Consequently, these reasons either are based solely on faith or a conclusion is drawn from them which is the very opposite of what they actually prove.

71. I reply that natural reason merely shows us that it is necessary for us to know definitely one part of this contradiction: "The enjoyment [of God] is [our] end; this enjoyment is not our end." In other words, our intellect must not remain in doubt or ignorance on this problem of whether such enjoyment is our end, for such would keep us from seeking the end. But natural reason does not reveal just which part we must know. In this way, then, the aforementioned reasons in so far as they are natural, reveal that one part of the contradiction must be true. Either it is this or it is that. But a definite answer is possible only from what we believe.

[*IV. Reply to the arguments of the philosophers*]

72. As to the arguments for the opinion of Aristotle, I say to the first[100] that knowledge depends upon the soul knowing and the object known, for according to Augustine (*On the Trinity,* IX, last chapter):[101] "Knowledge is born of the knower and the known." Hence, even though the soul may possess sufficient active and passive faculties so far as its own activity in knowing is concerned, still it does not have in itself active powers that would suffice to take the place of the ob-

---

99 Cf. par. 13-41.
100 Cf. par. 6.
101 *On the Trinity*, IX, ch. 12 (PL 42, 970).

ject's action for it is like a blank writing-tablet, as the third book, *On the Soul*[102] tells us. Hence to say that the agent intellect is that by which [the mind] makes all things [known], is true only in so far as this 'making' something known is an action of the soul and not in so far as it involves an action on the part of the object.

73. To the confirmation by reason,[103] I say to the major that "nature" at times is taken in the sense of an intrinsic principle of movement and rest—as is described in the second book of the *Physics*[104]—at other times, for a naturally active principle, in so far as nature is distinguished from art[105] and deliberate intention[106] on the basis of the different ways these proceed from their principle. In this latter sense, "nature" may or may not be intrinsic, just so long as it is natural [i.e. not deliberate or the result of art]. According to the first meaning of "nature," the major is not true, because not everything that is naturally passive has a corresponding intrinsic active principle or nature, for many things lack an intrinsic active power to produce some act they are able to receive naturally. If nature be taken in the second sense, the major is also false in certain instances, namely when a nature because of its excellence is naturally ordained to receive a perfection so eminent that it could be caused by an agent that is natural in the second sense. And so it is in our case.

74. To the proof given for the major, I say that the passive potency is not in vain for even though it could not be reduced to act by a natural agent as the principal cause, still a natural agent can dispose it for such an act. And there is some agent in nature, i.e. in the universe as a whole, that can completely reduce it to act, namely the First or Supernatural Agent.

75. Someone may object that to be incapable of attaining its perfection through what is natural devaluates [our] nature, for according to the second book *On the Heavens and*

---

[102] Aristotle, *On the Soul*, III, ch. 4 (429b 30).
[103] Cf. par. 7.
[104] *Physics*, II, ch. 1 (192b 20-23).
[105] *Ibid.* (193a 31-33).
[106] *Ibid.*, ch. 5 (196b 17-22).

Earth:[107] "The more noble nature, the less it should lack." I reply: if our happiness consisted in the highest speculation that is naturally attainable, the Philosopher would not say our nature lacked anything necessary. But I admit that we can naturally possess such perfection at present. But I go further when I say that there is another higher form of speculation that can be received naturally. Consequently, nature in this regard is honored even more than if one were to claim that the highest possible perfection it could receive is that which is naturally attainable. Nor is it surprising that some nature has the ability to receive a perfection greater than that which lies within the reach of its own active causality.

76. The above citation from the second book *On the Heavens and Earth* is not to the point, because the Philosopher is speaking here of organs corresponding to the power of movement, if this be present in the stars. Now I concede universally that nature gives an organ to everything to which it gives an organic power (I am speaking of things that are not deformed). In our case, however, it is a question of giving a non-organic power, and still not giving naturally all the other requisites for the act. From the Philosopher's statement here, then, it can be said that if a nature can be ordained for a certain act or object, this nature has a natural faculty for the act and also a corresponding organ, if the faculty is organic. But the same cannot be said of the other requisites for the act.

77. The major[108] could be answered in another way, namely that it is true if one speaks of a natural passive potency with respect to an active power, but it is false if passive potency is taken with respect to the act received. The difference between these two is clear from the first part of the solution to this question.[109]

78. The minor[110] is true in the second way [*viz.* if the possible intellect is taken in respect to the act received], but not

---

[107] *On the Heavens*, II, ch. 8 (290a 29), ch. 11 (291b 12).
[108] Cf. par. 7.
[109] Cf. par. 57.
[110] Cf. par. 7.

in the first. There is a third and easy way of answering the minor, namely: to deny it. For even though absolutely speaking the possible intellect is naturally receptive of this intellection, this is not so in its present state. The reason for this, however, will be explained later in distinction 3.[111]

79. To the third reason[112] see Thomas' reply in the *Summa* I, question 1[113] where he says: "Sciences are diversified according to the diverse nature of their knowable objects. For both the astronomer and the physicist demonstrate the same conclusion, for example, that the earth is round. The astronomer does so by means of mathematics (i.e. abstracting from matter), but the physicist does so by means of the matter considered. Hence, there is no reason why the same things treated by the philosophical sciences inasmuch as they can be known by the light of natural reason, may not also be treated by another science inasmuch as they are known by the light of divine revelation."

To the contrary: If the knowledge of those things which can be known in theology is, or can be, treated in other sciences, even though it be in another light, it follows that theological knowledge of such things is unnecessary. The consequence is evident from his own example, for anyone who knows that the earth is round by means of physics has no absolute need of a mathematical knowledge [of the same].

80. This reply [of Thomas], to the third argument, however, is explained in this way. Habit is both a form and a habit. In so far as it is a habit, it is distinguished by reason of the object. In so far as it is a form, however, it can be distinguished by reason of the active principle. Now principles are the efficient causes of a habit of knowledge. Consequently, even though the same object of knowledge (for example, that the earth is round), is not distinguished by reason of the object, there is still a distinction by reason of the different principles which the mathematician and physicist use to prove

---

111 *Ordinatio*, I, d. 3, part 1, q. 2.
112 Cf. par. 8.
113 *Summa theol.* I, q. 1, a. 1 ad 2.

this. And so there will be a distinction of habits in so far as they are forms, but not in so far as they are habits.[114]

81. To the contrary: Form is a common [or generic term] with reference to habit. Now it is impossible that anything be distinct by reason of some superior classification and yet not be distinct by reason of some subordinate classification. Therefore, it is impossible that anything be distinct by reason of form (and hence distinct in form) and still not be distinct by reason of habit. This is like saying that certain things differ as animals but not as men. Furthermore, he assumes that principles distinguish habits[115] according to some other type of causality than as efficient principles, which is false. For if the distinguishing causes have any relation to habits, it is none other than as efficient causes. Furthermore, the [basic] reason always holds, for no matter how cognitive habits may be distinguished, so long as other habits are possible, there would still be no need of any one habit [e.g. theology], in the sense that without it knowledge would be impossible.

82. Therefore, I reply to the argument that even though these speculative sciences [*viz.* physics, mathematics and metaphysics] treat of all speculative things, they still do not exhaust all that can be known about these objects, for they fail to treat of what is proper to them, as has been made clear in the third argument against the first opinion. See above.[116]

83. The fourth argument[117] is answered in this way. First principles cannot be applied to any conclusions other than those which deal with what can be perceived by the senses, both because their terms are abstracted from sensible objects and so partake of their nature, and because the agent intellect, through which this application [of principles] takes place, is limited to objects that can be perceived by the senses.

84. To the contrary: The intellect is certain that these first

---

114 *Ibid.*, I-II, q. 54, a. 2.
115 Namely, when habits are distinguished as habits and not merely in so far as they are forms.
116 Cf. par. 40 ff.
117 Cf. par. 9.

principles are true not only of what can be perceived by the senses, but also of what cannot be so perceived. For the intellect has no doubt that contradictories cannot be simultaneously true of spiritual things any more than of material things. And there is no value in the statement that the term of the first principle is the "being" which is divided into the ten categories and does not apply to theological objects. For we have not the slightest doubt that contradictories are not simultaneously verified about God (e.g. God is happy; God is not happy, etc.) any more than of something white.

85. Another solution is offered, namely, that the conclusions follow from the major premises only when the latter are combined with a minor premise. But the minors to which they must be joined are not naturally evident.

To the contrary: The minors subsumed under the first principles predicate of the things subsumed, the subject terms of the first principles. But the terms of the first principles are known to be predicated about everything, for these terms are most common, therefore, etc.[118]

86. Therefore, I reply that the second part of the minor[119] is false, *viz.* that all the conclusions that can be known are virtually included in the first principles. To the proof, I say that just as the subject terms are common, so also are those of the predicate. Therefore, when the subject terms, since they are distributed, stand for [supposit for] all things, they stand for them only in regard to the predicate terms, which are most common. In virtue of such principles, then, only the most common predicates are known of those things which fall under such principles.

87. This is evident from reason, because the middle term cannot give the reason why any attribute inheres in its respective subject, unless the attribute in question is included virtually in the notion of the middle term. But the notion of the subject of a most common principle includes the reason

---

118 That is, if the first principles (major premises) are known, the minor premises are also known.
119 Cf. par. 10.

for the inherence of only the most universal attributes and not those which are particular. Therefore, it is only under this most general aspect that such a subject can be the means or the reason why anything is known. But in addition to the most general attributes, there are many other attributes that can be known. Because these are not included in the attributes of the first principles, however, the latter will yield no knowledge of them. Consequently there are many things that can be known which are not included in the first principles.

This is clear from an example. Although the proposition: "Every whole is greater than its part," includes "A quarternion is greater than a binary" and other similar propositions with the same predicate, it does not include these: "A quarternion is twice as much as a binary" or "A ternary is one and a half times a binary," for these propositions would require some special middle terms which include them.

88. The third proof is from logic.[120] Although it is licit to descend from a universal affirmative subject, it is not licit to do so from the predicate. Now there are many predicates contained under the predicates of the first principles that can be known of those things which fall under the subjects of these principles. Therefore, these predicates are not known of these subjects through the first principles.

89. Against this it is objected: "Anything can be either affirmed or denied, but nothing can be both affirmed and denied."[121] It follows: "Therefore, this is white or not white," so that it is permissible in this case to descend both from the predicate and from the subject.

I reply that this principle, "Anything can be affirmed or denied, etc. . . ." is equivalent to this: "Concerning anything one part of any contradiction is true and the other is false," where there is a double distribution [*viz.* "concerning anything" and "of any contradiction"], and it is lawful to descend from both distributed terms: "Therefore, of this thing, [one part] of this contradiction [is true, the other false; of

[120] The first proof is in par. 86; the second in par. 87.
[121] *Topics*, VI, ch. 6 (143b 15).

that thing, one part of this contradiction is true, etc.; of that thing, one part of that contradiction is true, etc.] etc. But it is not lawful to descend [distributively] from a predicate with confused supposition," because it does not follow "Concerning everything, one part of every contradiction [is true and the other false], therefore, this part [is true and the other false]." And so it is with other principles. The predicate of a universal affirmative proposition always has only confused supposition, whether there is a double or only one distribution of the subject.

And in the example proposed it is clear that this still holds true. For it can be known of man that he is risible. From this principle "Of anything, etc. . . ." we can never infer anything more than: "Therefore, man is either risible or not risible." Hence, the other part of this disjunctive predicate will never be known of the subject through this principle. On the contrary another special principle is required such as the definition of the subject or the attribute, which is in truth a means and reason for knowing definitely that man is risible.

[*Solution of the initial arguments*]

90. To the arguments at the beginning.—To the first:[122] I distinguish natural objects. For a natural object can mean one which the faculty can attain naturally, i.e. by the action of causes that are naturally active, or it may mean an object toward which the faculty is naturally inclined, whether such an object can be naturally attained or not. The major, then, could be denied if natural is taken in the first sense, for the first object is equal to the faculty, and therefore this object is abstracted from everything concerning which the faculty is able to function. Still it does not follow necessarily that just because the intellect could know such a common object naturally, it could know everything contained under it, because the knowledge of some of the things contained is much more

---

122 Cf. par. 1.

perfect than the confused knowledge of the common object itself. And so, even granting the minor in either sense of natural knowledge, the intended conclusion about what can be naturally attained does not follow, for the major is not true of the object that can be naturally attained.

91. Against this answer, I contend that it destroys itself. For according to him,[123] the primary object is one that is equal to the power. Now this is true: a power regards as its object [a] only those things of which the notion of its first object is verified and [b] anything of which this notion is verified. Therefore, it is impossible that something should be the primary natural object without everything of which it is verified being of itself a natural object. For grant the opposite and then the object is not naturally adequate but exceeds [the faculty] and something inferior is adequate and therefore the first object.

The reason given for [Henry's] answer, however, is a fallacy of figure of speech. For although, in so far as "being" is something that can be grasped by the intellect in a single act (as "man" can be grasped in one intellectual act), "being" can be known naturally (for this one concept of being in so far as it is a concept of one object is something natural), still it cannot be maintained that "being" is the primary object naturally attainable. For "being" is the first object in so far as it is included in all objects known of themselves, and as such it would be naturally attainable only if each of these objects were naturally attainable. Therefore, he [Henry] interchanges "this something," [without qualification], with "of a certain kind" when he argues: "Being is naturally knowable; therefore, being in so far as it is the first (i.e. adequate) object of the intellect, is naturally attainable." For the antecedent is true in so far as "being" is one single intelligible [object], e.g. a white thing, but the consequent makes a conclusion about being in so far as it is included in every intelligible object, and not "being" as conceived without this qualification.

123 Namely, Henry of Ghent, *Summa*, a. 19, q. 1.

92. To the argument, therefore, there is another, a real, answer, namely, the minor is false in regard to the object naturally attainable, but it is true in the other sense (namely, the object to which the power is naturally ordered or inclined). In this way the quotation from Avicenna must be understood. (It will be pointed out later in distinction 3[124] what must be held to be the first object naturally attainable.) This answer is confirmed by Anselm in Chapter 4, *On Free Will:*[125] "We have no power, I believe, which alone suffices for an act." By "power" he means what we commonly call a faculty, as is evident from his example about sight. Therefore, it is not unfitting that a power should be naturally ordered to an object which it cannot attain naturally by natural causes, any more than it is for a power or faculty to be ordained by its very nature [for an act] and nevertheless be unable to produce this act by itself alone.

93. As to the second argument, I deny its consequence.[126] What is to be said of its proof, is clear from the reply given the second argument for the opinion of the Philosopher,[127] because superior natures are ordained passively to receive something greater than they can actively produce. Consequently, their perfection cannot be achieved except by some supernatural agent. But this is not so with the perfection of less perfect things whose ultimate perfection could fall under the action of inferior agents.

94. As to the third,[128] I say some of the propositions we must firmly hold to be true, are disproportionate to the possible intellect, that is to say, the intellect is not equal to being moved [to know them] by what can be known from sense images and the natural light of the agent intellect.

When you argue: "Therefore, the intellect becomes proportionate by means of something else," I concede that there is

---

124 *Ordinatio*, I, d. 3, part 1, q. 3.
125 *On Free Will*, ch. 3 (PL 158, 494).
126 Cf. par. 2.
127 Cf. par. 73-74.
128 Cf. par. 3.

something else—both something that moves it (for, moved supernaturally by the one revealing, the intellect assents to this truth), and something else in the sense of a form (for there is the assent produced in the intellect, which is a kind of inclination in the intellect toward this object which brings the intellect into proportion with the latter).

But when you press further, "Is this 'something else' natural or supernatural?" I reply that it is supernatural, and this is so whether you understand this "something else" in the sense of agent or form.

When you infer: "Therefore, the intellect is disproportionate to it and must be made proportionate through something else," I declare that the intellect by its very nature is in obediential potency toward the agent, and thus is sufficiently proportionate to it to the extent that it can be moved by this agent. Also of itself, the intellect is capable of the act of assent caused by such an agent and this capability is natural. Hence, it is not necessary that it be proportioned by something in order that it be able to receive this assent.

Therefore, we stop not with the first [*viz.* something natural] but with the second [*viz.* something supernatural]. For this revealed truth of itself is insufficient to incline the intellect to assent to it, and hence neither the agent nor the patient is proportionate to this truth. But a supernatural agent suffices to incline the intellect toward this truth by causing in it the act of assent which makes the intellect proportionate to this truth. Hence, an additional something is not required to make the intellect proportionate to such an agent or to the form it impresses, in the same way that something is required in addition to the intellect that it be made proportionate to such an object in the twofold manner mentioned above.

Suggestions for Further Reading

Harris, C. R. S. *Duns Scotus.* 2 vols. Oxford, 1927; Grajewski, M. J. *The Formal Distinction of Duns Scotus.* Washington, 1944; *FCC* vol. II, 476-551; *EG* 454-465; *AAM* 220-241; *RMcK* vol. II, 303-350.

William Ockham

William of Ockham was born around 1280, probably at Ockham, a village in the county of Surrey, near London. He entered the Franciscan Order, studying and lecturing at Oxford University from about 1309 to 1323. In 1324 he was summoned to Avignon by Pope John XXII to answer charges of having expounded heretical doctrines. It appears, however, that the commission appointed to investigate the charges against him reached no final agreement concerning the orthodoxy of his teachings.

Ockham was still in detention in 1327, the year that Michael of Cesena, the General of the Franciscan Order, arrived at Avignon to answer for his attacks upon the papal position concerning Evangelical poverty. Ockham became involved in the issue, siding with his General against the Pope. In May of 1328, evidently fearing the worst, Ockham, along with Michael and several others, fled for protection to the court of the Pope's political enemy, Louis of Bavaria. The Pope promptly excommunicated the refugees. Ockham retaliated with the pen: over the course of the next twenty-odd years he directed a bitter series of polemics against John XXII as well as his successors, Clement XII and Benedict VI.

With the death of Louis of Bavaria in 1347, Ockham's position became hopeless, and he appears to have taken steps to reconcile himself with the Church. A formula of submission was drawn up, but it is not known whether Ockham actually signed it. He died in Munich around 1349, probably a victim of the Black Death.

Ockham was enormously influential in shaping and giving impetus to the empirical trend which came to dominate thought in the late Middle Ages. The selection presented below is typical of Ockham's philosophical approach.

OCKHAM ON EPISTEMOLOGICAL PROBLEMS*

EPISTEMOLOGICAL PROBLEMS

[*The basis of immediate cognition*]

1. First I intend to show that our intellect, even in this life, can have two specifically distinct kinds of non-complex knowledge even when it is concerned with the same object under the same aspect. The one may be called intuitive, the other abstractive cognition. . . .

In order to explain this first conclusion, I shall present a few preliminary distinctions and conclusions; after that I shall prove the conclusion which is principally intended.

The first distinction is between two acts of the intellect. The first act is an act of apprehension and relates to everything that can be the term of an act of the intellective power, whether this be something complex or non-complex. For we apprehend not only that which is non-complex, but also propositions and demonstrations, and impossibilities and necessities, and, in general, anything within the scope of the intellective power. The second act may be called an act of judgment, by which the intellect not only appprehends its object, but also gives its assent or dissent to it. This act has to do with a proposition [*complexum*] only. For our intellect does not assent to anything unless we believe it to be true, nor does it dissent from anything unless we believe it to be false. It is clear, therefore, that in reference to a proposition, a twofold

* Reprinted by permission of Thomas Nelson and Sons from *Ockham's Philosophical Writings*, published by Thomas Nelson and Sons Ltd. Edinburgh, 1957.

act is possible, namely an act of apprehension and an act of judgment.

Proof: It is possible that someone apprehends a proposition, but nevertheless gives neither assent nor dissent to it; this is clearly true, for instance, of indifferent propositions, to which the intellect gives neither assent nor dissent, because otherwise they would not be indifferent for it.

Likewise, a layman who does not know Latin may hear many propositions in this language to which he gives neither assent nor dissent. On the other hand, it is certain that the intellect can give its assent to one proposition and its dissent to another proposition. Therefore, apprehension and judgment are distinct.

The second distinction is, that just as in regard to a proposition there can be a twofold act, so also there can be two corresponding *habitus;* the one inclines the intellect toward an act of apprehension; the other towards an act of judgment.

This distinction is manifest. For after someone has frequently apprehended an indifferent proposition, he finds himself more inclined to apprehend and think about this proposition than he was before. Therefore he has now a *habitus* inclining him towards acts of apprehension. The fact that there is also a *habitus* inclining one toward acts of judgment is clear from the statement of the Philosopher in the sixth book of the *Ethics,* where he affirms the existence of [the several *habitūs* of] understanding, knowledge, etc.

First preliminary conclusion: The act of judgment in reference to a proposition (*complexum*) presupposes an act of apprehending the same proposition. . . .

Second conclusion, following from the preceding discussion [here omitted]. Every act of judgment presupposes in the same faculty a non-complex cognition of the terms; for it presupposes an act of apprehension, and the act of apprehending a proposition presupposes non-complex cognition of the terms. . . .

Third conclusion: No act of the sensitive part of the soul is either partially or totally the immediate and proximate cause of the intellect's own act of judgment.

A persuasive argument can be adduced for this conclusion. If we assume that contents of the intellect suffice as proximate and immediate causes to produce some act of judgment, then they suffice to produce every such act. Now contents of the intellect suffice for some act of judgment, namely a conclusion; because when the knowledge of the premises is in the intellect, the conclusion is immediately known without the help of anything else. Therefore contents of the intellect suffice as the proximate cause of every act of judgment.

Furthermore, since the causes existing in the intellective part can be sufficient, the assumption of other causes is superfluous.

Given these premises I shall prove the main conclusion as follows. Any non-complex cognition of terms that can cause evident cognition of a proposition composed of these terms, is specifically distinct from a non-complex cognition which, no matter how intense it is, cannot cause evident cognition of the same proposition. This is manifest. For things of the same kind that are equally perfect can produce effects of the same kind in the same object when this is equally disposed to receive the effect. This the Philosopher shows in the seventh book of the *Topics*. Now it is certain, as experience teaches, that the intellect can have a non-complex cognition of both Socrates and whiteness, on the strength of which it cannot know evidently whether Socrates is white or not. But besides this knowledge, the intellect can have another cognition by which it is able to know evidently that Socrates is white, if he is white. Hence the intellect can have two non-complex cognitions of these things: the one cognition can cause evident knowledge of this contingent proposition; and the other cannot, no matter how intense it is. Therefore these two cognitions are specifically distinct. . . .

The second main proof: Whenever an intelligible thing can be known only by intellect and in no way by sense, if there can be one non-complex cognition of the thing that suffices for evident knowledge of a contingent truth and another that does not suffice, then the two cognitions are specifically distinct. But acts of intellect, emotions, pleasures, griefs and the like, can be apprehended only by the intellect and not by the sense-faculty. Now some non-complex knowledge of them suffices for evident knowledge of whether they exist or not, and whether or not they exist in such and such a subject. Yet not all non-complex knowledge of them suffices for this; therefore, etc. The first part of the minor premise is shown thus: Everyone experiences in himself that he understands, loves, is pleased, is sad. Since such knowledge concerns contingent facts, it cannot be obtained from necessary propositions. Therefore, either (1) it must be obtained from a non-complex knowledge of the terms, or the things for which the terms stand, or (2) from a contingent proposition obtained from non-complex cognition of the terms or things, or (3) we can go on *in infinitum* with such contingent propositions. The third case is impossible, since there must be an end in the series of such propositions. If the second case is assumed, then the contingent proposition either contains some term which can be obtained from a sensible object, or it does not. The first alternative cannot be admitted; for there is no proposition about a sensible thing from which it would necessarily follow that love is occurring in the will, as will be made clear elsewhere, and consequently there is no contingent proposition in virtue of which it is evidently knowable that this man loves. If the second alternative is conceded, we have the result we wanted: that a non-complex knowledge of purely intelligible terms is sufficient for evident knowledge of such a contingent truth. The second part of the minor premise is shown thus: There is no inconsistency in the supposition that someone does not know whether a certain intelligible thing exists or does not exist, and has nevertheless a non-complex cognition of it; this is no more inconsistent than the corresponding supposition about a certain sensible thing. If, therefore, someone's intellect should directly perceive another person's love and he were thus as certain of this other person's love as of his own love, then there would not be any difficulty about supposing that later on he could still think of this love and nevertheless not know whether it continued to exist, even though it did still exist; just as may happen with some sensible thing which is first seen and then thought of.

This second argument proves that it is possible for the intellect to have this twofold cognition and to have it about purely intelligible facts, whereas the first proves that our intellect actually has this twofold cognition in the present life, and has it even as regards sensible facts. . . .

I maintain, therefore, . . . that there are two ways of knowing something non-complex. The one can be called "abstractive cognition," the other "intuitive cognition." But I am not concerned whether others wish to call this non-complex cognition "intuitive cognition" or not. For what I intended to prove in the first instance was just that our intellect can have two specifically different non-complex cognitions of the same thing.

We must realise, however, that the term "abstractive cognition" can be taken in two senses. In one sense it means cognition that relates to something abstracted from many singulars; and in this sense abstractive cognition is nothing else but cognition of a universal which can be abstracted from many things. We shall speak about this later. If such a universal is a true quality existing in the mind as its subject—which is a probable opinion—then it must be conceded that such a universal can be intuitively known and that the same knowledge is intuitive and also abstractive, according to this first meaning of "abstractive." And in this sense "intuitive" and "abstractive" are not contrasted.

Abstractive cognition in the second sense abstracts from existence and non-existence and from all the other conditions which contingently belong to or are predicated of a thing. This does not mean that something may be known by intuitive cognition which is not known by abstractive cognition; rather, the same thing is known fully, and under the same aspect, by either cognition. But they are distinguished in the following manner. Intuitive cognition of a thing is cognition that enables us to know whether the thing exists or does not exist, in such a way that, if the thing exists, then the intellect immediately judges that it exists and evidently knows that it exists, unless the judgment happens to be impeded through the imperfection of this cognition. And in the same way, if the divine power were to conserve a perfect intuitive cognition of a thing no longer existent, in virtue of this non-complex knowledge the intellect would know evidently that this thing does not exist.

Then, too, intuitive cognition is such that when one thing known by means of it inheres as an accident in another, or is locally distant from the other, or stands in some other relation to the other, then non-complex cognition of these things gives us an immediate knowledge whether a certain thing inheres or does not inhere in another, or whether it is distant from it or not, and so for other contingent truths; unless this cognition is too weak, or there be other impediments. For instance, if Socrates is in reality white, then knowledge of Socrates and of whiteness is called intuitive cognition, when it can be evidently known in virtue of such knowledge that Socrates is white. Generally speaking, any non-complex cognition of one or more terms or things, is an intuitive cognition, if it enables us to know a contingent truth, especially about present facts.

Abstractive cognition, on the other hand, is that knowledge by which it cannot be evidently known whether a contingent fact exists or does not exist. In this way abstractive cognition abstracts from existence and non-existence; because, in opposition to intuitive cognition, it does not enable us to know the existence of what does exist or the non-existence of what does not exist.

Likewise, through abstractive cognition no contingent truth, in particular none relating to the present, can be evidently known. This is clear from the fact that when Socrates and his whiteness are known in his absence, this non-complex knowledge does not enable us to know whether Socrates exists or does not exist, or whether he is white or is not white, and the same for other contingent truths. But yet it is certain that these truths can be evidently known. And any complex knowledge of terms, or of things signified by terms, is ultimately reduced to non-complex knowledge of terms. Hence these terms or things can be known by a cognition which is different from that which cannot give us knowledge of such contingent truths; and this will be intuitive cognition. And it is from this that empirical knowledge begins; for, generally speaking, he who is enabled by observation to know a contingent truth and, by means of this, a necessary truth, has non-complex knowledge of some term or thing which another who is unable to make this observation cannot have. And therefore, just as the knowledge of sensible facts that is obtained from experience (as the Philosopher says in the first book of the *Metaphysics* and in the second book of the *Posterior Analytics*) begins with the senses, i.e. from a sense-intuition of these sensible facts, so in general the scientific knowledge of these purely intelligible facts of experience begins with an intellective intuition of these intelligible facts.

Still, it is to be noted that at times it may happen that no contingent truths, or only a few, can be known about a thing that we know intuitively, owing to the imperfection of the intuitive cognition (it being very imperfect or very obscure), or because of some impediment on the part of the object, or some other impediment.

[*Intuitive cognition of non-existing things*]

2. *Whether intuitive cognition can be had of an object that does not exist?*

It cannot: For it is a contradiction that there should be an act of seeing and nothing be seen; therefore it is a contradiction that there should be an act of seeing but the seen object not exist.

On the contrary: Vision is a non-relative quality distinct from the object; without contradiction, therefore, it can occur without an object.

On this question I lay down two conclusions. First: Intuitive cognition of a non-existent object is possible by the divine power. I prove this first by the article of faith "I believe in God the Father almighty," which I understand in the following sense: Anything is to be attributed to the divine power, when it does not contain a manifest contradiction. But that this [i.e. cognition of a non-existent object] should be produced by the power of God, does not contain a contradiction; therefore, etc.

Again, on this article is based the famous maxim of the theologians: "Whatever God can produce by means of secondary causes, He can directly produce and preserve without them." From this maxim I argue thus. Every effect which God can produce by means of a secondary cause He can produce directly on His own account. God can produce intuitive sense cognition by means of an object; hence He can produce it directly on His own account.

Furthermore, every non-relative reality that differs in its place and its subject [of inherence] from another non-relative reality can still exist by virtue of the divine power when the other non-relative reality is destroyed. But seeing a star in the sky, whether by sense or by intellect, is such a reality; therefore, etc.

You may object that according to this argument it follows that there could be an intuitive and beatific vision of God without His actual presence as an object actually present to the intellect; which is false and erroneous. I answer that there is no logical connexion in the following way of arguing: "Because God can make such an act of seeing without a created object (on which this act depends only as a secondary cause), therefore, there can be an intuitive and beatific vision of God without His actual presence as an object actually present to the intellect (an object on which this is dependent as its first cause)." For though, according to the Doctors, God can make the proper effects of secondary causes without these secondary causes, nevertheless He cannot make any effect without its first cause. For this reason, just as it is not possible that a colour should, as efficient cause, cause itself to be seen in the eye unless it is actually present, so in like manner it is not possible that God should cause an act of seeing Him in the intellect unless His actual presence is given.

Second conclusion: So far as natural causes are in question, an intuitive cognition cannot be caused or preserved if the object does not exist. The reason is this. A real effect cannot be caused, or brought from nothing into being, by that which is nothing. Hence, if we are speaking of the natural mode of causation, it requires for its existence both a productive and a preservative cause.

You may object: "If someone sees the sun and then enters a dark room, it appears to him that he sees the sun in the same place and of the same size. Hence a sight of the sun remains, when the sun is absent; and for the same reason would remain, even if it did not exist." To this I answer: "No sight of the sun does remain; but there does remain a quality, viz. the light-impression in the eye, and it is this quality that is seen. And if the intellect formulates such a proposition as 'Light is seen at the same place, etc.' and gives its assent to it, it is deceived by this quality or impression which it sees."

To the main argument I answer: It is a contradiction that an act of seeing should exist while that which is seen neither exists nor can exist in reality. Hence it is a contradiction that a chimera should be intuitively seen. But it is no contradiction that what is seen should be nothing actually existing outside its cause, provided only that it can exist in reality or has once been in the universe. And so it is in our case. It was thus that God from all eternity saw all things that could be made, and nevertheless they were then nothing.

[*The primacy of cognition of singular things*]

3. *Whether the singular is the first thing known, as regards the origin of cognition?*

It is not the first thing known: for the universal is the first and proper object of the intellect; and is, therefore, the first thing known, as regards the origin of cognition.

On the contrary: Both intellect and sense have the very same object; but if we are speaking of the origin of cognition, a singular thing is the first object of the sense faculty; therefore, etc.

Answer: We must first clarify the meaning of the question, and then answer it.

Concerning the first point we have to realize that here

"singular thing" does not mean everything that is numerically one; for, in this sense, *everything* is singular. Instead we take "singular thing" here for a thing which not only is numerically one, but in addition is not a natural or conventional sign belonging in common to many things signified. In this sense neither a written expression nor a concept nor a significant oral utterance, but only a thing which is not a common sign, is a singular thing.

Secondly, we should know that our question does not refer indiscriminately to any cognition of a singular thing. For in a sense every universal cognition is a cognition of a singular thing, since such a universal cognition gives us knowledge only of a singular thing or singular things. Our question rather refers to a proper and simple cognition of a singular thing.

On the second point: Granted that the question is taken to be about proper cognition of a singular thing, I maintain in the first place that a singular thing, taken in the above sense, is what is first known, in a cognition that is simple and proper to this singular thing.

This conclusion is proved in the following manner: What is first known by such cognition is an extra-mental thing which is not a sign; but everything outside the mind is singular; therefore, etc.

Furthermore, the object precedes the act which is proper to it and that comes first in order of origination; but only a singular thing precedes such an act; therefore, etc.

Secondly, I maintain that this cognition which is simple, proper to a singular thing, and the first to be acquired, is an intuitive cognition. That such a cognition is first, is clear; for abstractive cognition of a singular thing presupposes an intuitive cognition of the same object, and not vice versa. The fact that it is proper to one singular thing is likewise clear; for it is immediately caused, or is of such a nature as to be so caused, by this singular thing; it cannot naturally be caused by another singular thing, even of the same species.

Thirdly, I maintain that the abstractive cognition which is simple and comes first in order of origination is not proper to a singular thing, but is sometimes, indeed always, a cognition common to many. The first part of this thesis is shown thus: We have no proper and simple cognition of a singular thing, as long as we can get no specific knowledge of it. Now this is sometimes the case, for instance, when somebody, approaching from a distance, causes in me a sense-perception with the help of which I can judge only that what I see is an existent. In this case it is clear that my first abstractive cognition (first, that is, in order of origination) is the cognition of existence, and of nothing less general; consequently it is not a specific concept nor a concept proper to a singular thing. The second part of the thesis is likewise clear. For no simple abstractive cognition is more a likeness of one singular thing than of another thing very similar to this thing, nor is such cognition caused by a thing or of such nature as to be caused by a thing; therefore no such cognition is proper to a singular thing, but every such cognition is universal.

But here some doubts arise.

First: It seems that intuitive cognition is not proper knowledge. For any assigned intuitive cognition will have no more likeness to one singular thing than to another very similar one, and will represent the one as much as the other. Therefore it does not seem to be a cognition of one rather than the other.

Second doubt: If the first abstractive cognition is at times a cognition or concept of existence, as you hold in the instance of a man coming from afar, then the first intuitive cognition in such a case will also be cognition of existence in general, since it is impossible to have several simple concepts of the same thing. Nevertheless, in the case of one coming from afar, I can have one look from which I judge that this is an existent, another from which I judge that this is an animal, a third one from which I judge that this is a man, and a fourth one from which I judge that this is Socrates. Yet these various looks are different in kind; therefore, it is not possible that all of them are proper to the singular thing seen.

Third doubt: It seems that the first abstractive cognition is a proper one, especially when the object is sufficiently close, because by the first abstractive cognition I can recall the same thing as I saw before. But this could not happen, unless my abstractive cognition were proper to the thing.

Fourth doubt: According to what has been said it seems possible that the concept of a genus could be abstracted from one individual, let us say, the concept "animal"; as is clear from the case of one coming from a distance, when I see enough to judge that what I am seeing is an animal.

To the first doubt, I say that we have a cognition proper to one singular thing, not on account of a greater likeness to one than to another, but because this intuitive cognition is naturally caused only by the one and not by the other, and cannot be caused by the other.

If you say that it may be caused by God alone, I admit that this is true. Nevertheless, where created things are concerned, it is always of the nature of such a look to be caused by one object and not by another; and if it is naturally caused, it can be caused only by the one object and not by the other. Therefore the reason why intuitive cognition, rather than the first abstractive cognition, is said to be proper to the singular thing, is not similarity, but only causality; no other reason can be assigned.

To the second doubt, I say that sometimes such looks are of the same species and differ only as the more or less perfect differ within the same species. For instance, if we saw something composed only of homogeneous parts, where no more than one accident, let us say whiteness, is visible, then as this thing approaches, our vision becomes stronger and clearer, and accordingly different judgments are possible, viz. that what we see is an existent, or a body, or a colour, or whiteness, etc.

You object, perhaps: "Things which cannot cause the same specific effect differ specifically. But clear and obscure vision cannot; therefore, etc." I answer: "If certain causes, no matter how much they are intensified and increased, cannot cause an effect specifically the same, then they are specifically different; otherwise not. But this vision, if increased and intensified, can produce every effect that clear vision can. Consequently obscure and clear vision are of the same kind." Sometimes, however, clear and obscure vision are specifically different: for instance, if different objects are seen, as when something like a many-coloured shield is viewed from a greater or lesser distance. But these views are not of the same object but of different objects.

To the third doubt, I say that when I see something, I do have a proper abstractive cognition; only it will not be a simple cognition, but one composed of simple cognitions. This composite knowledge is the basis of recollection; for I recall Socrates because I have seen him with such a figure, colour, height and width, and in such a place, and by putting these together I recall having once seen Socrates. But if you leave out all simple concepts except one, you cannot by means of this have memory relating to Socrates rather than any other man who is very similar to him; I can well recall having seen someone, but whether it was Socrates or Plato, I do not know. Therefore a simple abstractive cognition is not proper to a singular thing; however, a composite cognition may well be proper to one.

To the fourth doubt I answer: "The concept of a genus is never abstracted from only one individual." Concerning the instance of a man coming from a distance, I say that I judge him to be an animal, since I am already in the possession of the concept "animal," a concept that is a genus; and therefore, by means of this concept I am led to recognition. Hence, if I did not already possess the concept of the genus "animal," I would judge only that this which is seen is something.

If you ask, which abstractive cognition is first obtained by the help of intuitive cognition, I answer: "Sometimes only the concept 'existent,' sometimes the concept of a genus, sometimes the concept of the ultimate species; but it all depends on whether the object is more or less remote." However, we always get an impression of the concept "existent," because if the object is sufficiently close, a concept of the species and the concept "existent" are simultaneously caused by the extramental singular thing.

To the principal objection I answer: A universal is the first object in the order of adequacy [i.e. of adequacy as object of the intellect], but not in the order of origin of cognition.

The problem of universals

4. A general knowledge of terms is not sufficient for the logician; he must also know terms more in detail. Therefore, having dealt with the general divisions of terms [in the previous chapters of the *Summa logicae*], we must turn to some of the things that come under members of this division.

First we have to treat terms of second intention; secondly, terms of first intention. It has been said that terms of second intention are those like "universal," "genus," "species," etc. Hence we must say something about those which are set up as the five predicables. But first we must speak of the general term "universal," which is predicated of every universal, and of the term "singular," which is opposed to it.

First we must realize that "singular" is taken in two senses. In one sense the name "singular" signifies whatever is one thing and not several. If it is so understood, then those who hold that a universal is a certain quality of the mind predicable of many things (but standing for these many things, not for itself) have to say that every universal is truly and really a singular. For just as every word, no matter how common it may be by convention, is truly and really singular and numerically one, since it is one thing and not many, so likewise the mental content that signifies several things outside is truly and really singular and numerically one, since it is one thing and not many things, though it signifies several things.

In another sense the name "singular" is taken for that which is one and not several things and is not of such a nature as to be the sign of several things. If "singular" is understood in this sense, then no universal is singular, since every universal is of such a nature as to be a sign of, and to be predicated of, several things. Hence, if a universal is that which is not numerically one—a meaning attributed by many to "universal"—then I say that nothing is a universal, unless perhaps you wish to abuse this word by saying that a population is a universal, since it is not one but many. But that would be childish.

Hence we have to say that every universal is one singular thing. Therefore nothing is universal except by signification, by being a sign of several things. This is what Avicenna says in the fifth book of the *Metaphysics:* "One form in the intellect has reference to a multitude, and in this sense it is a universal, since the universal is a content in the intellect which is equally related to anything you take." And later on: "This form, though universal in reference to individuals, is nevertheless individual in reference to the particular mind in which it is impressed, for it is one of the forms in the intellect." He wishes to say here that the universal is one particular content of the mind itself, of such a nature as to be predicated of several things; therefore, it is by the very fact that it is of such a nature as to be predicated of several things (standing not for itself, but for those many things), that it is called a "universal." By the fact, however, that it is one form really existing in the intellect, it is called a "singular." Hence "singular" in the first sense is predicated of the universal, but not "singular" in the second sense. In like manner, we say that the sun is a universal cause, and nevertheless it is in truth a particular and singular thing, and consequently a singular and particular cause. For the sun is called "universal cause," because it is the cause of many things, namely of all that can be generated and corrupted here below. It is, on the other hand, called "particular cause," because it is one cause and not several causes. Likewise the content of the soul is called "universal," because it is a sign predicable of many; on the other hand, it is called "singular," because it is one thing and not many things.

It must, however, be understood that there are two sorts of universal. There is one sort which is naturally universal; in other words, is a sign naturally predicable of many things, in much the same way as smoke naturally signifies fire, or a groan the pain of a sick man, or laughter an inner joy. Such a universal is nothing other than a content of the mind; and therefore no substance outside the mind and no accident outside the mind is such a universal. It is only of such a universal that I shall speak in the chapters that follow.

The other sort of universal is so by convention. In this way, an uttered word, which is really a single quality, is universal; for it is a conventional sign meant to signify many things. Therefore, just as the word is said to be common, so it can be said to be universal. But it is not so by nature, only by convention.

A universal is not a thing outside the mind

5. Since it is not sufficient merely to assert this without proving it by manifest reasoning, I shall advance a few reasons for what has been said above and I shall confirm by arguments from authority.

That a universal is not a substance existing outside the mind can in the first place be evidently proved as follows: No universal is a substance that is single and numerically one. For if that were supposed, it would follow that Socrates is a universal, since there is no stronger reason for one singular substance to be a universal than for another; therefore no singular substance is a universal, but every substance is numerically one and singular. For everything is either one thing and not many, or it is many things. If it is one and not many, it is numerically one. If, however, a substance is many things, it is either many singular things or many universal things. On the first supposition it follows that a substance would be several singular substances; for the same reason, then, some substance would be several men; and thus, although a universal would be distinguished from one particular thing, it would yet not be distinguished from particular things. If, however, a substance were several universal things, let us take one of these universal things and ask "Is this one thing and not many, or is it many things?" If the first alternative is granted, then it follows that it is singular; if the second is granted, we have to ask again "Is it many singular or many universal things?" And thus either this will go on *in infinitum*, or we must take the stand that no substance is universal in such a way that it is not singular. Hence, the only remaining alternative is that no substance is universal.

Furthermore, if a universal were one substance existing in singular things and distinct from them, it would follow that it could exist apart from them; for every thing naturally prior to another thing can exist apart from it by the power of God. But this consequence is absurd.

Furthermore, if that opinion were true, no individual could be created, but something of the individual would pre-exist; for it would not get its entire being from nothing, if the universal in it has existed before in another individual. For the same reason it would follow that God could not annihilate one individual of a substance, if He did not destroy the other individuals. For if He annihilated one individual, He would destroy the whole of the essence of the individual, and consequently He would destroy that universal which is in it and in others; consequently, the other individuals do not remain, since they cannot remain without a part of themselves, such as the universal is held to be.

Furthermore, we could not assume such a universal to be something entirely extrinsic to the essence of an individual; therefore, it would be of the essence of the individual, and consequently the individual would be composed of universals; and thus the individual would not be more singular than universal.

Furthermore, it follows that something of the essence of Christ would be miserable and damned; since that common nature which really exists in Christ, really exists in Judas also and is damned. Therefore, something is both in Christ and in one who is damned, namely in Judas. That, however, is absurd.

Still other reasons could be advanced which I pass over for the sake of brevity.

The same conclusion I will now confirm by authorities. . . .

From these and many other texts it is clear that a universal is a mental content of such nature as to be predicated of many things. This can also be confirmed by reason. All agree that every universal is predicable of things. But only a mental content or conventional sign, not a substance, is of such nature as to be predicated. Consequently, only a mental content or a conventional sign is a universal. However, at present I am not using "universal" for a conventional sign, but for that which is naturally a universal. Moreover, it is clear that no substance is of such nature as to be predicated; for if that were true, it would follow that a proposition would be composed of particular substances, and consequently that the subject could be in Rome and the predicate in England. That is absurd.

Furthermore, a proposition is either in the mind or in spoken or written words. Consequently, its parts are either in the mind or in speech or in writing. Such things, however, are not particular substances. Therefore, it is established that no proposition can be composed of substances; but a proposition is composed of universals; hence universals are in no way substances.

Scotus's opinion on universals and its refutation

6. Although it is clear to many that a universal is not a substance existing outside the mind in individuals and really distinct from them, still some are of the opinion that a universal does in some manner exist outside the mind in individuals, although not really but only formally distinct from them. Hence they say that in Socrates there is human nature, which is "contracted to" Socrates by an individual difference which is not really but only formally distinct from this nature. Hence the nature and the individual difference are not two things, although the one is not formally the other.

However, this opinion appears to me wholly untenable. Proof: In creatures no extra-mental distinction of any kind is possible except where distinct things exist. If, therefore, some kind of distinction exists between this nature and this difference, it is necessary that they be really distinct things. I prove the minor premise in syllogistic form as follows: This nature is not formally distinct from itself; this individual difference is formally distinct from this nature; therefore this individual difference is not this nature.

Furthermore, the same thing is not common and proper; however, according to them, the individual is proper, but the universal is common; therefore the individual difference is not common; consequently no universal is the same thing as the individual difference.

Furthermore, opposites cannot belong to the same created thing; "common" and "proper" are opposites; therefore the same thing is not common and proper, as would follow if individual difference and common nature were the same thing.

Furthermore, if common nature were really the same as the individual difference, then there would be in reality as many common natures as there are individual differences, and hence none of them would be common, but each one would be proper to the difference with which it is really identical.

Furthermore, everything which is distinguished from something else is distinguished either of itself or by some thing intrinsic to itself; but the humanity of Plato is one thing and the humanity of Socrates another; therefore they are distinguished of themselves; therefore *not* by having differences added to them.

Furthermore, according to Aristotle, things specifically different are also numerically different; but the nature of a man and the nature of a donkey are of themselves specifically different; therefore, of themselves, they are numerically different; consequently, each of these natures is on its own account numerically one.

Furthermore, what no power can cause to belong to several things no power can make predicable of several things; now no power can make such a nature, if it is really the same as the individual difference, belong to several things, because in no manner can [something really identified with one individual] belong to another individual; therefore, no power can make it predicable of several things, and consequently no power can make it universal.

Furthermore, I take this individual difference and the nature that it "contracts" and ask "Is the distinction greater or less than between two individuals?" It is not greater, since they do not differ really; whereas individuals do differ really. Nor is it less, for then the two things said to be distinct would fall under the same concept, just as two individuals fall under the same concept. Consequently, if the one is numerically one on its own account, the other will also be so on its own account.

Furthermore, I ask "Is the nature the individual difference, or is it not?" If it is, then I shall argue in syllogistic form as follows: This individual difference is proper and not common, this individual difference is the nature; consequently the nature is proper and not common, which is what we intended to prove. Likewise I argue in syllogistic form as follows: This individual difference is not formally distinct from this individual difference; this individual difference is the nature; therefore, this nature is not formally distinct from the individual difference. If, however, the other alternative is granted, namely "This individual difference is not the nature," our thesis is admitted, since this therefore follows: The individual difference is not the nature, therefore the individual difference is not really the nature. For from the opposite of the consequent the opposite of the antecedent follows, by this argument: The individual difference is really the nature, therefore the individual difference is the nature. The inference is clear, since it is a valid inference to argue from a determinable as qualified by a determination which does not cancel or diminish it, to the determinable without the qualification. "Really," however, is not a cancelling or diminishing determination, hence this follows: The individual difference is really the nature, therefore the individual difference is the nature.

Therefore it must be said that in creatures there is no such formal distinction; but whatever in creatures is distinct, is really distinct, and constitutes a distinct thing, if each of the two things distinguished is truly a thing. Just as in creatures we must never deny the validity of such modes of arguing as "This is *A*, this is *B*, consequently a *B* is *A*," or "This is not *A*, this is *B*, consequently a *B* is not *A*," so also as regards creatures whenever contradictory predicates are true of certain things, we must not deny that the things are distinct; unless of course some determination or some syncategorematic term should be what causes this to be true, as should not be assumed in our present case.

Therefore we must say with the Philosopher that in a particular substance nothing whatsoever is substantial except the particular form and the particular matter or a compound of matter and form. Hence we must not imagine that in Socrates we have human nature or humanity distinct in any way from Socrates, to which is added an individual difference that "contracts" this nature. But any imaginable substantial reality that exists in Socrates is either the particular matter or the particular form or a compound of the two. Therefore every essence and quiddity and everything substantial, if it really exists outside the mind, is either simply and absolutely matter or form, or a compound of them, or it is a separate immaterial substance, according to the teachings of the Peripatetics.

[*A universal is a thought-object*]

7. Another theory [different from those opinions concerning the nature of universals previously criticized by Ockham] could be advanced. I maintain that a universal is not something real that exists in a subject [of inherence], either inside or outside the mind, but that it has being only as a thought-object in the mind. It is a kind of mental picture which as a thought-object has a being similar to that which the thing outside the mind has in its real existence. What I mean is this: The intellect, seeing a thing outside the mind, forms in the mind a picture resembling it, in such a way that if the mind had the power to produce as it has the power to picture, it would produce by this act a real outside thing which

would be only numerically distinct from the former real thing. The case would be similar, analogously speaking, to the activity of an artist. For just as the artist who sees a house or building outside the mind first pictures in the mind a similar house and later produces a similar house in reality which is only numerically distinct from the first, so in our case the picture in the mind that we get from seeing something outside would act as a pattern. For just as the imagined house would be a pattern for the architect, if he who imagines it had the power to produce it in reality, so likewise the other picture would be a pattern for him who forms it. And this can be called a universal, because it is a pattern and relates indifferently to all the singular things outside the mind. Because of the similarity between its being as a thought-object and the being of like things outside the mind, it can stand for such things. And in this way a universal is not the result of generation, but of abstraction, which is only a kind of mental picturing.

I shall first show that something exists in the mind whose being is that of an object of thought only, without inhering in the mind as an independent subject.

This is clear from the following: According to the philosophers, existence is primarily divided into existence in the mind and existence outside the mind, the latter being subdivided into the ten categories. If this is admitted, then I ask "What is understood here by 'existence in the mind'?" It means either existence as a thought-object, and then we have our intended thesis, or it means existence as in a subject. The latter, however, is not possible; for, whatever exists truly in the mind as a subject, is contained under existence that is divided into the ten categories, since it falls under quality. For an act of intellect, and indeed in general every accident or form of the mind, is a true quality, like heat or whiteness, and hence does not fall under the division of existence that is set over against existence in the ten categories. [Consequently the main distinction of the philosophers would be futile.]

Furthermore, fictions have being in the mind, but they do not exist independently, because in that case they would be real things and so a chimera and a goat-stag and so on would be real things. So some things exist only as thought-objects.

Likewise, propositions, syllogisms, and other similar objects of logic do not exist independently; therefore they exist only as thought-objects, so that their being consists in being known. Consequently, there are beings which exist only as thought-objects.

Again, works of art do not seem to inhere in the mind of the craftsman as independent subjects any more than the creatures did in the divine mind before creation.

Likewise, conceptual relations are commonly admitted by the [scholastic] doctors. If this is conceded, then I ask "Do they exist only in a subject?" In that case they will be genuine things and real relations. Or do they exist only as thought-objects? In that case we have our intended thesis.

Again, according to those who think differently, the term "being" means a univocal concept, and nevertheless does not mean a distinct reality.

Likewise, practically all men distinguish second intentions from first intentions, and they do not call the second intentions real qualities of the mind. Since they are not in reality outside the mind, they can only exist as thought-objects in the mind.

Secondly, I maintain that this mental picture is what is primarily and immediately meant by the concept "universal," and has the nature of a thought-object, and is that which is the immediate term of an act of intellection having no singular object. This mental picture, in the manner of being that a thought-object has, is just whatever the corresponding singular is, in the manner of being proper to a subject; and so by its very nature it can stand for the singulars of which it is in a way a likeness. . . .

I maintain, therefore, that just as a spoken word is universal and is a genus or a species, but only by convention, in the same way the concept thus mentally fashioned and abstracted from singular things previously known is universal by its nature. . . .

[*A universal is an act of the intellect*]

8. There could be another opinion, according to which a concept is the same as the act of knowing. This opinion appears to me to be the more probable one among all the opinions which assume that these concepts really exist in the soul as a subject, like true qualities of the soul; so I shall first explain this opinion in its more probable form.

I maintain, then, that somebody wishing to hold this opinion may assume that the intellect apprehending a singular thing performs within itself a cognition of this singular only. This cognition is called a state of mind, and it is capable of standing for this singular thing by its very nature. Hence, just as the spoken word "Socrates" stands by convention for the thing it signifies, so that one who hears this utterance, "Socrates is running," does not conceive that this word, "Socrates," which he hears, is running, but rather that the thing signified by this word is running; so likewise one who knew or understood that something was affirmatively predicated of this cognition of a singular thing would not think that the cognition was such and such, but would conceive that the thing to which the cognition refers is such and such. Hence, just as the spoken word stands by convention for a thing, so the act of intellect, by its very nature, and without any convention, stands for the thing to which it refers.

Beside this intellectual grasp of a singular thing the intellect also forms other acts which do not refer more to one thing than to another. For instance, just as the spoken word "man" does not signify Socrates more than Plato, and hence does not stand more for Socrates than Plato, so it would be with an act of intellect which does not relate to Socrates any more than to Plato or any other man. And in like manner there would be also a knowledge whereby this animal is not more known that that animal; and so with other notions.

To sum up: The mind's own intellectual acts are called states of mind. By their nature they stand for the actual things outside the mind or for other things in the mind, just as the spoken words stand for them by convention. . . .

. . . By such a common or confused intellection, singular things outside the mind are known. For instance, to say that we have a confused intellection of man, means that we have a cognition by which we do not understand one man rather than another, but that by such a cognition we have cognition of a man rather than a donkey. And this amounts to saying that such a cognition, by some kind of assimilation, bears a greater resemblance to a man than to a donkey, but does not resemble one man rather than another. In consequence of the aforesaid, it seems necessary to say that an infinity of objects can be known by such a confused cognition. Still this seems no more untenable than that an infinity of objects can be liked or desired by the same act of liking or desiring. Yet the latter does not seem to be untenable. For a man may like all the parts of a continuous thing, which are infinite in number, or he may desire that all these parts remain in existence. Now in such a case, what was desired would simply be a part of the continuous thing, but not one part rather than another; therefore all parts must be desired; these parts, however, are infinite in number. Likewise, somebody can desire the existence of all men who can exist. Now these are infinite in number, since an infinity of men can be generated.

And so it could be said that one and the same cognition refers to an infinite number of singulars without being a cognition proper to any one of them, and this is so because of some specific likeness between these individuals that does not exist between others. However, no singular thing can be distinguished from another by such a cognition.

Suggestions for Further Reading

Moody, E. A. *The Logic of William Ockham.* London, 1935; Shapiro, H. *Motion, Time and Place According to William Ock-*

ham. New York, 1957; Boehner, P. *Collected Articles on Ockham*. E. M. Buytaert (ed.). New York, 1958; Webering, D. *Theory of Demonstration According to William Ockham*. New York, 1953; *FCC* vol. III, 43-121; *EG* 489-499; *AAM* 265-286; *RMcK* vol. II, 351-421.

Nicolaus of Autrecourt

Nicolaus was born around 1300 at Autrecourt, near Bar-le-Duc, in France. He studied at the University of Paris, being a member of the Sorbonne from about 1320 to 1327. After having obtained the degree of Master of Arts and a licentiate in theology, Nicolaus became a prebendary of the Cathedral of Metz.

Nicolaus' philosophical theories early aroused determined opposition. There is extant a letter from Pope Benedict XII to the Bishop of Paris, dated 1340, in which the Pope directed the Bishop to see that Nicolaus, along with several others, put in an appearance at Avignon to explain certain questionable views. Owing to the death of Benedict XII, Nicolaus' hearing dragged on until it was reopened by Benedict's successor, Clement VI. Nicolaus, apparently anticipating the worst, fled Avignon before any decision concerning the orthodoxy of his opinions was reached. It is not known for sure where he went; but tradition has it that he sought refuge at the court of Louis of Bavaria. In 1346 Nicolaus was sentenced to burn his writings before the assembled University of Paris and to recant his condemned theses. Further, he was expelled from the teaching faculty of the University of Paris. Nicolaus complied with the sentence of the curia in 1347. We know nothing more of his later life except that he became Dean of the Cathedral of Metz in 1350.

The most noteworthy of Nicolaus' few surviving writings are his first two letters to Bernard of Arezzo, one of his most trenchant critics. These letters—reprinted below in their entirety—contain such a powerful critique of the notions of causality and substance that they have led a recent scholar to dub Nicolaus "the medieval Hume."

NICOLAUS OF AUTRECOURT'S CRITIQUE OF CAUSALITY AND SUBSTANCE *

I. FIRST LETTER TO BERNARD

With all the reverence which I am obligated to show to you, most amiable Father Bernard, by reason of the worthiness of the Friars, I wish in this present communication to explain some doubts—indeed, as it seems to some of us, some obvious contradictions—which appear to follow from the things you say, so that, by their resolution, the truth may be more clearly revealed to me and to others. For I read, in a certain book on which you lectured in the Franciscan school, the following propositions which you conceded, to whoever wished to uphold them, as true. The first, which is set forth by you in the first book of the *Sentences,* Dist. 3, Qu. 4, is this: *"Clear intuitive cognition is that by which we judge a thing to exist, whether it exists or does not exist.* Your second proposition, which is set forth in the same place as above, is of this sort: *The inference,* 'An object does not exist, therefore it is not seen' *is not valid; nor does this hold,* 'This is seen, therefore this exists'; *indeed both are invalid, just as these inferences,* 'Caesar is thought of, therefore Caesar exists,' 'Caesar does not exist, therefore he is not thought of.' The third proposition, stated in that same place, is this: *In-*

* Translation and notes by Professor Ernest A. Moody of the University of California at Los Angeles, printed with his permission. The translation is from the text edited by J. Lappe, *Beiträge zur Geschichte der Philosophie des Mittelalters.* Bd. VI, Hft. 2, Münster i.-W. 1908, pp. 2-14.

tuitive cognition does not necessarily require the existing thing." [1]

From these propositions I infer a fourth, that every awareness which we have of the existence of objects outside our minds, can be false; since, according to you it [the awareness] can exist whether or not the object exists. And I infer another fifth proposition, which is this: By natural cognitive means [*in lumine naturali*] we cannot be certain when our awareness of the existence of external objects is true or false; because, as you say, it represents the thing as existing, whether or not it exists. And thus, since whoever admits the antecedent must concede the consequent which is inferred from that antecedent by a formal consequence, it follows that you do not have evident certitude of the existence of external objects.[2] And likewise you must concede all the things

[1] Bernard's definition of "clear intuitive cognition," as that by which we judge a thing to exist, whether or not it does in fact exist, is not the definition given by William of Ockham, though a number of historians have failed to appreciate this point. Ockham defines intuitive cognition in the following way: "Intuitive cognition of a thing is cognition that enables us to know whether the thing exists or does not exist, in such a way that, if the thing exists, then the intellect immediately judges that it exists and evidently knows that it exists, unless the judgment happens to be impeded through the imperfection of this cognition. And in the same way, if the divine power were to conserve a perfect intuitive cognition of a thing no longer existent, in virtue of this non-complex knowledge the intellect would know evidently that this thing does not exist." (Translation from Ockham's *Ordinatio*, Prologue, Qu. 1, by Philotheus Boehner, *Ockham: Philosophical Writings*, Edinburgh, 1957, p. 23.) Whereas Bernard of Arezzo defines intuitive cognition in such manner that it can yield a false judgment, Ockham defines it in such a way that it cannot yield a false judgment; thus Ockham's definition does not entail the skeptical consequences that Nicolaus of Autrecourt finds in the definition of Bernard.

[2] In fourteenth-century logic, a *consequence* is a conditional proposition of the form "If p, then q" (or, alternatively, "p, therefore q"); the protasis of the conditional was called the *antecedent*, and the apodasis the *consequent* (not the *consequence*, which designates the conditional as a whole). The medieval logic of *consequentiae*, corresponding to the modern sentential calculus, but normally interpreted in terms of entailment rather than in terms of truth-functions, is used regularly by Nicolaus of Autrecourt in his arguments against Bernard of Arezzo in these letters. Cf. Ernest A. Moody, *Truth and*

which follow from this. But it is clear that you do not have evident certitude of the existence of objects of the senses, because no one has certitude of any consequent through an inference which manifestly involves a fallacy. But such is the case here; for according to you, this is a fallacy, "Whiteness is seen, therefore whiteness exists."

But you will perhaps say, as I think you wished to suggest in a certain disputation over at the Preaching Friars', that although from the fact of seeing it cannot be inferred, when that seeing is produced or conserved by a supernatural cause, that the seen object exists, nevertheless when it is produced precisely by natural causes—with only the general concurrence of the First Agent—then it can be inferred.

But to the contrary: When from some antecedent, if produced by some agent, a certain consequent cannot be inferred by a formal and evident inference, then from that antecedent, no matter by what thing it be produced, that consequent cannot be inferred. This proposition is clear, by example and by reason. By example in this way: If, whiteness being posited as existing by the agency of A, it could not be formally inferred "Whiteness exists, therefore color exists," then this could not be inferred no matter by what agency the whiteness be posited as existing. It is also clear by reason, because the antecedent is not in itself modified by whatever it is that causes it to be—nor is the fact which is signified by that antecedent.

Further, since from that antecedent it cannot be inferred evidently by way of intuitive cognition, "therefore whiteness exists," we must then add something to that antecedent—namely, what you suggested above, that the [vision of] whiteness is not produced or conserved in existence supernaturally. But from this my contention is clearly established. For when a person is not certain of some consequent, unless in virtue of some antecedent of which he is not evidently certain whether or not the case is as it states it to be—because it is not known by the meaning of its terms, nor by experience,

Consequence in Mediaeval Logic, Amsterdam, 1953, for a detailed exposition of the structure and terminology of this branch of medieval logic.

nor is it inferred from such knowledge, but is only believed —such a person is not evidently certain of the consequent. It is clear that this is so, if that antecedent is considered together with its condition; therefore etc.[3] On the other hand, according to your position, whoever makes the inference from that antecedent without adding that condition, makes an invalid inference—as was the case with the philosophers, and Aristotle, and other people who did not add this condition to the antecedent, because they did not believe that God could impede the effects of natural causes.

Again, I ask you if you are acquainted with all natural causes, and know which of them exist and which are possible, and how much they can do. And I ask how you know evidently, by evidence reducible to that of the law of contradiction, that there is anything such that its coming to pass does not involve contradiction and which nevertheless can only be brought to pass by God? On these questions I would gladly be given certitude of the kind indicated.

Again, you say that an imperfect intuitive cognition can be had in natural manner, of a non-existent thing.[4] I now ask how you are certain (with the certitude defined above) when your intuitive cognition is of a sufficiently perfect degree such that it cannot naturally be of a non-existent thing. And I would gladly be instructed about this.

Thus, it is clear, it seems to me, that as a consequence of your statements you have to say that you are not certain of the existence of the objects of the five senses. But what is

---

3 Bernard has argued that the inference "A is seen, therefore A exists" is valid on the assumption that God is not interfering with the natural causal relation between existing visible objects and acts of seeing them. But since we can never know, in any particular case, whether God is or is not interfering with the course of nature, Nicolaus argues that the above inference is never valid. Given three propositions, p, q, and r, we may concede the statement "If p, then if q then r," but if we cannot know whether p is true or false, we cannot know whether "if q then r" is valid or invalid.

4 The distinction between "imperfect intuitive cognition" and "clear intuitive cognition" is equivalent to the distinction between memory and direct perception. Ockham held that direct perception (or "clear intuitive cognition") was infallible, but admitted that memory (or "imperfect intuitive cognition") might be mistaken.

even harder to uphold, you must say that you are not certain of your own actions—e.g., that you are seeing, or hearing—indeed you must say that you are not sure that anything is perceived by you, or has been perceived by you. For, in the *Sentences, Book I, Dist. 3,* in the place above cited, you say that your intellect does not have intuitive cognition of your actions. And you prove it by this argument: Every intuitive cognition is clear; but the cognition which your intellect has of your acts, is not clear; therefore etc. Now, on this assumption, I argue thus: The intellect which is not certain of the existence of things of which it has the clearest cognition, will not be certain concerning those things of which it has a less clear cognition. But, as was said, you are not certain of the existence of objects of which you have a clearer cognition than you have of your own acts; therefore etc.

And if you say that sometimes some abstractive cognition[5] is as clear as an intuitive cognition—e.g., that every whole is greater than its part—this will not help you, because you explicitly say that the cognition which we have of our own acts is not as clear as intuitive cognition; and yet intuitive cognition, at least that which is imperfect, is not naturally of evident certainty. This is clear from what you say. And thus it follows evidently, that you are not certain of what appears evident to you, and consequently you are not certain whether anything appears to you.

And it also follows that you are not certain whether any proposition is true or false, because you are not evidently certain whether any proposition exists, or has existed. Indeed it follows that if you were asked whether or not you believed some articles of the Faith, you would have to say, "I do not know," because, according to your position, you could not be certain of your own act of believing. And I confirm this, be-

---

[5] Abstractive cognition is defined by Ockham (and presumably by Bernard and Nicolaus as well) as "that knowledge by which it cannot be evidently known whether a contingent fact exists or does not exist" (Ph. Boehner, *op. cit.*, p. 23). All judgments not based on immediate perception, including all general or "universal" statements, were held to be based on abstractive cognition; though ultimately abstractive cognitions arise from intuitive cognitions.

cause, if you were certain of your act of believing, this would either be from that very act itself, in which case the direct and reflective act would be identical[6]—which you will not admit—or else it would be by some other act, and in that case, according to your position, you would in the same way be uncertain, because there would then be no more contradiction than that the seeing of whiteness existed and the whiteness did not exist, etc.

And so, bringing all these statements together, it seems that you must say that you are not certain of those things which are outside of you. And thus you do not know if you are in the heavens or on the earth, in fire or in water; and consequently you do not know whether today's sky is the same one as yesterday's, because you do not know whether the sky exists. Just as you do not know whether the Chancellor or the Pope exists, and whether, if they exist, they are different in each moment of time. Similarly, you do not know the things within you—as, whether or not you have a beard, a head, hair, and so forth. And *a fortiori* it follows from this that you are not certain of the things which occurred in the past—as, whether you have been reading, or seeing, or hearing. Further, your position seems to lead to the destruction of social and political affairs, because if witnesses testify of what they have seen, it does not follow, "We have seen it, therefore it happened." Again, I ask how, on this view, the Apostles were certain that Christ suffered on the cross, and that He rose from the dead, and so with all the rest.

I wish that your mind would express itself on all these questions, and I wonder very much how you can say that you are evidently certain of various conclusions which are more obscure—such as concern the existence of the Prime Mover,

---

6 The distinction between the "direct act" (*actus rectus*) and the "reflective act" (*actus reflexus*), corresponds to the distinction between the act of knowing or believing expressed in the sentence "A is B," and the act of knowing or believing expressed in the sentence "I know (or I believe) that A is B." Ockham, and most fourteenth-century philosophers (as well as St. Thomas Aquinas), held that the direct and the reflective act are not identical and do not have the same objects.

and the like—when you are not certain about these things which I have mentioned. Again, it is strange how, on your assumptions, you believe that you have shown that a cognition is distinct from what is cognized, when you are not certain, according to your position, that any cognition exists or that any propositions exist, and consequently that any contradictory propositions exist; since, as I have shown, you do not have certainty of the existence of your own acts, or of your own mind, and do not know whether it exists. And, as it seems to me, the absurdities which follow on the position of the Academics, follow on your position. And so, in order to avoid such absurdities, I maintained in my disputation at the Sorbonne, that I am evidently certain of the objects of the five senses, and of my own acts.

I think of these objections, and of so many others, that there is no end to them, against what you say. I pray you, Father, to instruct me who, however stupid, am nevertheless desirous of reaching knowledge of the truth. May you abide in Him, who is the light, and in whom there is no darkness.

II. THE SECOND LETTER OF NICOLAUS OF AUTRECOURT TO BERNARD OF AREZZO

Reverend Father Bernard, the depth of your subtlety would truly bring forth the admiration of my mind, if I were to know that you possess evident knowledge of the separated substances[1]—the more so if I know this, but even if I had in my mind a slight belief. And not only, if I should think that you possess true cognition of the separated substances, but even of those conjoined to matter. And so to you, Father, who assert that you have evident cognition of such lofty objects of knowledge, I wish to lay bare my doubtful and anxious mind, so that you may have the materials for leading me

[1] The "separated substances" are immaterial substances, such as angels, or God, or Aristotle's "intelligences" associated with the celestial spheres were thought to be. Material bodies were called "conjoined" or "composite" substances, their forms being determinations of matter, and not capable of existing separately from matter.

and other people toward acquaintance with such great things.

And the first point is, that at the foundation of discourse this principle is primary: Contradictories cannot be simultaneously true. And with respect to this, two things hold: the first is, that this is the first principle, taken negatively as that than which nothing is more primary. The second is, that this is first, taken positively, as that which is prior to every other principle.

These two statements are proved by argument, as follows: Every certitude possessed by us reduces to this principle, and it in turn is not reduced to any other in the way that a conclusion is reduced to its premise; it therefore follows that this principle is first, with the twofold primacy indicated. This consequence is known from the meaning of the term "first," according to each of the expositions given. The antecedent is proved with respect to both of its parts. And first, with respect to its first part, namely that every certitude possessed by us, short of this certitude, reduces to this principle of which you say you are certain, I set forth this consequence: It is possible, without any contradiction being implied, that something will appear to you to be so, and yet that it will not be so; therefore you are not evidently certain that it is so. It is clear to me that if I were to admit this antecedent to be true, I would concede the consequent to be true; and therefore I would not be evidently and unqualifiedly certain of that of which I was saying that I was certain.[2]

From this it is clear that every one of our certitudes is resolved into our said principle, and that it is not resolved into another, as a conclusion into its premise. From this it is plain that all certitudes are resolved into this one, as was said, and that this consequence is valid: If this is prior to everything

---

2 This appears to be an argument *ad hominem* against Bernard's simultaneous claims that he is certain of the law of contradiction, and that it is possible for something to appear to him to be so, when it is not so. Nicolaus argues that if Bernard's second claim is conceded—namely that one can be certain of something that is not so —then it follows that he is conceding that contradictories can be simultaneously true; for he admits that that of which he is certain (the law of contradiction) is something of which he is uncertain.

other than itself, then nothing is prior to it. And thus it is first, with the twofold primacy above stated.

The third point is, that a contradiction is the affirmation and negation of the same (predicate) of the same (subject), etc., as is commonly said.

From these things I infer a corollary—namely, that the certitude of evidence which we have in the natural light, is certitude in the unqualified sense; for it is the certitude which is possessed in virtue of the first principle, which neither is nor can be contradicted by any true law. And hence whatever is demonstrated in the natural light of reason, is demonstrated without qualification; and, just as there is no power which can make contradictories simultaneously true, so there is no power by which it can come to pass that the opposite of the consequent is compatible with the antecedent.

The second corollary which I infer, with regard to this, is that the certitude of evidence has no degrees. Thus, if there are two conclusions, of each of which we are evidently certain, we are not more certain of one than of the other. For as was said, every certitude is resolved into the same first principle. Either, then, those first conclusions are reduced with equal immediacy to the same first principle—in which case there is no ground for our being more certain of one than of the other; or else one is reduced mediately, and the other immediately. But this makes no difference, because, once the reduction to the first principle has been made, we are certain of the one equally with the other—just as the geometrician says that he is as certain of a second conclusion as of the first, and similarly of the third and so on, even though in his first consideration, because of the plurality of the deductions, he cannot be as certain of the fourth or third as of the first.

The third corollary which I infer, in connection with what has been said, is that with the exception of the certitude of faith, there is no other certitude except the certitude of the first principle, or the certitude which can be resolved into the first principle. For there is no certitude except that in which there is no falsity; because, if there were any in which falsity could exist, let it be supposed that falsity does exist in it—

then, since the certitude itself remains, it follows that someone is certain of something whose contradictory is true, without contradiction.[3]

The fourth corollary is this: that a syllogistic form is immediately reducible to the first principle; because, by its demonstration, the conclusion is either immediately reduced (in which case the thesis holds), or else mediately; and if mediately, then either the regress will be infinite, or else it must arrive at some conclusion which reduces immediately to the first principle.

The fifth corollary: In every consequence which reduces immediately to the first principle, the consequent, and the antecedent either as a whole or in part, are really identical; because, if this were not so, then it would not be immediately evident that the antecedent and the opposite of the consequent cannot both be true.[4]

The sixth corollary is this: In every evident consequence reducible to the first principle by as many intermediates as you please, the consequent is really identical with the antecedent or with part of what is signified by the antecedent. This is shown because, if we suppose some conclusion to be

---

3 This is a similar argument to the previous one—namely, that if one can be certain of something which is false, he would be certain of something whose contradictory is true; and if this is possible, it follows that it is not self-contradictory to be certain of that whose contradictory is true. Hence Bernard cannot be certain of the law of contradiction, as he claims.

4 The statement that in every evident consequence whose evidence is based on the law of contradiction, the antecedent and consequent are "really identical," appears to refer to the type of consequence which was known as "simple material consequence." In such conditionals, the consequential relation is determined by what is now called "analytic necessity," or necessity due to inclusion of what one term signifies in what the other term signifies. For example, in the conditional "If a man walks, an animal walks," what is signified by the term "man" is included in what is signified by the term "animal"; hence the consequence holds by reason of the identity of the things designated by the subject-term of the antecedent, with things (or with part of the things) designated by the subject-term of the consequent. This identity is expressed by the additional proposition (needed to convert the above conditional into a formally valid syllogism), "Every man is an animal." Cf. E. A. Moody, *Truth and Consequence in Mediaeval Logic*, pp. 73-79.

reduced to the certitude of the first principle by three intermediates, the consequent will be really identical with its (immediate) antecedent or with part of what is signified by that antecedent, by the fifth corollary; and similarly in the second consequence, by the same reason; and thus, since in the first consequence the consequent is really identical with the antecedent or with part of what is signified by the antecedent, and likewise in the second one, and likewise in the third, it follows that in these consequences, ordered from first to last, the last consequent will be really identical with the first antecedent or with a part of what is signified by that antecedent.

On the basis of these statements, I laid down, along with other conclusions, one which was this: From the fact that some thing is known to exist, it cannot be evidently inferred, by evidence reduced to the first principle or to the certitude of the first principle, that some other thing exists.

Aside from many other arguments, I brought forth this argument. In such a consequence, in which from one thing another thing is inferred, the consequent would not be really identical with the antecedent or with part of what is signified by the antecedent; therefore it follows that such a consequence would not be evidently known with the said evidence of the first principle. The antecedent is conceded and posited by my opponent; the consequence is plain from the description of "contradiction," which is affirmation and negation of the same of the same, etc. Since therefore in this case the consequent is not really identical with the antecedent or its part, it is evident that if the opposite of the consequent, and the antecedent, be simultaneously true, this would not be a case of one thing being affirmed and denied of the same thing, etc.

But Bernard replies, saying that although in this case there is not a formal contradiction, for the reason given, yet there is a virtual contradiction; he calls a contradiction virtual, however, if from it a formal contradiction can be evidently inferred.

But against this we can argue manifestly, from the fifth

and sixth of the above corollaries. For it has been shown that in every consequence reducible either immediately or mediately to the certitude of the first principle, it is necessary that the consequent—whether the first one or the last—be really identical with the first antecedent or with a part of it.

Again, we may argue conclusively from another premise. For he says that, although in a consequence in which from one thing another thing is inferred, there is not a formal contradiction,[5] there is nevertheless a virtual one from which a formal one can be evidently inferred. Then let there be, for example, the following consequence propounded: "A exists, therefore B exists." If, then, from the propositions, "A exists," "B does not exist," a formal contradiction could be evidently inferred, this would be through a consequent of one of these propositions, or through a consequent of each of them. But whichever way it is, the thesis is not established. For these consequents would either be really identical with their antecedents, or they would not. If identical, then there will not be a formal contradiction between those consequents, since there will not then be an affirmation and a negation of the same predicate of the same subject, and hence not between the antecedents either. Just as it is not a formal contradiction to say that a rational animal exists and that a neighing animal does not exist; and for the same reason. But if it be said that these consequents differ from their antecedents, we argue the same way as before, that this is not a consequence evidently reduced to the certitude of the first principle, since the opposite of the consequent is compatible with whatever is signified by the antecedent, without contradiction. And if it be said that there is a virtual contradiction, from which a formal one can be inferred, we argue as before, either there is a regress with-

[5] The meaning is obviously that it would not involve a formal contradiction to affirm the existence of one thing and to deny the existence of another thing—since the affirmation and negation of the same predicate would not be of the same subject. If A and B are distinct things, the conjunctive statement "A exists and B does not exist" is not logically impossible; consequently the conditional "If A exists, then B exists" is not logically necessary. And the reason for this, according to Nicolaus of Autrecourt, is simply the fact that A is not identical with B.

out end, or else we must say that in a consequence evident without qualification the consequent is identical in its signification with the antecedent, or with part of what is signified by the antecedent.

And it is true that the reverend Father has said, with regard to this question, that it would not be true to say that in a consequence evident without qualification it is required that the opposite of the consequent, and the antecedent, cannot simultaneously be false, and that they are therefore not opposed as contradictories. But in actual fact this does not in any way prevent what I am maintaining. For I do not wish to say that the opposite of the consequent must be the contradictory of the antecedent—for in many consequences the antecedent can signify more than does the consequent, though the consequent signifies a part of what is signified by the antecedent—as in this consequence, "A house exists, therefore a wall exists." And on this account the opposite of the consequent, and the antecedent, can both be false. But I wish to say that in an evident consequence the opposite of the consequent, and the antecedent or a part of what it signifies, are opposed as contradictories. It is plain that this is the case in every valid syllogism; for since no term occurs in the conclusion which did not occur in the premises, the opposite of the conclusion, and something signified by the premises, are opposed as contradictories. And so it must be in every valid inference, because an enthymeme is only valid in virtue of a proposition presupposed—so that it is a kind of incomplete syllogism.[6]

Further, I offer this argument for my main conclusion: Never, in virtue of any inference, can there be inferred a greater identity of the extreme term, than that which is be-

---

[6] The type of consequence which was called a "material consequence" in fourteenth-century logic was assimilated to what Aristotle called an enthymeme or incomplete syllogism, because the validity of the material consequence depends on an identity of *designata* of the subject terms of the antecedent and consequent, which is made explicit by a "suppressed premise" which, if introduced as an additional antecedent, reduces the material consequence to a formally valid syllogism.

tween the extreme term and the middle term, because the former is only inferred in virtue of the latter. But the opposite of this will occur, if from the fact that one thing is a being, it could evidently be inferred that something else is a being; because the predicate of the conclusion, and the subject, signify what is really identical, whereas they are not really identical with the middle term which is posited as another thing.[7]

But Bernard objects to this proposed rule, because it follows evidently, with an evidence reduced to the certitude of the first principle, "Whiteness exists, therefore something else exists"—because whiteness cannot exist unless some subject maintains it in existence. Likewise it follows, "Whiteness is not a being in the primary sense, therefore some other thing exists." Or likewise, "Fire is brought into contact with the fuel, and there is no impediment, therefore there will be heat."

---

[7] Given a statement of the form "A exists," Nicolaus argues that another term B, designating something other than A, could not serve as a middle term through which the predicate "exists" (or "is a being") could be demonstrated of A; for if the conclusion "A is a being" is true, then the predicate "is a being" denotes what is denoted by the subject-term "A," whereas the alleged middle term "B," denoting something other than A, does not denote what is identical with A or with the being which is A. The subsequent argument applies this principle as follows: if a sensible quality such as a particular whiteness, is not identical with the substance that is said to be white or to have whiteness, one cannot validly infer from the sentence "Whiteness exists," the sentence, "A substance, in which whiteness inheres, exists." Since Bernard of Arezzo maintained that a sensible quality is an entity distinct from the substance to which it is attributed, Nicolaus here argues that inference from the existence of such a quality, to the existence of an underlying substance, is invalid; for the existence of one thing does not formally imply the existence of another distinct thing. And on the assumption that Aristotle also considered that sensible qualities are entities distinct from substances (which is perhaps a questionable assumption), Nicolaus argues that Aristotle never had evident knowledge of the existence of any material substance. Not by direct perception, since the direct objects of perception are qualities; and not by any valid inference from direct perception, because from the existence of one thing the existence of another distinct thing cannot be validly inferred. This is, of course, Hume's well-known argument against the possibility of establishing the existence of substances either by experience or by reason.

To these objections I have elsewhere given many answers. But for the present I say that if a thousand such objections were adduced, either it must be said that they are irrelevant, or, if relevant, that they conclude nothing against my position. Because in these consequences which he states, if the consequent is really identical in its signification with the antecedent as a whole or with a part of the antecedent, then the argument is not to the point, because in that case I would concede the consequences to be evident, and nothing against my position would be adduced. But if it be said that the consequent is not identical with the antecedent or part of it, then, if I concede the opposite of the consequent, and the antecedent, to be simultaneously true, it is plain that I am not conceding them to be contradictories, since contradictories are of the same predicate of the same subject, etc. And thus such a consequence is not evident by the evidence of the first principle, because the evidence of the first principle was understood to be had when, if it were conceded that the opposite of the consequent is compatible with the antecedent, contradictories would be admitted as simultaneously true. For though one might concede, with respect to this consequence "A house exists, therefore a wall exists," that a house exists and a wall does not exist, he does not thereby concede contradictories to be simultaneously true, because these propositions are not contradictories, "A house exists," "A wall does not exist," since both of them may be false; yet he does concede contradictories on another ground, because to signify that a house exists is to signify that a wall exists, and then it is a contradiction that a house exists and that a wall does not exist.

From this rule, so explained to anyone having the grasp of it, I infer that Aristotle never possessed an evident cognition concerning any substance other than his own soul—taking "substance" as a thing other than the objects of the five senses, and other than our formal experiences. And this is so, because he would have had a cognition of such a thing prior to every inference—which is not true, since they (substances) are not perceived intuitively, and since (if they were) rustics would know that such things exist; nor are they known by inference, namely as inferred from things perceived to exist antecedently to discursive thought—because from one thing it cannot be inferred that another thing exists, as the above conclusion states.

And if he did not have evident cognition of conjoined (material) substances, much less did he have it of abstract substances.[8] From which it follows, whether you like it or not, and not because I make it so but because reason determines it, that Aristotle in his whole natural philosophy and metaphysics had such certitude of scarcely two conclusions, and perhaps not even of one. And Father Bernard, who is not greater than Aristotle, has an equal amount of certitudes, or much less.

And not only did Aristotle not have evident cognition (of these things)—indeed, though I do not assert this, I have an argument which I cannot refute, to prove that he did not have probable knowledge. For a person does not have probable knowledge of any consequent, in virtue of some antecedent, when he is not evidently certain whether the consequent will at some time be true together with the antecedent. For let anyone really consider well the nature of probable knowledge—as for example that because it was at one time evident to me that when I put my hand in the fire I was hot, therefore it is probable to me that if I should put it there now I would be hot. But from the rule stated above, it follows that it was never evident to anyone that, given these things which are apparent without inference, there would ex-

---

[8] The "abstract substances" in question are those elsewhere called "separated substances," these being immaterial beings such as angels, God, Aristotle's "separated intelligences," and presumably rational souls. Of these direct perception (except possibly in the case of one's own soul) was not admitted by any of the Aristotelian philosophers of the Middle Ages; and since such abstract substances were not considered to have any sensible qualities inhering in them, even the inference from the existence of a perceived quality, to the substance underlying it, would not be applicable. And since this sort of inference has been shown by Nicolaus to be invalid, in the case of material substances with sensible accidents, *a fortiori* any inferential knowledge of the abstract substances is invalid or impossible.

ist certain other things—namely those others which are called substances. It therefore follows that of their existence we do not have probable knowledge. I do not assert this conclusion; but let this argument be resolved, for a solution will surely occur.[9]

And that we do not possess certitude concerning any substance conjoined to matter, other than our own soul, is plain—because, pointing to a piece of wood, or a stone, this conclusion will be most clearly deduced from a belief accepted at the same time. For by the divine power it can happen, with these things which appear prior to all inference, that no substance is there; therefore in the natural light of reason it is not evidently inferred from these appearances that a substance is there. This consequence is plain from what we explained above. For it was said that a consequence is evident only if it is a contradiction for it to occur, through any power, that the opposite of the consequent is true along with the antecedent. And if it is said that the consequence is evident, if to the antecedent we add "God is not performing a miracle," this is disproved by what we have said on this point in our first letter to Bernard.

I ask, Father, that you take up these doubts and give counsel to my stupidity; and I promise that I will not be stubborn in evading the truth, to which I adhere with all my strength.

---

[9] The distinction between certain and probable knowledge is here assimilated to the distinction between a *consequentia simplex* (or consequence valid without qualification), and a *consequentia ut nunc*, valid for a particular time. Cf. E. A. Moody, *Truth and Consequence in Mediaeval Logic*, pp. 74-75 and 79. Thus, during the time when my hand is in the fire, the consequence "If my hand is in the fire, my hand feels hot" is valid; but it is not necessary, though probable, that the consequence holds for any time in the future. The point here made by Nicolaus is that if at no time one can validly infer from the existence of a sensible quality, that a substance exists, such an inference cannot be even probable, because a probable inference is one which, on the basis of repeated evident experimental judgments in particular cases at particular times, asserts that the same connection will hold for all similar cases at other times. For a very full discussion of the arguments of these letters of Nicolaus of Autrecourt, see the book by Julius Weinberg, *Nicolaus of Autrecourt*, Princeton University Press, Princeton, N.J., 1948.

Suggestions for Further Reading

Weinberg, J. *Nicolaus of Autrecourt.* Princeton, 1948; Rashdall, H., "Nicholas de Ultricuria, A Mediaeval Hume," in *Proceedings of the Aristotelian Society,* 8 (1907); O'Donnell, J. R., "The Philosophy of Nicholas of Autrecourt and His Appraisal of Aristotle" in *Mediaeval Studies,* 4 (1942); *FCC* vol. III, 135-148; *EG* 505-511; *AAM* 289-291.

Jean Buridan

The known facts concerning Jean Buridan's life and career are extremely sparse. He seems to have been born at Béthune, France, at an unknown date. The first documentary mention of him is found in a statute of the University of Paris, dated 1328, in which his name is listed as Rector of the University. In 1340, Buridan was again appointed Rector. The last known date in his life is 1358, in which year he affixed his signature to a document concerning an agreement between Picard and English students at the University of Paris. It is generally assumed that Buridan died in that same year, 1358, of plague.

After William Ockham, philosophy as such became strongly oriented to the positive sciences and the mathematical disciplines. According to the estimates of modern scholars, Buridan was responsible for originating or developing some of the most essential ideas of the modern scientific tradition. The selection below, in which Buridan deals with special problems in dynamics, kinematics, and celestial mechanics, will provide the reader solid evidence of Buridan's scientific interest and genius.

JEAN BURIDAN AND THE IMPETUS THEORY OF PROJECTILE MOTION*

1. BOOK VIII, QUESTION 12. It is sought whether a projectile after leaving the hand of the projector is moved by the air, or by what it is moved.

It is argued that it is not moved by the air, because the air seems rather to resist, since it is necessary that it be divided. Furthermore, if you say that the projector in the beginning moved the projectile and the ambient air along with it, and then that air, having been moved, moves the projectile further to such and such a distance, the doubt will return as to by what the air is moved after the projectile ceases to move. For there is just as much difficulty regarding this (the air) as there is regarding the stone which is thrown.

Aristotle takes the opposite position in the eighth [book] of this work (the *Physics*) thus: "Projectiles are moved further after the projectors are no longer in contact with them, either by antiperistasis, as some say, or by the fact that the air having been pushed, pushes with a movement swifter than the movement of impulsion by which it (the body) is carried towards its own [natural] place." He determines the same thing in the seventh and eighth [books] of this work (the *Physics*) and in the third [book] of the *De caelo*.

2. This question I judge to be very difficult because Aristotle, as it seems to me, has not solved it well. For he touches on two opinions. The first one, which he calls "antiperistasis," holds that the projectile swiftly leaves the place in which it was, and nature, not permitting a vacuum, rapidly sends air

---

* Reprinted with the permission of the copyright owners, the Regents of the University of Wisconsin, from M. Clagett, *The Science of Mechanics In The Middle Ages*, 1959, The University of Wisconsin Press.

in behind to fill up the vacuum. The air moved swiftly in this way and impinging upon the projectile impels it along further. This is repeated continually up to a certain distance. . . . But such a solution notwithstanding, it seems to me that this method of proceeding was without value because of many experiences (*experientie*).

The first experience concerns the top (*trocus*) and the smith's mill (i.e. wheel—*mola fabri*) which are moved for a long time and yet do not leave their places. Hence, it is not necessary for the air to follow along to fill up the place of departure of a top of this kind and a smith's mill. So it cannot be said [that the top and the smith's mill are moved by the air] in this manner.

The second experience is this: A lance having a conical posterior as sharp as its anterior would be moved after projection just as swiftly as it would be without a sharp conical posterior. But surely the air following could not push a sharp end in this way, because the air would be easily divided by the sharpness.

The third experience is this: a ship drawn swiftly in the river even against the flow of the river, after the drawing has ceased, cannot be stopped quickly, but continues to move for a long time. And yet a sailor on deck does not feel any air from behind pushing him. He feels only the air from the front resisting [him]. Again, suppose that the said ship were loaded with grain or wood and a man were situated to the rear of the cargo. Then if the air were of such an impetus that it could push the ship along so strongly, the man would be pressed very violently between that cargo and the air following it. Experience shows this to be false. Or, at least, if the ship were loaded with grain or straw, the air following and pushing would fold over (*plico*) the stalks which were in the rear. This is all false.

3. Another opinion, which Aristotle seems to approve, is that the projector moves the air adjacent to the projectile [simultaneously] with the projectile and that air moved swiftly has the power of moving the projectile. He does not mean by this that the same air is moved from the place of projection to the place where the projectile stops, but rather that the air

joined to the projector is moved by the projector and that air having been moved moves another part of the air next to it, and that [part] moves another (i.e., the next) up to a certain distance. Hence the first air moves the projectile into the second air, and the second [air moves it] into the third air, and so on. Aristotle says, therefore, that there is not one mover but many in turn. Hence he also concludes that the movement is not continuous but consists of succeeding or contiguous entities.

But this opinion and method certainly seems to me equally as impossible as the opinion and method of the preceding view. For this method cannot solve the problem of how the top or smith's mill is turned after the hand [which sets them into motion] has been removed. Because, if you cut off the air on all sides near the smith's mill by a cloth (*linteamine*), the mill does not on this account stop but continues to move for a long time. Therefore it is not moved by the air.

Also a ship drawn swiftly is moved a long time after the haulers have stopped pulling it. The surrounding air does not move it, because if it were covered by a cloth and the cloth with the ambient air were withdrawn, the ship would not stop its motion on this account. And even if the ship were loaded with grain or straw and were moved by the ambient air, then that air ought to blow exterior stalks toward the front. But the contrary is evident, for the stalks are blown rather to the rear because of the resisting ambient air.

Again, the air, regardless of how fast it moves, is easily divisible. Hence it is not evident as to how it would sustain a stone of weight of one thousand pounds projected in a sling or in a machine.

Furthermore, you could, by pushing your hand, move the adjacent air, if there is nothing in your hand, just as fast or faster than if you were holding in your hand a stone which you wish to project. If, therefore, that air by reason of the velocity of its motion is of a great enough impetus to move the stone swiftly, it seems that if I were to impel air toward you equally as fast, the air ought to push you impetuously and with sensible strength. [Yet] we would not perceive this.

Also, it follows that you would throw a feather farther than a stone and something less heavy farther than something heavier, assuming equal magnitudes and shapes. Experience shows this to be false. The consequence is manifest, for the air having been moved ought to sustain or carry or move a feather more easily than something heavier. . . .

4. Thus we can and ought to say that in the stone or other projectile there is impressed something which is the motive force (*virtus motiva*) of that projectile. And this is evidently better than falling back on the statement that the air continues to move that projectile. For the air appears rather to resist. Therefore, it seems to me that it ought to be said that the motor in moving a moving body impresses (*imprimit*) in it a certain impetus (*impetus*) or a certain motive force (*vis motiva*) of the moving body, [which impetus acts] in the direction toward which the mover was moving the moving body, either up or down, or laterally, or circularly. *And by the amount the motor moves that moving body more swiftly, by the same amount it will impress in it a stronger impetus.* It is by that impetus that the stone is moved after the projector ceases to move. But that impetus is continually decreased (*remittitur*) by the resisting air and by the gravity of the stone, which inclines it in a direction contrary to that in which the impetus was naturally predisposed to move it. Thus the movement of the stone continually becomes slower, and finally that impetus is so diminished or corrupted that the gravity of the stone wins out over it and moves the stone down to its natural place.

This method, it appears to me, ought to be supported because the other methods do not appear to be true and also because all the appearances (*apparentia*) are in harmony with this method.

5. For if anyone seeks why I project a stone farther than a feather, and iron or lead fitted to my hand farther than just as much wood, I answer that the cause of this is that the reception of all forms and natural dispositions is in matter and by reason of matter. *Hence by the amount more there is of matter, by that amount can the body receive more of that impetus and more intensely* (intensius). *Now in a dense and heavy body,*

other things being equal, there is more of prime matter than in a rare and light one. Hence a dense and heavy body receives more of that impetus and more intensely, just as iron can receive more calidity than wood or water of the same quantity. Moreover, a feather receives such an impetus so weakly (*remisse*) that such an impetus is immediately destroyed by the resisting air. *And so also if light wood and heavy iron of the same volume and of the same shape are moved equally fast by a projector, the iron will be moved farther because there is impressed in it a more intense impetus, which is not so quickly corrupted as the lesser impetus would be corrupted. This also is the reason why it is more difficult to bring to rest a large smith's mill which is moving swiftly than a small one, evidently because in the large one, other things being equal, there is more impetus.* And for this reason you could throw a stone of one-half or one pound weight farther than you could a thousandth part of it. For the impetus in that thousandth part is so small that it is overcome immediately by the resisting air.

6. From this theory also appears the cause of why the natural motion of a heavy body downward is continually accelerated (*continue velocitatur*). For from the beginning only the gravity was moving it. Therefore, it moved more slowly, but in moving it impressed in the heavy body an impetus. This impetus now [acting] together with its gravity moves it. Therefore, the motion becomes faster; and by the amount it is faster, so the impetus becomes more intense. Therefore, the movement evidently becomes continually faster.

[The impetus then also explains why] one who wishes to jump a long distance drops back a way in order to run faster, so that by running he might acquire an impetus which would carry him a longer distance in the jump. Whence the person so running and jumping does not feel the air moving him, but [rather] feels the air in front strongly resisting him.

Also, since the Bible does not state that appropriate intelligences move the celestial bodies, it could be said that it does not appear necessary to posit intelligences of this kind, because it would be answered that God, when He created the world, moved each of the celestial orbs as He pleased, and in moving them He impressed in them impetuses which moved them without His having to move them any more except by the method of general influence whereby He concurs as a co-agent in all things which take place; "for thus on the seventh day He rested from all work which He had executed by committing to others the actions and the passions in turn." And these impetuses which He impressed in the celestial bodies were not decreased nor corrupted afterwards, because there was no inclination of the celestial bodies for other movements. Nor was there resistance which would be corruptive or repressive of that impetus. But this I do not say assertively, but [rather tentatively] so that I might seek from the theological masters what they might teach me in these matters as to how these things take place. . . .

7. The first [conclusion] is that that impetus is not the very local motion in which the projectile is moved, because that impetus moves the projectile and the mover produces motion. Therefore, the impetus produces that motion, and the same thing cannot produce itself. Therefore, etc.

Also since every motion arises from a motor being present and existing simultaneously with that which is moved, if the impetus were the motion, it would be necessary to assign some other motor from which that motion would arise. And the principal difficulty would return. Hence there would be no gain in positing such an impetus. But others cavil when they say that the prior part of the motion which produces the projection produces another part of the motion which is related successively and that produces another part and so on up to the cessation of the whole movement. But this is not probable, because the "producing something" ought to exist when the something is made, but the prior part of the motion does not exist when the posterior part exists, as was elsewhere stated. Hence, neither does the prior exist when the posterior is made. This consequence is obvious from this reasoning. For it was said elsewhere that motion is nothing else than "the very being produced" (*ipsum fieri*) and the "very being corrupted" (*ipsum corumpi*). Hence motion does not result when it *has been* produced (*factus est*) but when it *is being* produced (*fit*).

8. The second conclusion is that that impetus is not a purely successive thing (*res*), because motion is just such a thing and the definition of motion [as a successive thing] is fitting to it, as was stated elsewhere. And now it has just been affirmed that that impetus is not the local motion.

Also, since a purely successive thing is continually corrupted and produced, it continually demands a producer. But there cannot be assigned a producer of that impetus which would continue to be simultaneous with it.

9. The third conclusion is that that impetus is a thing of permanent nature (*res nature permanentis*), distinct from the local motion in which the projectile is moved. This is evident from the two aforesaid conclusions and from the preceding [statements]. And it is probable (*verisimile*) that that impetus is a quality naturally present and predisposed for moving a body in which it is impressed, just as it is said that a quality impressed in iron by a magnet moves the iron to the magnet. And it also is probable that just as that quality (the impetus) is impressed in the moving body along with the motion by the motor; so with the motion it is remitted, corrupted, or impeded by resistance or a contrary inclination.

10. And in the same way that a luminant generating light generates light reflexively because of an obstacle, so that impetus because of an obstacle acts reflexively. It is true, however, that other causes aptly concur with that impetus for greater or longer reflection. For example, the ball which we bounce with the palm in falling to earth is reflected higher than a stone, although the stone falls more swiftly and more impetuously (*impetuosius*) to the earth. This is because many things are curvable or intracompressible by violence which are innately disposed to return swiftly and by themselves to their correct position or to the disposition natural to them. In thus returning, they can impetuously push or draw something conjunct to them, as is evident in the case of the bow (*arcus*). Hence in this way the ball thrown to the hard ground is compressed into itself by the impetus of its motion; and immediately

after striking, it returns swiftly to its sphericity by elevating itself upward. From this elevation it acquires to itself an impetus which moves it upward a long distance.

Also, it is this way with a cither cord which, put under strong tension and percussion, remains a long time in a certain vibration (*tremulatio*) from which its sound continues a notable time. And this takes place as follows: As a result of striking [the chord] swiftly, it is bent violently in one direction, and so it returns swiftly toward its normal straight position. But on account of the impetus, it crosses beyond the normal straight position in the contrary direction and then again returns. It does this many times. For a similar reason a bell (*campana*), after the ringer ceases to draw [the chord], is moved a long time, first in one direction, now in another. And it cannot be easily and quickly brought to rest.

This, then, is the exposition of the question. I would be delighted if someone would discover a more probable way of answering it. And this is the end.

JEAN BURIDAN ON THE FREE FALL OF BODIES

1. BOOK II, QUESTION 12. Whether natural motion ought to be swifter in the end than the beginning. . . . With respect to this question it ought to be said that it is a conclusion not to be doubted factually (*quia est*), for, as it has been said, all people perceive that the motion of a heavy body downward is continually accelerated (*magis ac magis velocitatur*), it having been posited that it falls through a uniform medium. For everybody perceives that by the amount that a stone descends over a greater distance and falls on a man, by that amount does it more seriously injure him.

2. But the great difficulty (*dubitatio*) in this question is why this [acceleration] is so. Concerning this matter there have been many different opinions. The Commentator (Averroës) in the second book [of his commentary on the *De caelo*] ventures some obscure statements on it, declaring that a heavy body approaching the end is moved more swiftly because of a great

desire for the end and because of the heating action (*calefactionem*) of its motion. From these statements two opinions have sprouted.

3. The first opinion was that motion produces heat, as it is said in the second book of this [work, the *De caelo*], and, therefore, a heavy body descending swiftly through the air makes that air hot, and consequently it (the air) becomes rarefied. The air, thus rarefied, is more easily divisible and less resistant. Now, if the resistance is diminished, it is reasonable that the movement becomes swifter.

But this argument is insufficient. In the first place, because the air in the summer is noticeably hotter than in the winter, and yet the same stone falling an equal distance in the summer and in the winter is not moved with appreciably greater speed in the summer than in the winter; nor does it strike harder. Furthermore, the air does not become hot through movement unless it is previously moved and divided. Therefore, since the air resists before there has been movement or division, the resistance is not diminished by its heating. Furthermore, a man moves his hand just as swiftly as a stone falls toward the beginning of its movement. This is apparent, because striking another person hurts him more than the falling stone, even if the stone is harder. And yet a man so moving his hand does not heat the air sensibly, since he would perceive that heating. Therefore, in the same way the stone, at least from the beginning of the case, does not thus sensibly heat the air to the extent that it ought to produce so manifest an acceleration (*velocitatio*) as is apparent at the end of the movement.

4. The other opinion which originated from the statements of the Commentator is this: Place is related to the thing placed as a final cause, as Aristotle implies and the Commentator explains in the fourth book of the *Physics*. And some say, in addition to this, that place is the cause moving the heavy body by a method of attraction, just as a magnet attracts iron. By whichever of these methods it takes place, it seems reasonable that the heavy body is moved more swiftly by the same amount that it is nearer to its natural place. This is because, if place is the moving cause, then it can move that body more strongly

when the body is nearer to it, for an agent acts more strongly on something near to it than on something far away from it. And if place were nothing but the final cause which the heavy body seeks naturally and for the attainment of which the body is moved, then it seems reasonable that that natural appetite (*appetitus*) for that end is increased more from it as that end is nearer. And so it seems in every way reasonable that a heavy body is moved more swiftly by the amount that it is nearer to [its] downward place. But in descending continually it ought to be moved more and more swiftly.

But this opinion cannot stand up. In the first place, it is against Aristotle and against the Commentator in the first book of the *De caelo,* where they assert that, if there were several worlds, the earth of the other world would be moved to the middle of this world. . . .

Furthermore, this opinion is against manifest experience, for you can lift the same stone near the earth just as easily as you can in a high place if that stone were there, for example, at the top of a tower. This would not be so if it had a stronger inclination toward the downward place when it was low than when it was high. It is responded that actually there is a greater inclination when the stone is low than when it is high, but it is not great enough for the senses to perceive. This response is not valid, because if that stone falls continually from the top of the tower to the earth, a double or triple velocity and a double or triple injury would be sensed near the earth than would be sensed higher up near the beginning of the movement. Hence, there is a double or triple cause of the velocity. And so it follows that that inclination which you posit not to be sensible or notable is not the cause of such an increase of velocity.

Again, let a stone begin to fall from a high place to the earth and another similar stone begin to fall from a low place to the earth. Then these stones, when they should be at a distance of one foot from the earth, ought to be moved equally fast and one ought not to be swifter than the other if the greater velocity should arise only from nearness to [their] natural place, because they should be equally near to [their] natural place. Yet it is manifest to the senses that the body which should fall from the high point would be moved much more quickly than that which should fall from the low point, and it would kill a man while the other stone [falling from the low point] would not hurt him.

Again, if a stone falls from an exceedingly high place through a space of ten feet and then encountering there an obstacle comes to rest, and if a similar stone descends from a low point to the earth, also through a distance of ten feet, neither of these movements will appear to be any swifter than the other, even though one is nearer to the natural place of earth than the other.

I conclude, therefore, that the accelerated natural movements of heavy and light bodies do not arise from greater proximity to [their] natural place, but from something else that is either near or far, but which is varied by reason of the length of the motion (*ratione longitudinis motus*). Nor is the case of the magnet and the iron similar, because if the iron is nearer to the magnet, it immediately will begin to be moved more swiftly than if it were farther away. But such is not the case with a heavy body in relation to its natural place.

5. The third opinion was that the more the heavy body descends, by so much less is there air beneath it, and the less air then can resist less. And if the resistance is decreased and the moving gravity remains the same, it follows that the heavy body ought to be moved more swiftly.

But this opinion falls into the same inconsistency as the preceding one, because, as was said before, if two bodies similar throughout begin to fall, one from an exceedingly high place and the other from a low place such as a distance of ten feet from the earth, those bodies in the beginning of their motion are moved equally fast, notwithstanding the fact that one of them has a great deal of air beneath it and the other has only a little. Hence, throughout, the greater velocity does not arise from greater proximity to the earth or because the body has less air beneath it, but from the fact that that moving body is moved from a longer distance and through a longer space.

Again, it is not true that the less air in the aforementioned case resists less. This is because, when a stone is near the earth, there is still just as much air laterally as if it were farther from the earth. Hence, it is just as difficult for the divided air to give way and flee laterally [near the earth] as it was when the stone was farther from the earth. And, in addition, it is equally difficult or more difficult, when the stone is nearer the earth, for the air underneath to give way in a straight line, because the earth, which is more resistant than the air, is in the way. Hence, the imagined solution (*imaginatio*) is not valid.

6. With the [foregoing] methods of solving this question set aside, there remains, it seems to me, one necessary solution (*imaginatio*). It is my supposition that the natural gravity of this stone remains always the same and similar before the movement, after the movement, and during the movement. Hence the stone is found to be equally heavy after the movement as it was before it. I suppose also that the resistance which arises from the medium remains the same or is similar, since, as I have said, it does not appear to me that the air lower and near to the earth should be less resistant than the superior air. Rather the superior air perhaps ought to be less resistant because it is more subtle. Third, I suppose that if the moving body is the same, the total mover is the same, and the resistance also is the same or similar, the movement will remain equally swift, since the proportion of mover to moving body and to the resistance will remain [the same]. Then I add that in the movement downward of the heavy body the movement does not remain equally fast but continually becomes swifter.

From these [suppositions] it is concluded that another moving force (*movens*) concurs in that movement beyond the natural gravity which was moving [the body] from the beginning and which remains always the same. Then finally I say that this other mover is not the place which attracts the heavy body as the magnet does the iron; nor is it some force (*virtus*) existing in the place and arising either from the heavens or from something else, because it would immediately follow that the same heavy body would begin to be moved more swiftly from a low place than from a high one, and we experience the contrary of this conclusion. . . .

From these [reasons] it follows that one must imagine that a heavy body not only acquires motion unto itself from its principal mover, i.e., its gravity, but that it also acquires unto itself a certain impetus with that motion. This impetus has the power of moving the heavy body in conjunction with the permanent natural gravity. And because that impetus is acquired in common with motion, hence the swifter the motion is, the greater and stronger the impetus is. So, therefore, from the beginning the heavy body is moved by its natural gravity only; hence it is moved slowly. Afterwards it is moved by that same gravity and by the impetus acquired at the same time; consequently, it is moved more swiftly. And because the movement becomes swifter, therefore the impetus also becomes greater and stronger, and thus the heavy body is moved by its natural gravity and by that greater impetus simultaneously, and so it will again be moved faster; and thus it will always and continually be accelerated to the end. And just as the impetus is acquired in common with motion, so it is decreased or becomes deficient in common with the decrease and deficiency of the motion.

And you have an experiment [to support this position]: If you cause a large and very heavy smith's mill [i.e., a wheel] to rotate and you then cease to move it, it will still move a while longer by this impetus it has acquired. Nay, you cannot immediately bring it to rest, but on acount of the resistance from the gravity of the mill, the impetus would be continually diminished until the mill would cease to move. And if the mill would last forever without some diminution or alteration of it, and there were no resistance corrupting the impetus, perhaps the mill would be moved perpetually by that impetus.

7. And thus one could imagine that it is unnecessary to posit intelligences as the movers of celestial bodies since the Holy Scriptures do not inform us that intelligences must be posited. For it could be said that when God created the celestial spheres, He began to move each of them as He wished, and they are still moved by the impetus which He gave to them because, there being no resistance, the impetus is neither corrupted nor diminished.

You should note that some people have called that impetus "accidental gravity" and they do so aptly, because names are for felicity of expression. Whence this [name] appears to be harmonious with Aristotle and the Commentator in the first [book] of this [work, the *De caelo*], where they say that gravity would be infinite if a heavy body were moved infinitely, because by the amount that it is moved more, by that same amount is it moved more swiftly; and by the amount that it is moved more swiftly, by that amount is the gravity greater. If this is true, therefore, it is necessary that a heavy body in moving acquires continually more gravity, and that gravity is not of the same constitution (*ratio*) or nature as the first natural gravity, because the first gravity remains always, even with the movement stopped, while the acquired gravity does not remain. All of these statements will appear more to be true and necessary when the violent movements of projectiles and other things are investigated. . . .

JEAN BURIDAN ON THE DIURNAL ROTATION OF THE EARTH

1. BOOK II, QUESTION 22. It is sought consequently whether the earth always is at rest in the center of the universe. . . .

This question is difficult. For in the first place there is a significant doubt as to whether the earth is directly in the middle of the universe so that its center coincides with the center of the universe. Furthermore, there is a strong doubt as to whether it is not sometimes moved rectilinearly as a whole, since we do not doubt that often many of its parts are moved, for this is apparent to us through our senses. There is also another difficult doubt as to whether the following conclusion of Aristotle is sound, namely, if the heaven is by necessity to be moved circularly forever, then it is necessary that the earth be at rest forever in the middle. There is also a fourth doubt whether, in positing that the earth is moved circularly around its own center and about its own poles, all the phenomena that are apparent to us can be saved (*possent salvari omnia nobis apparentia*). Concerning this last doubt let us now speak.

2. It should be known that many people have held as probable that it is not contradictory to appearances for the earth to be moved circularly in the aforesaid manner, and that on any given natural day it makes a complete rotation from west to east by returning again to the west—that is, if some part of the earth were designated [as the part to observe]. Then it is necessary to posit that the stellar sphere would be at rest, and then night and day would take place through such a motion of the earth, so that that motion of the earth would be a diurnal motion (*motus diurnus*). The following is an example of this [kind of thing]: If anyone is moved in a ship and he imagines that he is at rest, then, should he see another ship which is truly at rest, it will appear to him that the other ship is moved. This is so because his eye would be completely in the same relationship to the other ship regardless of whether his own ship is at rest and the other moved, or the contrary situation prevailed. And so we also posit that the sphere of the sun is everywhere at rest and the earth in carrying us would be rotated. Since, however, we imagine that we are at rest, just as the man located on the ship which is moving swiftly does not perceive his own motion nor the motion of the ship, then it is certain that the sun would appear to us to rise and then to set, just as it does when it is moved and we are at rest.

3. It is true, however, that if the stellar sphere is at rest, it is necessary to concede generally that the spheres of the planets are moving, since otherwise the planets would not change their positions relative to each other and to the fixed stars. And, therefore, this opinion imagines that any of the spheres of the planets moved evidently like the earth from west to east, but since the earth has a lesser circle, hence it makes its rotation (*circulatio*) in less time. Consequently, the moon makes its rotation in less time than the sun. And this is universally true, so that the earth completes its rotation in a natural day, the moon in a month, and the sun in a year, etc.

4. It is undoubtedly true that, if the situation were just as this position posits, all the celestial phenomena would appear to us just as they now appear. We should know likewise that those persons wishing to sustain this opinion, perhaps for

reason of disputation, posit for it certain persuasions. . . . The third persuasion is this: To celestial bodies ought to be attributed the nobler conditions, and to the highest sphere, the noblest. But it is nobler and more perfect to be at rest than to be moved. Therefore, the highest sphere ought to be at rest. . . .

The last persuasion is this: Just as it is better to save the appearances through fewer causes then through many, if this is possible, so it is better to save [them] by an easier way than by one more difficult. Now it is easier to move a small thing than a large one. Hence it is better to say that the earth, which is very small, is moved most swiftly and the highest sphere is at rest than to say the opposite.

5. But still this opinion is not to be followed. In the first place because it is against the authority of Aristotle and of all the astronomers (*astrologi*). But these people respond that *authority does not demonstrate,* and that it suffices astronomers that they posit a method by which appearances are saved, whether or not it is so in actuality. Appearances can be saved in either way; hence they posit the method which is more pleasing to them.

6. Others argue [against the theory of the earth's diurnal rotation] by many appearances (*apparentiis*). One of these is that the stars sensibly appear to us to be moved from the east to the west. But they solve this [by saying] that it would appear the same if the stars were at rest and the earth were moved from west to east.

7. Another appearance is this: If anyone were moving very swiftly on horseback, he would feel the air resisting him. Therefore, similarly, with the very swift motion of the earth in motion, we ought to feel the air noticeably resisting us. But these [supporters of the opinion] respond that the earth, the water, and the air in the lower region are moved simultaneously with diurnal motion. Consequently there is no air resisting us.

8. Another appearance is this: Since local motion heats, and therefore since we and the earth are moved so swiftly, we should be made hot. But these [supporters] respond that mo-

tion does not produce heat except by the friction (*confricatio*), rubbing, or separation of bodies. These [causes] would not be applicable there, since the air, water, and earth would be moved together.

9. But the last appearance which Aristotle notes is more demonstrative in the question at hand. This is that an arrow projected from a bow directly upward falls again in the same spot of the earth from which it was projected. This would not be so if the earth were moved with such velocity. Rather before the arrow falls, the part of the earth from which the arrow was projected would be a league's distance away. But still the supporters would respond that it happens so because the air, moved with the earth, carries the arrow, although the arrow appears to us to be moved simply in a straight line motion because it is being carried along with us. Therefore, we do not perceive that motion by which it is carried with the air. But this evasion is not sufficient because the violent impetus of the arrow in ascending would resist the lateral motion of the air so that it would not be moved as much as the air. This is similar to the occasion when the air is moved by a high wind. For then an arrow projected upward is not moved as much laterally as the wind is moved, although it would be moved somewhat. . . .

10. Then I come to the other doubts. One would be whether the earth is situated directly in the middle of the universe. It should be answered in the affirmative. For we suppose that the place [designated] absolutely (*simpliciter*) as "upward," insofar as one looks at this lower world, is the concave [surface] of the orb of the moon. This is so because something absolutely light, i.e., fire, is moved toward it. For since fire appears to ascend in the air, it follows that fire naturally seeks a place above the air, and this place above the air is at the concave [surface] of the orb of the moon; because no other element appears to be so swiftly moved upward as fire. Now the place downward ought to be the maximum distance from the place upward, since they are contrary places. Now that which is the maximum distance from the heaven is the middle of the universe. Therefore the middle of the universe is absolutely

downward. But that which is absolutely heavy—and earth is of this sort—ought to be situated absolutely downward. Therefore, the earth naturally ought to be *in* the middle of the universe or *be* the middle of the universe.

11. But it is a significant difficulty as to whether the center of magnitude in the earth is the same as the center of gravity (*medium gravitatis*). It seems according to some statements that it is not. This is because if a large region of the earth is not covered with waters due to the habitation of animals and plants, and the opposite part is covered with waters, it is clear that the air which is naturally hot, and the sun, make hot the noncovered part, and thus they make it to some degree more subtle, rarer, and lighter. The covered part remains more compact and heavier. Now if one body in one part is lighter and in an opposite part heavier, the center of gravity will not be the center of magnitude. Rather with the center of gravity given, the greater magnitude will be in the lighter part, just as in the case of balances if on one side a stone is placed and on the other side wool [and they balance], the wool will be of a much greater magnitude.

12. With this understood, it ought to be seen which of those centers is the center of the universe. It should be answered immediately that the center of the universe is the center of gravity of the earth. This is because, as Aristotle says, all parts tend toward the center of the universe through their gravity, and a part which is heavier would displace another, and thus finally it is necessary that the center of the universe coincide with the center of gravity. From these arguments it follows that the earth is nearer to the heaven in the part not covered with waters than in the covered part, and thus at the covered part there is greater declivity, and so the waters flow to that part. So, therefore, the earth, with respect to its magnitude, is not directly in the center of the universe. We commonly say, however, that it is in the center of the universe, because its center of gravity is the center of the universe.

13. By this another doubt is solved, evidently, whether the earth is sometimes moved according to its whole in a straight line. We can answer in the affirmative because from this

higher [part of] the earth many parts of the earth (i.e., debris) continually flow along with the rivers to the bottom of the sea, and thus the earth is augmented in the covered part and is diminished in the uncovered part. Consequently, the center of gravity does not remain the same as it was before. Now, therefore, with the center of gravity changed, that which has newly become the center of gravity is moved so that it will coincide with the center of the universe, and that point which was the center of gravity before ascends and recedes, and thus the whole earth is elevated toward the uncovered part so that the center of gravity might always become the center of the universe. And just as I have said elsewhere, it is not apparent how it could be saved unless the mountains were consumed and destroyed sometimes, nay infinite times, if time were eternal. Nor is any other way apparent by which such mountains could be generated. This was spoken of elsewhere, so I shall now desist. . . .

Suggestions for Further Reading

Thorndike, Lynn. *History of Magic and Experimental Science.* Vols. I-IV. New York, 1929-34; Clagett, M. *Science of Mechanics in the Middle Ages.* Madison, 1959; Sarton, G. *Introduction to the History of Science.* Vol. III. Baltimore, 1927-48; *FCC* vol. III, 154 *et passim; EG* 511-516; *AAM* 254-264.

The Best of the World's Best Books

COMPLETE LIST OF TITLES IN

THE MODERN LIBRARY

76 ADAMS, HENRY: *The Education of Henry Adams*
310 AESCHYLUS: *The Complete Greek Tragedies*, Vol. I
311 AESCHYLUS: *The Complete Greek Tragedies*, Vol. II
101 AIKEN, CONRAD (Editor): *A Comprehensive Anthology of American Poetry*
127 AIKEN, CONRAD (Editor): *20th-Century American Poetry*
145 ALEICHEM, SHOLOM: *Selected Stories*
104 ANDERSON, SHERWOOD: *Winesburg, Ohio*
259 AQUINAS, ST. THOMAS: *Introduction to St. Thomas Aquinas*
248 ARISTOTLE: *Introduction to Aristotle*
228 ARISTOTLE: *Politics*
246 ARISTOTLE: *Rhetoric and Poetics*
160 AUDEN, W. H.: *Selected Poetry*
263 AUGUSTINE, ST.: *Confessions*
264 AUSTEN, JANE: *Pride and Prejudice* and *Sense and Sensibility*

256 BACON, FRANCIS: *Selected Writings*
299 BALZAC: *Cousin Bette*
193 BALZAC: *Droll Stories*
245 BALZAC: *Père Goriot* and *Eugénie Grandet*
116 BEERBOHM, MAX: *Zuleika Dobson*
22 BELLAMY, EDWARD: *Looking Backward*
184 BENNETT, ARNOLD: *The Old Wives' Tale*
231 BERGSON, HENRI: *Creative Evolution*
285 BLAKE, WILLIAM: *Selected Poetry and Prose*
71 BOCCACCIO: *The Decameron*
282 BOSWELL, JAMES: *The Life of Samuel Johnson*
64 BRONTË, CHARLOTTE: *Jane Eyre*
106 BRONTË, EMILY: *Wuthering Heights*
198 BROWNING, ROBERT: *Selected Poetry*
15 BUCK, PEARL: *The Good Earth*
32 BURCKHARDT, JACOB: *The Civilization of the Renaissance in* [*Italy*
241 BURK, JOHN N.: *The Life and Works of Beethoven*
289 BURKE, EDMUND: *Selected Writings*
136 BUTLER, SAMUEL: *Erewhon* and *Erewhon Revisited*
13 BUTLER, SAMUEL: *The Way of All Flesh*
195 BYRON, LORD: *Selected Poetry*
24 BYRON, LORD: *Don Juan*

295 CAESAR, JULIUS: *The Gallic War and Other Writings*
51 CALDWELL, ERSKINE: *God's Little Acre*

249 Caldwell, Erskine: *Tobacco Road*
109 Camus, Albert: *The Plague*
339 Camus, Albert: *Resistance, Rebellion and Death*
79 Carroll, Lewis: *Alice in Wonderland,* etc.
165 Casanova, Jacques: *Memoirs of Casanova*
150 Cellini, Benvenuto: *Autobiography of Cellini*
174 Cervantes: *Don Quixote*
161 Chaucer: *The Canterbury Tales*
171 Chekhov, Anton: *Best Plays*
50 Chekhov, Anton: *Short Stories*
272 Cicero: *Basic Works*
279 Coleridge: *Selected Poetry and Prose*
251 Colette: *Six Novels*
235 Commager, Henry Steele & Nevins, Allan: *A Short History of the United States*
306 Confucius: *The Wisdom of Confucius*
186 Conrad, Joseph: *Lord Jim*
275 Conrad, Joseph: *Nostromo*
34 Conrad, Joseph: *Victory*
105 Cooper, James Fenimore: *The Pathfinder*
194 Corneille & Racine: *Six Plays by Corneille and Racine*
130 Crane, Stephen: *The Red Badge of Courage*
214 Cummings, E. E.: *The Enormous Room*

236 Dana, Richard Henry: *Two Years Before the Mast*
208 Dante: *The Divine Comedy*
122 Defoe, Daniel: *Moll Flanders*
92 Defoe, Daniel: *Robinson Crusoe* and *A Journal of the Plague Year*
43 Descartes, René: *Philosophical Writings*
173 Dewey, John: *Human Nature and Conduct*
110 Dickens, Charles: *David Copperfield*
204 Dickens, Charles: *Pickwick Papers*
308 Dickens, Charles: *Our Mutual Friend*
189 Dickens, Charles: *A Tale of Two Cities*
25 Dickinson, Emily: *Selected Poems*
23 Dinesen, Isak: *Out of Africa*
54 Dinesen, Isak: *Seven Gothic Tales*
12 Donne, John: *Complete Poetry and Selected Prose*
205 Dos Passos, John: *Three Soldiers*
293 Dostoyevsky, Fyodor: *Best Short Stories*
151 Dostoyevsky, Fyodor: *The Brothers Karamazov*
199 Dostoyevsky, Fyodor: *Crime and Punishment*
55 Dostoyevsky, Fyodor: *The Possessed*
5 Douglas, Norman: *South Wind*
206 Doyle, Sir Arthur Conan: *The Adventures and Memoirs of Sherlock Holmes*
8 Dreiser, Theodore: *Sister Carrie*
69 Dumas, Alexandre: *Camille*
143 Dumas, Alexandre: *The Three Musketeers*
227 Du Maurier, Daphne: *Rebecca*

338 Ellison, Ralph: *Invisible Man*
192 Emerson, Ralph Waldo: *The Journals*
91 Emerson, Ralph Waldo: *Essays and Other Writings*
331 Erasmus, Desiderius: *The Praise of Folly*

314 EURIPIDES: *The Complete Greek Tragedies*, Vol. V
315 EURIPIDES: *The Complete Greek Tragedies*, Vol. VI
316 EURIPIDES: *The Complete Greek Tragedies*, Vol. VII

271 FAULKNER, WILLIAM: *Absalom, Absalom!*
175 FAULKNER, WILLIAM: *Go Down, Moses*
88 FAULKNER, WILLIAM: *Light in August*
61 FAULKNER, WILLIAM: *Sanctuary*
187 FAULKNER, WILLIAM: *The Sound and the Fury* and *As I Lay [Dying*
324 FAULKNER, WILLIAM: *Selected Short Stories*
117 FIELDING, HENRY: *Joseph Andrews*
185 FIELDING, HENRY: *Tom Jones*
28 FLAUBERT, GUSTAVE: *Madame Bovary*
102 FORESTER, C. S.: *The African Queen*
210 FRANCE, ANATOLE: *Penguin Island*
298 FRANK, ANNE: *Diary of a Young Girl*
39 FRANKLIN, BENJAMIN: *Autobiography*, etc.
96 FREUD, SIGMUND: *The Interpretation of Dreams*

36 GEORGE, HENRY: *Progress and Poverty*
327 GIDE, ANDRÉ: *The Counterfeiters*
177 GOETHE: *Faust*
40 GOGOL, NIKOLAI: *Dead Souls*
291 GOLDSMITH, OLIVER: *The Vicar of Wakefield and Other [Writings*
20 GRAVES, ROBERT: *I, Claudius*
286 GUNTHER, JOHN: *Death Be Not Proud*

265 HACKETT, FRANCIS: *The Personal History of Henry the Eighth*
163 HAGGARD, H. RIDER: *She* and *King Solomon's Mines*
320 HAMILTON, EDITH: *The Greek Way*
135 HARDY, THOMAS: *Jude the Obscure*
17 HARDY, THOMAS: *The Mayor of Casterbridge*
121 HARDY, THOMAS: *The Return of the Native*
72 HARDY, THOMAS: *Tess of the D'Urbervilles*
233 HART & KAUFMAN: *Six Plays*
329 HART, MOSS: *Act One*
250 HARTE, BRET: *Best Stories*
93 HAWTHORNE, NATHANIEL: *The Scarlet Letter*
239 HEGEL: *The Philosophy of Hegel*
223 HELLMAN, LILLIAN: *Six Plays*
26 HENRY, O.: *Best Short Stories*
255 HERODOTUS: *The Persian Wars*
328 HERSEY, JOHN: *Hiroshima*
334 HESSE, HERMAN: *Steppenwolf*
166 HOMER: *The Iliad*
167 HOMER: *The Odyssey*
141 HORACE: *Complete Works*
302 HOWARD, JOHN TASKER: *World's Great Operas*
277 HOWELLS, WILLIAM DEAN: *The Rise of Silas Lapham*
89 HUDSON, W. H.: *Green Mansions*
35 HUGO, VICTOR: *The Hunchback of Notre Dame*
340 HUME, DAVID: *Philosophy*
209 HUXLEY, ALDOUS: *Antic Hay*
48 HUXLEY, ALDOUS: *Brave New World*
180 HUXLEY, ALDOUS: *Point Counter Point*

305 IBSEN, HENRIK: *Six Plays*

307	Ibsen, Henrik: *The Wild Duck and Other Plays*
240	Irving, Washington: *Selected Writings*
16	James, Henry: *The Bostonians*
107	James, Henry: *The Portrait of a Lady*
169	James, Henry: *The Turn of the Screw*
269	James, Henry: *Washington Square*
244	James, Henry: *The Wings of the Dove*
114	James, William: *The Philosophy of William James*
70	James, William: *The Varieties of Religious Experience*
234	Jefferson, Thomas: *The Life* and *Selected Writings*
124	Joyce, James: *Dubliners*
300	Jung, C. G.: *Basic Writings*
318	Kafka, Franz: *The Trial*
283	Kafka, Franz: *Selected Stories*
297	Kant: *Critique of Pure Reason*
266	Kant: *The Philosophy of Kant*
233	Kaufman & Hart: *Six Plays*
273	Keats: *Complete Poetry and Selected Prose*
303	Kierkegaard, Søren: *A Kierkegaard Anthology*
99	Kipling, Rudyard: *Kim*
74	Koestler, Arthur: *Darkness at Noon*
262	Laotse: *The Wisdom of Laotse*
148	Lawrence, D. H.: *Lady Chatterley's Lover*
128	Lawrence, D. H.: *The Rainbow*
333	Lawrence, D. H.: *Sons and Lovers*
68	Lawrence, D. H.: *Women in Love*
252	Lewis, Sinclair: *Dodsworth*
221	Lewis, Sinclair: *Cass Timberlane*
325	Livy: *A History of Rome*
56	Longfellow, Henry W.: *Poems*
77	Louys, Pierre: *Aphrodite*
95	Ludwig, Emil: *Napoleon*
65	Machiavelli: *The Prince* and *The Discourses*
321	Mailer, Norman: *The Naked and the Dead*
317	Malamud, Bernard: *Two Novels*
33	Malraux, André: *Man's Fate*
309	Malthus, Thomas Robert: *On Population*
182	Marquand, John P.: *The Late George Apley*
202	Marx, Karl: *Capital and Other Writings*
14	Maugham, W. Somerset: *Best Short Stories*
270	Maugham, W. Somerset: *Cakes and Ale*
27	Maugham, W. Somerset: *The Moon and Sixpence*
176	Maugham, W. Somerset: *Of Human Bondage*
98	Maupassant, Guy de: *Best Short Stories*
46	Maurois, André: *Disraeli*
119	Melville, Herman: *Moby Dick*
253	Meredith, George: *The Egoist*
134	Meredith, George: *The Ordeal of Richard Feverel*
138	Merejkowski, Dmitri: *The Romance of Leonardo da Vinci*
296	Michener, James A.: *Selected Writings*
322	Mill, John Stuart: *Selections*
132	Milton, John: *Complete Poetry and Selected Prose*
78	Molière: *Eight Plays*
218	Montaigne: *Selected Essays*

343 Nash, Ogden: *Verses From 1929 On*
235 Nevins, Allan & Commager, Henry Steele: *A Short History of the United States*
113 Newman, Cardinal John H.: *Apologia Pro Vita Sua*
9 Nietzsche, Friedrich: *Thus Spake Zarathustra*
81 Nostradamus: *Oracles*

67 Odets, Clifford: *Six Plays*
42 O'Hara, John: *Appointment in Samarra*
211 O'Hara, John: *Selected Short Stories*
323 O'Hara, John: *Butterfield 8*
342 O'Neill, Eugene: *Ah, Wilderness! and Two Other Plays*
146 O'Neill, Eugene: *The Emperor Jones, Anna Christie* and *The Hairy Ape*
111 O'Neill, Eugene: *The Long Voyage Home: Seven Plays of the Sea*

232 Palgrave, Francis (Editor): *The Golden Treasury*
123 Parker, Dorothy: *Collected Short Stories*
237 Parker, Dorothy: *Collected Poetry*
267 Parkman, Francis: *The Oregon Trail*
164 Pascal, Blaise: *Penseés* and *The Provincial Letters*
86 Pater, Walter: *The Renaissance*
103 Pepys, Samuel: *Passages from the Diary*
247 Perelman, S. J.: *The Best of S. J. Perelman*
153 Plato: *The Republic*
181 Plato: *The Works of Plato*
82 Poe, Edgar Allan: *Selected Poetry and Prose*
196 Polo, Marco: *The Travels of Marco Polo*
257 Pope, Alexander: *Selected Works*
284 Porter, Katherine Anne: *Flowering Judas*
45 Porter, Katherine Anne: *Pale Horse, Pale Rider*
120 Proust, Marcel: *The Captive*
220 Proust, Marcel: *Cities of the Plain*
213 Proust, Marcel: *The Guermantes Way*
278 Proust, Marcel: *The Past Recaptured*
59 Proust, Marcel: *Swann's Way*
260 Proust, Marcel: *The Sweet Cheat Gone*
172 Proust, Marcel: *Within a Budding Grove*

194 Racine & Corneille: *Six Plays by Corneille and Racine*
62 Reade, Charles: *The Cloister and the Hearth*
215 Reed, John: *Ten Days That Shook the World*
140 Renan, Ernest: *The Life of Jesus*
336 Renault, Mary: *The Last of the Wine*
10 Richardson, Samuel: *Clarissa*
200 Rodgers & Hammerstein: *Six Plays*
154 Rostand, Edmond: *Cyrano de Bergerac*
243 Rousseau, Jean Jacques: *The Confessions*
53 Runyon, Damon: *Famous Stories*
137 Russell, Bertrand: *Selected Papers of Bertrand Russell*

280 Saki: *Short Stories*
301 Salinger, J. D.: *Nine Stories*
90 Salinger, J. D.: *The Catcher in the Rye*
292 Santayana, George: *The Sense of Beauty*
335 Sartre, Jean-Paul: *The Age of Reason*
52 Schopenhauer: *The Philosophy of Schopenhauer*
281 Schulberg, Budd: *What Makes Sammy Run?*
2,3 Shakespeare, William: *Tragedies*—complete, 2 vols.

4,5 Shakespeare, William: *Comedies*—complete, 2 vols.
6 Shakespeare, William: *Histories* } complete, 2 vols.
7 Shakespeare, William: *Histories, Poems* }
19 Shaw, Bernard: *Four Plays*
294 Shaw, Bernard: *Saint Joan, Major Barbara,* and *Androcles* [*and the Lion*
112 Shaw, Irwin: *The Young Lions*
319 Shaw, Irwin: *Selected Short Stories*
274 Shelley: *Selected Poetry and Prose*
159 Smollett, Tobias: *Humphry Clinker*
312 Sophocles I: *Complete Greek Tragedies,* Vol. III
313 Sophocles II: *Complete Greek Tragedies,* Vol. IV
60 Spinoza: *The Philosophy of Spinoza*
332 Stein, Gertrude: *Selected Writings*
115 Steinbeck, John: *In Dubious Battle*
29 Steinbeck, John: *Of Mice and Men*
216 Steinbeck, John: *Tortilla Flat*
157 Stendhal: *The Red and the Black*
147 Sterne, Laurence: *Tristram Shandy*
254 Stewart, George R.: *Storm*
31 Stoker, Bram: *Dracula*
11 Stone, Irving: *Lust for Life*
261 Stowe, Harriet Beecher: *Uncle Tom's Cabin*
212 Strachey, Lytton: *Eminent Victorians*
188 Suetonius: *Lives of the Twelve Caesars*
100 Swift, Jonathan: *Gulliver's Travels and Other Writings*
49 Symonds, John A.: *The Life of Michelangelo*

222 Tacitus: *Complete Works*
230 Tennyson: *Selected Poetry*
80 Thackeray, William: *Henry Esmond*
131 Thackeray, William: *Vanity Fair*
38 Thompson, Francis: *Complete Poems*
155 Thoreau, Henry David: *Walden and Other Writings*
58 Thucydides: *Complete Writings*
85 Thurber, James: *The Thurber Carnival*
37 Tolstoy, Leo: *Anna Karenina*
346 Tolstoy, Leo: *Short Stories*
41 Trollope, Anthony: *Barchester Towers* and *The Warden*
21 Turgenev, Ivan: *Fathers and Sons*
162 Twain, Mark: *A Connecticut Yankee in King Arthur's Court*

190 Vasari, Giorgio: *Lives of the Most Eminent Painters, Sculptors and Architects*
63 Veblen, Thorstein: *The Theory of the Leisure Class*
156 Vinci, Leonardo Da: *The Notebooks*
75 Virgil: *The Aeneid, Eclogues* and *Georgics*
47 Voltaire: *Candide and Other Writings*

178 Walpole, Hugh: *Fortitude*
170 Warren, Robert Penn: *All The King's Men*
219 Webb, Mary: *Precious Bane*
225 Weidman, Jerome: *I Can Get It for You Wholesale*
197 Wells, H. G.: *Tono Bungay*
290 Welty, Eudora: *Selected Stories*
299 Wharton, Edith: *The Age of Innocence*
97 Whitman, Walt: *Leaves of Grass*
125 Wilde, Oscar: *Dorian Gray* and *De Profundis*

83 WILDE, OSCAR: *The Plays of Oscar Wilde*
84 WILDE, OSCAR: *Poems* and *Fairy Tales*
126 WODEHOUSE, P. J.: *Selected Stories*
268 WORDSWORTH: *Selected Poetry*

44 YEATS, W. B. (Editor): *Irish Fairy and Folk Tales*
179 YOUNG, G. F.: *The Medici*

207 ZIMMERN, ALFRED: *The Greek Commonwealth*
142 ZOLA, ÉMILE: *Nana*

MISCELLANEOUS

288 *An Anthology of Irish Literature*
330 *Anthology of Medieval Lyrics*
326 *The Apocrypha*
201 *The Arabian Nights' Entertainments*
87 *Best American Humorous Short Stories*
18 *Best Russian Short Stories*
129 *Best Spanish Stories*
Complete Greek Tragedies
310 Vol. I (Aeschylus I); 311 Vol. II (Aeschylus II); 312 Vol. III (Sophocles I); 313 Vol. IV (Sophocles II); 314 Vol. V (Euripides I); 315 Vol. VI (Euripides II)
101 *A Comprehensive Anthology of American Poetry*
226 *The Consolation of Philosophy*
94 *Eight Famous Elizabethan Plays*
345 *Eight Spanish Plays of the Golden Age*
224 *Eighteenth-Century Plays*
73 *Famous Ghost Stories*
139 *The Federalist*
30 *Five Great Modern Irish Plays*
144 *Fourteen Great Detective Stories*
108 *Great German Short Novels and Stories*
168 *Great Modern Short Stories*
238 *Great Tales of the American West*
203 *The Greek Poets*
118 *Stories of Modern Italy*
217 *The Latin Poets*
149 *The Making of Man: An Outline of Anthropology*
183 *Making of Society*
344 *Medieval Philosophy*
133 *Medieval Romances*
1 *The Modern Library Dictionary*
258 *New Voices in the American Theatre*
152 *Outline of Abnormal Psychology*
66 *Outline of Psychoanalysis*
287 *Restoration Plays*
337 *Roman Comedies*
158 *Seven Famous Greek Plays*
57 *The Short Bible*
276 *Six Modern American Plays*
38 *Six American Plays for Today*
127 *Twentieth-Century American Poetry*—revised
341 *Twenty German Poets*

G38 MURASAKA, LADY: *The Tale of Genji*
G30 MYERS, GUSTAVUS: *History of the Great American Fortunes*
G34 NIETZSCHE, FRIEDRICH: *The Philosophy of Nietzsche*
G88 O'HARA, JOHN: *49 Stories*
G55 O'NEILL, EUGENE: *Nine Plays*
G68 PAINE, TOM: *Selected Work*
G86 PASTERNAK, BORIS: *Doctor Zhivago*
G5 PLUTARCH: *Lives* (The Dryden Translation)
G40 POE, EDGAR ALLAN: *Complete Tales and Poems*
G29 PRESCOTT, WILLIAM H.: *The Conquest of Mexico* and *The Conquest of Peru*
G62 PUSHKIN: *Poems, Prose and Plays*
G65 RABELAIS: *Complete Works*
G12 SCOTT, SIR WALTER: *The Most Popular Novels* (Quentin Durward, Ivanhoe & Kenilworth)
G4 SHELLEY & KEATS: *Complete Poems*
G32 SMITH, ADAM: *The Wealth of Nations*
G61 SPAETH, SIGMUND: *A Guide to Great Orchestral Music*
G75 STEVENSON, ROBERT LOUIS: *Selected Writings*
G53 SUE, EUGENE: *The Wandering Jew*
G42 TENNYSON: *The Poems and Plays*
G23 TOLSTOY, LEO: *Anna Karenina*
G1 TOLSTOY, LEO: *War and Peace*
G49 TWAIN, MARK: *Tom Sawyer* and *Huckleberry Finn*
G50 WHITMAN, WALT: *Leaves of Grass*
G83 WILSON, EDMUND: *The Shock of Recognition*

MISCELLANEOUS

G77 *An Anthology of Famous American Stories*
G54 *An Anthology of Famous British Stories*
G67 *Anthology of Famous English and American Poetry*
G81 *An Encyclopedia of Modern American Humor*
G47 *The English Philosophers from Bacon to Mill*
G16 *The European Philosophers from Descartes to Nietzsche*
G31 *Famous Science-Fiction Stories: Adventures in Time and Space*
G85 *Great Ages and Ideas of the Jewish People*
G89 *Great Classical Myths*
G72 *Great Tales of Terror and the Supernatural*
G9 *Great Voices of the Reformation*
G87 *Medieval Epics*
G48 *The Metropolitan Opera Guide*
G46 *A New Anthology of Modern Poetry*
G69 *One Hundred and One Years' Entertainment*
G21 *Sixteen Famous American Plays*
G63 *Sixteen Famous British Plays*
G71 *Sixteen Famous European Plays*
G45 *Stoic and Epicurean Philosophers*
G22 *Thirty Famous One-Act Plays*
G66 *Three Famous Murder Novels*
Before the Fact, Francis Iles
Trent's Last Case, E. C. Bentley
The House of the Arrow, A. E. W. Mason
G10 *Twelve Famous Plays of the Restoration and Eighteenth Century* (1660–1820)
(Congreve, Wycherley, Gay, Goldsmith, Sheridan, etc.)
G56 *The Wisdom of Catholicism*
G59 *The Wisdom of China and India*
G79 *The Wisdom of Israel*